BLACK CHARLESTONIANS

BLACK CHARLESTONIANS
A Social History, 1822-1885

BERNARD E. POWERS JR.

The University of Arkansas Press
Fayetteville   1994

98 97 96 95 94   5 4 3 2 1

Designed by Gail Carter

The paper used in this publication meets the minimum
requirements of the American National Standard for
Permanence of Paper for Printed Library Materials
Z39.48–1984. ⊛

Library of Congress Cataloging-in-Publication Data

Powers, Bernard Edward.
    Black Charlestonians : a social history, 1822–1885 /
    Bernard E. Powers, Jr.
        p.   cm.
    Includes bibliographical references and index.
    ISBN 1-55728-364-8
    1. Afro-Americans—South Carolina—Charleston—
    History—19th century. 2. Charleston (S.C.)—History.
    I. Title.
    F279.C49N4   1994
    975.7'91500496073—dc20   94-7861
                                                CIP

This book is dedicated to
Bernard Sr., Mildred, Brian, Brenda, and Lorraine,
whose love and devotion made it possible.

ACKNOWLEDGMENTS

In the course of researching and writing, I have amassed a considerable debt to many individuals and groups. At Northwestern University, Professor Sterling Stuckey initially urged me to study black life in Charleston, and his brilliant insights then and now have heightened my appreciation for the rich culture of the African-derived population there. Professor George Fredrickson supervised my investigations as they took the form of a doctoral dissertation and provided keen insights into the nature of southern race relations. In more recent years, scholars such as Norrece Jones, Daniel Littlefield, James Anderson, William Hine, and Gregory Mixon have offered useful criticism of conference papers that embodied various aspects of this study. Willard Gatewood, a consummate scholar, also read a version of this study and took the time to provide much needed encouragement and support at critical junctures. I owe a special debt to Edmund Drago, who set aside a frenetic schedule to read the manuscript and share insights based on his research on this important community.

Without the support of various libraries and archival personnel, this study would not have been possible. The assistance of Donald West, Rebecca Graebner, and Curtis Franks of the Avery Research Center for African American History and Culture at the College of Charleston has been indispensable. At the Special Collections Division of the College of Charleston Library, Oliver Smalls' professionalism has been unexcelled and Bill Finley's assistance unusually generous. At the University of South Carolina Caroliniana Library, Allan Stokes' and Eleanor Richardson's familiarity with the manuscript and photographic sources of South Carolina history is exceptional. I would also like to thank Michelle Baker of the South Carolina State Museum, Donna Wells of the Moorland-Spingarn Collection of Howard University, and Rita Reynolds for expeditious assistance locating photographs. Many thanks also go to the staffs of the Library of Congress, the South Carolina Historical Society, the Charleston Library Society, and the Charleston County Library.

The generosity of others has also been valuable. Cheryle Drago and Alisandra Ravenel contributed suggestions or materials that proved vital contributions to my efforts. Reverend Alphonso R. Blake and Deacon Alfonso Evans, Bishop Zedekiah L. Grady and the late Reverend Marion Stroble extended the hand of fellowship and provided useful records pertaining to the black church.

Technical support was provided by Mrs. Joanne Diaz, whose mastery of computerized word-processing skills solved even the most challenging problems with ease. The maps were produced by Mr. Cornell Mack. The easygoing style, the sharp eye, and literary talents of my editor, Scot Danforth, improved the final manuscript immensely. The patience and diligent efforts of Karen Johnson of the editorial staff were also invaluable. Certain portions of this book originally appeared in the January 1994 issue of the *South Carolina Historical Magazine* as an article entitled "Community Evolution and Race Relations in Reconstruction Charleston, S.C." I am grateful to Stephen Hoffius, editor of the *Magazine,* and the South Carolina Historical Association for permission to reprint them here. A faculty research grant and a summer research stipend from the College of Charleston helped defray some of the costs of publication.

Finally, special thanks go to my wife, Lorraine, who has endured my long hours and the vacation-research jaunts, but who has willingly made the sacrifices necessary to see this work come to fruition.

BERNARD E. POWERS JR.
Charleston, S.C.

CONTENTS

LIST OF TABLES

INTRODUCTION

Although Afro-Americans have always been a significant presence in this country's major cities, for the greater part of the nation's history they were typically found in the countryside. In fact at the end of the Civil War, 90 percent of the black population resided in the rural South. Yet, a dramatic redistribution of that population has occurred over the last century, producing a complete reversal of the traditional residential pattern. In 1980 approximately 80 percent of all American blacks were urbanized.[1] Such a dramatic transformation could not escape the notice of scholars, many of whom were sensitive to the problems in America's urban places and especially those problems fundamentally grounded in American race relations. Based upon these concerns, scholars interested in the phenomenon of black urbanization traditionally directed their research efforts to the forces of the late 1890s and the first half of the twentieth century, forces which contributed to the rise of major northern black communities. This body of research has devoted particular attention to such issues as the Great Migration of blacks from the South, the consequences of racially restrictive housing policies, and the rise of the physical and institutional ghetto. The greatest emphasis has been on the conditions of black life within the peculiar ecology of northern, industrialized cities in this century.[2]

This traditional focus has been invaluable and contributed much to the body of literature on black urbanization. In the last decade or so, scholars have realized that the crucial issues faced by black urbanites in twentieth-century northern cities were not necessarily identical to those they faced in other regions and during earlier phases of urbanization and industrialization. While twentieth-century northern black communities continued to draw the greatest interest, a number of path-breaking studies have enabled us to appreciate the broad diversity of black urban life by focusing on places or aspects of the experience that have received insufficient attention. Typically these works devoted significantly more attention to the nineteenth century in the attempt to examine the texture of black urban life before the advent of the modern ghetto. Interest in the black urban experience below the Mason Dixon line grew also.[3]

The comparatively small, mainly commercial cities of the South always contained substantial black populations and comparatively few immigrants. Given these characteristics, along with the South's racial ideology and the heritage of slavery, we might expect the cities that developed in the region to have produced experiences that were somewhat different from their northern counterparts. Only after sufficient studies of Old South and New South cities have been done in the nineteenth and twentieth centuries will we fully begin to grasp the totality of the southern black urban experience or the general urban experience. No comprehensive view of black urban life in the South would be complete without giving proper consideration to the pivotal city of Charleston, South Carolina. This study, in part the result of the comparatively recent interest in nineteenth-century southern cities, is designed to explore the major social and economic features of the black community there.

In the early nineteenth-century South, Charleston was second only to Baltimore in population and in commercial prominence. But by the end of the antebellum period, the city had declined in relative importance as its commercial preeminence fell victim to the southwestward spread of the cotton kingdom and the rivalry of the emerging southern river towns that profited from the steamboat trade. Despite its declining economic fortunes, Charleston maintained an atmosphere of gentility because its location in the heart of the South Carolina Low Country made it the resort of the region's most affluent planters. Many of them maintained homes in the city to which they came every summer, as they fled the malarial miasmas that they supposed emanated from the swamps surrounding their plantations.[4] In Charleston the planters surrounded themselves with the pleasures of elegant restaurants, the theater, and the race track, or enjoyed the breezes that aerated their palatial mansions in the lower part of the city.

Charleston's large enslaved black population was a marked contrast to the planters' polished and refined society. As a major seaport, Charleston had always been a center for the importation and distribution of slaves. South Carolina was the only southern state to reopen the foreign slave trade from 1803 to 1807. During this period it is estimated that forty thousand Africans were brought to the city. The continued heavy importation of people from the African continent ensured that the Low Country region along with coastal Georgia would be the seat for the most Africanized slave communities in America. Most slaves brought to Charleston were resold to nearby plantations just outside the city and on the Sea Islands that dotted the coast. The sprawling Low Country plantations grew rice and Sea Island cotton and were characteristically worked by very large gangs of slaves. No other region of the South contained such a large and densely concentrated population of blacks, and in 1830 slaves outnumbered whites by approximately three to one in Charleston County.[5] Some of the imported Africans remained in the city to be integrated into the urban slave system, which was quite different from the form servitude took on the Low Country plantations.

Not all black Charlestonians were enslaved, and the antebellum city contained a significant number of free blacks. Most existed near the lowest stratum of society and were not vastly better off than the slaves. The more privileged members of the group acquired real and sometimes even slave property, created an array of social institutions, and developed quite distinctive lifestyles. Even so, the quality and character of their lives was conditioned by the stark reality of existence within a slaveholding society.

The decision was made to begin this study of Charleston's black community in the early 1820s because this period was marked by national and local events that had serious consequences for the community's members. The year 1819 witnessed the rekindling and escalation of sectional conflict between the North and South over the admission of Missouri to statehood. This was the early phase of a protracted sectional conflict, the byproducts of which were a growing southern self-consciousness, a strengthened commitment to slavery, and the twin perceptions that the institution of slavery was jeopardized by northern abolitionists and by the presence of free blacks. Those who shared the latter apprehension had their greatest suspicions confirmed when a major slave conspiracy was discovered in Charleston in 1822. These events contributed to the demand for more stringent control of the city's black population, both slave and free.[6] For the remaining antebellum years,

Charleston slaves attempted to enlarge the modicum of freedom afforded by urban life, while free blacks struggled against attempts to limit the freedom they already enjoyed. The precariousness of free black life in Charleston was revealed in the late 1850s. By then, members of the free black community were caught between the white hostility engendered by the mounting sectional conflict and the inexorable logic of the South's proslavery argument.

The discussion of the antebellum community is intended to provide background for the main focus of this study, which is on the Reconstruction years. Attention is also given to the early years of the New South to take advantage of sources that only became available then. There are several useful monographs that analyze specific aspects of black Reconstruction in South Carolina, including the Freedmen's Bureau, the South Carolina Land Commission, and black political involvement, but none of these examines the black urban experience. Joel Williamson's pioneering study, *After Slavery: The Negro in South Carolina During Reconstruction, 1861–1877,* surveys the black experience in the entire state, and while references are made to Charleston, the scope of the study prevents any detailed or systematic analysis of life in any one location. This study of an urban black community thus provides another perspective on the process of Reconstruction in South Carolina and follows a course similar to that of John Blassingame's perceptive study of New Orleans' black community.[7]

The primary emphasis upon the social and economic evolution of the Charleston black community was also dictated by the tenor of earlier studies. Of the many facets of Reconstruction in South Carolina, politics and those developments of the era that largely depended upon the political process have received the most extensive attention. But in the state, the period of political Reconstruction (although longer than in most states) was of short duration, lasting less than a decade before the Republicans were turned out of office by the Democrats' campaign of fraud, intimidation, and violence. The primacy of politics in the traditional analyses of the era has led many historians to conclude that important aspects of Reconstruction were at best qualified or glorious failures. Several reasons are put forth to explain the failure of this unprecedented experiment, including the overt hostility of the white South and the lack of a firm commitment to racial equality on the part of the national government.[8]

But all too often, those who have discussed the failures of Reconstruction view blacks merely as victims caught between a vacillating and insensitive federal government and the rising tide of southern racial violence. While these tragic circumstances were essential features of the era, it is necessary to extend the analysis of the period beyond such portrayals that implicitly view the black community as a dependent variable and its members as essentially responding to the actions of whites, rather than taking initiatives themselves. A major exception to the pattern of seeing blacks only as victims is an analysis of the failure of political Reconstruction in South Carolina by Thomas Holt in his book *Black Over White: Negro Political Leadership in South Carolina During Reconstruction.* Herein the author argues that part of the failure can be attributed to the inability of Republicans to formulate a coherent legislative program. Moreover, the difficulty on this front was exacerbated by cleavages between black leaders of different socioeconomic backgrounds that translated into destructive intraparty rivalries and decreased the political effectiveness of the Republicans.[9] The importance of socioeconomic status for the analysis of political Reconstruction in South Carolina points to the need for a much more thorough examination of class, status, and the socioeconomic circumstances of southern black communities in general. Such an examination can help us understand the political developments of the era more fully, while illuminating other equally important aspects of black life.

This emphasis on socioeconomic issues attempts to ask and answer fundamental questions that still require detailed study. Charleston shared common attributes, problems, and opportunities with other southern cities and also had its unique qualities. We still need to know precisely how workers were affected by emancipation and the economies of the specific places where they resided. We don't know enough yet about their ability to acquire property, their mobility experiences, and the relationship between urban and "suburban" workers. We also need to know much more about how they attempted to protect their economic interests. These are only some examples of directions further work might take.

A thorough analysis of black Charleston, and by implication other urban black communities during Reconstruction, represents the logical extension of the useful insights scholars have provided into the world of the antebellum slave. In general, the slaves were legally and physically subordinated to the master class, but wherever possible they resisted becoming the mere extensions of their owners' will. Scholarship on slave communities demonstrates that the bondsmen showed remarkable determination and creativity in their attempts to maintain normal human relationships with one another while enduring the burdens of their enslavement.[10] It seems likely that the same resourcefulness and determination that shaped the slave community would be brought to bear upon the problems and new circumstances stemming from the Civil War and its results. Given their special position in antebellum society, free blacks had even greater latitude than the slaves to organize their lives, and the heritage of freedom often proved a vital resource during the postbellum years.

The following pages assess the way black Charlestonians responded to the consequences of the Civil War and Reconstruction while delineating the basic social and economic contours of the community they created during the postbellum years. During the period, Congress passed legislation that theoretically granted blacks the rights of free and full citizens. But black Charlestonians demonstrated a keen awareness that equality could only come about if they were willing to act on their own behalf to give a theoretical freedom substantive and enduring form. Members of the black community immediately moved to take advantage of the new circumstances created by emancipation in several ways. Workers availed themselves of new employment opportunities and pooled their collective strength to challenge outmoded assumptions about black-white relations in the work place. Others took initiatives at the earliest opportunity to stand up for their community and demand equal treatment before the law and inclusion in the body politic.

Black Charlestonians gave even greater institutional form to their community by helping to establish schools for their children, churches where they could practice their religion, and a myriad of lesser organizations that served social, intellectual, and recreational purposes. The new churches and schools, workingmen's associations, fire companies, and sports clubs provided much of the infrastructure that bound the community together. The officers of these organizations were considered community leaders, although they were not necessarily politicians. Their roles were as important as those of the black officeholders Reconstruction studies typically focus on and they survived the erosion of black political rights.

There was always a significant degree of social distinction among Charleston blacks, but emancipation accelerated the rate of social differentiation, and the community that emerged was markedly stratified along traditional socioeconomic lines. Emancipation undercut the peculiar social position of the free black group and created legal parity among all blacks. Nevertheless, the heritage of freedom brought with it certain social advantages and attitudinal correlates that the more privileged members of the antebellum free black group easily translated into their upper-class status during subsequent years. Certain aspects of the antebellum heritage had to be overcome; given the ambivalence that sometimes had existed between free blacks and slaves, the precise relationship they would have after emancipation wasn't immediately clear and had to be worked out. In the process of doing so the lines of status and class were clarified.

Although this study is about the condition of black lives, goals, strategies, and attitudes, the circumstances in which these developed were influenced by blacks' interaction with whites. The examination of black Charleston's development would be incomplete without exploring the evolving pattern of race relations. The emancipation of the slaves was a forcible act, and usually whites relinquished their full control of the black community only grudgingly. Violence sometimes occurred as attempts were made to resurrect the antebellum arrangement of race relations. There is also evidence that whites used de facto racial segregation as a substitute for the now moribund antebellum racial strictures. However, the physical separation of the races was not as starkly drawn or as extensive as it would become by the end of the nineteenth century.[11] This was because while whites generally preferred separation of the races, they were not as fully committed to this principle as they would later become. Equally important is the fact that black men and women so valued their freedom that they aggressively resisted the attempts to treat them as inferiors. The vigor with which black Charlestonians pursued their equal rights as citizens stemmed from the same determination that led them to form a cohesive community.

While it is widely recognized that the policies of Reconstruction failed to secure the civil and political rights of black Americans permanently, less is known about the other aspects of social change and continuity for the period. The postwar history of black Charleston reveals several important patterns of institutional growth and social development that continued long after the demise of the Republican party in the South. It is to these areas that historians and others must look if they are ever to have a full understanding of Reconstruction's lasting impact.

CHAPTER ONE

SLAVERY IN ANTEBELLUM CHARLESTON

During the antebellum years, slavery was the most important feature of Afro-American life in the South. Dehumanization and cruelty were endemic features of the institution, but while these characteristic oppressions were manifest throughout the region, Charleston's slaves found themselves in a rather unique situation. As a major seaport city, this location posed unique problems for the master class while simultaneously providing opportunities available only to blacks in other major southern cities. In many respects, urban slavery was quite different from its rural counterpart. The latter found strength in the isolation of the slave from elements foreign to plantation life. By contrast, city slaves were not isolated, and this critical difference made the development of attitudes and activities antithetical to slavery possible.[1] Charleston's slaves were quick to seize every opportunity to live normal lives and continually acted to enlarge the cracks in the wall of oppression, wherever these were found. The contradictions inherent within the system, coupled with the initiatives taken by the slaves themselves, produced a complex and variegated slave community. As a result of the relatively independent lifestyles made possible by city life, Charleston slaves were able to mitigate the full impact of what would have otherwise been an even more debilitating existence.

One of antebellum Charleston's most distinctive features was its large and diffuse black population. The black population reached a high point of 22,973 in 1850, and blacks had outnumbered whites in seven of the eight decades from 1790 to 1860. Such a large and highly visible segment of the population evoked the continual comment of both residents and visitors to the city. When the Swedish traveler Fredrika Bremer, who visited the South in the 1850s, arrived in Charleston, she immediately observed that "negroes swarm in the streets" and "two thirds of the people whom one sees out in the town are negroes or mulattoes." On another occasion, Rev. John B. Adger, a prominent minister, commented on the interaction between slaves and masters in Charleston: "They belong to us. We also belong to them. They are divided out among us and mingled up with us and we with them in a thousand ways."[2] Because of its size and characteristics, Charleston's black population affected almost every aspect of the city's life.

Although it had certain distinctive features, urban slavery, like its rural counterpart, was first and foremost a system of labor organization, a system to which Charleston was more firmly wedded than any other major southern city. Charleston had a much broader occupational structure than its rural hinterland, and, although the majority of its slaves worked as domestics or unskilled laborers, the diversity of their occupations was striking. In the year 1848, Charleston slaves were involved in at least thirty-eight different occupations. Many of these required considerable skill and included the needlecraft trades for women and bricklayers, blacksmiths, carpenters, tailors, bakers, plasterers, coopers, shoemakers, and miscellaneous mechanical trades for men.[3]

Slaves were used in Charleston's various manufacturing enterprises. Mill owners preferred using slaves in unskilled or semiskilled capacities, and their operations relied heavily upon black labor. The majority of workers employed by the Gibbes and Williams Steam Saw Mill, Bennett's Mill, and Chisolm's Mill were slaves. Slaves with skills also found work in the milling industry. The West Point Rice Mills on the Ashley River was the largest and considered the most efficient rice mill in antebellum South Carolina. In 1860 it owned 160 slaves, and among them were included many engineers, carpenters, blacksmiths, and coopers. Slaves were also employed in the manufacture of bricks; Horlbeck's brickyard, certainly one of the largest in 1850, employed eighty-five hands, most of whom were slaves. Charleston's modest shipbuilding industry used slaves in various skilled and unskilled capacities.[4]

In this port city, slaves were extensively involved in maritime occupations. They were naturally employed as wharf hands and stevedores, and they did the rough, physically demanding work on the waterfront. In addition, they worked as hands and pilots on steamboats and sloops engaged in coastal trade as far north as Washington, D.C. As a slave, Robert Smalls' first job on the waterfront was as a dock hand and he eventually became a foreman. In the winter he obtained employment in the shop of John Simmons where he learned the trades of rigging and sail making. To complete his nautical education, Smalls hired out as a sailor on coastal schooners. In this capacity, he learned how to read maps and charts, studied complex channel currents and tides, and finally came to know the location of the major shoals and reefs in Charleston harbor.[5]

Other aspects of the transportation industry also relied on slave labor. The Charleston Bridge Company and the South Carolina Canal and Railroad Company hired slave laborers and carpenters. When the white employees of the Northeastern Railroad left the city during the summer months of 1855 to seek a healthier environment, the company was forced to hire slave replacements. Immigrant labor failed to meet the needs of the South Carolina Railroad Company and it turned to slaves, purchasing 111 between 1845 and 1865. The company's confidence in the efficiency of slave labor was revealed when in 1836 the president suggested that trains be run by slave engineers under the supervision of white conductors. Although this measure was adopted by the board of directors, it was never implemented perhaps to avoid the wrath of skilled white labor.[6]

Sometimes slaves acquired skills and training from their owners, who in turn utilized those skills in their own businesses. This must have been the case with William Rouse, a Charleston leather craftsman, who in 1825 owned at least four tanners, a currier, and seven shoemakers. Christopher Werner was a German blacksmith who was highly regarded for his ornamental ironwork. His five slaves were instrumental in producing his commissioned work, and some became well known for their skills. White artisans frequently advertised their willingness to train slave apprentices, and most skilled slaves probably received their training in this way.[7] Once the apprenticeship had been served, the owner could then hire the person out and expect a much higher return on the slave's labor.

Many masters who owned more slaves than they could effectively use in a single enterprise hired them to others who could better employ their services. Owners could benefit handsomely from this practice, and in 1849 the South Carolina Railroad earned over one thousand dollars from hiring out its slaves. Although it was an economically rational method of allocating labor resources, the hiring-out system became quite controversial because masters often allowed their slaves to procure their own work and literally "hire themselves out." These slaves had far greater autonomy and latitude to obtain work, to negotiate wages and hours, and perhaps even to determine living arrangements. This was certainly the case with Samuel Robertson, a slave shoemaker owned by a resident of Alabama. Left in the care of Mrs. Louisa Lord of Charleston, who only collected his wages and forwarded them to his owner, Robertson had complete freedom in obtaining employment and housing. The slave Monday Gell operated a harness shop on Meeting street, and according to observers enjoyed "all the substantial comforts of a free-man." Since he was "much indulged and trusted by his master," much of "his time and a large proportion of the profits of his labour were at his own disposal." Some female slaves in Charleston organized their own commercial network for marketing vegetable produce. These Charleston women acted as distribution agents for products grown in the countryside, brought to the city, and then sold by awaiting market women or street vendors.[8]

As early as 1712, hiring slaves from anyone other than their owners was made illegal. The widespread violation of this regulation was an ongoing problem, however, and as late as 1864 legislation was proposed to prevent a dangerous independence on the part of slave jobbers. A Charleston belle, the victim of such slave independence, recalled she was forced to sell her slave Big Jack "on account of his own folly—he owed upwards of $100 for wages—and would not pay me one Cent—but said he wished to be Sold[.] So he has got a good master—and I hope he will treat him better than he has me."[9]

Slave labor was hired by the Charleston city government. Its scavenger service used slave laborers as early as 1806, but the most interesting use of slaves was as firemen. Charleston's fire department was made up of two segments. One segment consisted of volunteer companies that were staffed by whites and used the best equipment. The city or ward engine companies, as the other component was known, consisted of black slaves that were hired by the city. In 1848 there were eight hand-powered fire engines and one elevating ladder unit which were operated by 243 slaves, under the management of 23 whites. It seems that the slave manned city engines, and the volunteer companies carried on many of the same functions. The slaves also acted to supply the volunteer companies and relieved them when the major portion of a fire had been subdued.[10] In attempts to minimize "disagreeable contact and competition" with the whites and to preserve that critical distinction between masters and slaves, the white volunteers and the city engine hands received different rates of pay. Highly prized rewards were offered to the first engines to arrive at the scene of a fire, and in keeping with contemporary racial etiquette, these were separate and unequal for city and volunteer engine companies.[11]

The importance of slave labor to Charleston's fire department—clearly evident to contemporaries—was revealed by the unforeseen consequences of changes in city council policies. All slaves that hired their time out were required by law to obtain a license in the form of a badge issued by the city. In 1846 the Charleston City Council passed a resolution requiring that before slaves could hire out to the fire department, they must have the written permission of their masters. This greatly increased the difficulty of procuring slaves for such potentially dangerous work and triggered complaints from the city engine managers.[12] The resolution was finally amended to eliminate the need for a master's written consent and allowed any slave who had obtained a badge to hire his time to the fire department. This revision did not completely solve the department's labor problems because neither the Board of Firemasters nor its subordinate officers had ever enforced the badge requirement. In 1850, the firemaster complained that as a result of the city council regulations, the department "has been much crippled." In fact, "in the two last fires this Board has seriously felt the want of Engines to Supply & Hose [*sic*] to Loan the Volunteer Companies." Furthermore, the Board believed "it of interest to the City even should they occasionally have to pay for hands injured at Fires" to continue hiring slaves without necessarily securing the prior approval of their masters. In keeping with the letter of the law, but certainly not its spirit, the fire department did furnish badges for the slaves it employed, if they did not already possess them.[13]

White workingmen, ever sensitive to the challenge of slave labor, often protested and vigorously acted to protect their interests. At the turn of the eighteenth century, white laborers managed to obtain legislation that required each white mechanic to employ a white journeyman or apprentice for every six slaves employed or taught. Likewise, in 1793 white coopers, apprehending the evils of slaves "selling their commodities and working at their Trades much lower, and at much cheaper Rates" than they could reasonably afford to, incorporated themselves as the Society of Master Coopers of Charleston. As a body they intended to protect their interests as laboring men and to prevent those concomitants of slave labor that "tend to the Injury of any part of the Community."[14]

Slave labor competition was but the single edge of a double-edged sword that cut deeply into the very heart of the urban slave system. White workers' grievances went beyond the fact that slaves could be employed more cheaply. They also claimed that the relative autonomy and responsibility they were sometimes accorded gave slaves an unfair competitive advantage. In one case from the 1820s, a group of skilled whites complained that wealthy slaveholders with work to be done would often "leave it to their Domestics to employ what workmen they please." This was troubling because "it universally happens that those Domestics prefer men of their own color and condition." The result was that "the Black Mechanics enjoy as complete a monopoly, as if it were secured to them by Law."[15] When he spoke to the Agricultural Society of South Carolina in the early 1830s, Edward Laurens pointed out that slaves "are often allowed of carrying on occupations, the very nature of which relieves them in great measure from the wholesome restraint of a master's eye." White master stevedores protested that slaves organized labor gangs on the docks and argued along the same lines. Although slaves were by law prohibited from assembling in large numbers, they could do so below the decks of a ship without the presence of a white person. Furthermore, unattended slaves often unloaded northern ships with black crews, which placed them "in direct communication with any emisary [sic] the North may think proper to send among us."[16]

Some slave occupations were viewed with dismay because of the particular responsibilities and skills they entailed. In 1826, in a memorial to the legislature, the Charleston City Council decried the ever-increasing use of slaves as clerks and salesmen in shops. This practice not only drove whites out of work but also "introduces the slaves, into situations which are inconsistent with their condition." The city fathers had no objections to the employment of slaves as domestics, laborers, or mechanics, but viewed with great trepidation slave involvement in "any engagements which require the exercise of greater intelligence & improvement." Left unchecked, they continued, this trend would "prepare the seeds of disquietude in the very constitution of our society." In another similar yet exceptional case, a wealthy Charleston master relied on his favorite slave to arrange his financial affairs, including maintaining his accounts, drawing checks on the local bank, and receiving the money.[17] It is easy to see how the diversity and extent of slave labor aroused the ire of white workingmen. Equally important, many whites feared the nature of certain slave employments because these jobs physically or intellectually removed the bondsmen from the masters' complete control and thereby threatened the viability of the slave system.

Charleston not only provided a wide range of occupations; the city itself proved to be a diverse learning environment for slaves. In addition to the skills and education necessary for the performance of some of their tasks, as Carter G. Woodson points out, "What the master did not seem disposed to teach the slave so situated, they usually learned by contact with their fellowmen who were better informed." In Charleston, slaves used church gatherings as occasions to educate themselves, the opposing efforts of the white community notwithstanding. In 1827, slaves learned to read while attending one of the local Methodist Sunday schools. As pastor of the Anson Street Chapel for Presbyterian slaves, Rev. John Adger opposed the legal restrictions on slave and free black literacy in South Carolina. Like many religious whites, he believed it especially cruel to hinder a slave from learning the word of God. In defiance of the law, he allowed his children to instruct the family slaves and ordered large quantities of Bible tracts for his black congregation. John Henry Vessey underscored the futility of prohibiting slaves from learning to read while allowing them to attend churches. When visiting the Anson Chapel under the charge of a successor minister, he reported, "Among those 2,000 blacks in Mr. Girardeau's church I noticed many of them take out their Bibles and follow the minister." But even those masters who favored literacy for religious instruction thought it should be confined to reading.[18]

Slaves maintained schools clandestinely or enlisted the aid of free blacks in their educational efforts. Daniel Payne, a free black teacher, counted three adult slaves whom he taught at night among his first scholars. Further, when slaves were apprenticed to free blacks for the purpose of learning trades, they often learned to read and write in the course of their work activities. One slave apprenticed to the free black tailor Samuel Weston during the 1850s recalled studying signs and names on doors when making deliveries. En route, he said, "[I] asked people to tell me a word or two at a time; till, in 1860, I found I could read the papers. . . . I took some time to look in the measuring books to see how the writing letters were made. In this way I learned to write." This slave became so proficient in reading that in 1860 he was sometimes hired by local whites to read the *New York Tribune* or *Herald* to them.[19]

Charleston was a bustling center of intellectual activity, and this atmosphere promoted the slave's enlightenment. James Henry Hammond estimated that at any given public political rally or discussion, at least 10 percent of those present were blacks who listened attentively. The slaves were even aware of the latest Congressional debates because, as one pointed out, "What was going on was printed in all the papers, so that every body [*sic*] black as well as white might read it." No wonder that during John C. Calhoun's funeral procession, slaves were observed leaping about the streets, "looking quite entertained." Fredrika Bremer, a witness to such scenes of rejoicing, recorded slaves as having said, "Calhoun was indeed a wicked man, for he wished that we might remain slaves."[20]

Charleston slaves were often well traveled compared to their rural counterparts. The slaves hired by the Charleston and Savannah Railroad made an annual three-week steamboat excursion to North Carolina and Virginia, where they visited both owners and friends. Many could be considered genuinely cosmopolitan because of their backgrounds. One fugitive slave advertisement revealed that a slave spoke both French and English fluently and another spoke Spanish and French intelligibly. The case of the slave Omar ibn Seid is especially revealing in this respect. Although he was in Charleston in 1807, Seid had been born to a wealthy family in Futa Toro, West Africa, where he studied with learned scholars for twenty-five years. As a devout Muslim, he had made the pilgrimage to Mecca and also had participated in an annual jihad. Even in America, Seid kept the celebration of Ramadan and "deemed a copy of the Koran in Arabic . . . his richest treasure." Other slaves traveled with their masters. Philander Michaw was taken to England by his master where he was offered his liberty but chose to return to Charleston to purchase his freedom. Forrest, the body servant of Judge Prioleau, traveled throughout Europe with his master. Thomas Middleton served as valet to his master's sons when they attended school in Oxford, England. The white boys shared their lessons with him, and Thomas learned both Greek and Hebrew. Thomas, in turn, instructed his slave sons James and Abram in these languages.[21]

The church proved an invaluable avenue of enlightenment, and Charleston's slaves enjoyed regular access to churches representing several major denominations. Masters usually arranged for the slaves to attend church along with them, but they did often allow slaves to seek church affiliations according to their individual preferences. By the late antebellum period, the growing pressure of large numbers of slaves who attended white churches led to the establishment of special churches for them. This was a controversial step, and many whites greeted the prospect with skepticism. The biggest fear was that these facilities would become the seedbeds for rebellion and for the propagation of incendiary ideas.[22]

Suspicions deepened in 1849 when construction neared completion for Calvary Protestant Episcopal Church for slaves. That summer an insurrection broke out among the slave inmates at the workhouse one block from the church. Thirty-seven prisoners escaped, including one who had been convicted of assaulting a policeman with a deadly weapon. After linking the construction of the church and insurrection, a mob of angry whites attacked the church, disrupted construction, and almost destroyed the edifice. After a public meeting and subsequent investigation explained the benefits of the church and revealed the safeguards proposed to preserve order and discipline, white fears were assuaged. Construction was completed, and Calvary Protestant Episcopal Church was dedicated just before Christmas in 1849. By 1857 the church maintained one of the largest Sunday schools in the city. Zion Presbyterian Church began as the Anson Street Mission for slaves in 1850. It grew rapidly, and by 1860 Zion had relocated near the intersection of Calhoun and Meeting streets. With a congregation of between one thousand and fifteen hundred, it was housed in the largest church in Charleston, built at a cost of twenty-five thousand dollars.[23]

In addition to allowing them to fulfill their Christian duty as masters, whites generally believed that proper religious instruction had a salutary effect on slave behavior. With specific reference to Zion Church, the Rev. James H. Thornwell believed it would "prove a stronger fortress against insubordination and rebellion than weapons of brass or iron." In recognizing the impossibility of stifling the slave's religion and religious meetings, Thornwell recommended tolerance and cautioned:

> If our laws and the public sentiment of the community tolerate them, they will be open, public, responsible. If our laws prohibit them, they will be secret, fanatical, dangerous. Teachers they will have—if we supply them, their teachers will be teachers indeed. . . . If they are compelled surreptitiously to supply themselves, they will heap to themselves teachers after their own lusts, who will give them fanaticism for piety, excitement for devotion and enthusiasm for faith.

Above all, Thornwell believed slaves must be saved "from secret convocations which the white man cannot witness from appeals which madden rather than instruct—from a religion which puffs up but does not edify."[24]

Secret religious meetings resulted not only from the slaves' need for greater autonomy but also from their desire for spiritual fulfillment. The religious lives of Charleston slaves, like the religious lives of so many slaves throughout the Low Country, illustrate in varying degree the ubiquitous vitality of the region's Gullah culture.[25] The Afro-Christianity they practiced was a syncretism of Christianity and traditional African elements. For example, the highly rational, intellectual, and detached sermonic style of most white ministers failed to satisfy Afro-Christians. True to the African traditions, they continued to believe in emotive and exuberant forms of worship. Rev. Paul Trapier encapsulated the difficulty when he explained that the Gospel could satisfy the slaves' spiritual yearnings except that "in the form of its presentation" it was "not adapted to his comprehension." Sam Polite illustrated the sentiments of the slaves when he observed, "De Book say, 'They that worship me must worship me in spirit and in truth.' There might be some truth in deys—all religion, but there ain't much spirit in a religion that's all in de head." The slaves' worship services could last all night, as the shouts, hand clapping, foot stomping, spirituals, and fervent prayers were offered up in an ecstatic display of praise. Sometimes the exuberance caught the attention of neighbors, and in 1816 a white man complained about the "noisy, frantic worshippers" who continuously disturbed the midnight atmosphere near his residence.[26]

One observer noted that the density of the slave population in the Low Country allowed slaves to "more easily preserve their heathenish ideas and customs." Many African practices shaped the slave's Christianity. It was not at all unusual for slaves to believe that seeing visions necessarily accompanied the process of spiritual rebirth or conversion. Other professing Christians retained African beliefs that were only tangentially related to their new faith and sometimes antithetical to it. Their spirit world was filled with hags, the spirits of ancestors, and other malevolent spirits, such as haunts, that could cause nightmares and otherwise produce chaos for humans on earth. Some people, known as conjurers, had special metaphysical powers that could be used for good or evil, could cast or break spells, could foretell the future, and could cure illnesses. The slaves' world view became Christianized, but the infusion of African elements made the metaphysical world and this one more intelligible to them. The resultant Afro-Christianity was not only the basis for new values but also the basis for leadership. Therein resided a problem, though, because in certain contexts a figure such as a conjurer became more influential than a master.[27]

Sometimes the church organization itself provided an important forum for the exercise of leadership and collaborative effort among the slaves. Although they couldn't legally own property, slaves sometimes held burial grounds through burial societies in their churches. This was the case with one of Charleston's largest Baptist churches, and when the slave members met and collectively agreed to the sale of the property, they were reimbursed by the white membership. Although receptive to the church's otherworldly offerings, the slaves used its organization to mitigate their condition on earth. Through their missionary and charity funds, slaves collected and dispersed monies for spreading the Gospel among their fellows as well as for the care of their indigent. Although the law prohibited unsupervised meetings of blacks, Robert Smalls reported that while he was a slave he was a member of seven charitable societies that held secret meetings and sometimes even discussed methods by which the slaves could obtain their freedom. According to one minister, slaves made regular contributions to church associations that had as their main purpose "purchasing their members and thus virtu-ally emancipating them." Such collective efforts necessitated a change in the rules governing the black membership of Charleston's Methodist Church in 1815. On the eve of the Civil War, however, blacks continued to use church funds for the purpose of liberating their friends and family members still in bondage.[28]

Although the Presbyterian and Episcopal churches doubted the wisdom of relying on black leadership in administering their slave congregations, the Baptists and Methodists evidenced few such reser-vations. Black Methodists were divided into classes with either a slave or a free black leader. In 1822 Trinity Methodist Episcopal Church had seventy such classes. It was the responsibility of the class leaders, where possible, to visit their charges weekly and attend to their spiritual and moral needs. In the First Baptist Church of Charleston, slaves and free black leaders collaborated with the all-white Committee on Colored Persons in deciding to admit new members or to grant letters of dismissal to those leaving the church. The leadership also summoned members to appear before religious hearings, usually to adjudicate some moral offense committed by the more indiscreet members.[29]

Such activities and organizations, when maintained by blacks and especially slaves, became concerns of the gravest kind for whites. Rev. Paul Trapier, an Episcopalian minister, warned that the "assumption of authority by one colored person over another" was "at variance with their servile condition, and apt in persons so situated, to foster some of the vilest passions, and afford opportunities for gross abuses." He feared the immediate result of such indulgences would be "self-conceit" and ultimately the indirect undermining of slavery.[30]

Once having exercised a degree of autonomy over important church affairs, however, Charleston's blacks were resolved to maintain it. Until 1815, the city's black Methodists had their own quarterly conferences and raised funds that were disbursed by their own leaders and preachers. As in the Baptist Church, the black congregants also convened church trials that were held exclusively among themselves. In 1815 an investi-gation was held that revealed monetary irregularities among the blacks because class leaders had used funds to buy and emancipate slaves. As a result, the rules governing the black members were changed. In the future, they would be required to deliver their funds directly to the stewards, and church trials would be allowed only in the presence of the white minister in charge.[31]

Quite naturally the decision of the Methodist Church aroused considerable opposition among the blacks, who responded by sending Morris Brown, a free black lay preacher, and another delegate to Philadelphia to be ordained as ministers of the newly organized African Methodist Episcopal Church. In 1818, under Brown's leadership, 4,367 blacks seceded from the Methodist Church and formed the African Church, which was affiliated with the African Methodist Episcopal Church in Philadelphia. The secession involved over three-fourths of all the city's black Methodists, and a contemporary minister disparingly remarked, "The galleries, hitherto crowded, were almost completely deserted, and it was a vacancy that could be felt." In the same year the trustees of the African Society bought land on Hanover at Reid Street, upon which a church was built. There were also missionary branches on Anson Street near Boundary and in Cow Alley. At this time the number of African Methodists grew so rapidly that the Charleston membership was only exceeded by that of the church in Philadelphia.[32]

The formation of the African Church in Charleston was a rebellious act of revolutionary proportions.[33] The city authorities recognized the full import of the initiatives taken by this group of slaves and free blacks and responded with harassment. For instance, in June 1818, one hundred and forty members were arrested by the city guard. Five ministers, among them Morris Brown, were sentenced and given the choice of either leaving the state or suffering imprisonment for one month. Eight other ministers were sentenced to pay five dollars or leave the state. Morris Brown, dedicated to his fledgling church, elected imprisonment and remained. Finally, it was only the discovery of the Denmark Vesey slave conspiracy in 1822 that precipitated the final demise of the African Church. Although Morris Brown had no part in plotting the rebellion, several of the conspirators were either class leaders or active in the African Church. As a result, he had to be secreted from the city to avoid bodily harm, and by orders of the city authorities the church building was destroyed.[34]

In addition to the activities they were involved in, the outward appearance of Charleston's slaves often seemed to belie their proscribed condition. As many were engaged in domestic service, their appearance was of concern to their owners, who not only dressed them appropriately but also gave them clothing that had previously been worn by members of their families. Slave women could be especially well dressed, and one observer found those from Santo Domingo worthy of special comment. In the early nineteenth century, John Lambert found these "distinguished from the rest, by their coloured handkerchiefs tastily tied about their heads, the smartness of their dress, and long flowing shawls or muslin handkerchiefs thrown carelessly over their shoulders, a la Francoise [*sic*]." On Sundays, slaves donned their finest clothes to attend church and promenade on the main streets. George Gordon, a newcomer to Charleston, remarked that on Sundays, blacks "crowd the streets in the height of fashion. . . . All through the week they sweat and bark in the sun with a slouch hat, shirt sleeves rolled up & on Sundays they dress up in fine clothes, wear a silk hat and gloves." While visiting the Circular Church in 1818, Rev. Abiel Abbott observed slaves not only decently but "many handsomely dressed" while worshiping in the galleries.[35]

The well-dressed domestics who served affluent masters developed a sense of their own importance that was anathema to their owners. On more than one occasion, a mistress found it necessary to tell her "very gentlemanly dining room servant that he carries his head too high." Often such slaves felt themselves better than whites. A visitor to Charleston was repulsed by scenes of the "sleek, dandified negroes who lounge on the streets" making fun of the poor and tattered "cracker." The relationship between the dress of slaves and their behavior did not escape the observation of the Charleston City Council. In 1822 it found "the expensive dress worn by many of them" not only "highly destructive to their honesty & industry" but more importantly, "subversive of that subordination which policy requires to be enforced." The council requested special state legislation as a means of regulating the appearance of slaves and hence their "insolent" behavior.[36]

Despite the best efforts of masters, Charleston's slaves proved a difficult lot to manage. In amazement, Sir Charles Lyell remarked that "the negroes here have certainly not the manners of an oppressed race." Although slaves were not permitted to be on the streets without a pass after the evening curfew, between September 1836 and September 1837, 573 were convicted of this offense or for being at large in some illegal place. At this time, according to the mayor, slaves violating the curfew were sometimes fined one dollar, and where corporal punishment was meted out at all, it was considered comparatively moderate.[37] Sometimes their violation of the law was flagrant. In 1804 one early morning observer reported his astonishment to witness the arrival of about forty slave men and women by boat from Sullivan's Island, across the Cooper River. When querried, they admitted having been "dancing and carousing all night" with a large number of others. At precisely this moment, a woman whose slave had recently absconded came up and she caught him as he exited the boat. The stunned observer described this incident as only the most recent episode in a "growing evil" and denounced those boatmen who carried slaves without passes to the island.[38]

The slaves' disregard for the curfew was an even greater problem in Charleston Neck, an infrequently patrolled unincorporated area just north of Boundary Street. It would be annexed to the city in December 1849 in part to gain greater control over the activities of slaves in the vicinity. Lamenting the situation there several years earlier, one frustrated master asked:

> How many of us retire on a night under the impression that all our servants are on the premises, and will continue there till morning. And how often is it quite the reverse, especially with our men servants, who are wandering to and fro all night, or are quietly ensconced in some dark retreat of villany [sic], exposed to all sorts of vices and temptations, alike destructive of their morals and their usefulness. It is thus that some of our best servants become cast-aways.[39]

The laws clearly prohibited the disorderly gathering of slaves, yet these were regularly abused. In the mid-1840s one Charlestonian was "constantly annoyed, especially on Sundays, with most unruly and profane mobs; setting all law at defiance, and, if dispersed from one vicinity, re-collecting, with increased numbers, at another." Residents complained about the ineffectiveness of the punishments and laxity of law enforcement in the Neck area. But for at least two years after the area's incorporation, law enforcement remained ineffective. This was because there had been a special police force in the Neck and the extent of regular city police authority there wasn't immediately clear.[40]

Although it was illegal to sell liquor to slaves without their masters' consent, the local grog shop proved to be a favorite gathering spot for slaves. With the contrivance of local authorities, merchants, and shop-keepers, the slave was able to buy a drink there, play a game of cards or dominoes, and sometimes spend the entire night in debauchery. One concerned citizen pointed out that it was not unusual to find "gangs of drunken and riotous negroes lounging, pitching cents, playing marbles, cursing and blaspheming" in the vicinity of these grog shops. This wasn't the only concern of the masters, however. The conviviality that pervaded the atmosphere of such establishments destroyed the critical distance between master and slave. This was especially the case with immigrant grog shop keepers and their black clientele. It was charged that the former "become courteous to the negro and submit to an equality of sociability." Slaves, on the other hand, took advantage of the familiarity, and when they were provoked, used abusive and insulting language toward the tavern keepers as a means of asserting themselves. Masters saw the demoralization of the slave and the erosion of his sense of respect and subservience toward all whites as the end result of the "unrestrained intercourse" between black and white in the grog shop.[41]

Along with the time slaves spent in the grog shops, they engaged in several other pleasurable activities. Gambling was a favorite amusement for some, who participated in lotteries or played "rattle and snap," one of several popular card and dice games. Parties and balls extended into the wee hours of the morning and provided another source of entertainment. At one such ball, the participants "played waltzes and quadrilles, which were danced with great zest." Another popular dance was "Jump Jim Crow" in which a slave would jump up and down while tripping and dancing in the same spot and sometimes sing, "Every time I jump, I jump Jim Crow." The horse races were also quite popular among Charleston's slaves, who were on occasion known to outnumber whites at the race track. After the main races they could be seen enjoying refreshments at the concession stands and watching the less popular horses run.[42]

The diverse social life of the slaves was in large part made possible by the anonymity of living in Charleston. Although most slaves lived in out buildings, located in the master's yard, a significant number did not. Approximately 15 percent of all Charleston's slaves lived away from their masters by 1861. In that same year, Claudia Goldin calculates that one of every thirteen of Charleston's residences was occupied by slaves alone and one of every twelve either by slaves or by both slaves and free blacks. With the privacy of their own quarters, slaves could come and go more freely and also could carry on a variety of activities that would have otherwise been impossible. In a revealing case, after the Charleston Police entered a house they found six slaves gambling, two of which were runaways that had been missing for several weeks. On another occasion, only the orders of the patrol dispersed a late-night prayer meeting at a slave residence.[43]

Despite the city's comparatively large and dispersed white population, slave housing sometimes formed enclaves where the residents lived or visited, safely beyond the masters' constant scrutiny. One such place was Clifford's Alley, which ran west from King Street between Queen and Clifford. Here, in 1861, seventy-six slaves and one white lived in wooden houses, on both sides of the street. Other areas where slaves enjoyed this kind of security were located on Charleston Neck, particularly around the upper edge of the city. In 1856 slave housing there came to the attention of the Grand Jury because:

> In these negro rows as many as fifty to one hundred negroes, or persons of color, are sometimes residing, shut out from the public street by a gate, all the buildings having but one common yard, and not a single white person on the premises. The impolicy of allowing so many persons of color to live together without the presence of a responsible white person, is not the only objection against these places for the neighborhoods of these rows are constantly disturbed by the fights, quarrels, and the turbulence of the inmates. The law of the State declares the assemblage of more than seven male negros [sic], without the presence of a responsible white man, to be an unlawful gathering; but in these rows from twenty to fifty male slaves live together in one house, with only board partitions separating the tenements from each other, and with a common yard to all the tenements.[44]

The grand jurors' concern no doubt extended to such streets as Grove and Hester. Grove Street, located just above the Washington Race Course, almost at the northern boundary of Charleston, had only two white residences but forty-eight slave residents, while Hester, just north of Grove, provided homes for twenty-nine slaves exclusively in 1861.[45]

The possibility of establishing a private residence in the city away from whites and the master particularly, coupled with the quasi-independence of the hiring-out system, gave the urban slave family advantages that were rarely obtained on the plantation. These were only two beneficent features of the urban milieu.

The proximity of churches was of critical importance for the slave family also. Slaves attended church in families, and in church, as one observer surprisingly pointed out, they "make the most formal and particular inquiries after each other's families." Many slaves were married in Charleston's churches. That such church weddings had special significance for them was revealed in the conversations the Rev. Abiel Abbott had with a runaway slave in Charleston's Work House. When Abbott inquired why he had run away, the slave replied that his master desired to sell him to a man in Columbia. Protesting, the slave begged not to be sold, arguing "because I have a *companion* in this city & two children yes . . . & because I am *married according to church.*" When his words fell on deaf ears, the only recourse was to run away. According to Abbott, "there are hundreds of cases of the kind continually occurring" in Charleston.[46]

The church used its moral authority to bolster the slave family, and black members were expected to be faithful in marital affairs and to accept the ideal of the monogamous family unit. The authority of the church and the pressure of peers within it exercised a significant influence on slave families. Illustrative in this respect are the cases of slaves who first requested permission from the church to remarry because they had been separated from their spouses by their masters. Nevertheless, punitive sanctions sometimes had to be taken, and the unfortunates were excluded from the fellowship of the church until their moral indiscretions were recanted.[47]

On balance, the slave family in Charleston was subject to tremendous centrifugal pressures. Family formation and maintenance must have been greatly hampered by the low ratio of males to females in the slave population. In 1861 there were only 77.7 males for every 100 female slaves in the city.[48] In addition and more importantly, it was the master who ultimately held sway over the family's destiny, and the auction block was all too familiar to Charleston's slaves.

With no legal restrictions, white men sometimes gratified their sexual desires with female slaves, and the children of such illicit relations were sometimes accorded special treatment. One master gave his mulatto offspring "the best victuals from the table" and "treated them as his own children." Another master attempted in vain to have his mulatto progeny educated in a school with the other white children.[49]

The female participants in such liaisons were sometimes able to turn them to their advantage and thus command special privileges. Amy, who bore Elijah Willis five mulatto children, rode to the store in his carriage where she was seen "trading largely and as freely as a white woman." In another similar example, a white man named Farr had cohabited with Fon his slave for years. Fon controlled all the domestic arrangements of the household, and it was reported she influenced him as "a white woman and a wife." Farr bought and sold slaves only after Fon had been consulted and had approved. He was even known to have agreed to the sale of a slave that she somehow represented as her own property. Sometimes the master's affection for his slave paramour even led to hostility toward his legal wife. This was the case with Francis Jelineau, who, while lavishing affection on his slave woman and mulatto offspring, "daily insulted" his wife "and encouraged his slave to do the same."[50]

By no means docile, Charleston's bondsmen mounted a continual resistance to slavery. The anonymity of the city and its position as a major seaport made running away one of the most common modes of resistance. In fact, 115 runaways were apprehended in 1838–39 alone. One unfortunate runaway apprehended in Charleston had intended to stow away aboard a ship bound for Massachusetts. Once there, the slave planned to work and accumulate enough money to return to his home in Africa.[51] Morris, a Charleston hotel servant, was more successful. In 1851, with the aid of a white friend who represented him as a free black, he was able to board a ship "without concealment" and sailed to freedom in Philadelphia. In addition to running away, on numerous occasions slaves physically assaulted, maimed, murdered, and poisoned masters in their quest for freedom.[52]

Slave resistance sometimes had as its object not a single master but the entire system. Charleston's slaves were involved in numerous plots to burn the city. In 1797, such a plot was discovered. Also, in 1825–1826 slaves were accused and three convicted of several arson fires which caused serious damage, even engulfing a portion of King Street, a major business thoroughfare and destroying $100,000 in property.[53]

Another cause of uneasiness arose in 1791 when free blacks and whites with slaves fleeing from Toussaint L'Ouverture's military successes in St. Domingue sought refuge in Charleston. By 1794 the presence of Haitian slaves had become a matter of the gravest concern for white Charlestonians, who contemplated their expulsion. "Rusticus," a white who gave such fears their greatest articulation, wrote:

> The circumstances which occasion'd their introduction gave new ideas to our slaves which the opportunities of conversation with the new comers could not fail to ripen into mischief. It may be perhaps true that the generality of those admitted were not immediately concerned in the revolt— their hands were free from blood but they had wittnessed [sic] all the horrors of the scene—they saw the dawning hope of their countrymen to be free—the rapidity with which the flame of liberty spread among them—the enthusiasm with which it was cherished had scarcely perceiv'd it, before they saw too, that their triumph was complete, that it needed but the wish of a trifling struggle to effect their freedom.[54]

Some even came to believe that an organization similar to the Amis de Noirs of Paris existed in Charleston and had encouraged the slaves to take their freedom. But not only the instrumentality of the French Revolution but also its very ideas (which contributed to the temporary abolition of slavery in the French colonies) were unsettling. The logical outcome of the notions of liberty, equality, and fraternity was the attitude of some slave refugees who were overheard to say that "if they continued to serve it was from pure good will for . . . the right of Freedom was theirs."[55]

The subversive actions of the Haitian blacks did not fail to materialize. In 1793, Thomas Jefferson warned the governor of South Carolina that Castaing, "a small dark mulatto," and the quadroon La Chaise, both Frenchmen, had left Philadelphia and were en route to Charleston "with a design to excite an insurrection among the negroes."[56] Burdened with such fears, the intendant of Charleston thought it best to arrest Joukain, "a very dangerous negro," because he formerly "headed a parcel of colored people in Santo Domingo and engaged in a pitched Battle with the Whites." But the spirit of resistance did not die easily. In December 1797, between ten and fifteen French slaves led by Figaro and Jean Louis, were implicated in a conspiracy to burn Charleston and act "as they had formerly done at St. Domingue." The plot was discovered by two mulatto fellows who feared the bloody consequences and urged their master to move away from Charleston before it was too late. Instead he encouraged one of the slaves to win the conspirators' confidence to learn the details of the plan. Based on information he provided, two of the ringleaders were executed and the other participants jailed.[57]

In Charleston, the Denmark Vesey slave conspiracy of 1822 remains the example of slave resistance *par excellence*. Although informants betrayed the plot, the conspirators intended to overpower the city guard, to take control of the arsenals, and once slaves from the country and surrounding islands were supplied with weapons, to fire the town in several places and slay all the whites.[58] The conspiracy, of great importance in itself, is equally significant for the insights it provides into certain aspects of Afro-American life in Charleston.

Although most of the leaders were slaves, Denmark Vesey was a free black. At the time of the American Revolution, Denmark was the property of Captain Vesey, who engaged in the slave trade between St. Thomas and St. Domingue. In 1781 he was sold to St. Domingue, but shortly thereafter because of epileptic seizures he was returned to Captain Vesey. In his twenty years of service to the captain, Denmark had occasion to sail to ports throughout the world. In 1800, after winning a prize of fifteen hundred dollars from the East Bay lottery, he purchased his freedom.[59]

In many respects, the leaders of the conspiracy were exceptional men. Most of them were artisans, and some even maintained their own shops. For instance, Tom Russell was a toolmaker and Monday Gell a harness maker, and both maintained shops. These blacks also possessed a high degree of literacy, often communicating to each other by letter. According to observers, Monday Gell "could read and write with facility, and thus attained an extraordinary and dangerous influence over his fellows." Vesey was not only literate but had some knowledge of classical literature, knowledge that he aptly applied to the plight of slaves.[60]

In Charleston, literacy and the freedoms some slaves enjoyed proved fallow ground in which the awareness of the outside world germinated easily. These slaves were well aware of Rufus King and the controversy over the admission of Missouri to statehood in 1820. The slave William and many others often went to Monday Gell's shop "to hear what was going on in Congress," as they believed that body would shortly grant their emancipation.[61]

It is not surprising that such privileged and exceptionally well-informed slaves devised a complex scheme of resistance that was informed with an equally sophisticated ideology. One element in the ideology of the conspiracy was the monumental example of successful slave revolt in St. Domingue. This was an outstanding source of encouragement to the designs of Charleston's slaves. Vesey had been a slave there, and in addition, there were allegedly one hundred French blacks in and around the city "trained armed and impatient for the conflict." Vesey and his slave conspirators were convinced that they would receive military support from Haiti, if they would only make the first move toward securing their freedom. To this end, Vesey and Monday Gell prepared a letter directed to President Boyer of Haiti. This they delivered to a black sailor on board a vessel then in Charleston harbor. The sailor was formerly a military officer in St. Domingue and vowed to have the letter delivered. As preparation for the task ahead, some slaves even began to read and study descriptions of the battles, tactics, and strategies used by Haitian military leaders.[62]

The logic of rebellion was strengthened by ideological elements borrowed from the Christian religion. Vesey and his fellow leaders artfully used the tenets of Christianity as a justification for revolt. According to Mingo Harth, Vesey devoted considerable time to studying the Bible and teaching blacks that slavery was incompatible with it. Benjamin Ford, a white neighbor, remembered that Vesey spoke frequently about religious matters "which he would apply to Slavery." For example, "he would speak of the creation of the world in which he would say all men had equal rights, black as well as whites and all his religious remarks were mingled with Slavery." At the meetings of the conspirators, Vesey read from the Bible, using the example of the Israelites' delivery from the hands of the Egyptians to bolster the confidence of his fellows in their own deliverance. Vesey skillfully manipulated such themes, themes that had originally led blacks to unite together and establish the African Church in Charleston. Religious references were appealing in that many of the conspirators were church members. In addition to Vesey, Peter Poyas, Ned Bennett, and Charles Shubrick were all class leaders in the African Church.[63]

Although obtaining great strength from Christian tenets, the force of the conspiracy also derived from traditional African religious belief systems. Gullah Jack, an Angolan and one of the most prominent leaders in the conspiracy, was widely acknowledged as a conjure man. According to Mingo Harth, Jack "couldn't be killed shot or caught" because of his magical powers. Jack gave the rebels magical mixtures of parched corn and ground-nuts, instructing them to eat only the mixtures on the morning the rebellion occurred. Then, according to his prescriptions, as the troops assembled, they were each to place a crab claw in their mouths to keep from being wounded. Gullah Jack's presence was important: it was only after Harry Haig and another slave had been "charmed" by Jack that they consented to join the rebellion.[64]

In 1822 there were still many first-generation Africans in the Charleston area.[65] Their interactions with indigenous Afro-Americans allowed many of Charleston's slaves to maintain a profound sense of their original heritage and culture. In addition to religious Africanisms that informed the Vesey conspiracy, the ethnic consciousness of these uprooted Africans also played a role in its logistical organization. Over ten thousand blacks were supposedly enlisted by the conspirators for the purpose of rebellion. Many of these were organized into companies that were based upon the ethnic divisions of the slave community. Monday Gell, an Ibo, organized the Ibo company; Gullah Jack, an Angolan, led the Angolans; and Mingo Harth led the Mandingo. Ethnic consciousness was sometimes skillfully used by the conspirators to coerce reluctant slaves into joining the rebellion. One slave who vacillated about joining the conspiracy recalled Peter Poyas' warning that "he would turn all my Country people against me" if he didn't join. Combined with the influence of a powerful African religious tradition, this evidence clearly revealed a profound African presence. African cultural vestiges were not merely incidental to the conspiracy but in fact provided much of its force. Simultaneous with the use of ethnically based companies, Vesey's collaboration with the leaders of each reveals in microcosm, the process by which many different African people became one.[66]

The nature of Vesey's appeal prefigured several concerns that were later frequently articulated by nineteenth-century black nationalists. Vesey believed that blacks were primarily responsible for their own liberation and often emphasized this. One slave recalled his admonition "that if we did not put our hand to the work, & deliver ourselves, we would never come out of Slavery." Vesey's comparison of the plight of the slaves to that of the Israelites suggests that he conceived of the former as a separate and distinct people suffering under the burdens of an oppressive and racist society. Vesey and those that came after him found hope in the example of successful black nationalist revolution that established Haiti. They drew upon this event not only for encouragement but also as a potential source of military and political aid. Finally, the diversity of African peoples that came together to effect a common plan of liberation belie categorization as a narrow, nationalist thrust in the traditional sense. Such a co-mingling of African humanity reveals the conspiracy's essentially Pan-African dimension.[67]

The Vesey conspiracy never reached fruition because advanced information and assistance in discovering its details were provided to the authorities. The mulatto Peter Desverneys and George Wilson, both slaves, were vital informants and were rewarded with freedom and annual stipends from the state and exemption from taxes. William Pencil, a mulatto and another free black, played critical roles by either providing additional information or by encouraging the slave informants. They were provided with large cash rewards.[68] The conspirators fared far worse. Although it appeared for a while that Vesey had escaped, he was eventually apprehended with seventy-one others. Thirty-five were executed, including Vesey, and thirty-seven others were sentenced to banishment. Not only had the conspiracy failed, but the role played by the informants widened the cleavage that already existed between free blacks and slaves, mulattoes, and those Africans of darker hue in Charleston.[69]

A white Charlestonian confided that "our minds were kept in continual agitation" because of Vesey's plot, and the authorities acted swiftly to provide more effective security. Steps were taken to further repress free blacks. In December 1822 the legislature passed a new law that, among other things, required recent free black migrants to pay special taxes, to secure white guardians, and subjected free black sailors from out of state to arrest once they arrived in port. In 1823 the Negro Seaman's Act eliminated loopholes in the 1822 law and enacted harsher penalties against free blacks who violated its provisions. Also in 1823, the South Carolina Association was formed among wealthy whites to assist in controlling the black population.[70]

The city council established a large municipal police force to preserve order, and it eventually grew to two hundred fifty members by the mid-1850s. In late 1822 the city petitioned the general assembly for a new arsenal to ensure the safety of life and property. A temporary installation was established on Boundary Street, which was the northern border of the city. In the mid-1820s a much more substantial arsenal and barracks surrounded by a high wall and mounted cannons were under construction. In 1842 the newly chartered South Carolina Military Academy, also known as the Citadel, was established here. Charlestonians understood that the nature of a society predicated on slavery made a well-trained military cadre essential for survival.[71]

The martial atmosphere in the city at night was striking to visitors, who commented on the steps taken to guard against the slaves' potential intrigues. Frances Kemble visited in the late 1830s, and, upon learning of the slave patrol, she immediately understood "the meaning of a most ominous tolling of bells and beating of drums, which, on the first evening of my arrival . . . made me almost fancy myself in one of the old fortified frontier towns of the Continent." These "nightly precautions" were not actuated by the fear of foreign invasion but of "domestic insurrection." Two decades later, the European traveler William Russell found many Charlestonians stressed the docility of their slaves. He remained suspicious of "the constant never-ending statement that 'we are not afraid of our slaves.'" Russell found that all the elaborate precautions taken by Charleston's white citizenry "prove that strict supervision, at all events, is needed and necessary."[72]

Although the machinery of law enforcement became more elaborate, even in the final antebellum years, Charleston's resourceful slaves still found ways to circumvent it. Citizens still complained about slaves who frequented interdicted places, especially in the more isolated neighborhoods, where they obtained liquor and disrupted the city's tranquility. Religious services and churches for slaves came in for criticism again because it seemed that these only provided more opportunities for the slaves to violate the law. So seriously did Rev. John Girardeau and the Elders of Zion Presbyterian Church take these charges that they responded to the criticisms in the columns of the *Daily Courier,* reiterating their credentials as southerners and slaveholders.[73]

These reassurances weren't sufficient to convince many by the late

---

1850s; in fact, some whites even charged that slave behavior had deteriorated over the years and openly questioned the direction of slaveholding society. "ANOTHER SLAVEHOLDER" was a skeptic who voiced his concerns to a local newspaper in 1859. He asked, "Can any one recognize for the same people, the slaves and free negroes of the present day with those who filled our streets twenty years ago?" Some of the problems he identified were the illegal emancipation of slaves, slaves who kept bank accounts and travelled freely, including those seen driving the city thoroughfares "in stylish equipages, rivalling those of the less favored white man." Only days after John Brown's infamous raid at Harper's Ferry, Virginia, "ANOTHER SLAVEHOLDER" wrote to urge immediate remedial action to avert the kind of dangers to the community that would require the severest repression of the slaves.[74] The writer couldn't have known it then, but it was already too late; in 1859 slavery had entered upon its final days.

The nature of bondage in the city ensured that even though urban slaves were oppressed, they would enjoy advantages over their rural counterparts. While most of its slaves were unskilled laborers or domestics, Charleston's occupational structure was sufficiently broad to use slaves in a variety of occupations, some of which required a fair amount of skill. The nature of certain slave occupations, along with the pervasiveness of slave hiring practices and housing arrangements, often removed them from the master's constant scrutiny and allowed them to take initiatives unheard of in the countryside.

Often free to determine significant aspects of their daily lives, many urban slaves had important experiences that mitigated some of slavery's most debilitating effects. Charleston, like other urban places, proved a difficult environment in which to thwart slave literacy and awareness of the outside world. The presence of churches was an especially important feature of the city because in addition to their orthodox functions, they served as educational forums, involved slaves in leadership roles, and provided the basis for a modest organizational life. Ultimately, however, it was the master who exercised complete legal authority over the slave. Even so, slaves drank and cavorted with whites, and had sex with them on too many occasions to be completely overawed by their absolute authority.

Unfortunately, some slaves were crushed by the oppressive, racist society in which they existed. These had their aspirations quashed or lacked the self-confidence that was necessary for independent action. Most slaves were illiterate; still others were improvident and possessed with a pathological self-hatred. Fortunately, most were not so debilitated. In the post-emancipation years, the limited self-reliance Charleston slaves had experienced and the values they maintained enabled them not only to survive but also to make substantial contributions to the organization of a new black community.

CHAPTER TWO

FREE BLACK LIFE IN ANTEBELLUM AND CIVIL WAR CHARLESTON

A free black community emerged in Charleston by the 1690s, and by 1850 it had grown to 3,441 persons. Although it was small by northern standards, of ten major southern cities, only Baltimore, New Orleans, and Washington contained larger free black communities on the eve of the Civil War. Many of the slaves emancipated in the countryside eventually found their way to the Port City. Attracted by the anonymity and diversity of Charleston, many also found opportunities to develop the requisite skills, institutions, and attitudes around which a meaningful community life could be built. The free black's penchant for city life indicates that where similar opportunities existed at all in the countryside, they were perceived as comparatively limited. This is why in 1850, approximately 40 percent of all free blacks in the state lived in Charleston and 89 percent of all free blacks in Charleston County lived in the city.[1]

Regardless of their location in the antebellum South, the character of free black communities and their quality of life were dictated by the region's commitment to slavery. All free blacks suffered from the oppressive burdens of that system, but, despite its strictures, in Charleston a comparatively prosperous, cultured, mulatto elite developed. Sometimes it's members even owned slaves. Members of this free brown elite sometimes maintained close relationships with influential whites, received special privileges, and were viewed as a buffer against the much darker and more "dangerous" slave majority. As long as free blacks' existence was at the sufferance of whites, their lives and freedom would be precarious. This became abundantly clear when, during the final antebellum years, even the elite's special status was called into question and their community thrown into a full-scale crisis. As the escalating sectional conflict reached its apogee and war ensued, free blacks, regardless of refinement, appeared anomalous and were forced to answer questions about loyalty and destiny.

Natural increase through births contributed to the growth of Charleston's free black population, but several other factors were also significant. As many urban slaves were allowed to hire their time out, some managed to accumulate enough money to purchase freedom for themselves and for their relatives. As an important southern seaport, Charleston became a focal point for free black migrants from other states and from foreign countries. James Mitchell, for example, was from Portugal, and Robert Gordon fled to Charleston along with many others in the wake of Toussaint L'Ouverture's revolution in St. Domingue. Slaves were also granted their freedom for meritorious services rendered to the state or to local communities. Moses Irvin received freedom as a reward for faithfully serving in the Revolutionary War under Gen. Francis Marion. Likewise, when a slave saved St. Michael's Church from a fire that threatened the entire city, the mayor granted his freedom on the spot.[2]

It seems that the largest single group of emancipated slaves gained freedom by the last will and testament of their masters. Faithful service could be rewarded with freedom, and sometimes emancipation granted under these circumstances was intended to assuage a master's guilt-ridden conscience. In other cases, masters emancipated their mistresses along with their illicit offspring. Joseph Bixby emancipated his slave paramour and her mulatto son Charles, "as no person ever had the right to hold him in Slavery." Philip Stanislas Noisette, an accomplished French horticulturist who migrated to Charleston from St. Domingue, had several children by his slave housekeeper, Celestine. Accordingly, his will provided that the mother and her children be sent to a place where they all might be emancipated.[3]

One consequence of the large-scale manumission of children sired by slaveholders is clearly reflected in the demography of the free black population. In 1860, 75 percent of the free black residents of Charleston County were mulattoes. This contrasts sharply with the county's slave population, 8 percent of which was mulatto. In addition, Charleston, like other southern cities, contained a disproportionate number of mulattoes among its free Negroes. For the South at large, free Negroes of mixed blood amounted to 40 percent of all free blacks, or only roughly one-half the Charleston percentage. This explains why in South Carolina and throughout the Lower South, free Negroes were usually designated free persons of color. According to a South Carolina jurist, this term was "of as settled significance and import as any to be found in our laws . . . and is never applied to any persons but those of mixed blood and who are descended from negroes."[4]

Amicable relations and intimacy with whites assured many manumitted slaves that their transition from slavery to freedom would be aided by the master's benevolence. The amorous relationship between the slave Tabatha Singleton and her master survived the manumission decree. According to observers, after her emancipation, he "maintained the same intercourse" as before: he paid the rent for her tenement and eventually conveyed a house, lot, and two slaves to her. When William Turpin, the former slaveholder turned abolitionist supporter emancipated his Charleston slaves, he provided the newly freed Jenny with a lot and two-story brick house on Society Street. He bequeathed another lot and brick house on Magazine Street to five slaves who were to collectively occupy it. Sarah Gray, a white woman, was allowed the use of one tenement in the house "on condition only, that She Shall Reside therein, and act as Guardian & protector to these coloured people." Another master desired that one of his recently freed slaves "be Sent to School until he has acquired a tolerable English Education in reading, Writing and Arithmetic and then be bound out to Some good trade for Seven Years or until he understands the business he is put to."[5]

In spite of the master's intentions, the ease with which a slave could be emancipated was subject to regulation by the state. Since they lived in a society that not only accepted slavery as necessary but extolled its positive good, free persons of color became increasingly anomalous and found access to their ranks gradually restricted. In 1800, in an attempt to reduce the number of superannuated or undesirable slaves emancipated, the legislature required that candidates for manumission prove their capacity for self-support before a court of magistrates and freeholders. It was not until 1820, however, that legislation specifically designed to curtail the growth of the free black population was passed. After that year, slaves could only be emancipated by the state legislature, free blacks were prohibited from immigrating to the state, and those already there had their egress and ingress severely restricted.[6]

Though they faced a vexatious problem, free blacks found methods to circumvent the restrictions on manumission. Sometimes slaves were sold to trustees who then held them as nominal slaves. In this way, they could not only gain virtual freedom but could also inherit property through their trustees. In other cases, blacks bought their relatives outright, holding them as slaves. By his frugality and industriousness, James Patterson, a free person of color, managed to buy both his wife and children whom he continued to hold as nominal slaves. When Charles Benford was given the opportunity to purchase his freedom in 1832, he found that the laws prevented this and called upon Richard Holloway to hold him as a slave while he paid the money to his original owner. As both Benford and Holloway were friends and leaders in the Methodist Church, the latter man readily assumed the obligation. This was not the first time Richard Holloway had helped secure freedom for a slave. In 1829 he bought Betty from Thomas Bonneau for the same purpose and upon his death willed her exclusively to his wife, "as she knew of the circumstances and would faithfully guard the trust." Betty remained in the family as a nominal slave until the Civil War. Samuel Weston and both William and George McKinlay are known to have also held friends as nominal slaves, circumventing the restrictions against emancipation.[7]

Whites participated in subterfuges by which slaves secured virtual freedom. One Charleston mistress sold her two slaves to a friend for the nominal fee of one dollar but explicitly provided that "Kitty & Mary shall enjoy full free and undisturbed liberty as if they had been regularly emancipated." Others, like Elijah Willis, had their slaves sent to northern states and emancipated there. Another master who found the legislature unwilling to manumit his slave Henry, sent him to Indiana, provided him with considerable sums of money, and financed his education.[8]

As a means of closing all avenues to emancipation, in 1841 the legislature passed the "Act To Prevent The Emancipation of Slaves." By its provisions, any bequest, trust, or conveyance for the removal and emancipation of slaves out of the state was declared void. Bequests or conveyances of slaves that either implied or explicitly made provisions for their nominal servitude were also voided. Finally, all legal agreements designed to allow slaves to inherit property or gifts of any kind through a trustee were nullified.[9]

As only two slaves were officially emancipated in the entire state of South Carolina in 1850, it seemed on its face that the Act of 1841 had effectively closed the remaining avenues to freedom. However, free blacks continued to circumvent the law. Francis Mishaw willed his slave Sally, her children, and his property to three wealthy white executors. The bequest made no provisions for the division of the estate among them, implying that the executors would act as guardians for the family. In 1848 a South Carolina jurist indicated that the restrictive legislation had "done more harm than good" and "caused evasions without number." These succeeded "by vesting the ownership in persons legally capable of holding it and thus substantially conferring freedom, when it was legally denied." Neither was trusteeship effectively curtailed, and the tax records for 1859 and 1860 reveal that free persons of color continued to hold and acquire slaves in trust.[10]

The lengths to which free blacks went to redeem relatives from slavery attests to the importance of the family among them. The church promoted adherence to the monogamous family unit and censured those who acted contrary to its dictates. Many free blacks took pride in their family traditions. The Holloways prided themselves upon the maintenance of a family homestead that not only provided shelter but also housed the family business for several generations. Other free blacks kept detailed family genealogies or records of all births, deaths, illnesses, and important events affecting the family members. The marriage rite was tremendously important to free blacks, many of whom were married in Charleston's most prestigious churches. Among the brown elite, the process by which marriage partners were selected was as elaborate and ritualistic as that of the most aristocratic whites and was designed to ensure that only families of similar socioeconomic backgrounds intermarried. Thus Sarah Ann, daughter of Thomas S. Bonneau, an important free black teacher, married Jacob Weston, a prominent and wealthy free black tailor. Similarly, Frances Pinckney Bonneau married Richard Holloway Jr., a free black teacher. Not all free blacks could afford to be so selective, and although most free blacks married free persons of color, some married slaves. The fact that free black families were protected by law gave them advantages over their slave counterparts but could not eliminate a common problem faced by both: the greater chances women had for emancipation, coupled with the employment opportunities Charleston afforded them, led to a free black sex ratio that was even lower than that of the slaves. In 1861 there were only fifty-six free black men for every one hundred free black women aged twenty to fifty. This contrasts with the sex ratio of the white community, which was much closer to parity (one hundred and eight men to every one hundred women). The low sex ratio of free black men to women must have affected family formation, but even so the modal free black family had two parents and proved to be a remarkably stable institution.[11]

With their personal liberty provided for, free blacks were left to themselves to secure their economic well-being. The method by which emancipation occurred often had a direct bearing on free blacks' ability to retain their freedom. Selective manumission based on its close affiliations with whites and directed toward favorite and often skilled slaves assured free persons of color a significant place in Charleston's economic order.

In 1860 Charleston's free black men engaged in at least sixty-five different occupations, many of which required a considerable amount of skill; free blacks were carpenters, painters, coopers, tailors, shoemakers, brick masons, blacksmiths, butchers, bakers, and barbers. During the antebellum years, the range of occupations for free black women was far narrower. Most were employed as domestics, and the most highly skilled females practiced needlecraft trades. Because of their origins, free blacks were undoubtedly a more skilled group than the slaves of Charleston. More striking are the comparative skill levels of free blacks and immigrants. The occupational structure of free black men is compared with that of German and Irish workers in 1850 in Table 1. Almost 82 percent of all free black workers were engaged in either skilled or semiskilled occupations in 1850. This figure compares quite favorably with both the Irish and German groups. The Irish immigrants had approximately 27 percent and the German immigrants 28 percent of their workers in these categories. The range of skilled occupations available to free blacks was not very broad, though. By 1860 ten occupations provided employment for almost one-half of all free black workers and for 81 percent of all free black skilled workers.[12]

TABLE 1

OCCUPATIONAL DISTRIBUTION OF FREE BLACK, GERMAN, AND IRISH MALES IN CHARLESTON, 1850

	Free Black		German		Irish	
	N	%	N	%	N	%
Proprietary/ Professional	21	3.7	615	68.1	229	21.8
Skilled	388	68.0	224	24.8	230	21.9
Semiskilled	78	13.7	27	3.0	52	5.0
Service-Unskilled	83	14.6	37	4.1	539	51.3
TOTAL	570	100.0	903	100.0	1050	100.0

Source: *U.S. Manuscript Census of Population 1850,* City of Charleston.

As slaves, certain favorites acquired skills or were given liberties that would later aid them as free persons. One free black recalled that as a slave he had been responsible for maintaining his master's accounts and managing many of his financial affairs. In another case, before his manumission, Toney Weston, a slave millwright, was accustomed to working for himself from May to November of every year. Around the year 1831, Weston was employed by Col. Benjamin Franklin Hunt, a distinguished Charleston lawyer, to improve the performance of a threshing machine. After boosting its productivity by 100 percent, his reputation spread among the Low Country planters, who employed his services extensively throughout the antebellum period. The farming and horticultural techniques employed by Alexander and Peggy Noisette initially must have been acquired from Philip Stanislaus Noisette, their former botanist master.[13]

Some free persons of color had such established reputations as skilled workers and tradesmen that whites utilized their services to train their slaves. Richard Holloway, a highly skilled carpenter regularly provided such services. For example, in 1829 Ann Timothy bound her slave Carlos to him for a period of four years to learn the carpenter and house joiner trades. Dr. Benjamin B. Simmons called on Holloway to provide the same service in 1835. Similarly, free blacks used their skills to train one another in various trades. Sometimes one family member trained other members in a specific craft which over time became the family's hallmark. This was the case with the Ingliss family, which, beginning as early as 1819, contained at least one barber. The Holloways established their reputation as carpenters and harness makers. The availability of skilled labor within the free black community enabled young apprentices to acquire much needed training. At age thirteen, Daniel Alexander Payne went into the carpenter's trade along with his brother-in-law James Holloway. While continuing at this for four-and-one-half years, Payne managed to help support himself by selling the various articles of furniture he had crafted. Later, after tiring of the carpenter's trade, he obtained training as a tailor from other free blacks in the city.[14]

Although the white collar, professional, and proprietary class was very small (comprising less than 4 percent of all free black male workers in 1860), Charleston did provide some opportunities for free blacks in this category. As a free person of color, Alonzo J. Ransier was employed as a shipping clerk for a prominent white merchant in Charleston. Some others were able to become small-scale entrepreneurs and operate their own businesses. Richard Dereef and Robert Howard were wood factors operating an extensive business in the city and surrounding area providing residents, factories, and steamers with fuel. They employed many laborers who procured wood and operated several vessels, a regular clerk, and also a bookkeeper. According to Martin R. Delany, Howard and Dereef were "men of great business habits, and command a great deal of respect and influence" in Charleston.[15]

Jehu Jones, another prominent free black, operated his own hotel. Jones' Hotel, as it came to be known, with its "antique and mixed" architecture and large convex windows, was situated in a choice location on Broad Street adjacent to the aristocratic St. Michael's Church. The hotel had a widespread reputation, and according to one Charlestonian "was unquestionably the best in the city . . . few persons of note ever visited Charleston without putting up at Jones', where they found, not only the comforts of a private house, but a table spread with every luxury that the country afforded." With such a reputation, it became the resort of the South Carolina elite and attracted past and contemporary governors, prominent military officials, and a host of European travelers, including the famed British actor Tyrone Power. During Charleston's famous Race Week, Jones' rooms were always completely filled. So far in advance were the decor and fare of Jones' Hotel over any other encountered between New Orleans and Charleston that a commentator declared, "The luxury of Jones' iced claret might have converted Diogenes into a gourmet." In addition to his Broad Street site, Jones operated a resort hotel on Sullivan's Island.[16]

Jones was not the only black hotel keeper in Charleston. Mrs. Eliza Lee, another free person of color, owned the Mansion House, also located on Broad Street. Like Jones' Hotel, it was frequented by Charleston's elite, and its owner's reputation for good management and excellent cooking went unchallenged.[17]

Francis St. Marks, one of Charleston's finest barbers, maintained his salon in the fabulous Charleston House. St. Marks had long established his reputation and accordingly developed an extensive patronage among white Charlestonians. Many wealthy clients like George Gilliland maintained standing accounts with the barber for their shaves, haircuts, and shampoos.[18]

Although highly skilled and sometimes successful enough to have established independent businesses, free black workers encountered several critical problems which in varying degrees impeded their progress. Much of the legislation regarding black workers was actually meant to render them subservient to their employers. The Charleston City Council attempted to freeze the wages of free blacks. According to its regulations, the maximum amount that they could be paid for a full day's work was one dollar. For time periods of less than a full day, the worker was to be paid at the rate of twelve-and-one-half cents per hour. If a free black was convicted of asking for greater wages, the person was to be fined and, if necessary, incarcerated until the fine was paid. Although legislation prohibiting the testimony of blacks against whites in courts of law was not passed with free black laborers specifically in mind, it affected their economic viability nonetheless. In 1791 Thomas Cole, P. B. Mathews, and Mathew Webb, all free black butchers, petitioned the state legislature seeking redress from this discriminatory legislation. Such legal impediments prevented black laborers and businessmen "in recovering Debts due to them, or in establishing Agreements made by them except . . . in cases where Persons of Colour are concerned, whereby they are subject to great Losses and repeated injuries without any means of redress."[19]

Although free blacks constituted a much smaller segment of the labor force than slaves, their high level of skill made whites equally hostile to their employment in certain occupations. The basis for white laborers' apprehensions was well founded, since free blacks had greater mobility than slaves and sometimes engaged in certain occupations in disproportionate numbers. The degree to which free black, German, Irish, and native white male workers participated in ten major occupations for 1850 is revealed in Table 2. Although free blacks constituted approximately 9 percent of Charleston's total free male labor force, they were over-represented in nine of the ten important occupations. Certain occupations reveal a marked concentration of free blacks, such as butchers and tailors, half of whom were free blacks, and coopers, who were slightly less than one-third free blacks.[20]

When he spoke before the Agricultural Society of South Carolina in 1832, Edward R. Laurens, a state legislator, decried the domination of certain skilled occupations by free persons of color in no uncertain terms. He believed anyone could "walk through the streets of our ill-fated city, and see how certainly—how surely, and . . . how rapidly, all the mechanical arts, and all the ordinary avocations" were "becoming overstocked by persons of colour, to the ultimate exclusion of the bone and sinew of our population." Laurens believed that if the current trend forced whites to quit the city, as it seemed it necessarily would, the results would be catastrophic for Charleston "where worse than savage massacre may yet be the consequence of their absence."[21]

The skills that free blacks acquired were protected to a degree because many white workers desired to avoid identification with jobs performed by them. This was understandable according to Laurens and others because "we first degrade the occupation by employing colored persons, and are then surprised that our young men (whose spirit and high-mindedness we endeavor almost daily to excite), will not enter the arena with them." If free blacks were prohibited from the mechanical trades, he continued, "an honorable emulation among themselves [the whites] will immediately take the place of their present apparent apathy."[22]

The stigma of "nigger work" was not sufficient to prevent completely the displacement of free black with white labor. The decade from 1850 to 1860 witnessed both native white and immigrant increases in Charleston's free male labor force. The concomitant to such increases was the decline of free blacks in several critical occupations. Of the ten occupations listed in Table 2, the participation of free black laborers declined in seven from 1850 to 1860. For example, free blacks, as well

TABLE 2

SELECTED OCCUPATIONS IN CHARLESTON ACCORDING TO RACE AND NATIVITY, 1850

Occupation	Free Black		Irish		German		Native White		Total Charleston
	N	%	N	%	N	%	N	%	
Carpenter	107	30.3	23	6.5	14	4.0	188	53.2	353
Painter	11	12.8	13	15.1	7	8.1	36	41.9	86
Cooper	11	31.4	5	14.3	0	0.0	15	42.8	35
Tailor	84	51.5	7	4.3	28	17.2	26	15.9	163
Shoemaker	38	24.2	20	12.7	55	35.0	23	14.6	157
Brick Mason	15	14.8	27	26.7	0	0.0	57	56.4	101
Blacksmith	11	10.0	11	10.0	13	11.8	60	54.5	110
Butcher	21	46.6	4	8.9	6	13.3	12	26.6	45
Baker	1	1.4	8	11.6	32	46.4	18	26.1	69
Barber	26	100.0	0	0.0	0	0.0	0	0.0	26
TOTAL	324		118		155		435		1145

Source: *U.S. Manuscript Census of Population 1850, City of Charleston.*

as native whites, lost approximately 7 percent and 6 percent respectively of their jobs as carpenters. Their losses were balanced by the percentage gains both the Irish (9 percent) and German immigrants (4 percent) made in the occupation. In the case of coopering, an occupation that also evidenced declines of free black labor, their places were assumed by a combination of immigrant and native white workers. In spite of such losses in individual occupations, by 1860, 76 percent of all free black workers were still engaged in either skilled or semiskilled occupations.[23]

The problems faced by free black workers notwithstanding, a significant number succeeded economically and eventually became property holders. In 1860 Charleston had 299 free black taxpayers who owned a total of $759,870 in real property. The group's median property holding was $1,665, but the distribution of holdings among the propertied group was highly skewed. Forty-one free blacks owned $4,000 or more in real estate, and the mean and median property values for this group were $9,278 and $6,000 respectively. Many elite property holders had accumulated real estate when the restrictions against free blacks were less stringent and opportunities greater. This elite comprised 13.7 percent of all free persons of color owning property, and their holdings were worth $380,395, which was 50 percent of the total real property owned by free persons of color in 1860.[24]

Jehu Jones, one member of Charleston's free colored elite, began his career as a tailor and owned property on Coming Street that he inherited from his wealthy mother. Beginning in the early 1800s, Jones began to acquire property in Wraggsboro, which was a new township and also on Logan and Beaufain Streets. In 1809 he purchased a choice lot on Broad Street and in 1815 acquired the house and lot adjacent to it for thirteen thousand dollars. The Broad Street properties were located near the prestigious St. Michael's Episcopal Church. This was the beginning of Jones' Lot, which was expanded into Jones' Long Room and eventually became the famous Jones' Hotel. At his death, Jones' total estate was valued at over forty thousand dollars. Many elite free blacks found real estate speculation and investment lucrative fields of endeavor. The Holloway family supplemented its carpentry enterprise with extensive investments in real estate. Thomas Small owned much land in the city and engaged in extensive speculation. In one transaction, Small purchased a lot on Morris Street for one hundred dollars. The next day he sold the lot for five hundred dollars, realizing a profit of 400 percent overnight. Some free blacks not only held land in Charleston but in other places as well. Thomas S. Bonneau, for instance, owned an extensive plantation outside the city, and Peter Desverneys owned several lots in the town of Aiken in Barnwell County.[25]

Real estate was not the only form of property held by free persons of color. In addition to his commercial and residential property, Robert Howard's personal property was valued at $3,200 in 1860. Others maintained personal bank accounts, and by 1860 Peter Desverneys had saved $1,145.37 in the Charleston Savings Institution. Members of Charleston's free brown elite were sometimes integrally involved in the financial life of the city and state. A case in point is Captain Williamson, a wealthy farmer who owned 128 shares in the Bank of the United States and invested $1,460 in City of Charleston stock.[26]

Free blacks utilized their collective strength to promote their economic interests. The Brown Fellowship Society, an exclusive organization among Charleston's free brown elite acquired a considerable amount of real estate from Charleston College over the period from 1794 to 1820. After the latter date, the organization determined that the return on their investment could be increased by converting the real property to bank stocks. The funds continued to accumulate throughout the antebellum period, until in 1856 the society's initial investment was worth six thousand dollars, which was dispersed among its membership. The Brown Fellowship Society also served as a credit union for its members, allowing them to borrow money from its treasury to make home improvements or finance business endeavors.[27]

In a society that vested the ownership of one man in another, slaves represented another form of property held by free blacks. In 1860 there were 131 Charleston free blacks who owned a total of 388 slaves. The ownership of slaves, like the ownership of real estate, was concentrated in the hands of a few. Among free blacks, 9 percent of the slaveholders controlled 31 percent of the slaves. Furthermore, those free blacks that owned large amounts of real property also owned a disproportionate number of slaves. Of the top forty-one owners of real property in 1860, thirty-one owned slaves. This group, while making up 24 percent of all black slaveholders in Charleston, controlled 43 percent of the slaves owned by free blacks in 1860. During the period from 1820 to 1860, women predominated among the free black slaveholding heads of households in Charleston: two-thirds of the free black slaveholding heads of households were women in 1850. This is probably because women made up the majority of the free black population and were given slaves by their former white masters or inherited them from relatives or spouses.[28]

It has already been established that free blacks often held relatives as slaves to circumvent the laws restricting emancipation. It is also certain that slaves were held for purely economic reasons. Sometimes they were viewed merely as assets by which a deceased spouse could provide comfort for the surviving family members. The case of Richmond Kinloch is revealing in this respect. Upon his death he provided that Peggy "be hired out to pay all my lawful debts, but should my Creditors demand immediate . . . payment then it is my wish and desire that Peggy shall be sold & after all my debts is [sic] paid the balance of sale shall go to the purchase of a small girl which shall be the same to My beloved wife if [sic] Peggy had not been sold as well as all issues from her."[29] Peter Desverneys' case is an especially ironic one as he was a former slave who obtained his freedom by informing on a slave conspiracy. His last will gave the slave Lavinia to his wife during her lifetime. At her death, he ordered his executors to sell the slave "with her issue and increase at public auction . . . and the proceeds . . . I give and bequeath unto my son William Desverneys and my step daughters." Thomas S. Bonneau owned slaves who resided in Charleston and others that worked on his plantation outside the city. Alexander Noisette owned three slaves who worked on his farm in Charleston Neck. Upon his death, the trustee of the estate was given authority to sell all or some of the slaves if necessary and to distribute the proceeds to Noisette's widow and children. In 1859 one of the slaves was sold for fourteen hundred dollars.[30]

The largest group of black slaveholders worked in the various garment trades; in 1850 there were twenty-nine free black garment makers. Most were female mantua makers and seamstresses and were unmarried or widows who depended on their own income and headed households. They saw the value of slave labor for their enterprises and generally purchased adult women who were employed in their businesses. In addition to employing slaves in their own businesses, free black slave owners often hired them out to others. There are many examples of male and female owners who hired out skilled slave artisans and domestics to supplement their incomes. Between 1840 and 1846, William McKinlay bought sixteen slaves of both sexes, all of which were hired out, many undoubtedly as domestics. The extensive use of slaves as domestics and in the garment industry ensured that women would predominate among the enslaved. In 1850, of 755 slaves owned by free persons of color, 452 were female.[31]

Free black slaveholders sometimes had special difficulties. Such was the case with Anthony Weston, one of the wealthiest of Charleston's colored masters. Anthony was emancipated by his master for faithful service in 1826, contravening the Act of 1820, which required state approval. Fortunately for Weston, though, he was allowed to enter upon a new life as a de facto free man. Despite the fact that he was listed in the census as free, and he paid the state capitation tax, he still couldn't legally own property. He used slaves extensively in his millwright business but these were purchased by his wife Maria and held in her name. Between 1834 and 1845 she purchased twenty slaves valued at $8,950 and several already possessed skills. In 1860 Maria Weston's real estate holdings were worth $40,075 and she owned fourteen slaves. Apparently the Weston's sometimes purchased slaves at their request to prevent family separations. Anthony was likely one of the more benevolent masters and allowed his slaves the kind of liberties he enjoyed and may have even assisted some to purchase their freedom.[32]

Unlike other forms of property holding, the ownership of slaves by free persons of color in Charleston had special consequences. This practice increased the social distance between free persons of color and the slaves in general and certainly increased slave suspicions of the free group. But also 85 percent of Charleston's free persons of color who held slaves were mulattoes, while the slaves were a predominantly black group. By the act of holding slaves the gulf between mulattoes and blacks was widened.[33] Both consequences would make it more difficult for free Negroes and slaves to forge a united front during the antebellum years.

Elite free persons of color formed a highly group conscious and exclusive segment within the larger free Afro-American population. They had an appreciation for Charleston's aristocratic traditions, but this did not necessarily lead to a disavowal of racial pride or heritage. As an artisan-elite, they were imbued with the Protestant ethic and confidently embraced the idea of self-help as the vehicle for individual and group advancement. In this sense, their approach to socioeconomic problems rested on assumptions and strategies that they shared with contemporary northern black communities.[34]

Members of Charleston's free brown elite evidenced a high-spirited sense of noblesse oblige even rivaling that of many aristocratic whites. Maria Creighton, a wealthy free black woman, bequeathed her house as a meeting place for the society maintained by black Baptists in Charleston. The remainder of her estate was to go to the Baptist Church for the support of indigent blacks in the city. Captain Williamson likewise willed two hundred dollars to the Circular Church for the same purpose and bequeathed one hundred dollars to support its Colored Sabbath School. Another free person of color named Creighton accumulated considerable wealth in all forms that he decided to devote to the colonization of blacks in Liberia. When he disposed of all his property, he offered to emancipate his slaves and pay their transportation there.[35]

Although free persons of color sometimes benefited from public and private relief services, they generally had to rely upon their own efforts to ameliorate social problems in their community. Fortunately, the elite's beneficent concerns led to the formation of several mutual benefit and charitable societies. One such organization, the Minor's Moralist Society was formed in 1803 by such prominent men as James Mitchell, Joseph Humphries, William Cooper, Thomas S. Bonneau, and Richard Holloway. Its main object was "to educate orphan or indigent colored children, and also to provide for their necessary wants." Its members totaling fifty paid a five dollar initiation fee and twenty-five cents per month dues. The Christian Benevolent Society was another organization created to cope with the problem of indigence among free blacks. Organized in 1839, according to the members, its purpose was "the commiseration and aid of the sick poor of our free Colored Community in the City, by pecuniary grants, and Judicious Council." From its inception until 1856, the organization spent $1,228 and aided seventy persons.[36]

The elite's sense of noblesse oblige was sometimes tempered by class consciousness, the case in point being the Brown Fellowship Society. According to James Holloway this organization, made up of male members of Charleston's free brown elite, had "as its foundation-stone Charity and Benevolence, and its capstone Social Purity."

Membership in this exclusive society was limited to free mulattoes and their descendants. Its members and their families had the benefit of the organization's cemetery. If any member died and left an insufficient estate to care for his children, the children would be fully supported and educated until age fourteen. Then the children would be apprenticed to craftsmen until adulthood. The records of the society reflect that Daniel Alexander Payne was one of the earliest boys taken in, clothed, educated, and put to a trade.[37] The Society of Free Dark Men (also known as the Humane Brotherhood), likewise of benevolent purpose, admitted only "respectable Free Dark Men" to its ranks. Its members viewed with disdain the pretensions of the mulatto elite, and they were especially disdainful of those females who either actively courted or tacitly approved the attentions of white men. The Unity and Friendship Society and the Brotherly Association are other prototypical examples of associations designed to provide for the insurance and charitable needs of their members.[38]

Several of Charleston's free blacks, themselves men of cultivation and refinement, showed a keen interest in both contemporary and classical literature. At his death Richmond Kinloch bequeathed to various persons his *Polyglot Bible,* a two-volume set of *Blair's Sermons*, six volumes of *Scots Family Bible*, *The Life of Josephus*, *The Teacher's Assistant*, and *Brewer's Travels in Turkey*. Organizations were formed to pursue the literary interests of wealthy free blacks. According to its articles of organization, the Bonneau Literary Society was formed "for the purpose of obtaining further progress in Literary Improvement & . . . for the Improvement of Our Mental Faculties." The Clionian Debating Society established in 1847 maintained its own library, and its debates and proceedings were very similar to counterparts at Charleston College at the time. Two of the college's graduates, John and Francis Mood, sometimes attended the Clionian meetings and donated books to its library.[39] The Library Society and the Amateur Literary and Fraternal Association were other free black organizations dedicated to intellectual growth.

The natural outgrowth of such concerns was the establishment of schools for free persons of color. Around 1807, at the request of the Brown Fellowship Society, Thomas Bonneau established a schoolhouse to educate the members' children in Richard Holloway's yard. Bonneau enjoyed such popularity as a teacher and his school attracted such a following that he was required to hire William McKinney and Frederick K. Sasportas as assistants.[40]

Daniel Alexander Payne was trained for two years in a school maintained by the Minor's Moralist Society. Later, he received his advanced education in Thomas S. Bonneau's school. Payne continued the work of his mentor: he opened his own school in 1829 with three students. Although he taught slaves clandestinely, Payne attracted children from Charleston's leading free black families. His school was the most popular of five then in existence because of its advanced curriculum. In addition to the three R's, descriptive astronomy, natural philosophy, biology, grammar, map skills, and history were among the subjects Payne taught. After several relocations, the school obtained a permanent building and eventually served sixty pupils.[41]

On more than one occasion free blacks enlisted the services of white teachers to educate their children. One of the most popular schools operated by whites for free blacks was conducted by Mr. W. W. Wilburn. He was paid a regular salary arranged for by a board of trustees that managed all the financial affairs of the school. Some of the earliest trustees were such prominent free persons of color as Benjamin Huger, Joseph Sasportas, and William McKinlay. Sometimes students from Charleston College were hired as tutors for those free blacks engaged in advanced study. Samuel and William Weston, along with other men of "means and character," hired Henry Mood, a college student, to organize an afternoon school. Located in a house rented by its trustees, the school prospered and later utilized Thomas Mood, also a Charleston College student, as an assistant teacher.[42]

While visiting Charleston's free black schools in the 1850s, Fredrika Bremer was impressed with the breadth of study they offered and noticed that in one, the texts were exactly the same as those used by white children. These schools, with their advanced subjects and exceptional advantages, attracted students from other nearby cities, several of whom were from Augusta, Georgia. Just as Charleston's schools attracted students from other places, the lure of the North and the hope of increased opportunities led some Charleston free blacks to travel there in pursuit of advanced studies. One such individual was Allen M. Bland, who, after completing his education at a local school maintained by a Charleston College graduate, moved to Philadelphia in hopes of studying further and obtaining suitable employment. Edward M. Brawley, another Charleston free black, was sent to the Institute for Colored Youth in Philadelphia where he pursued advanced study.[43]

The free black quest for education was not without its obstacles. In a slave society increasingly attacked by abolitionists and convulsed by slave rebellion or its threat, the educational efforts of free blacks were viewed with suspicion and fell prey to restrictive legislation. Such legislation was offered in direct response to the level of educational activity maintained by Charleston's blacks. In 1834, fearful politicians framed laws making it illegal for free persons of color to maintain schools either for themselves or for slaves. Because of this legislation, Daniel Payne became so disenchanted with his continued prospects as an educator in Charleston that he closed his school and moved to Philadelphia. Although the exact degree to which the restrictions impaired black education is difficult to assess, they must have made it more difficult. But no amount of legislation could completely squelch the free black's attempts to seek education. As late as 1859, a slaveholder was appalled as he observed the ineffectiveness of legislation to end "the crowds of black children who throng our streets every morning on their way to school, with satchel well filled with books." The initial efforts of Charleston's free black educators laid the groundwork for moderate levels of literacy within the community. In this respect, Charleston's free black community compared quite favorably with others throughout the South, and only 1 percent of its adult population could neither read nor write in 1850.[44]

The church provided its own special kind of education for free blacks. Although its purpose was spiritual, the effective imparting of its message in the black community called for able and dedicated leadership. Cumberland Street Methodist Church housed one of the earliest Sunday Schools controlled by free blacks. Prominent among its teachers were Ann, Jacob, and Samuel Weston, Daniel A. Payne, Edward Beard, F. W. Wilkinson, and Richard, Charles, and Isaac Holloway. Later, during the years 1862 and 1863, free black superintendents and teachers assumed control of their Sunday School at Trinity Methodist Church.[45]

Free blacks in the Methodist Church served as class leaders, and several were exceptional spiritual leaders. After Daniel A. Payne felt the impression of God on his soul, he was assigned to the class of Samuel Weston. In Payne's own words, Weston "from that time became the chief religious guide of my youth." Payne continued his religious studies and later became a bishop in the African Methodist Episcopal Church.[46]

Among antebellum Charleston's black churchmen, men of national prominence, like Daniel Payne and Morris Brown, were exceptions, but its local leadership was quite respectable nonetheless. Among the city's black Baptists, Jacob Legare was a well-known minister. In addition to preaching the Gospel, he attended to the spiritual and moral needs of his charges and often acted as an intermediary between them and the white church officials. In one case, the slave Amelia requested a letter of dismissal so that she might join a church in Augusta. After examining her character and providing counseling, Legare reported favorably on her request.[47]

By virtue of their status, free blacks were usually able to assume more authority in the church than slaves. Bishop William Capers, recounting the quality of free black leadership among Charleston's Methodists, pointed out that "we had belonging to the Church in Charleston . . . as if raised up for the exigencies of the time, some extraordinary colored men." Among these were Castile Selby, Smart Simpson, Harry Bull, Richard Holloway, and Alek Harleston. These were "men of intelligence and piety, who read the Scriptures and understood them, and were zealous for religion among the negroes." Known to many of the planters in rural South Carolina, they were permitted to preach to the slaves, while white Methodist ministers were sometimes denied the privilege because it was suspected they harbored antislavery views. Richard Holloway traveled as far as Savannah to preach for the Methodist Episcopal Church. Free black Methodist preachers were authorized to accept and exclude members and to exercise other important church functions, even though these activities were contrary to the church regulations set forth in its Discipline. Such assumptions of authority were permissible, even needed, according to Bishop Capers, because "we knew them to be good men," and there was no other alternative. Although short-lived, the African Church in Charleston provided unique opportunities for free blacks, many of whom were active in the Philadelphia organization and served as deacons and elders at its annual conference.[48]

Although many free persons of color fared well, in several respects the group's existence was an imperiled one, even in Charleston. Free blacks were sometimes kidnapped and sold as slaves. This had been the case with Phillis Cox. While this unfortunate black woman was born free in Pennsylvania, a tragic series of events resulted in her being sold and being held as a slave in Charleston. As a boy, Daniel Payne's father met the same fate and remained a slave in Charleston until he reached adulthood and purchased his freedom for one thousand dollars. Moreover, free blacks could legally be sold into slavery. Burdened with a special capitation tax and also subjected to the taxes that were regularly laid on whites, free blacks who failed to pay these assessments could be enslaved. The inability to pay jail fees or court fines brought the same result. In one case, when four free blacks convicted of harboring two slave girls found themselves unable to pay their fines, they were sold to the South Carolina Association.[49]

A society predicated upon the perpetual bondage of Afro-Americans perceived free blacks as a particularly enigmatic group. Rather than adjust to their peculiar situation as free blacks, some blacks attempted to lose their racial identity by passing for white. In one interesting case from the 1820s, a man was required to defend himself in court and would have received all the civil rights of a white person were it not for a witness who was accused of being a mulatto. Testimony regarding this matter was elicited, and it was determined that not only was the witness a mulatto but that the defendant was also. According to the court, such instances were by no means rare.[50]

Ironically, while antebellum South Carolina, like the South at large, was deeply concerned with the issue of race, miscegenation had so blurred racial boundaries that no firm guidelines for their determination could be maintained. Color proved a deceptive measure of racial purity, and pure genealogical analysis presented certain problems, as observed by a South Carolina court, which, in 1835, declared:

> If we should say that such an one is to be regarded as a person of color, on account of any mixture of negro blood, however . . . remote, we should be making, instead of declaring the law, and making a very cruel and mischievous law. . . . We cannot say what admixture . . . will make a colored person . . . the condition is not to be determined solely by visible mixture . . . but by reputation . . . and it may be . . . proper, that a man of worth . . . should have the rank of a white man, while a vagabond of the same degree of blood should be confined to the inferior caste.[51]

One case reveals that the descendant from the union of a mulatto and a white woman, "although of dark complexion, had been recognized as a white man, received into society, and exercised political privileges." His daughter was treated as white, and his grandchildren, although they were one-sixteenth black, passed for white and married into some of the most respected families in South Carolina. Judicial determination of racial status sometimes divided families. Elijah Bass was either a mulatto or a dark quadroon. Of two children by his wife, the daughter "shewed plainly the corrupt blood," but her brother "appeared an ordinary white sand hill boy." Interestingly, in 1846 a jury found these two children free mulattoes, while in a separate decision a different jury found another of Bass's sons to be a free white person. The determination of racial status was a vexatious problem, and, according to one court, the attempts by free persons of color to assimilate represented an unfortunate yet "constant tendency" that frequently embarrassed the white community.[52]

As objects of suspicion in the slaveholding South, free blacks became painfully aware that their freedom was exercised only at the sufferance of whites. Thus many perceived the maintenance or advancement of their social positions as dependent upon how successfully they distinguished themselves from the slave population. When he was asked to join with Denmark Vesey's conspirators, one free black responded that "as he was a free man he would have nothing to do with slaves." In some of Charleston's Methodist Churches, free blacks were reluctant to sit with slaves. This tendency to dissociate from slaves was greatest among the free brown elite. As a member of this group, Jehu Jones interacted with whites whenever possible, seldom kept the company of even light-complexioned free blacks, and never of slaves. Conditioned by such attitudes, slaves reciprocated in kind. Rev. W. H. Barnwell found it "difficult to get slaves to attend meetings in the week [because] they seem as reluctant to attend meetings frequented by the free people of color as those of the white." Already separated from slaves by color, wealth, and slave ownership, the attitudes of many free persons of color reinforced these distinctions.[53]

An outstanding example of this behavior can be found in the records of the Friendly Moralist Society, an important elite benevolent association. In June 1848, Michael Eggart, the incoming vice president, gave the annual address, which focused on the distinctive identity and problems of Charleston free persons of color. He identified the problematic nature of the group: they occupied a "middle ground" between white prejudice and "the deepest hate of our more sable brethren." In his view, there was little chance of overcoming the "foul hate" of blacks, but it was possible to win the esteem of whites while further distinguishing themselves from the slaves. Both purposes could be accomplished by making sacrifices to hire more teachers capable of fostering the intellectual and moral development of the group. Eggart believed "by so doing we add bone and sinew to our strength *as a people*" (emphasis added). Eggart rhetorically asked, "And what but Education raises us Above the level of the slaves[?]" The problem was that the most ignorant persons were often taken as representative of all free blacks. He contended that if they could only be educated, "how much *more* vivid how much brighter would the line of separation be between us and the slaves. it [*sic*] would be so bright that it would Eventually triumph over the prejudices of the white man." To succeed, Michael Eggart urged elite organizations to arrive at common goals and coordinate their efforts.[54]

Sometimes persons of color took calculated steps to prove their sense of civic responsibility and loyalty. In 1814 a large number of free blacks, including the free brown elite, volunteered to aid in the preparations for the defense of Charleston from the British. The mayor accepted, using their services to build an extensive breastwork in the eastern part of the city. On other occasions, free blacks took steps to minimize those matters that might be perceived as potential threats to the larger society. It was such concerns that led Edward P. Wall to decline to serve as orator for the Friendly Moralists. The secretary reported, "He is opposed to having addresses before the society believing the same to be dangerous to the Pease [*sic*] and security of the Society." The Brown Fellowship Society prohibited the discussion of any ecclesiastical or political matters during its meetings for the same reasons.[55]

By demonstrating their fidelity, and by acquiring wealth, literacy, and, in some cases, slaves, members of the free brown elite hoped to carve out a special niche for themselves. To a certain extent, they were successful, and in lower South cities, such as Charleston, something approaching a three tier model of racial stratification developed. In this model—a model that typified Caribbean slave societies—whites occupied the top of the hierarchy and black slaves the bottom. Free persons of color (who were often mulatto) occupied a position intermediate between the others and were accorded special privileges. In various ways, whites bolstered this intermediate position to secure the loyalty of free persons of color.[56]

Both the property and privileges free blacks were allowed to enjoy were seen as effective tools of racial policy. The right to hold slave property was perceived as especially useful in this respect because, according to the Charleston *Courier* in 1835, "it identified his [the free person of color] interests and his feelings . . . with those of the white population." This explains why, in the late 1820s, at least one of the free Holloway men was required to serve with the Charleston Neck Rangers. One of the main functions of this unit was to police the slaves in that suburban area. When free blacks were threatened with additional restrictive legislation in the 1830s, the *Courier*'s editor warned against "breaking down the barrier which now separates the free colored man from the slave, and assigns him an intermediate caste between the slave and his master." The continued privileged status of the group was important because, as one Charleston pamphleteer reminded his readers, "in case of revolt they would be more likely to prove allies of the whites." In 1858 Alfred Huger, postmaster of Charleston, espoused the same views. He described free persons of color as the best "intermediate class in the world," and he went on to say that "they are our natural allies [and] . . . make an insurmountable barrier between the right of the master and the sedition of the slave." The group's other value for Huger was its possession of mechanical skills, which could help keep the white working class in check.[57]

The free blacks, and especially the members of the free brown elite who enjoyed the confidence and preferment of influential whites, had important advantages. In 1843 Elias W. Garden, a mulatto slaveholder, had such a highly respected reputation that local authorities declared that "all persons with whom he may sojourn and desire to receive his attestation [should] grant to [him] . . . the benefits of common kindness and the rights and privileges of a free white citizen." He was still considered a mulatto but was not required to pay the state capitation tax required of adult free persons of color. William Rollin maintained a lumberyard in Charleston, employed several whites in his business, and often obtained city contracts. The demands of his business required him to travel north, which he did regularly even during the 1850s. His trips clearly violated the law, but his daughter Frances explained, "My father's business interest was so interwoven with that of the most influential element of both races no account was taken of the law in his case."[58]

Daniel Payne so impressed Dr. John Bachman, the distinguished naturalist, that Payne was able to use the scientist's laboratory and discuss complex zoological problems with him. The amity between the two encompassed Bachman's family with whom Payne conversed "as freely as though all were of the same color and equal rank." Daniel Payne was respected by whites, several of whom he conferred with after deciding to quit the city. From them, he obtained letters of introduction to prominent northerners who would aid in his relocation. The conservative policy of the Brown Fellowship Society that prohibited the discussion of political and church-related issues proved beneficial in the mid-1830s. Legislation passed at this time made it more difficult for free blacks to meet together. After he heard of the society's meetings, Mayor Hayne sent for the minutes. Upon their review he commended the organization's purpose and declared its members exempt from the restrictive legislation.[59]

In one outstanding case, members of the Noisette family were able to secure their freedom from slavery with the aid of prominent white friends. Peggy, the wife of Alexander Noisette, along with her children Celestina, Margaret, and Philip were held as nominal slaves by their trustees the Rev. John Bachman and John Seigling. These trustees were sincerely interested in the family and desired "to keep up the name of Noisette in a respectable position for future years." Upon the death of her husband, Peggy occupied and cultivated land Alexander had arranged Dr. Elias Horlbeck to hold in trust. The farm became a model for all others on Charleston Neck, and although in reality the farm was managed by Peggy, it remained the official charge of Horlbeck. When they feared discovery that the liberties enjoyed by the Noisettes ran counter to the Act of 1841, the trustees, along with James L. Petigrew, devised a scheme to obtain the slaves' emancipation. The plan was for the trustees to grant Peggy and all her children deeds of manumission that would be certified in Philadelphia. According to Petigrew, this would secure their manumission "even in a Court as at present constituted." Apparently, the plan worked, as both Peggy and Celestina are reported as free persons of color in the federal census of 1860.[60] The support of aristocrats was critical if concessions were to be won by free persons of color. Importantly, though, such support and protection could only be granted on terms dictated by whites, thus ensuring its extension only to conservative and unobtrusive elements in the black community.

The vast majority of free blacks did not have the colored elite's special interests to protect. With few hopes of passing from their caste-like position they interacted freely and naturally with the slave population. Free blacks and slaves mingled in the grog shops, at nocturnal balls, and at the race track, and participated in a variety of amusements together. They were also often connected by marriage and by a broad network of family relationships. Free blacks and slaves collaborated in the church, acting as spiritual leaders, collecting and dispersing funds and purchasing burial grounds. Charleston's African Church was especially significant in this respect, forging a unity of purpose between members of the elite, like Morris Brown, the middle class, poorer elements within the free black group, and the slaves.[61]

It was also the whites' shared notion of a society predicated upon the degradation of all Afro-Americans that brought the interests of slaves and most free blacks closer together. Some free blacks enjoyed privileges, but they were exceptional. Moreover, free blacks were identified with the enslaved group by a common racial heritage and were made to share in the slaves' degradation at every turn. Free persons of color were tried in slave courts along with their fettered brethren and likewise were subject to the arbitrary justice of the slave patrol. They found many of Charleston's institutions inaccessible to them. Mentally disabled and superannuated slaves had been accommodated in the Charleston Poor House, but by the 1830s all other black indigents were excluded, although they were still legally entitled to its services. Blacks were also excluded from hotels, restaurants, and theaters. According to a traveler, minstrel shows and the play *Othello* were even prohibited "lest the negroes in Charleston should conceive, from being represented on the stage, and having their colour, dress, manners, and customs imitated by the white people that they were very important personages."[62]

The institutions that did admit blacks did so in ways calculated to reinforce the distinctions between the races. Calvary Episcopal Church provided accommodations for whites who entered the edifice by a separate door. They would sit in seats "set apart and raised keeping before the eyes of the congregation, at all times, a sensible image of the subordination that is due to those to whom by the course of Providence, they are to look up to as their rulers." When in 1842 the city councilmen contemplated how indigent free blacks could best be served, they decided to remodel the old workhouse to provide a separate building from that used by the whites, because they believed "the distinction of castes must be strictly and broadly preserved in slave-holding communities."[63] The concerted steps taken to maintain the distinctions between castes ensured that slaves and most free blacks would have more common interests than either group would have with whites.

This shared plight explains why whites found the presence of free blacks especially problematic during times of crisis. While their egress and ingress was already limited by the Act of 1820, in 1822 (the year of the Vesey conspiracy), free persons of color were required to register twice a year with the intendant and to explain any prolonged period of absence from the city. That same year, the Charleston delegation introduced a bill to the legislature to banish all free blacks who had come to the state in the previous five years. Many whites believed that free blacks could not long endure a situation that allowed certain rights and prohibited others. Convinced that partial freedom necessarily created "a thirst for its perfection" this situation would "inevitably drive them, in every desperation, to obtain that by force which can be effected in no other way."[64]

Congenital suspicion of free blacks was transformed into hostility and fear by two related series of events that occurred during the 1850s. The first involved white workers, a group that had always decried the employment of slaves in skilled trades. White workers complained about free black competitors, and they especially complained about the extensive contracting businesses blacks operated in the construction trades. In the years immediately preceding the Civil War, white artisans tried to strengthen their hand by winning favorable legislation. In December 1858, three white workingmen's associations petitioned the legislature to restrict or eliminate slave competition. The Committee on the Colored Population readily admitted that a problem existed because hired slaves were making their own contracts and generally conducting themselves as free workers. Nevertheless, it flatly refused to recommend excluding them from crafts but instead proposed penalties for employers who hired slaves directly, rather than through their masters. Even so the Committee stipulated that exceptions had to be made because strict enforcement "would . . . drive away all slave labor from any employment in the towns." White workers were persistent, and they made similar appeals to the Charleston City Council, where they were no more successful. The aldermen shared the same reservations as the legislators and also deemed it improper to interfere with the masters' control over their slave property.[65] Although their attempts to obtain legislative relief failed, the level of white labor's hostility toward black competition was undiminished.

A second series of events was the escalation in the sectional conflict during the final decade before the Civil War; because of this sectional conflict, the social position of free blacks deteriorated markedly throughout the South. In South Carolina as early as 1850, the governor recommended the removal of all free blacks, except those who owned real estate or slaves. Since many free blacks were former slaves and interacted with slaves, they were viewed as the entering wedge by which abolitionist doctrines surreptitiously spread throughout the South. These apprehensions explain the attempts to restrict their movement, particularly outside the state. Free blacks regularly evaded such restrictions, thereby seeming to confirm their ascribed roles as abolitionist emissaries. John Brown's raid on Harper's Ferry, Virginia, in October 1859 signaled the need for greater regulation of the entire black population. Like Vesey's earlier conspiracy, it especially focused the attention of whites on Charleston's free black community and the threat it posed.[66]

An influential segment of white public opinion increasingly lumped all free blacks together regardless of class and even denounced the activities and liberties of the most affluent as threats to the slave system. One anxious slaveholder rhetorically asked city officials for an explanation of "the negro visitors to northern cities and watering places, who go and come regularly every season under the very eye of the law, and who return, possibly, with the personal acquaintance of the black Douglas [sic] and the white Greeley." Strict adherence to the law had been neglected for too long. Given the volatile political climate, there was now a need to "purge our community and punish its lawbreakers. Neither talents, social position or wealth should screen them from public exposure and denunciation." In January 1860 the Charleston Grand Jury even expressed concern over the practice of slaves and free blacks riding on public conveyances driven by whites. The jury warned that "it is proper that the line of demarcation between the castes should be broad and distinct, more particularly at this time for reasons which need not be mentioned." Now more than ever before, it was necessary that slaves and free persons of color "know and understand their position" in southern society.[67]

By spring 1860 the specific grievances of white workers and those of Carolinians who viewed free Negroes as a dangerous fifth column converged with devastating effect on Charleston's free persons of color. At this time, Charles McBeth, the recently elected mayor, fulfilled campaign promises to uphold the interests of white mechanics and to gain control over the city's black population. He initiated a crackdown on slaves working without badges, and, during the spring and summer months, arrests for this offense soared. Free blacks were affected by the new, stringent enforcement policies in two ways. First, the same vigor was used to enforce the capitation tax, and arrests for failure to pay also escalated. Second, many free persons of color had been illegally emancipated and had worked for years unmolested. But now they were required to *prove* their freedom. Those unable to do so were required to obtain badges just like other slaves, and were required to at least have an owner in trust. In August the Charleston *Courier* reported that within two or three days, some sixty or seventy blacks had been arrested for working without badges, and three to four hundred badges were sold by the city. Most of those arrested, according to the paper, "were under a mistaken notion that they were free and did not require it [a badge]." In contrast to the *Courier*'s dispassionate reportage of this situation, its reporter noted the episode "created considerable commotion" amongst those affected most directly.[68]

In the heat of the South's reaction to John Brown's raid, some whites were not satisfied with the mere enforcement of the laws. For such persons, only the complete removal or enslavement of the free black population could eliminate its threat. In 1859–60 at least four different bills for this purpose were introduced in the state legislature. One would have replaced extant punishments with enslavement for free blacks convicted of certain crimes. Others would have re-enslaved free blacks who remained in the state after certain dates (March 1860 and January 1, 1862, were both contemplated). Free blacks were assailed in other ways also. Their livelihoods came under attack when the legislature's Committee on the Colored Population recommended free blacks' exclusion from the mechanical trades. A bill was also introduced to prohibit them from owning slaves. A full-scale crisis ensued in Charleston's free black community. The old informal arrangements with influential whites that protected the de facto free began to break down. Many of the whites who had in the past acted as guardians for free blacks refused to challenge the group's detractors and acquiesced in the wave of persecution. Even members of the mulatto elite were made to understand that their positions were vulnerable as the tolerance of the past seemed to vanish before their eyes.[69]

Free persons of color employed different strategies to cope with their increasingly precarious status in South Carolina. A small number sought the protection of benevolent masters and petitioned the legislature for voluntary enslavement. Other free blacks, including representatives from some of the most affluent families, contemplated emigration. Some actually left, emigrating to the North, to Canada, and to Liberia, but most were not from elite families. In this "enslavement crisis," others continued to place their faith in white men of influence whose support they still hoped to marshal. One important source of support was the Charleston *Mercury,* which opposed the legislation, describing it as "mischievous" and "ill timed." Free black Charlestonians mounted a petition campaign that protested the impending bills, and they still found succor among important white aristocrats. The ability to enlist the aid of sympathetic legislators was absolutely crucial and the free brown elite was successful in doing this. One of the most important allies of free blacks was Christopher Memminger of the Charleston delegation. In the halls of the legislature, Memminger espoused all the traditional arguments on behalf of the community, even pointing out that white workers were a greater threat to the state's tranquility. The tactics employed by their allies in the legislature, as well as its need to consider more pressing issues connected with the secession crisis, derailed the hostile bills.[70]

Even as South Carolina moved inexorably toward secession and war, many free persons of color continued to profess their loyalty to the South, hoping to further disarm their detractors and bolster their eroded social niche. Only a few weeks after the state seceded, members of the brown elite, such as Robert Howard, Richard and Joseph Dereef, and Anthony Weston, petitioned the governor. Their message proclaimed that "in our veins flows the blood of the white race, in some half, in others much more than half white blood . . . our allegiance is due to South Carolina and in her defense, we will offer up our lives, and all that is dear to us."[71] But the social position of the free black group would never be the same, not just because of the logic of the South's proslavery argument but because of the Civil War and its consequences.

Charleston's entire black population rendered essential service to the Confederate war effort. City slaves were heavily relied upon to build defensive fortifications in and around Charleston. To augment the city's work force, slaves were brought in from the countryside and were utilized not only in Charleston but also at Fort Sumter and at several other forts strategically located in Charleston harbor. As the war languished, white men volunteered or were drafted into the Confederate army and slaveholders withdrew their slaves into the interior, as Union forces moved nearer to the city. Both these developments created a labor shortage that increased the importance of free blacks.[72]

Even before the actual fighting began, a group of one hundred and fifty free blacks volunteered their services to the city government and began to erect coastal defenses and redoubts in Charleston. Later, the city council required free blacks to work on military fortifications, and the Confederate army sometimes impressed reluctant free blacks into the corps of military laborers. The construction of ironclad vessels for the defense of the harbor in 1862 relied on unskilled slaves and free black ship carpenters. During the war, the city fire engines were understaffed, and some had to be abandoned because of inadequate manpower. To compensate for the labor deficit, in late 1862 the city government enacted provisions to enroll free blacks into the fire department. Within a year and for the remainder of the war, virtually all the city engines were operated by free blacks (though some whites continued to operate the volunteer engines).[73]

Free black cooperation with the Confederacy sometimes extended beyond providing labor. Charles C. Leslie became involved in the lucrative gun-running operations during the war. The butcher Francis Sasportas served his own vested economic interests and the Confederacy by acting as a purchasing agent for the city council, which bought cattle from him. Some free blacks supported the Confederacy monetarily. The Charleston *Mercury* noted that, during the first year of the war, "THE FREE COLORED MEN . . . contributed $450 to sustain the cause of the

South." In the summer of 1861, the elite Brown Fellowship Society called a special meeting at which the membership voted to give fifty dollars to the Ladies Relief Association for the care of injured and sick Confederate soldiers. The efforts of black women were evident also. On one occasion a group of "Colored Abandoned Women" used their considerable fund-raising ability to collect several hundred dollars, which they presented to the Y.M.C.A. for the Confederacy.[74]

Whites extolled the apparent loyalty of Charleston's black population and used it as evidence for the continued strength of the South's social system. But this perception did not necessarily reflect reality. In 1861 one newspaper reporter observed that the slaves that hadn't already escaped only feigned loyalty. He explained, "Some have told me how they said to their masters and mistresses on the day of the fight, 'The Yankees will be whipped, Massa and Missus,' but all the while they prayed and believed otherwise." There were numerous instances of otherwise "loyal" slaves who deserted the Confederates when given the opportunity. In 1862 the slave William Summerson worked as a boatman on a coastal steamer and later at one of the arsenals in Charleston where he stockpiled ammunition. After obtaining the assistance of friends, he and his wife were able to escape to federal gunboats at the Stono River. Once he was safely aboard a ship, Summerson provided valuable information about Charleston harbor and Confederate blockade-running operations.[75]

One of the most spectacular slave escapes was conducted by Robert Smalls. Before the war, he was employed along the wharves of Charleston and aboard coastal schooners. In 1862 Smalls worked on the Confederate ship *Planter*. In May that same year, Robert Smalls, along with several other black crewmen and their families, secretly took charge of the vessel and sailed it beyond Charleston's heavily fortified harbor to safety within the Union naval blockade. Smalls was later commissioned as a second lieutenant in the Thirty-third Regiment of the U.S. Colored Troops and given charge of the *Planter*. He used his invaluable knowledge of Charleston harbor to break enemy supply lines and to remove torpedoes he had earlier helped the Confederates lay.[76]

The Union navy began to shell Charleston in August 1863, but the city remained one of the strongest bastions of the Confederacy until almost the end of the war. In the face of an imminent Union invasion, Confederate troops burned railroad depots, warehouses, and stores of cotton and finally abandoned the city on February 17, 1865. On February 18 the Twenty-first United Stated Colored Infantry became the first Union soldiers to arrive in Charleston. They were later joined by the famous Fifty-fourth and Fifty-fifth U.S. Colored Infantry and several other regiments of black and white soldiers."[77]

The triumphant entry of black troops into Mount Pleasant on February 19, directly opposite Charleston and the response of the town's inhabitants, were unequivocal and dramatic evidence of the transforming power of the war. Colonel Charles Fox of the Fifty-fifth Massachusetts Regiment recalled: "The welcome given to a regiment of colored troops by their people redeemed from slavery. As shouts, prayers, and blessings resounded . . . all felt that the hardships and dangers of the siege were fully repaid. The few white inhabitants left in the town were either alarmed or indignant, and generally remained in their houses; but the colored people turned out *en masse*."[78] Two days later, at sunset, they left their encampments and landed at Charleston's east side wharves. After forming a line, they marched through the city to Charleston Neck. Few people were present at first, but soon the streets along the march route became crowded with blacks. As he continued with his description of the emotional scene, Colonel Fox heard:

> cheers, blessings, prayers, and songs . . . on every side. Men and women crowded to shake hands with men and officers. Many of them talked earnestly and understandingly of the past and present. The white population remained within their houses, but curiosity led even them to peep through the blinds at the "black Yankees". On through the streets of the rebel city passed the column, on through the chief seat of that slave power, tottering to fall. Its walls rung to the chorus of manly voices singing "John Brown," "Babylon is Falling," and the "Battle-Cry of freedom." . . . The glory and the triumph of this hour may be imagined, but can never be described. It was one of those occasions which happen but once in a lifetime, to be lived over in memory for ever.[79]

One month after the Confederate evacuation, in a dramatic display of unity, members of the black community held a grand march and celebration in honor of their recent emancipation. The two-and-one-half-mile procession was led by horseback-riding marshals who wore red, white, and blue sashes. They were followed by a band and the Twenty-first

Regiment of the U.S. Colored Troops under the lead of Colonel Bennet. Next came "a company of school boys, with the device: 'We know no masters but ourselves.' The Car of Liberty followed, bearing thirteen young girls dressed in white, with white head wreaths." After them came the Zion Bible Society of Zion Church and the "Preachers, Elders and Sunday School Teachers of the several colored congregations of Charleston, each bearing a Bible and Hymn Book." Approximately eighteen hundred schoolchildren participated in the march and some carried placards which read "We know no cast [*sic*] or color," "The Heroes of the War: Grant, Sherman, Sheridan." The tailors appeared next with their shears proudly displayed as the symbol of their occupation.

> They were followed by the coopers and the . . . "Zion Travel Society." The colored firemen, Nos. 2, 3, 6, 7, 8, followed, preceded by their band. . . . Carpenters, wheelwrights, blacksmiths, painters, barbers, masons, coach, carriage, wagon and dray drivers and farmers followed, all bearing some implement of their calling. After these came the auctioneer, mounted on a spring cart, accompanied by his driver with the auction bell and a number of "negroes for sale." Two colored women with their children were seated on the cart while the rest of "the gang to be sold" followed, their hands tied with ropes. As the procession moved along, the auctioneer was calling out vigorously "How much am I offered for this good cook." "She's an excellent cook, can make three kinds of mock turtle soup." "Two hundred, three hundred and fifty; four hundred," and so on until he had reached from twelve to fifteen hundred in Confederate money. Behind the auctioneer came a hearse, with the body of slavery; followed by the mourners all dressed in black. On the hearse, were the following inscriptions: "Slavery is Dead" "Who Owns Him." "No one" "Sumter Dug his Grave on the 13th of April, 1861." [80]

Black troops had been dispersed and quartered at various places in and around the city, including the Citadel, city arsenal, and the custom house, to restore order and provide security. Priority was given to the recruitment of additional black soldiers. Beginning in April, this responsibility largely fell to Maj. Martin R. Delany, who served on the staff of Gen. Rufus Saxton and later became commander of the 104th Regiment of the U.S. Colored Troops. Delany was widely known as one of the most influential abolitionists prior to the war. He was assisted by Capt. Orindatus S. B. Wall of the same regiment. Wall also had a distinguished record as a northern abolitionist. He was most well known for his work with the underground railroad and for having been indicted as a participant in the famous Oberlin-Wellington fugitive slave rescue of 1858.[81]

Sometimes squads of black soldiers were dispatched throughout the city to "impress" men into the ranks. Coercive measures generally were not necessary, though. Delany and Wall viewed their efforts as part of a racial mission. They appealed to area blacks by arguing that each of those eligible was duty-bound to "vindicate his manhood by becoming a soldier, and with his own stout arm to battle for the emancipation of his race." Black men responded so enthusiastically, the *Courier* reported that "the recruiting officers in Charleston are head over heels in business. The Colored men are flocking to the United States flag by the dozen and the score." By the end of the war in May, Major Delany and Captain Wall had completely organized the 103d and 104th Regiments and had also began organizing the 105th Regiment of the U.S. Colored Troops.[82]

The symbolism of Charleston's demise as a center of Confederate resistance was not lost on Union secretary of war Edwin Stanton, who ordered a memorial ceremony for April 14, 1865, in the harbor at Fort Sumter. The date was significant enough, occurring as it did exactly four years from the federal surrender of the fort; it took on added meaning as it approached, since Richmond fell and General Lee surrendered at Appomattox. Northern and foreign abolitionists, antislavery politicians, Union military leaders, and several thousand interested persons assembled a flotilla of boats and converged on the fort. During the celebration, Henry Ward Beecher, the abolitionist minister and brother of Harriet Beecher Stowe, gave the keynote speech, and Maj. Robert Anderson restored the American flag. One of the many vessels present was the *Planter,* piloted by Robert Smalls the war hero. Its deck was shared by Major Delany and Robert Vesey, the son of the late Denmark Vesey. All must have viewed the day's events with intense interest and emotion.[83]

The ceremony at Fort Sumter led to a week of celebrations, including one in which two or three thousand people gathered and rejoiced at Citadel Square before they moved to Zion Presbyterian Church for more formal speeches. On this occasion, when the abolitionist William Lloyd Garrison arrived, the crowd could not be restrained and one reporter noted, "The pressure and rejoicing was so great that Mr. Garrison was literally bourne on the shoulders of those present to the speaker's stand." Three decades earlier, Garrison had been burned in effigy on the downtown streets, but now he marveled with joyous and tear-filled eyes at the metamorphosis he had witnessed. The poignancy of the recent events was perhaps most cogently expressed when Maj. Martin Delany remarked simply, "This day should be the resurrection of John C. Calhoun."[84] This was the occasion for which so many had long waited. From this day of jubilee forward, black Charlestonians would challenge the restrictions of the past and march forward to creatively shape their destiny. While their new experiences differed greatly from those of the past, important continuities with the antebellum years persisted.

Almost two centuries prior to the Civil War, Charleston's free black community took shape. Free blacks found distinct advantages in Charleston, and by 1860, 40 percent of the state's free Negro population resided there. Slaves in the lower South were selectively emancipated, which ensured that favorite slaves, frequently the mulatto offspring of masters and their slave women, would be granted freedom. Such privileged slaves were often provided with special training and even property or money to facilitate their transition to freedom. This explains, in part, why, as a group, free blacks were relatively highly skilled and wealthy. Most male workers were artisans, women worked in the garment trades, and both depended upon the support and patronage of whites. Several acquired considerable property, and a few were able to begin their own businesses. The skills and property acquired by this free brown elite were translated into the post–Civil War years in many cases.

Free persons of color, especially those members of the brown elite, enjoyed a well-developed institutional and organizational life. The question of color was generally a significant issue in the free black community. Upper class mulattoes sometimes founded exclusive social organizations, and darker free blacks followed suit. Although slaves greatly valued their family relations, the free black family was a more viable institution since it was protected by law. The church provided free blacks with training as leaders, and by virtue of their superior social status, the church accorded them greater responsibilities than it did slaves. All blacks, both slave and free, would find such leadership skills helpful at critical junctures in the post-emancipation years. Free blacks also enjoyed the benefit of many secular organizations. These provided social, benevolent, and insurance functions. Schools made the education of black children possible, and literary associations provided intellectual activities for elite free blacks. The traditions and examples these organizations provided proved valuable during Reconstruction.

Tension existed between free blacks and their enslaved brethren. Since elite free blacks sometimes held slaves purely for economic reasons, slaves often viewed the entire group with suspicion. Such apprehensions were exacerbated by free blacks, who had attempted to dissociate themselves as completely as possible from slaves and to ingratiate themselves with whites. By the Civil War era, some free blacks even identified with the goals of the Confederacy. It is difficult to analyze the motives of those free blacks who professed sympathy with the southern war effort. Some seem to have done so because of their affinity for the southern aristocracy. Others benefited economically from their support of the Confederacy. But for many free blacks, supporting the Confederacy was merely an expedient decision resulting from the increased precariousness of life during the late 1850s and the crisis threatening to extinguish the group.

Ultimately, the Civil War brought emancipation to the slaves, which undermined the peculiar status of free blacks and made greater unity among all Charleston blacks more possible. But several troublesome and historically divisive problems had to be confronted before a more viable community could be constructed. The means by which Charleston blacks drew upon the antebellum heritage for strength and attempted to overcome the knotty problems imposed by it in the postwar years are the concerns of succeeding chapters.

Slave auction
in downtown Charleston.

*Avery Research Center for African
American History and Culture,
College of Charleston*

Slave tags.

*South Carolina
State Museum,
Columbia, S.C.*

Nancy Weston, a nominal
slave in Charleston, was
allowed to live as a free
black in the 1850s.
*Moorland-Spingarn Research
Center, Howard University*

Daniel A. Payne, a free black
educator, left Charleston in the
1830s when legislation prohibited
teaching Afro-Americans. He
later became an A.M.E. bishop.

*Black Charleston Photographic Collection,
College of Charleston Library*

Evacuation
of Charleston
before the
Union invasion.
*Black Charleston
Photographic
Collection, College
of Charleston
Library*

The Fifty-fifth
Massachusetts
Colored Regiment
arrives in
Charleston.
*Black Charleston
Photographic
Collection, College of
Charleston Library*

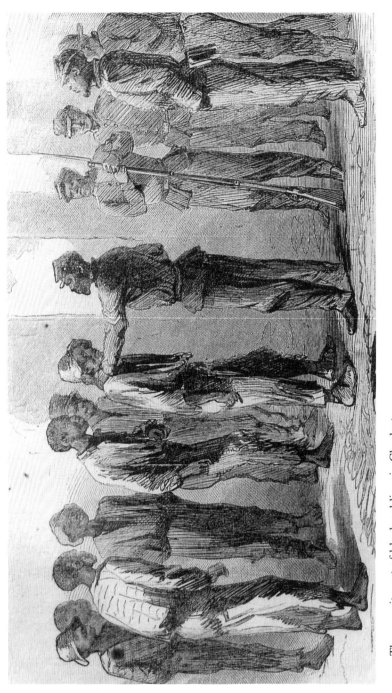

The recruitment of black soldiers in Charleston.

Caroliniana Library, University of South Carolina

Scenes from the Emancipation
Day celebration.

*Black Charleston Photographic
Collection, College of Charleston
Library*

One of the many racial clashes to occur in Charleston during 1865-66.
Black Charleston Photographic Collection, College of Charleston Library

CHAPTER THREE

"AN EARNEST ASSERTION OF MANHOOD"

The Quest for Civic and Political Equality

The Old South's leaders touted their region's "organic" social relationships as sources of strength. Ideally, masters, slaves, free blacks, and poor whites recognized and accepted their ascribed roles as well as those of the other groups with which they interacted. In this model, the ideal of Jeffersonian democracy was supplanted by John Calhoun's exaltation of human inequality and the hierarchical arrangement of social and racial groups ensured good order. Every group was consigned to a particular niche in the social hierarchy based upon its natural talents and relative importance. By meshing neatly together and fulfilling their respective roles, each added strength to the overall design of a complex human mosaic. Generally, all whites, regardless of economic status, occupied positions at the top of the hierarchy, while blacks, most of whom were slaves, were pushed to the bottom. Within this framework, some elite free persons of color could enjoy special privileges, occupying as they did a middle ground in an incipient three-tiered racial hierarchy.[1] The Civil War and the slaves' sudden emancipation threw these antebellum arrangements into chaos. In the three years that followed, the whites often clung to the vestiges of the old familiar order in confused apprehension. Yet, their intransigence was met by federal forces and by the determined resistance of black people. After emancipation former free persons of color and freedmen established new relations as they jointly asserted their right to political and civic equality with whites.

The result was a perplexing and uncertain transition that nevertheless laid the groundwork for new social and political relations that characterized the period of Reconstruction.

Violence and the threatened use of violence were central features of antebellum race relations. The slave master's authority ultimately resided in his superior ability to punish and physically coerce recalcitrant slaves. Yet, the masters were never completely at ease in the exercise of their authority, despite the command of superior coercive power. Many slaveholders realized that even an apparently contented slave had the capacity to become another Denmark Vesey. The dreaded possibility of violent slave rebellion was an ever-present threat, awaiting only the proper combination of events, to burst forth and drench the South in its own blood. These views led southern whites to believe that emancipation would be accompanied by an orgy of death and destruction. In the months after Appomattox, the South was gripped with fear as rumors swept through the region of the freedmen's plan to slaughter the whites and seize their land and property.[2]

South Carolina was no exception, and throughout the state the fear of insurrection was widespread. One man from Union District observed that the slaves had been controlled well until the arrival of federal troops, but now "the negroes were in a state of glad excitement, and everybody feared there would be bloody business right away." The migration of thousands of potentially rebellious freedmen to Charleston heightened the already tense relations that existed between former masters and newly freed slaves. In her correspondence with white Charleston residents in the summer of 1865, Harriott Middleton reported that "the Ravenels write from town that they live in a dreadful state of apprehension of insurrection, and Edward says that it is the general fear. It is the same all over the Low Country." Although she was encouraged because no major race riot had yet occurred, another correspondent revealed her underlying fears: "So far the poor wretches have behaved better than might be expected that is, they have not attempted to cut our throats as yet." According to John Dennett, who traveled to Charleston at this time, some whites were so fearful that they formed paramilitary organizations to protect themselves from the city's blacks.[3]

It was widely agreed that the most likely time for a general uprising was during the week of Christmas or early in January. This was traditionally a time when the normal discipline of slave life was relaxed, the slaves were granted special liberties, and they often came to Charleston to enjoy the holiday season. Asst. Adj. Gen. M. Burger believed that the Christmas season of 1865 had the potential to be different from any previous year because of the volatility of race relations and the general apprehension that there would be "some insurrectionary movement on the part of the colored people." According to him, "collisions" between the races were likely to occur, and "when commenced no one can tell where the conflict will end." Under these circumstances, Burger urged the local garrisons to be especially vigilant and to preserve order by arresting all disorderly and intoxicated persons.[4]

The presence of black troops proved unsettling to white citizens and heightened their fears of impending violence. In July 1865 one white Charlestonian wrote that "if the negro troops were only removed we could get on very well. They demoralize and excite the negroes who have been slaves and will not allow them to remain with their owners." A short time later, whites were outraged when a group of black soldiers from the city traveled up the Cooper River and were heard telling "the negroes that all the property of their former owners was theirs by right as they had worked for it." Henry W. Ravenel denounced the squads of black soldiers who visited the nearby plantations

> stealing and destroying property, insulting the whites in [*sic*] presence of the negroes, taking away all arms and leaving them in the hands of the negroes, encouraging the evil disposed to insubordination, and intimidating the well disposed by threats of death if they continued to serve their masters. In a short time they completed their devilish work, and left those whom they had found a quiet, contented, and happy people, dissatisfied, unruly, madmen intoxicated with the fumes of licentiousness, and ready for any outrage.[5]

It was such attitudes and activities that led another white resident to report disdainfully, "Speeches of the most inflammatory Kinds have been delivered by some of the negro soldiers, which have caused perfect insubordination among the negroes." While the occupation of Charleston by Union forces was intolerable enough, the excitement generated by black troops portended the most dire consequences. According to Dr. Benjamin Huger, who lamented the yoke under which white Charleston labored, "If providence does not interfere our history will yet be written in blood. . . . I am no alarmist, but it seems to me, that if the negro troops are not removed and our own negroes made to submit to the civil laws, massacre of white or black must soon come."[6]

Under these circumstances, mounting tensions flared into racial clashes during the year and a half prior to Military Reconstruction. In August 1865 Rev. Ennals J. Adams complained that "for the past two or three weeks this city has been disturbed and humanity shocked by serious and bloody riots, between white and colored citizens and troops." One year later the situation had not improved, and violent encounters punctuated the summer of 1866. Relations between the police and the black community were especially hostile, and the reasons for this hostility were numerous. The freedmen's homes were often indiscriminately searched by the city detectives at the request of former masters, who charged their ex-slaves with stealing. When the desired objects were not found, other possessions were sometimes confiscated.[7]

Blacks also complained about the excessive use of force by policemen and about the cruel and unmerciful beatings suffered at the policemen's hands. " Bona Nox," a black resident, believed that the potential was great for a riot as "bloody" as those that had occurred in Memphis and New Orleans, because "the policemen were inclined to maltreat our people, and only required a little encouragement from the civil authorities to butcher us like sheep." By September 1866 Gen. Daniel Sickles, military commander for South Carolina, finally ordered all policemen to turn over their weapons or be arrested. Whites were outraged, and "Bona Nox" sarcastically depicted them denouncing Sickles' order with the words, "O! Satan, how long? How long shall our noble hearted discharged policemen and confederate [*sic*] soldiers keep from murdering saucy negroes?"[8]

Black soldiers figured prominently in the violence of 1866, and sometimes even the most trivial event could precipitate a major confrontation. According to a reporter for the *Daily Courier,* on one occasion when rival groups of black and white boys began "forming alignments and pelting each other with stones" on the Battery, adults of each race joined in and began hurling sticks and other objects at each other. After the crowds were dispersed by the police, the blacks regrouped and summoned additional support from the neighborhood.

Once they were reinforced and "directed by some eight to ten negro soldiers," they "formed a procession of two or three hundred and riotously marched" through the streets. They were finally dispersed by a joint force of police and United States Regular Troops.[9] While this incident transpired without major consequences, all too often such occurrences ended in disaster. After another series of disturbances on the Battery between freedmen and the police, John Jenkins and Scipio Fraser (both discharged Union soldiers) organized a large group of blacks and attacked a detachment of policemen while threatening "to kill all of the D—d rebel sons of ___." When the mob saw a white man walking down Tradd Street, one of the ringleaders gave the order to "kill the son of a ___." The crowd pursued the man and, after knocking the victim down, battered his body with bricks. Scipio Fraser then ran into the yard of a nearby white witness, brandished a knife, and bragged that "he was the one that had killed the damned rebel, and that he would kill another one; that he had killed many a one in the army."[10]

The suspicion and hatred black soldiers and white Charlestonians displayed for each other was often exhibited between black and white Union troops, further straining the already volatile racial situation in the city. Black residents and soldiers found it difficult to view some white troops as liberators; the latter often shared the racism of the white South and in many cases were openly sympathetic to their erstwhile enemies. The black Rev. Richard H. Cain charged that all too often "the Military seem to be only here to aid the Civil authorities in inflicting wrongs upon an ignorant . . . and oppressed people." While commenting on the character of white Union soldiers, a correspondent for the *Christian Recorder* caustically noted blacks were "now in the hands of the police, now in the midst of soldiers, and it matters not which he falls into, he fares about the same (if the soldiers are white). It appears that all the jail birds of New York, and the inmates of Moyamensing had been left in this State to guard the freedmen's interest. No southern white man in Charleston, has heaped as much insult upon colored females passing the streets, as those foul-throated scamps who guard this city." Black leaders and army commanders complained that sometimes the soldiers were abusive and that they even physically assaulted and murdered freedmen in and around Charleston.[11]

Given the hostility between black and white troops, Charleston became the scene of several frays between these two groups. In fact local newspapers reported that Charleston was kept in "a state of continued excitement" because "day after day, and night after night, has the peace of the city been disturbed on account of the feuds existing between the white and colored troops." A very serious clash occurred in a city market in July 1865 between the 127th New York Volunteers, also known as the Zouaves, blacks from the 21st U.S. Colored Infantry, and the 54th Massachusetts Regiment. In the general melee that ensued, stones and bricks were hurled, and black soldiers fired a volley in the crowded market that killed one bystander and wounded three other persons, including a Zouave corporal. At least one black officer was arrested, and the Zouaves were transferred to Morris Island and later to Fort Sumter for mutinous and insubordinate behavior.[12]

Violence and its threat during the early postwar years was only one force arraying blacks and whites against each other in Charleston. The changed relations between former slaves and masters demonstrated that the latter had lost control well before Radical Reconstruction. In a city where interracial contact was constant, the erosion of white authority was matched by the growing assertiveness of blacks. This combination proved an endless source of irritation for white Charlestonians.

Many of the whites who fled the city prior to the Union occupation returned only to find their homes in the possession of freedmen who refused to relinquish them. In a typical case, Francis Parker wrote that when her husband visited Charleston, he found that their "beautiful house had been occupied by Charles Macbeth's plantation negroes, with their pigs & poultry. They were cooking in the drawing room, & as you may imagine everything was abused & soiled." Only after enlisting the aid of an armed soldier could the freedmen be driven out and the house repossessed. Such scenes were often repeated in the city's lower wards, where in 1865 one observer noted that there were few "decent" people residing in the mansions but only "negroes and low Irish."[13]

According to Caroline Gilman, the "Great Problem of The Times" was the insolent and disrespectful manner in which blacks now interacted with whites. A Charleston woman lamented that "the city is guarded entirely by negro troops, [and] one cannot go out without being jostled by flaunting mulattos [*sic*] with *their* soldier beaux (white sometimes). or [*sic*] having favorite songs shouted in your face such as 'Down with the rebel' 'Hang Jeff Davis on the sour apple tree' 'I'll never be a slave[.]'" Under similar circumstances one resident noted that as he passed black women and soldiers in the streets, he heard them "conversing about the d—d Rebels which word is constantly in their mouths." Another woman was outraged at the "insolent" behavior of blacks on the streets and complained that they "never pretend to give place to you [and] several times I have had them to squeeze themselves in the inside & say 'look at dat rebel.'"[14]

Whites' preoccupation with the ritual gestures of racial deference made even the slightest deviation from the "proper" etiquette of race relations seem insulting and offensive. In demonstrating extreme sensitivity to such matters, Caroline Gilman (a former Charlestonian who had moved to Greenville) wrote that

> the negroes are evidently aiming at supremacy. Juliet & Hester are teaching the little negroes to call them *Miss*. They talk openly of "when I have my house I mean to do this & that"—Amy gave birth to a son this week, & though mother & two children are clearly living on charity, Hester their sister said to Fransie, "my brother is just the same as you is." Fibbe & her children are all with us still, unable to get work, yet she told Caroline's white nurse, that when she went to Charleston she meant to wear *white morning gowns*. I mention these little things as symptoms.[15]

Unless the old symbols of deference were shown, whites usually found conversation with blacks quite repugnant. Shortly after the war, Daniel Heyward conversed with his former slaves, whom he found generally "kind enough," although he was annoyed that they remained seated while addressing him and refused to remove their hats. White men continued to demand that blacks address them as massa or boss. According to one South Carolinian, "Occasionally a pert maid or man servant will address their employers as Mr. and Mrs. instead of Master and Miss, but the whites are very jealous of such innovations." He knew of several nurses who were discharged because "they refused to prefix Master to the names of the children." Many blacks were also much concerned with the way whites addressed them. One perplexed white resident recounted the story of a friend who went to visit a black family and, in accordance with the old custom, addressed a woman who appeared at the door as "mauma." Because of this indiscretion and much to his surprise, the man was "assailed with such a torrent of abuse that he had no alternative but to hurry away."[16]

While the daily interaction of blacks and whites began to define a new racial accommodation, the freedmen's legal status remained uncertain. In the weeks and months following the Civil War, a variety of northern Republican officials and abolitionists visited Charleston and auspiciously described the place of blacks in the transformed South. Reuben Thomlinson of the Freedmen's Bureau, Supreme Court justice Salmon P. Chase, and Massachusetts senator Henry Wilson are all examples of northern whites who urged black Charlestonians to prepare themselves for a new day of civic and political equality. Ultimately, it was the unfolding of federal and state Reconstruction policy that determined their fate.[17]

By late summer 1865, white South Carolinians had begun the process of Reconstruction. In June President Johnson appointed the former Unionist and Confederate legislator Benjamin Perry as provisional governor of the state, to implement his Reconstruction policies. To this end, Perry convened a constitutional convention in mid-September that, among other things, recognized the abolition of slavery and forbade its re-establishment.[18]

The governor's address to the convention made it clear that slavery's demise would not entitle blacks to all the rights enjoyed by their white brethren. He pointed out that although northern Radical Republicans promoted the freedmen's right to vote, extending the franchise to them "in their present ignorant and degraded condition, would be little less than folly and madness." Were this to happen, the wealthiest men would manipulate the former slaves and thereby gain undue influence over elections at the expense of poor whites. While referring to the Dred Scott decision, the governor reminded the audience that the highest court in the land had excluded the Negro from the rights of citizenship under the Constitution. In concluding this topic, he urged the creation of "a white man's government, and intended for white men only . . . as the interest and honor of the state demand." The new constitution made no concessions to racial equality, limiting both voting and office holding to white males.[19]

It was difficult enough for whites to accept the demise of slavery and the loss of their perceived natural right to hold slaves. They certainly never believed it possible for the freedmen to be elevated much above the status of antebellum free persons of color. The constitutional convention empowered a special commission to recommend laws to the next legislature, codifying the freedmen's new legal status, regulating his labor, and generally providing for the "protection and government of the colored population." The convention also provided for the trial of blacks in special courts; the issue of accepting black testimony in the regular courts was deferred to the legislature.[20]

In the attempt to maintain the vestiges of legal and judicial control over the freedmen, the South Carolina legislature quickly passed a series of laws in the special session of September 1865 collectively known as the Black Code. This body of legislation regulated the activities of black workers in intricate detail to ensure employers a constant, dependable, and docile source of labor. It also seriously limited the ex-slaves' freedom while relegating them to a status of social and legal inferiority. By its criteria all persons with more than one-eighth Negro blood were defined as black. Blacks could not migrate into the state unless within twenty days of their arrival a one-thousand-dollar bond was obtained with two freeholders as sureties who would guarantee the person's good behavior.[21]

Those blacks who desired to practice trades or establish businesses had to satisfy special criteria. Interracial marriages were prohibited. The Black Code made it a felony for a black man to ravish a white woman or to have sexual intercourse with a white woman by impersonating her husband. Blacks were excluded from the state militia and also from keeping swords, firearms, or any other "weapon appropriate for purposes of war" without permission of a judge. It was illegal for them to manufacture or retail liquor, and if a black person was observed committing a crime, "any" person viewing the transgression could "arrest" the offender and bring him before a magistrate. Special district courts, provided for by the constitution, were established to adjudicate civil cases in which one or more parties were black and for all criminal cases in which the defendants were black. The testimony of black witnesses would only be considered credible in cases affecting them and their property.[22]

As a body of law, the Black Code represented the former masters' attempts at maintaining a paternalistic relationship with their former charges. If they were convinced of anything, it was that the freedmen required protection from their worst failings. Without the discipline and supervision whites could provide, the Negroes' capacity for indolence, self-indulgence, and barbarism would cause disaster. Such sentiments were not foreign to Dr. John Bachman, the Charleston cleric, and others like him. He believed that peaceful coexistence with an inferior species was possible only if regulations placed the black man "in the situation for which God intended him—[as] the inferior of the white man.[23]"

The objective of white policy makers was to preserve that which was salvageable from the past in order to minimize and restrain the consequences of emancipation. Black Carolinians, on the other hand, took steps to expand the meaning of their freedom and to place it on the broadest legal and political basis. As early as September 1865, a group of 103 Charleston blacks petitioned the state constitutional convention for the extension of impartial suffrage to them. These men were overwhelmingly artisans and had been free before the war. As if to underscore the moderation and reasonableness of their request, they quickly added that "we ask not at this time that the ignorant shall be admitted to the exercises [sic] of a privilege which they might use to the injury of the State." [24] They assured the audience that the petition was not offered in the spirit of antagonism. To the contrary, it was only an "earnest assertion of our manhood" and "notwithstanding the bitterness of the past, and of the present, we cherish feelings of respect and affection" for southern leaders. They concluded by pointing out that black Charlestonians would be satisfied with nothing less than equal rights, but if these weren't forthcoming immediately, they would wait patiently. According to the *Courier,* it was the "earnest desire" of the convention members to ignore "*in toto*" the issue of black suffrage, and the newspaper urged them to act accordingly. The moderation of the request and humility of the language notwithstanding, the petition failed to be seriously entertained at the convention.[25]

Despite rejection at the constitutional convention, black Carolinians remained undaunted in their quest for civic and political equality. In late November 1865, a statewide Colored People's Convention was held at Zion Presbyterian Church in Charleston. Specifically, the forty-five delegates assembled to formulate "plans best calculated to advance the interests of our people," to develop methods for "our mutual protection," and to promote the "industrial interests of the state." Almost one-half of the delegates were from Charleston. Nineteen of the city delegates— 86 percent of the city delegation—had been free before the war, and half worked in skilled occupations.[26] While similar in composition to the petitioners of the constitutional convention, this gathering was different because of the presence of northern blacks, who participated as honorary members. Of this group, Maj. Martin R. Delany and Capt. Orindatus S. B. Wall, both highly regarded abolitionists, ventured to South Carolina with the Union army. The other four honorary members were all ministers. Revs. Jonathan C. Gibbs, Ennals J. Adams, and Richard H. Cain were all northerners. Rev. Francis Cardozo was from Charleston. Each of these men were engaged in some missionary or educational efforts in Charleston's black community at this time.[27]

Throughout the convention, the delegates evinced a tone of moderation and hoped to demonstrate the unity of interests between the black and white populations. One early resolution informed whites that the convention bore neither "hatred [n]or malice toward those who have held our brethren as slaves." To the contrary, "we extend the right hand of fellowship to all, and make it our special aim to establish unity, peace and love amongst all men." More specifically, they tried to assuage the widespread fears of a Negro insurrection by reminding whites that they had always been "*law-abiding* SUBJECTS," while pledging to continue so as "law-abiding citizens." To the freedmen, the delegates counseled thrift, industriousness, and education.[28] While attempting to mollify whites and urging the freedmen to self-improvement, the delegates clearly recognized the seriousness of their plight in late 1865. One reason for convening the conclave was to discuss methods of "mutual protection," and Capt. O. S. B. Wall referred to the series of "emergencies" they had faced recently that had to be met with "firmness." Robert C. DeLarge, an antebellum free person of color and a tailor by training, incisively analyzed the challenge of the hour when he poignantly remarked that all that war could win for blacks had already been achieved; however, "the simple act of emancipation, if it stops there is not worth much." Black people would not be free until they enjoyed all the rights that they deserved. Without political equality "we will still have to be governed by laws that we have no voice in making, and submit to taxation without representation." This was what "the heroes of '76 fought" for, and the black struggle continued in that same spirit.[29]

One of the final products of the convention was an "Address" to the people of South Carolina. Therein, the delegates put forth the justification for political and civic equality based on the principles of Christian ethics and the ideals enshrined in the Declaration of Independence and the Constitution. Among these, the most important was that "all men are created equal" and, because of this, equally entitled to "life, liberty, and the pursuit of happiness." The "Address" continued by protesting the exclusion of blacks from citizenship rights that were "cheerfully" granted to "strangers." Denial of the right to testify in court deprived them of the means to safeguard their property. The exclusion from the right to vote left blacks without any means of political redress against those who governed their lives.[30]

The Black Code was a special object of protest because it subjected the freedmen to penalties and restrictions that only applied to them. The economic disabilities were especially burdensome upon those who hoped to continue practicing trades, to develop business enterprises, or to acquire land. In addition to these economic restrictions, exclusion from public schools limited their opportunities for social and intellectual improvement. In conclusion, the delegates declared that "we simply desire that we shall be recognized as men; that we have no special obstructions placed in our way; that the same laws which govern white men shall direct colored men." Despite all the effort they expended, when the convention petitioned the legislature that fall, its entreaties were rebuffed. The Committee on the Colored Population, which heard the plea, reported that the petitioners' concerns, including the right to vote were not properly within the purview of the legislature.[31]

Though these early organizational efforts failed, they were significant nonetheless. These meetings represented an important political debut for black Carolinians, who used them as forums for political education of the delegates and their constituents. The meetings were also important avenues for recruiting talented leadership. In fact, a number of the men active in these meetings would continue in local politics and others go on to hold elective and appointive office at various levels of government service. The character of political activism at this time also made it clear that former middle-class free persons of color joined their destiny with that of the freedmen. This was why, at the Colored People's Convention, Alonzo Ransier, a former free black, gave a speech defending the capacity and achievements of black people against their detractors. In one example of the freedmen's contributions, he observed that thousands had fought to preserve the Union and "by their strong arms and brave hearts the American Government stands to-day." Ransier's conclusion was "that man *is* capable of self-government."[32]

Two months after the convention, one of its participants, Samuel L. Bennett, another former free black, who described himself as "one of the representatives of my people," wrote directly to the governor. He requested an audience to discuss South Carolina's future, its policies toward blacks, the problems they now faced, and the needs of their community. Discussion was essential, he believed, "as there is at present no positive position to which they may refer." Bennett would write again when Governor Orr visited Charleston in April 1866, requesting that the governor convene a mass meeting with the freedmen. This was a time of crisis, according to Bennett, and "the people wants [*sic*] to hear from you, they still believes [*sic*] that you as the Executive is not for them." He advised Orr that, based on his inaction, it could only be presumed that the prejudiced newspapers represented his views. In continuing his lament, Bennett complained: "when we look around, we see all looking backward. no [*sic*] word of comfort for the Freedman. No one to point them with recommendations to the future, [*sic*] But one strain of continual abuse by all the journals in the State."[33]

One year later, after a third request by Charleston's black leaders, the governor finally consented to a meeting ,which was held at Emanuel A.M.E. Church. There he pledged to use the power of the state to protect the freedmen's rights and safety. He urged them to be frugal, honest, and hardworking. With regard to political rights, Governor Orr favored a literacy qualification for voting but warned freedmen against preoccupation with political affairs. Finally, he predicted that if they were productive and educated, their children should easily qualify for the franchise. His assumption was that most freedmen, and especially those from the rural districts, would not presently qualify.[34]

In early 1866 federal military intervention addressed some of black Carolinians' most basic grievances. Gen. Daniel Sickles, the military commander of South Carolina, found the Black Code so blatantly discriminatory and damaging to economic recovery that he nullified it. In its place, he decreed that all laws should be applied to the entire population without discrimination. Based on his prodding, the legislature modified the Black Code to eliminate its most egregious provisions. Charleston was partially restored to civilian rule by January 1866, when

Mayor Palmer Gaillard and the city council resumed their duties. According to Freedmen's Bureau commissioner Oliver Howard's directives, provost courts would continue to hear cases involving freedmen until they were accorded equal judicial rights. Accordingly, in September the legislature passed laws granting freedmen the same rights as those outlined in the federal Civil Rights Act of 1866. By October 1866, military authorities ordered the restoration of civil courts, and that month black witnesses were being sworn in in state courts.[35]

Beyond conferring basic civil rights on the freedmen, white Carolinians were unwilling to go. Extending the franchise to them was completely unacceptable, and the state's political leaders lined up behind President Johnson to resist the proposed Fourteenth Amendment. In an insightful letter to Gov. James Orr, Samuel L. Bennett, the Charleston activist, claimed that recent political events "should be sufficient to open the Eyes of the South Carolina Gentlemen for the future." He also warned the governor and others of the consequences of their political obstructionism. They should beware because "political procrastination is an evil and if you Gentlemen will not look to your political interest, you are lost, and for ever."[36] Bennett was a more astute judge of the evolving political climate than Governor Orr, whose administration would eventually be subordinated to the will of Congress through adoption of the Reconstruction Acts. Passed in March 1867, these acts restored military rule and directed military commanders to implement the program of Congressional Reconstruction. In this process, elections open to all qualified male citizens would be held to choose delegates. These delegates would rewrite the constitution, providing for male suffrage regardless of "race, color or previous condition." The new constitution was to be approved by the electorate and Congress; the legislature created by the new constitution was required to ratify the Fourteenth Amendment before South Carolina could be readmitted to the union.[37]

March witnessed a flurry of political activism in Charleston in response to the Reconstruction Acts. A series of meetings was held to organize the Republican party, which would elect officials to implement the requirements of Congressional Reconstruction. Between March 7 and March 21, the Committee of Thirteen was organized and developed a platform for the Union Republican party of South Carolina. The committee consisted of twelve blacks and one white, J. P. M. Epping, the U. S. Marshal. Service on this committee was not the first example of political involvement for many of its black members, as seven had participated in the 1865 Colored People's Convention. Three ministers, Revs. Francis L. Cardozo, Ennals J. Adams, and Benjamin F. Randolph, served on the committee, although most of its members seem to have been artisans. At least eleven of the twelve black men had been free before the war and most were South Carolina natives.[38]

At the March 21 meeting, Rev. Adams, stressing that "these are revolutionary times," read the platform of the Union Republican party. It called for recognizing the fundamental equality of all men, for ratification of the Fourteenth Amendment, and for enfranchisement of the freedmen; it also called for social reforms, such as an end to imprisonment for debt, and the creation of a system of public education that would be open to all, regardless of race. The platform also stressed the need for policies to assist the poor in acquiring land as well as policies for the protection of home owners against ejection for debt. In endorsing the platform, Rev. Francis L. Cardozo warned blacks to be skeptical of "the false pretensions of would-be friends," referring to southern whites. He acknowledged that he had been "treated with the greatest personal kindness by many Southern gentlemen . . . [and] received from them individual favors and acts of kindness. But this is no question of individual or personal consideration. It is one of those great national questions that rise up to affect us as a whole people."[39]

After discussing the value of the new rights and opportunities he expected blacks to enjoy soon, Cardozo switched to another topic and warned of a danger he described as "peculiar to ourselves." On the eve of their entry into the body politic, he saw "the colored people . . . divided and disunited by a variety of sentiments and feelings." Undoubtedly one of the divisions was between men of wealth and those of more modest means. Another important cleavage was between freedmen and former free persons of color. As a native of this community, Cardozo certainly knew of the historical tensions that existed between blacks and mulattoes. He recognized the consequences of the old disunity, counseled blacks against seeking personal position or aggrandizement and even urged them to forego class interests in favor of aiding the progress of "the race." As a former free person of color, Cardozo had done so and desired others to act similarly. The meeting ended by endorsing the platform and calling for a statewide convention. Several days later a mass meeting was held on Citadel Green, and the platform was submitted to a gathering of fifteen hundred to two thousand persons, primarily from the black community. The platform was endorsed again.[40]

In its early months, the Republican party was primarily organized by black Carolinians, with little participation by whites. H. Judge Moore provides one of the few examples of white involvement. A native Carolinian, he published the Northern Methodist organ, the *Charleston Advocate,* addressed the 1865 Colored People's Convention, and worked along with the Committee of Thirteen to develop the Republican platform. J. P. M. Epping was a member of that committee also. By late spring and summer, though, whites began to show greater interest and involvement. In a May address to a politically diverse audience, Massachusetts senator Henry Wilson warned against the creation of racially defined political parties in South Carolina. Blacks and whites were urged to unite on the basis of the Republican platform. In addition to Marshal Epping, a number of other white federal officeholders were present, such as Albert G. Mackey, collector of the Port of Charleston, Frederick A. Sawyer, collector of internal revenue, and Daniel T. Corbin, U. S. district attorney. With the exception of Epping, these men would subsequently assume prominent positions in the Republican party.[41]

A statewide convention of the Union Republican party convened in Charleston early in May. Richard H. Gleaves, a northern black, chaired the meeting and became president of the Committee on Permanent Organization. Christopher Columbus Bowen, a former Confederate, became interim chairman of the State Central Committee. One of its functions was to employ representatives in various locations throughout the state in order to expand the party organization. In this and other projects, the former free black Charlestonians Edward P. Wall, Paul Poinsett, and Robert C. Delarge played a role as committee members.[42]

After the May meeting, the state convention reassembled in Columbia, and the composition of Charleston's delegation is revealing. Four of the seven-member delegation were whites. This group consisted of Marshall Epping and Gilbert Pillsbury, both northerners, Edward William Mackey of Charleston, and Christopher Bowen. The black delegates, William J. McKinlay, Robert C. Delarge, and James D. Price, had been free before the war. William J. McKinlay, a tailor by training, was one of the few members of the antebellum free brown elite to have become actively involved in Republican politics at this time. After endorsing the party platform, a new State Central Committee was elected. The president was B. Frank Whittemore of Massachusetts, who came to South Carolina as part of the Freedmen's Bureau educational efforts. A black minister, Benjamin F. Randolph, was elected vice president. He had attended Oberlin College and had served as chaplain for the Twenty-sixth Regiment of the U.S.C.T. during the war. Once he was in South Carolina, Randolph assumed the role of an assistant superintendent of education for the Freedmen's Bureau. William J. McKinlay was secretary to the State Central Committee. Gilbert Pillsbury and Marshall Epping, representing Charleston, were among the other members of the State Central Committee.[43] By this time the role of whites in the party machinery had expanded considerably, while black Charlestonians, and especially former free blacks, continued to play a prominent role.

Gen. Edward Canby, who replaced Gen. Daniel Sickles as commander of the Second Military District (including North and South Carolina), ordered November 19 and 20 as dates for the election to decide whether a constitutional convention would be held and to select delegates. White conservatives continued to denounce the Reconstruction Acts as illegal, unconstitutional, and hypocritical. They vigorously objected to the call for a constitutional convention, believing it would cause the political degradation of the state and the establishment of "negro supremacy." Conservatives generally refused to promote candidates as delegates and even urged registered white voters to boycott the election.[44]

The freedmen prepared for the upcoming elections, which would be their first ever, with considerable zeal. The Freedmen's Bureau played an important role in preparing the electorate. While its agents weren't supposed to become directly involved in partisan politics, Assistant Commissioner Robert Scott directed his staff to inform the freedmen of their rights and to "advise and encourage" voter registration. The meetings and rallies sponsored by the Union League expanded after the Reconstruction Acts and build support for the Republican party. Charleston's black community also sponsored its own voter registration drives. On one occasion a reporter for the *Courier* observed a large crowd of blacks who marched through the streets playing instruments and carrying a banner that appealed to potential voters with the words: "Have you registered, if you have not do so[.]" By the time of the fall elections, 3,941 whites and 5,188 blacks from Charleston were registered, but comparatively few whites actually voted. Because of white apathy or passive resistance and heavy black voting, the call for a constitutional convention was upheld, and General Canby scheduled it to begin on January 14, 1868, in Charleston.[45]

On the appointed day, the 124 delegates from all over the state who converged on the city entered into a task that distinguished them from all previous political conventions in the state's history. Seventy black men were present, and Charleston's eclectic delegation consisted of eight members—three whites and five blacks. One of the whites, Dr. Albert Mackey, was a native Charleston Unionist, a university-trained physician, and had been the city's collector of customs since 1865. Gilbert Pillsbury, a Massachusetts abolitionist, was the brother of the more famous antislavery activist Parker Pillsbury. Awash with enthusiasm following the war, he entered the state as a superintendent of education for the Freedmen's Bureau and later became the first president of the South Carolina Union League. Christopher C. Bowen, a northerner who nevertheless became an officer in the Georgia cavalry during the Civil War, had been court-martialed and jailed for fraud and for instigating the murder of his commanding officer. The Union occupation of Charleston ended his incarceration, and Bowen embraced the Republican party while working as a clerk in the provost courts.[46] Of the blacks, four were native Charleston mulattoes and all had been free before the war. Although not as diverse as their white counterparts, these men's backgrounds were also varied. Alonzo J. Ransier had been employed as a shipping clerk before the war, while Robert DeLarge and William McKinlay (the wealthy father to William J.) had been employed as a barber and tailor respectively. The other two members of the delegation were ministers. Frances L. Cardozo was a native Charleston mulatto who had attended the University of Glasgow and Presbyterian seminaries at Edinburgh and London to prepare for the ministry. He returned to Charleston as a volunteer with the American Missionary Association schools. The Ohio-born Richard Harvey Cain was the sole northerner amongst the group. He had been an A.M.E. pastor in Brooklyn before joining the South Carolina

Conference in 1865 and leading its missionary effort in the city and nearby communities in the Low Country.[47] Based upon their occupational backgrounds, the artisans were generally representative of black Charleston's middle class, with the exception of William McKinlay, who represented the most well-heeled segment of the brown elite. The ministers represented the community's new educational elite.

The Charleston delegation played an important role at the convention, and the positions taken by its black members revealed priorities they set for their community and the perils they hoped to avoid in charting the state's future. One issue of great importance, which emerged early during the proceedings, was the role state government would or should assume in redistributing land ownership. There were immediate and long-term reasons for the convention to articulate a clear and decisive policy on this matter. An immediate concern was that of Freedmen's Bureau assistant commissioner Robert Scott, who lamented the planters' difficulty in getting freedmen to sign labor contracts for the coming year. They were willing to work but were reluctant to commit for an entire season, since they believed the constitutional convention would provide them with land or the means of acquiring it. Black delegates expressed a longer-term concern that emancipation without land consigned the freedmen to a tenuous future. No one in the Charleston delegation nor in the convention at large favored outright confiscation of planter land. In fact Richard Cain even opposed the taxation of land to compel its sale. He proposed that South Carolina petition Congress for the appropriation of one million dollars from the surplus funds of the Freedmen's Bureau. These monies would be used to purchase the largest plantations and subdivide them for sale to the landless.[48] Robert Delarge and Alonzo Ransier vigorously supported Cain's proposal because of its many advantages. It could assist all persons, black and white, who desired to own land, and this would reduce racial tensions. Once operational, the plan would reduce the need for the Freedmen's Bureau, which DeLarge and Ransier believed shouldn't be extended unnecessarily lest it encourage dependency. Finally, as the land had to be purchased, the freedmen would have additional motivation to work just as other men and thereby demonstrate the ability to survive on their own resources.[49]

Cain's proposal was passed overwhelmingly, but when the convention learned that Congress would not support the resolution, its leaders changed tactics. They passed an ordinance directing the legislature to establish a Board of Commissioners of Public Lands. This agency was empowered to expend public funds to purchase land for resale. One year later in March 1869, the first legislature fulfilled the provisions of the constitution by establishing the South Carolina Land Commission.[50]

The level of personal indebtedness was high after the war, and closely related to the land question was the issue of declaring a debt moratorium. On this question the Charleston delegation was sharply divided. In speaking forthrightly on this matter, Richard Cain and Francis Cardozo argued that contracts made legitimately ought to be honored and viewed stay laws (which would suspend the collection of debts) as unconstitutional abridgements of property rights. Cain even revealed that he could lose several thousand dollars in real estate if the moratorium wasn't enacted, but he was willing to sacrifice personal for principled interests. But each man's reasoning went further. Reverend Cain was opposed also because the proposed relief would reward those who had opposed Reconstruction all along. Furthermore, he believed only the rich would benefit; otherwise, they would be forced to sell land, and poor people would have an opportunity to buy. For Cardozo, the market working according to laissez-faire principles would contribute to the breakup of the plantation system. He was convinced that this was essential for black progress, even arguing, "Our freedom will be of no effect if we allow it [the plantation system] to continue." Francis Cardozo had an additional concern. He thought 90 percent of the debt had been incurred due to the sale of slave property or from raising funds "to maintain a war waged for the purpose of perpetually enslaving a people." The black cleric couldn't have been less charitable and only had one recommendation: "Now let them suffer for it," he said.[51]

Robert DeLarge led the supporters of the debt relief proposal. He and others argued that all classes, including Low Country planters and Up Country farmers, would benefit, and any hope of economic recovery would be impaired by the continued impoverishment of the planters. But even if planters were forced to sell land, DeLarge claimed it would probably come to market in parcels far too large for the impoverished masses to ever purchase. After lengthy debate, a proposal to petition Major General Canby for a minimum three-month stay of debts was passed by a vote of fifty-seven to fifty-two. The Charleston delegation divided evenly, with the three whites joining DeLarge in favor. In a related matter, Jonathan Jasper Wright of Beaufort introduced a proposal to exempt a personal homestead from sale for indebtedness except for taxes or the purchase costs. This constitutional provision had overwhelming support and passed. In the Charleston delegation, William McKinlay, a wealthy Charleston tailor, feared that the provision completely deprived creditors of redress but, in the end, voted along with the remaining members of the delegation in favor.[52]

Access to the ballot box was equally important, and the qualifications for voting elicited lively debate. The original proposal reported by DeLarge's Committee on Franchise and Elections extended voting rights to male citizens but required that voters be literate by 1875. Radicals on this issue supported an amendment, introduced by Robert Brown Elliott of Barnwell, to drop all literacy requirements. In the debate Francis Cardozo upbraided his colleagues for not giving sufficient attention to the implications of the original proposal and thereby jeopardizing the Republican party's future. In his opinion it would take ten years for the school system to become fully functional outside Charleston and would require the expenditure of millions of dollars. But the proposal assumed that literacy could be achieved in a mere seven years. He also stated that it was ill-advised for blacks to place such unrealistic restrictions on themselves and hypocritical on the part of whites, who tolerated or promoted black ignorance under the slaveholding regime. Ransier argued against any restrictions because whites hadn't placed similar impediments before themselves and because the proposal would deprive a large segment of the black community of its chief means of self-defense.[53] By contrast, William J. McKinlay believed the public school system would be sufficiently organized to provide the necessary instruction. He contended since taxes were levied to fund a school system, citizens should be compelled to use it. He was willing to compromise and suggested 1878 as a reasonable date for voters to attain literacy. In open debate he was convinced by DeLarge and others to accept a later date, 1890. The motion to consider this alternative date failed, and the vote on the Elliott amendment to eliminate all literacy requirements passed one hundred and seven to two. All of the Charleston delegation voted in favor.[54]

The convention established the state's first statewide publicly financed school system, and some of the issues relating to its operation were of concern to black delegates. Francis Cardozo's Education Committee report provided for a poll tax to raise school funds, and this tax proposal immediately raised questions about the penalty for non-payment. Payment of a real estate or poll tax had been required for voting during the 1850s, and Cardozo believed the freedmen were willing and capable of paying the dollar tax now, without compulsion. Benjamin Randolph of Orangeburg and William McKinlay of Charleston were the conservatives on this issue, and they favored allowing the legislature to decide on penalties. No harm would result, according to McKinlay, because blacks would form a majority in the state assembly. Reverend Randolph believed that only the threat of disfranchisement would force compliance. Robert DeLarge had great trepidations about the possibility that the tax could be used against the black electorate unless adequate safeguards were also instituted. Robert Brown Elliott amended Cardozo's proposal to prohibit deprivation of voting rights as a penalty for non-payment. William McKinlay voted against the amendment and was the only member of the Charleston delegation to oppose this part of the education report, which passed eighty-one to twenty-one.[55]

The compulsory attendance provision of the education report also triggered a lengthy debate. Some members of the Charleston delegation, such as Cain and DeLarge, were philosophically opposed to requiring children to attend school; moreover, they thought the plan was unworkable. Robert DeLarge observed that making the schools available to all children and then requiring attendance suggested racial integration might occur. He believed this would alienate whites. Francis Cardozo denied this, rejoining that parents would only be required to send their children to some school, but there was no requirement to send them to school with blacks. Finally, Cardozo arranged a compromise. In amended form, the educational provisions requiring compulsory attendance would go into effect only after the school system was completely organized.[56] This would assuage white fears by ensuring that enough schools would be available for both races to reduce the possibility of integration.

Black delegates wanted to ensure that the implementation of state laws would be free of racial discrimination. To accomplish this, Benjamin F. Randolph introduced a clause into the Bill of Rights that prohibited racial distinctions between citizens in the enjoyment of their common rights. Some white delegates claimed such a measure was superfluous, contending that equal rights were implicitly provided for already. Ransier and Cardozo, like Randolph, believed that an explicit prohibition against discrimination was required because the constitutions of the state and the United States were vaguely worded and subject to conflicting interpretations. Cardozo, specifically, wished to include the explicit prohibition so "that no lawyer, however cunning or astute, can possibly misinterpret the meaning." He charged that many white Carolinians hadn't accepted the consequences of emancipation yet and were waiting to undermine black citizens' new rights. No constitutional loophole should be afforded them. Randolph's proposal prohibiting racial discrimination was passed and incorporated into the constitution.[57]

During the last weeks of the constitutional convention, plans were being laid to bring a new regime to power. Elections scheduled by the military for mid-April would elect state officials and congressmen and would either accept or reject the new constitution. The Republicans convened their nominating convention in early March. Amongst Charleston's delegates were five blacks, all of whom had been free before the war; two were northerners and three were from Charleston. At the convention black leaders did not aggressively pursue office and of the eight statewide positions to be filled, only one went to a black candidate. Francis L. Cardozo won and accepted nomination as secretary of state. Nor did they pursue nomination for Congress or to the United States Senate later. The restraint they exercised was calculated to avoid offending the racial sensibilities of southern whites from whom they hoped to win at least grudging toleration if not a modicum of support.[58]

Francis L. Cardozo had been offered the nomination as lieutenant governor but declined, explaining that such a high profile position would be objectionable to whites. Likewise, when a supporter suggested Martin Delany for Congress from the Second Congressional District (which included Charleston), he demurred, although he was flattered. He believed blacks should be cautious so early in their enfranchisement and should avoid steps that might prove injurious to their cause. Besides, it wasn't necessary to have representatives of their own race in the national councils at this time, and as long as white prejudices opposed black representatives, Delany urged forbearance. Jonathan J. Wright took a different view, and when he pursued nomination as lieutenant governor,

Alonzo Ransier, Robert DeLarge, and Benjamin Bosemon all opposed him. Among their many reasons was the belief that "it would ruin the party to put a colored man in such a high office."[59] Black political leaders did pursue seats in the general assembly and local offices much more aggressively, even at this early date. Thirteen of the eighteen candidates for the general assembly from Charleston County were black men, and Richard Cain was a candidate for one of Charleston's two seats in the state senate.[60]

The mid-April elections ratified the constitution by a large margin, and the Republican state ticket was elected. Robert Scott, the former assistant commissioner of the Freedmen's Bureau would soon become the state's first Republican governor. On July 24, after the legislature ratified the Fourteenth Amendment, Maj. Edward Canby remitted his powers to the civil authorities, and South Carolina was declared fully reconstructed.[61]

The city of Charleston underwent a political transformation no less dramatic and consequential than the transformation that occurred at the state level. On February 20, 1868, Major Canby removed the civilian mayor Palmer Gaillard from office, replacing him with a series of three military appointees. In late May, Canby intervened in city politics again by replacing thirteen of Charleston's eighteen aldermen. Seven of the replacements were black men. These were William Weston, Richard Dereef, William McKinlay, Robert Howard, Edward P. Wall, and Revs. Ennals J. Adams and Richard H. Cain. All had been free before the war, and, except for the two ministers who were northerners, the remainder were generally representative of Charleston's free brown elite families. If Major Canby's objective was to ease the shock certain to result from the appointment of black officials, the selection from amongst Charleston's former free persons of color was an especially wise choice. Whites still objected, but many deemed these to be respectable, intelligent men, and Dereef and Howard stood out as being especially conservative.[62]

Municipal elections were originally scheduled for June 2 and 3, but when the state government failed to make sufficient progress toward Reconstruction, the election had to be postponed. After a period of uncertainty and local Republican dissatisfaction over the delay, the legislature arrived at November 10 as the date for the first city elections since the end of military rule.[63] Several months earlier in the year, the

Republicans chose Gilbert Pillsbury, the Massachusetts abolitionist and Freedmen's Bureau official, as their mayoral candidate. In the ensuing campaign, substantive policy issues did not play much of a role, but Pillsbury pledged to restore prosperity and to ensure equal justice for all. The Democrats, who by now had organized themselves into the Citizen's party, nominated Henry D. Lesesne, a local attorney and former state legislator, as their standard-bearer. He pledged to be impartial, to restore the city's credit, to stimulate business, and to protect property. The Democrats accused Pillsbury of being a dangerous fanatic who harbored the nativist's hatred for the Irish and who as mayor would bring economic disaster to the city.[64]

Although the Citizen's party appealed to black voters for support and stressed the common interests of freedmen and former masters, it failed to nominate a single black aldermanic candidate. The Republicans ran an aldermanic ticket comprised of equal numbers of blacks and whites. Of the nine black candidates, William McKinlay, Robert Howard, and Edward P. Wall were incumbents appointed by Major Canby. All the men were employed as artisans or entrepreneurs and had formerly been free before the Civil War. In fact, seven of the nine were substantial property owners who represented some of black Charleston's most substantial families.[65]

Gilbert Pillsbury won the mayor's seat by only twenty-two votes and became Charleston's first Republican mayor; the entire aldermanic slate was successful. It proved difficult to assume office because the Citizen's party disputed the electoral results and charged that there was vote fraud and procedural irregularities. The city council held an investigation and declared the election void. A protracted and divisive dispute ensued that was only settled after the legislature passed an act validating the election and after appeals were exhausted through the state courts. In May 1869, Gilbert Pillsbury and a racially integrated board of aldermen assumed office.[66] Reconstruction was now well under way.

Immediately following the war, black and white Carolinians grappled with the meaning and consequences of emancipation for their lives. Occupied as the city was by Union forces, a new assertiveness emerged among the freedmen as they rejected the physical and psychological burdens of the past. Black Charlestonians also began a systematic campaign to win full equality as citizens, including the right to vote.

Without the protection these rights afforded, they rightly believed their freedom would be seriously compromised. Their appeals were met with white recalcitrance though, and only the advent of Congressional Reconstruction provided the leverage to force further political change.

The avant garde of black political activism in Charleston was comprised of artisans, many of whom had been free before the war. They were leaders in the early petition drives and mass meetings. They also played important roles in the organization of the Republican party at the constitutional convention. Craftsmen represented the more talented segment of the working class and had demonstrably higher levels of literacy.[67] Antebellum free blacks were a highly skilled group, had higher levels of education than the freedmen, and had participated in a well-developed institutional life. Some of these artisans may have entered politics to supplement their incomes, which undoubtedly sagged during Charleston's postwar economic slump. Free black artisans may have felt especially threatened by the discriminatory labor regulations of 1865 and raised their collective voice in protest at the early political meetings. All these factors ensured that they would play a disproportionately large role in the politics of reconstruction.[68]

Generally, these leaders of free black background were members of the middle class. The examples of William McKinlay Sr., William J. McKinlay, and Edward P. Wall, all members of the antebellum brown elite who entered politics almost immediately following the war were exceptional. Most of the community's wealthiest members remained aloof from serious and sustained political involvement throughout Reconstruction. Even though elite men such as Richard Dereef and Malcolm Brown held aldermanic seats briefly, neither could be considered an activist political leader. The reasons are unclear, but some of these wealthy men may have been preoccupied with routine business affairs. Others may have suffered financial losses because of the war and consequently chose to concentrate on rebuilding assets. According to one report, William McKinlay seemed to balk at accepting an interim aldermanic appointment, questioning the wisdom of losing personal friends and clients to fulfill its obligations. Others had owned slaves, and the Republican party was responsible for the destruction of this species of property. This factor, combined with other characteristics of the local party leadership, may have repulsed some of the former free brown elite.[69]

The absence of the old elite was more than compensated for by the participation of northern blacks. They entered the South with the army, through the relief efforts of freedmen's aid societies, or as missionaries from various northern churches. They joined with native middle-class leaders and with whites at the early political meetings and at the constitutional convention to promote the interests of their adopted community. Together they backed clearly middle-class objectives to secure voting rights, to provide educational opportunities, and to guarantee equal protection under the law. They were unwilling to consider radical schemes for land redistribution, choosing to create a land commission instead.

During the antebellum years, the free black group's existence was predicated upon its members' ability to distinguish themselves from slaves. The final years before the war witnessed the erosion of the unique social position free blacks had occupied, and emancipation completely destroyed it. During Reconstruction, more than ever before, the challenges of the day and the changed racial climate, which tended to view all blacks collectively, required racial unity.[70] The concerns and actions of Charleston's black activists qualified them as mass leaders. Their many accomplishments laid the groundwork for election of the first black elected officials, significantly affected the subsequent development of Charleston's black community, and symbolized a new level of cohesion possible only in the postbellum era.

CHAPTER FOUR

THE SEARCH FOR ECONOMIC SECURITY

Labor and Work in Reconstruction Charleston

Simultaneous with the struggle to define their rights as full citizens, the freedmen took other vital initiatives to give structure and new meaning to their lives. Certainly some of the most important, though still the least examined, are the initiatives taken by blacks to promote their economic interests in the city. When writing about Reconstruction in the 1930s, W. E. B. DuBois observed that blacks desired "economic enfranchisement" and the "real abolition of slavery." In his view, Reconstruction was in part a "vast labor movement" of black men. Three centuries of exploitation notwithstanding, black workers now emerged from the dislocation of war to launch "a tremendous series of efforts to earn a living in new and untried ways" and thereby "achieve economic security."[1] The quest for economic advancement encouraged many to migrate to the city. Urban places typically provided a wider range of economic options than were available in the rural districts. Nevertheless, the problems faced by all former slave workers were thrown into the boldest relief by the exigencies of life in the city. Charleston was no exception. In Charleston the freedmen made significant efforts to overcome the limits of their antebellum heritage while capitalizing on the new opportunities resulting from emancipation. The economic results were modest at best, but the workers' energetic and creative use of their talents also contributed to the further institutional development of the black community.

Throughout Reconstruction and especially during the immediate postwar years, Charleston became the focal point for the migration of thousands of ex-slaves, who endured hardships and risked their lives to reach the city. These migrants were overwhelmingly poor, agricultural laborers and almost entirely accounted for the growth of the city's black population, which increased from 16,600 in 1860 to 25,994 by 1880. In the fall of 1865, one visitor to the city found it literally "full of country negroes." At the same time, an old Charleston resident lamented the fact that the city was being "overrun with negroes of all sorts and conditions." Many of these rural freedmen were "occupying some of the best residences" that had been abandoned by whites who had fled the city before its occupation by federal troops. Most of the freedmen were not so fortunate, and, as the migration assumed massive proportions, refugees crowded into "miserable shanties," often located in the most unhealthy areas of the city. Living conditions were especially bad in the freedmen's camps along the coal docks and wharves on the Cooper River. A Freedmen's Bureau officer who inspected one encampment of migrants on Commercial Wharf found it in a very filthy and dirty condition and reported: "The Negroes are crowded together as closely as They can be, —both under the Sheet and around The wharf obstructing The passage way, Pigs, chickens and children of all ages; are in one promiscous [sic] huddle; old clothes bedding etc. which is very dirty and filthy is [sic] heaped up in different places—Vermin can be seen crawling over all the inmates of the camp; They build fires under the Sheet and around The wharf to keep, Themselves warm and to cook Their Scanty rations with."[2]

In its attempts to alleviate such scenes of deprivation and suffering among the refugees, the Freedmen's Bureau, under the leadership of Assistant Commissioner Rufus Saxton, launched an extensive relief program. By mid-summer of 1865, food, clothing, and medical supplies were being requisitioned from the army and distributed to destitute residents, both black and white. The Bureau also embarked on two major projects. One was the establishment of an orphans' home to care for the many black children who, through the disruptions of war or by other means, were now left without parents. The other was the establishment of the Old Folks Home, which was devoted to the care of aged and infirm blacks. The burden of the Freedmen's Bureau was lightened by the organized efforts of private citizens. George W. Williams, a prominent Charleston merchant, worked with other citizens to distribute the remaining Confederate foodstuffs to the needy. Black residents acted in their own behalf also. The Colored Women's Relief Association obtained material from the Bureau that they made into clothing. Another group of black women from a local church secured and outfitted an "orphan house" for the children of parents who found employment in the countryside. Originally some additional funding was derived from the Freedmen's Bureau; by 1869 the ninety-five children there were supported by local black churches and the New England Aid Society. The black congregation of Zion Presbyterian Church collected and disbursed clothing for the children of destitute freedmen. Likewise, the Patriotic Association of Colored People and the Mutual Aid Association distributed essential supplies to the freedmen and provided burials for the indigent.[3]

Despite the wretched living conditions they encountered, and the efforts of the Freedmen's Bureau to discourage blacks from changing locations, the tide of migrants to Charleston continued to swell. There were several reasons why blacks felt compelled to leave the countryside. Some desired to gain new experiences and thus fled their old residences. More pressing concerns, however, led most to leave home. Many whites only reluctantly accepted the abolition of slavery, and, as Sidney Andrews observed, these whites held to "the brutal assumption that the negro cannot be controlled except by fear of the lash." According to a Charleston Freedmen's Bureau agent, the South's failure to immediately reestablish planter hegemony resulted in "a general hatred of the freedmen." The agent predicted that unless the freedmen were accorded better treatment, they would probably desert the countryside entirely.[4]

Since the logistics of war caused population dislocations, many freedmen came to Charleston seeking rations from the Freedmen's Bureau and transportation back to their old homes. Some freedmen were separated from relatives and journeyed to the city in search of them, while others desired the benefit of schools for their children. Shortly after the end of the war, many blacks believed that whites would be driven from the coastal regions and the lands would be divided among them. Consequently, it was observed that upcountry blacks supposed "freedom can only be found 'down-country,' i.e., in the neighborhood of Charleston." Finally, large numbers of rural freedmen found their jobs and working conditions on the plantations no longer tolerable and journeyed to Charleston in search of new employment opportunities.[5]

While rural freedmen were deserting the plantations, many Charleston blacks were similarly taking leave from their old employments and residences. An observer for the *Nation* pointed out that "they thought . . . that in this way only could they fully shake off old habits, and make a complete entry upon their new condition." These desertions reinforced whites' belief that the freedmen were inefficient, lazy, and unwilling to work without compulsion. Such predispositions blinded whites to the fact that their former slaves often used their freedom in productive ways. In one such case, Quash deserted the Porcher family shortly after their return to Charleston, having decided to use his time selling fish in the streets of the city. Caroline Gilman reported that even though many former servants had deserted their masters, they were often seen "seeking a day's work." Although adhering to contemporary notions about the efficiency of free black workers, one Charleston resident had to admit that of the slaves who had deserted him, two or three of the men had joined the army, three others worked on the docks, one woman had gone north to take a job as a cook, and another now worked as a chambermaid aboard a steamer. Even those rural migrants who, after a short stay in the city, decided to desert their positions often did so for other jobs and not for the purpose of remaining idle. A Charleston man reported that "this morning Rebecca & Andrew both bid us farewell, they say they wished to return back to their Plantation to attend to their planting." In another case a woman resigned her servant's position "to enjoy the balmy air of her old native home on the Plantation of Mr. Ferguson" located on the Cooper River.[6]

The desertion of Charleston's domestics was particularly widespread. One contemporary newspaper describes domestics as "perfect nomads" who seldom remained in a family's service for any appreciable length of time. In his own personal lament, a Charleston diarist recalled that during the year between October 1865 and October 1866, his family had employed eighteen different servants. The servants' desertions, like those of other black workers, were prompted by the desire to assert as well as test their freedom. A black cook resigned a position she had been perfectly satisfied with because to her "it look like old time [*sic*] to stay too long in one place." To whites, the desertions of servants were senseless because in their view domestics obtained better food, clothing, and lodging than they could have procured on their own. However, domestics suffered under the disadvantage of having their every move scrutinized by whites and of having to work long hours while attempting to satisfy their employers' every fleeting whim and fancy. In the spring of 1865, from a household just north of the city, Susan Jervey reported incredulously that most of the servants "say they are free and went off last night." This even included "one Uncle Henry trusted most." No wonder Henry Raymond wrote that "the most indulged negroes have been the most faithless. . . . In fact the more indulged they have been the more bitter they have been against their masters and especially their mistresses."[7]

Since many whites were unaccustomed to performing domestic chores, their households were thrown into disarray when black servants could not be procured. Jacob Schirmer wrote of beginning a new year with "very discouraging prospects" because his family had "been some time without a house servant." In another case a woman disgustedly reported that "we are literally our own servants except for cooking. We make up our own rooms, & Mamma has been at the wash tub for two or three weeks. It almost makes me cry to see her." Even when servants could be obtained, they often refused to accept the treatment they had been accorded while slaves. According to one employer, the servant Cornelia "contended that she has as much right, by virtue of her Freedom, to sit to our table to meals, and use our glassware as she had been to white people besides us, where those liberties were allowed." After Cornelia failed to obtain the desired privilege, she left. In another revealing observation, a Carolinian warned that "white ladies have to be very prudent with their tongues, for colored domestics give back word for word, and even follow up words with blows, if reprimanded too cuttingly." Because of the domestics' new assertiveness, Henry Raymond urged his mother to discharge Tyra; he cautioned, "it is very *dangerous* to have dissatisfied Servants about you."[8]

The diversity of Charleston's economy enhanced the efforts of the rural freedmen who sought new employment opportunities following emancipation. For instance, during Reconstruction many blacks refused to continue working the rice plantations north of Charleston. Of these, many joined with black workers in the city to find jobs in the new phosphate industry that developed after 1867. The mining of phosphates relied almost exclusively on black laborers who dug the rock when it was found on land. When it was extracted from river beds by dredges, the rock was collected by black boatmen and transported to railroad lines where it was taken to the mills. At the mills the phosphate rock was crushed into a fine powder and treated with acids to produce fertilizer. The refining operations also relied almost exclusively on black laborers from Charleston and the outlying areas. Other industrial employment possibilities could be found in Charleston's lumber and rice mills, which utilized blacks in a variety of skilled and unskilled capacities at wages that were unattainable in agricultural employment.[9]

The range of jobs performed by blacks extended well beyond the milling operations of the city, though. By 1870 black men in Charleston were engaged in 158 different occupations. As in the antebellum period, however, they were randomly distributed neither through the range of jobs nor between occupational status groups in the city's overall occupational structure. The occupational distribution for black males in Charleston in 1870 is shown in Table 3. One of the most unfortunate concomitants of slavery was the relegation of so many black workers to occupations that required little or no skill. Once freed, black men constituted 78 percent of the male laborers and 98 percent of the domestics in Charleston. These two occupations alone provided employment for slightly more than one-half of all Charleston's black male workers in 1870. The relegation of black women to these types of jobs was even more complete, with 83 percent employed as domestics (servants, laundresses, cooks, etc.) or in other unskilled capacities in 1870. While

TABLE 3

OCCUPATIONAL DISTRIBUTION OF BLACK MALES IN 1870

	N	%
Professional	357	5.8
Skilled	1701	27.9
Semiskilled	860	14.1
Unskilled and Service	3187	52.2
TOTAL	6105	100.0

Source: *U.S. Manuscript Census of Population 1870,* City of Charleston.

blacks were over-represented among menials, they were seriously under-represented in the professions. Less than 6 percent of all black men worked as professionals in 1870, which was considerably less than the number of white professionals. Less than 1 percent of black women were employed in professional or proprietary positions at this time.[10]

In spite of slavery's crippling effects, black men and women played important and often critical roles in Charleston's skilled occupations. The needlecraft trades represented the largest and most important category of skilled labor for black women. This had been the case during the antebellum years and continued to be the case during Reconstruction, with 16 percent of them performing such jobs in 1870. They were divided between seamstresses, dressmakers, mantua makers, milliners, and tailoresses, and each required a different level or kind of skill. For example, seamstresses performed a variety of sewing tasks, including darning, tacking, hemming, and stitching. In addition to working on clothing, they also did general household sewing tasks.[11] Dressmakers were capable of doing the basic work of seamstresses, but they were also trained to cut, fit, and make women's dresses. In Charleston the mantua makers were considered to be highly specialized and trained dressmakers. They were capable of producing women's formal dresses adorned with lace and embroidery as well as the accompanying fancy undergarments. The changing nature of women's fashion and the attention paid to couture in Charleston required these women to regularly adapt and expand their techniques to remain current. Comparatively few women practiced the needlecraft trades on a full-time basis and often supplemented their incomes by working as cooks or laundresses.[12]

Table 4 shows comparisons between the complete 1870 occupational distributions for black, native white, Irish, and German male workers. With approximately 28 percent of their number involved in skilled occupations, black men were slightly more skilled than any of the other groups. At a level of only 20 percent, it was the Irish workers who were the least represented in the skilled occupations. While black workers made up 52 percent of the male labor force, they controlled 55 percent of Charleston's skilled occupations. By contrast, the native white and immigrant workers were slightly under-represented among the skilled trades.[13]

As a result of the training many had received as slaves, black workers

TABLE 4

OCCUPATIONAL DISTRIBUTION OF CHARLESTON MALES
ACCORDING TO RACE AND NATIVITY, 1870

	Black		Native White		Irish		German	
	N	%	N	%	N	%	N	%
Professional	357	5.8	2057	58.5	241	28.8	559	64.2
Skilled	1701	27.9	863	24.6	172	20.4	214	24.5
Semiskilled	860	14.1	340	9.7	126	14.9	51	5.7
Unskilled and Service	3187	52.2	234	6.6	301	35.8	48	5.5
TOTAL[1]	6105	100.0	3494	100.0	840	100.0	872	100.0

Source: *U.S. Manuscript Census of Population 1870,* City of Charleston.
[1]Percentages have been rounded.

controlled disproportionate shares of certain skilled occupations, especially among the building trades. In 1870 black workers controlled 54 percent of all jobs as blacksmiths, 55 percent of all plasterers' jobs, and 60 percent of all jobs as shoemakers. Other skilled occupations evidenced an even greater concentration of black workers. Between 64 and 78 percent of the sail makers, gardeners, carpenters, tailors, millwrights, butchers, and brick masons in Charleston were black workers. Between 80 and 100 percent of the cotton menders, coopers, barbers, wood sawyers, mattress makers, and cotton samplers were black.[14]

The over-representation of black workers was not limited to the skilled and unskilled occupations. Several semiskilled occupations relied largely on black labor. Among these occupations the most prominent were mill hands, draymen, boatmen, and fishermen, of whom between 71 and 96 percent were black.[15]

Black men were highly regarded for their ability as fishermen. Before the war most fishermen seem to have been free blacks, but slaves had sometimes performed this work. Many of the fishermen made up a large body known as the "mosquito fleet." Its size has been variously estimated as at between one hundred and several hundred participants, all of whom were bound by a set of common operating procedures. In 1880 the fleet may have included as many as fifty vessels, each with crews ranging from two to seven members. The men set sail well before dawn and sometimes ventured as far as forty miles from the harbor. Along the wharves, market women and street hucksters listened attentively for the cadences of rowing songs that marked the fleet's return. After obtaining their choice of the day's catch, these local merchants hawked the fish at the public market or on the streets. In 1883 a State Board of Agriculture report identified the fleet's members as the principal suppliers of the city's fresh seafood.[16]

Charleston's black and white male workers maintained fundamentally different occupational structures throughout Reconstruction. Examination of skilled workers makes this readily apparent. The ranks of Charleston's black skilled workers were highly skewed toward ten major occupations. These jobs (carpenter, brick mason, tailor, baker, cooper, blacksmith, shoemaker, painter, barber, butcher) accounted for 76 percent of all black skilled workers in 1870. Although whites were represented in them, these occupations were less prominent in their overall occupational structures. While 59 percent of the Irish and 58 percent of the German skilled workers were employed in these occupations, only 37 percent of the native whites were so employed. Examination of a larger number of occupations illustrates even more graphically the racial and ethnic differences in the occupational distributions. Of twenty-four skilled and semiskilled occupations in which blacks were either represented at or above their expected levels, Irish workers were represented in five of these jobs, German workers were represented in three of these jobs, and native whites were so represented in only one.[17]

Racial differences in the occupational structures that existed during Reconstruction were directly inherited from the antebellum period. Native whites were generally averse to engaging in certain manual occupations, particularly if they had been largely performed by slaves. But immigrants, as a less-established economic group, were unable to avoid performing such jobs as often as native whites. Aside from the stigma of "nigger work," there seems to have been another fundamental reason why whites attempted to avoid occupations that attracted large numbers of blacks during Reconstruction. One white Charlestonian recalled that shortly after the war ended, "Able bodied negroes in abundance" came to the city "clamoring for work at wages that white people could not live upon decency, [sic] much less in comfort." Three years later, the *Daily News,* pondering the low wages paid to white workingmen, attributed the cause to the "active, pressing, and constant" competition of black workers "in almost every department of the mechanic arts." Since they doubted their ability to make a living at such pursuits, many whites logically attempted to avoid them. These factors must have insulated black workers from the full force of white competitors to a degree and allowed them to continue practicing the skills they had acquired when they were slaves.[18]

If some whites were reluctant to engage in the same manual pursuits as blacks, there were others who found the competition of freedmen less offensive than competition with the slave had been. At the end of 1865, a meeting of white workingmen in Charleston declared that the results of the Civil War "elevated the working man and made labor respected. Henceforth, it will not be considered degrading to fulfill the devine [sic] command to 'earn our bread by the sweat of our brow.'" These workers were not only relieved that the stigma had been removed from manual labor but rejoiced in the prospect that greater employment opportunities would be provided for them and for their children.[19]

One of the earliest attempts made by whites to expand and protect their economic interests and to make significant inroads into traditionally black occupations was embodied in the South Carolina Black Code of 1865. According to one of its provisions, blacks who desired to practice mechanical trades, to maintain shops, or to engage in any employment or business other than husbandry or domestic service were required to obtain a license from a district court judge. These licenses had to be renewed annually after reapplication and certification of the person's skill and moral character. Mechanics paid a license fee of ten dollars, but shopkeepers had to pay one hundred dollars. Furthermore, if any complaints were raised or abuses of the licenses proved, they could be revoked. The code also contained vagrancy provisions, which were attempts to limit the economic choices available to skilled workers in particular. According to these regulations, a freedman without an employer could be imprisoned. The black workers who left one job to seek better wages could be charged and proven guilty of vagrancy. Fortunately for black workers, these laws were set aside in early 1866 by Maj. Gen. Daniel Sickles.[20]

During the 1870s the increased opportunities some whites envisioned often came at the expense of black workers but not by means of proscriptive legislation. Cotton mending (the process by which loose cotton samples were bound and made into bales) was an operation that had traditionally been performed by blacks. However, shortly after the Civil War, John Robinson and Company attempted to use white laborers to replace blacks in this capacity. Since it had moderate success, the company won the support of several leading cotton factors and of many of the city's other "loyal" whites. Even in occupations where their numbers were small, black workers met with the determined efforts of whites to undermine them. When York Moultrie, a full branch pilot with twenty-five years experience, and several other black pilots attempted to have their warrants renewed, the Board of Commissioners of Pilotage for Charleston Harbor refused to do so. In representing this matter to Governor Moses in 1873, Samuel Bennett, a local black political activist, explained that the board's "determination is to distroy [sic] the Colored Pilots, if possible." The attempt by the Board of Pilotage was thwarted, but later, after York Moultrie was appointed a member of that body, white pilots petitioned for his removal, charging that he was incompetent. According to Moultire, the motive of the white pilots was "jealousy and objection to my colour" only.[21]

By 1880 the competition between workers contributed to the decline of blacks in certain occupations, and these declines were sometimes significant. An examination of eighteen important skilled occupations reveals black wood sawyers, bakers, carpenters, tailors, blacksmiths, engineers, cigar makers, machinists, printers, cotton menders, and wheelwrights decreased between 1 and 9 percent. Even larger declines occurred among masons, sail makers, millers, shipwrights, and saddlers. The deteriorating position of blacks in these occupations is even more significant because the absolute number of workers engaged in several of them actually increased during the period. Furthermore, black workers were already under-represented in several of these trades, and the declines of the decade from 1870 to 1880 exacerbated their tenuous positions.[22]

Among the occupations listed above, native whites made positive gains in all except one. German immigrant workers made the next highest number of percentage gains, increasing in nine of the eighteen occupations. With only five percentage gains, the Irish workers fared least well among the white groups. Just as certainly as native whites gained the largest share of these skilled jobs, in all but two categories black men lost the largest share. In the case of carpenters, while the native whites and Germans gained 9 and 1 percent respectively and the Irish declined by 2 percent, it was the black workers who lost the most ground with a decline of 7 percent. Among shipwrights and builders, native whites and Germans increased their proportions, while Irish and black workers decreased. Importantly, though, the rate of decrease for blacks was more than twice as high as that for Irish workers.[23]

Beginning early during Reconstruction, white Charlestonians supported numerous measures to attract primarily European and even Chinese immigrants to the city and state. By doing so, they hoped to reduce their dependence on black labor. The state established a Bureau of Emigration, and in 1867 John Wagener, who eventually became a Democratic mayor of Charleston, was appointed to head it. The *News and Courier* heartily endorsed the policy, especially as an alternate source of domestics. In 1874 its editors wrote, "It would not be amiss to induce white servants to come to the city to supply places made vacant by a thriftless and unsatisfied class amongst us." As commissioner of immigration, Wagener actively canvassed master mechanics and associations of white workingmen in Charleston to determine the demand for foreign labor and to encourage its use. In promoting the use of immigrants as carpenters, millwrights, wheelwrights, tailors, and shoemakers, he appealed to the employers' "patriotism" and reminded them of their pecuniary interests. Wagener also appealed to white fears by mid-1867, suggesting that without an influx of immigrant labor, the chances were great that black officials would be selected as their next rulers.[24]

As many of the foreign workers the immigrant societies procured were trained in the same specialties as black workers, the latter's reaction was one of immediate outrage. A meeting of blacks in 1865 castigated the immigration movement because its "clear intent" was in their view "to thrust us out, and reduce us" to an intolerable serfdom. Their declaration of sentiments further warned that any such attempt would ultimately prove ruinous to the prosperity of the entire state. In the face of blatant attempts to undermine them, not all black workers reacted so diplomatically. In 1874 when a master drayman hired three recent immigrants from Ireland, the black draymen also in his employ refused to work, declaring that "they would not work if the white men were hired." Unable to carry on his business without experienced hands, the employer was forced to concede. Before resuming work, though, the black draymen "threatened" the whites and warned "that if they did not leave, they would be waylaid and . . . severely dealt with."[25] Although the apprehensions of black workers were raised, the attempts to attract an alternate source of labor were unsuccessful; by 1880 the number of immigrant workers in Charleston had actually declined.

While Charleston's black workers were sometimes displaced by foreign-born whites, they generally fared well against their immigrant competitors. The analysis of labor force changes in black workers' ten most important skilled occupations is revealed in Table 5. Again, native whites gained the greatest number of those important skilled occupations, but while the black worker declined in six of these occupations, the immigrant group of Germans, Irish, and others declined in eight. Even in those occupations in which both black and immigrant workers declined, in all but one case the immigrant decline was greater. Such findings explain the disgust of an English immigrant, who was amazed that southerners "would persistently give employment to colored people, some of whom can scarcely write their names, in preference to white people better educated and of course knowing better how to behave themselves." After unsuccessfully attempting to secure several jobs, he concluded that the employers "have their favorites" and that these matters were "cut and dried . . . [because] in nine cases out of ten these

TABLE 5

PERCENTAGE CHANGES IN MAJOR OCCUPATIONS, 1870–1880,
ACCORDING TO RACE AND NATIVITY

Occupation	Black	Native White	All Immigrants
Carpenter	-7.1	+8.7	-1.5
Brick Mason	-12.2	+6.8	+5.3
Tailor	-4.4	+3.6	+1.0
Baker	-1.9	+14.6	-12.1
Cooper	+10.4	-5.9	-4.5
Blacksmith	-3.1	+7.2	-4.0
Shoemaker	+13.6	-4.1	-9.7
Painter	+3.2	+3.9	-8.9
Barber	+4.2	-1.3	-2.8
Butcher	-0.3	+0.9	-0.7

Source: *U.S. Manuscript Census of Population, 1870, 1880*, City of Charleston.

favorites" were black workers. Finally, the disgruntled job seeker warned that if the trend continued whereby "immigrants from the old countries of Europe" were "slighted in favor of negroes who are enemies to every white face" many would return home rather than remain unemployed in Charleston.[26]

Although the foregoing observation exaggerated the situation, the white market for black skills remained extensive throughout the period. Even though most of the master tradesmen were whites, some blacks worked as contractors on important jobs. When C. D. Ahrens, a very well-known grocer, erected a new three-story store in the heart of Charleston's business district, he enlisted the services of Henry Richardson, a black plastering contractor. In another case, two white gentlemen hired an unnamed black building contractor to erect two identical cottages in an exclusive area on Savage Street. When they were finished, the buildings were two stories tall, each with seven rooms, adjoining kitchens in the rear, porches on the street, and Mansard-style roofs. Even after the war, black workers were often able to draw on antebellum connections as sources of employment. Jacob Drayton, a boatman who provided transportation services for many of the factors in the antebellum period, continued to draw on that patronage after the war. Others, like Francis St. Marks, who opened a new tonsorial salon on King Street, and William Ingliss, the famed barber at the Charleston Hotel, drew patronage from a strictly white clientele, many of whom had been antebellum patrons. The West Point Rice Mills utilized the same black workers both before and after the war. These antebellum relationships were extremely important to black workers during Reconstruction and in some cases protected them against new competitors.[27]

In addition to the direct competition of whites, the black workers' ability to successfully pursue a livelihood was sometimes affected by factors that were not strictly economic. Since they were usually dependent upon Democratic whites as customers or for employment, the predominantly Republican blacks became the subjects of both blatant and subtle political discrimination. Black workers were the victims of economic retaliation for voting according to their own preferences. Edward P. Wall was a Charleston tailor and local political leader who had been active at the Colored People's Convention in 1865 and had assisted in the organization of the Republican party. In mid-1868 he found it necessary to apply for work in the Freedmen's Bureau because, as he explained, "Devotion to the Republican party have [*sic*] rendered it impossible for me to earn support for my family." In 1876 the Charleston *News and Courier* editorialized that only "when we make it to the direct interest of the colored people to vote with the Democracy" will they do so and urged whites to only employ or patronize blacks that voted the Democratic ticket. The paper singled out the black butchers who, with one exception, were committed Republicans and "contribute liberally to the Radical campaign fund at every election." The *News* urged whites to boycott them in favor of white butchers, stating that it was now time to "withdraw our patronage, custom and employment from those who make war upon us." It seems that some heeded the paper's advice because when W. G. Marts wrote from Charleston in 1877, he reported that many blacks "have tried to get work for months and can not because they can not show a piece of paper, indicating that they have voted the Democratic ticket."[28]

The losses suffered by black workers due to political discrimination and the competition of whites did not necessarily lead to under-representation in occupations in which they had been preponderant. Although declines were witnessed among wood sawyers, carpenters, tailors, cotton menders, and brick masons, by 1880 blacks still comprised from 66 to 94 percent of the workers in these occupations. Fortunately, though, black workers were able to increase their share in several skilled occupations. Among butchers, painters, firemen, gardeners, barbers, metal smiths, coopers, upholsters, pilots, shoemakers, and plasterers, blacks increased their proportions between 1 and 28 percent by 1880. Table 6 reveals that even with the changes occurring within individual occupational categories, in 1880 the overall occupational distribution of black, native white, and immigrant workers remained much as it had been in 1870.[29]

Black workers maintained their overall skill levels throughout Reconstruction, but few of them were upwardly mobile by the end of the period. A sampling of black unskilled laborers (N=184) who persisted in the city from 1870 to 1880 reveals that only 29, or 16 percent, had acquired skills by the latter date. Of 457 black workers in major skilled occupations, only 8, or 2 percent, held white collar or professional positions in 1880. Emanuel Gibson, a one-time shoemaker, moved

TABLE 6

OCCUPATIONAL DISTRIBUTION OF CHARLESTON MALES
ACCORDING TO RACE AND NATIVITY, 1880

	Black		Native White		German		Irish	
	N	%	N	%	N	%	N	%
Professional	366	5.2	2486	54.8	486	63.4	167	27.1
Skilled	1823	26.2	1172	25.8	177	23.1	147	23.9
Semiskilled	1437	20.6	618	13.6	63	8.2	131	21.3
Unskilled and Service	3330	47.8	256	5.6	40	5.2	169	27.5
Total[1]	6956	100.0	4532	100.0	766	100.0	614	100.0

Source: *U.S. Manuscript Census of Population 1880*, City of Charleston.

[1]Percentages have been rounded.

upward to become a minister and missionary, and by 1880 Isaac Bailey, a former carpenter, had become a professional musician.[30]

Upward mobility was sometimes directly attributable to the political influence Afro-Americans wielded during Reconstruction, and they held a variety of elective and appointive government positions during the 1870s. Their experience is not captured by year-to-year census comparisons. Nevertheless, even this temporary opportunity was important to them for a number of reasons. First, holding political positions afforded the old formerly free artisan elite a means to preserve its former status in the face of competition for influence, power, and prestige from the freedmen. Second, given the harsh economic realities confronting postwar Charleston, obtaining political offices was a viable way for skilled workers to supplement their incomes and to preserve their standard of living. Finally, given the widespread political discrimination that all Republican workers and entrepreneurs faced, a career in politics was often the only alternative once a person embraced the Republican party. In an attempt to deflect the criticism of those Democrats who charged Republicans with merely "LIVING BY OFFICE," the *Daily Republican* pointed out that "under these circumstances, the man who accepted office was forced to live by it or starve."[31]

Robert C. DeLarge, a tailor and barber, was elected to the general assembly in 1868, and in early 1870 he was appointed state land commissioner. Later that year he was elected to a term in Congress representing the Second Congressional District. After returning to Charleston in 1873, he received an appointment as a trial justice. At the local level, it wasn't unusual for those artisans who entered politics to hold more than one position simultaneously. For example, Alderman William Hampton was also appointed as assistant flour inspector and as a port warden. Between the years 1868 and 1873, William McKinlay had been a state legislator, a member of the city council and the board of equalization, and a trial justice. Of course, the opportunity for government service diminished considerably with the end of Reconstruction, but blacks were sometimes able to continue in such positions beyond 1876–77. Christopher Burke, a former barber, was a deputy sheriff by 1880. Similarly, James Fordham, a carpenter in 1870, was listed as a second lieutenant on the municipal police force in 1880, and Robert Fields, a former tailor, worked as a municipal constable by the end of the decade.[32] These were clearly exceptional cases. The transitory nature of office holding in this era is most tragically revealed by the case of Alonzo Ransier. This former middle-class free person of color held numerous elective and appointive positions during Reconstruction. At various times, he was chairman of the Republican State Central Committee, auditor of Charleston County, a member of the state general assembly, a member of the U.S. House of Representatives, and the lieutenant governor. Nevertheless, by 1880 Ransier had been reduced to performing common labor.[33]

To judge by the fate of skilled workers, not only were few black workers upwardly mobile, but the mobility experience for most moved in the opposite direction. Table 7 shows the rate of downward mobility by occupation. Although only one-tenth of the tailors were downwardly mobile, most occupations experienced rates of decline of one-fifth or more, even ranging as high as 46 percent among masons and bakers. By 1880, of 457 blacks in major skilled occupations, 117, or 26 percent, slid downward on the occupational scale. Of these, the vast majority fell all the way to unskilled jobs.[34]

Several factors account for such high rates of downward mobility among black skilled workers. It seems that although a skilled slave may have possessed sufficient training to practice his trade on the plantation, that same level of proficiency may have proved inadequate in the urban environment. In his study of black artisans in the late nineteenth century,

TABLE 7

RATE OF DOWNWARD MOBILITY FOR BLACK MALE WORKERS IN MAJOR SKILLED OCCUPATIONS, 1870–1880

Occupation	N Persisting	N Downwardly Mobile	Percent
Blacksmith	32	9	28.0
Tailor	36	4	11.1
Brick Mason	39	18	46.2
Baker	15	7	46.7
Butcher	49	14	28.6
Painter	37	12	32.4
Cooper	39	8	20.5
Carpenter	129	26	20.2
Barber	31	8	25.8
Shoemaker	50	11	22.0

Source: *U.S. Manuscript Census of Population, 1870, 1880,* City of Charleston; *Charleston City Directories,* 1878, 1879–80, 1881.

W. E. B. DuBois referred to the skilled plantation slave and concluded he "was rather a jack-of-all-trades than a mechanic in the modern sense of the term." Even allowing for overstatement by DuBois, there may have been a differential in the technical skills of rural compared to urban slave artisans, with those from cities possessing greater technical competence and producing higher quality work. The rural migrants to Charleston might have been displaced by the competition of the city's indigenous artisans.[35]

The foregoing is only a partial explanation for the marked downward mobility rates observed here. Many freedmen undoubtedly attempted to work as independent craftsmen. According to DuBois, another aspect of the problem such persons faced resulted from the fact that prior to emancipation, the business of the slave "had been to do work but not to get work, save in exceptional cases." Although a significant number of urban slaves hired their own time, most were probably hired out either directly by their masters or by a contractor. There were even fewer exceptions to this among those slave artisans from the rural areas. Suddenly, these freedmen were thrown into open competition for jobs with much more experienced whites. Rural freedmen also had to compete with the more knowledgeable former urban slaves. Regardless of their origins, those pursuing self-employment now had to act as their own contractors, bidding for jobs, negotiating for wages, purchasing materials, and keeping records, all tasks that were in large part new to them.[36]

The ability to make such independent judgments was aided or hampered by the workers' level of literacy. Table 8 provides an analysis of the 1870 literacy rates for black laborers and black workers in ten major skilled occupations. It is instructive that the tailors with the lowest rate of downward mobility also demonstrated one of the highest rates of literacy.[37] Although a certain proportion of black skilled workers would have been downwardly mobile during the period, that number must have been greatly increased by the rural migrants, who entered the city with perhaps lower levels of skill and literacy and less experience in the way of functioning as free and often independent craftsmen.

It was not only their sometimes insufficient skills, lack of experience as independent workers, or the competition from whites that impeded the success of skilled black workers. Many of Charleston's black workers constantly complained about the incessant stream of migrants who came to the city either to reside permanently or for short periods of time. Although most came from the immediate vicinity of the city on

TABLE 8

LITERACY RATES OF BLACKS
IN MAJOR SKILLED OCCUPATIONS, 1870

Occupation	Either Reads or Writes		Both		Neither	
	N	%	N	%	N	%
Blacksmith	5	6.8	31	42.4	37	50.6
Tailor	10	18.1	36	65.4	9	16.3
Brick Mason	13	17.3	24	32.0	38	50.6
Baker	7	17.5	16	40.0	17	42.5
Butcher	15	16.1	48	51.6	30	32.2
Painter	13	16.8	40	51.9	26	33.7
Cooper	10	12.6	17	21.5	52	65.8
Carpenter	48	19.5	102	41.4	96	39.0
Barber	3	5.5	42	77.7	9	16.6
Shoemaker	14	25.0	27	32.5	42	50.6
Laborer	39	10.1	74	19.2	271	70.5

Source: *U.S. Manuscript Census of Population, 1870,* City of Charleston.

James and John's Islands, many came from Wadmalaw and some from as far away as Edisto. Charleston men argued that this surfeit of workers at best kept wages low and at worst made it difficult to continue working at skilled jobs. Six years after the war, a black alderman complained about the "strange negroes who came in from the country." The influx of rural blacks to the city proved an ongoing problem, and in 1886, when their numbers increased by the earthquake that year, one Charleston man denounced those who continued to flock to the city:

> You see those men? Well, they come from John's Island and Jeems Island and Wadmalaw and Edisto. They don't belong here. . . . Every man brings a hatchet with him, because every man thinks he is a bricklayer, and in case he can't get rations he will go to work for a day or two cleaning bricks. The colored people can't complain, because it's their own race that is going back on them. The white people are willing enough to pay fair wages, and there are enough colored laborers here to do all the work and at fair prices, but these lazy niggers from the islands keep coming here in the hope of getting rations, and when they get here, they will just work long enough to earn a dollar or two and will loaf around till they spend it. How can we expect to get good wages when our own people flock into town, leaving the cotton fields, where they belong . . . and come here to take the bread out of our mouths?[38]

At least one group of workers enlisted the direct aid of the city council in their attempt to limit the competition from country rivals. The Charleston wood sawyers cut and hauled wood from the surrounding countryside to be used for a variety of commercial and household purposes in the city. High levels of skill were not required to engage in this occupation, and, as Edward P. Wall, a black member of the city council observed, "Certain persons from the country and the islands in the neighborhood of the city" migrated to Charleston "and during the few weeks that they remain interfere materially with the business of the professional woodsawyers." In the fall of 1869, wood sawyers in Charleston petitioned the city council "to require that all persons who saw wood in the city . . . shall take out a license" under penalty of fine. The petitioners also requested that the council "fix the price for sawing a cord of wood, according to the number of cuts." In response, the city council required wood sawyers to take out licenses at a cost of one dollar. Curiously, the council also declared that the charge for sawed wood should not exceed one dollar per cut per cord. Violations would incur a ten-dollar fine. Although the licensing requirement had begun to produce the desired effect, the wood sawyers were not completely satisfied. One year later they requested that the license fee be raised to two dollars and fifty cents and also called for the incarceration of anyone convicted of charging less than one dollar per cord per cut of wood. These additional provisions were never instituted.[39]

Even when black workers were able to establish themselves against the encroachments of competitors, they remained captives of Charleston's sluggish economy. The war dealt the city a severe economic blow, although the relative decline in Charleston's economic prominence began in the early antebellum period. The rise of competing commercial centers and rural cotton entrepots that exported products via railroads after the Civil War delivered the coup de gras to the city's commercial leadership. These developments along with the decline of the antebellum cotton factorage system, explain why as late as 1871, the volume of Charleston's cotton exports had not reached the 1860 level. Nor had banking capital returned to its prewar levels. The lack of funds undoubtedly was one reason why as late as 1880 the city was still unable to completely repair the burnt district that had been destroyed by the fire of 1861. The city would never regain its antebellum proportion of shipping tonnage that entered American ports, and at the turn of the century Charleston was one of the two major southern ports that continued to decline significantly.[40]

In the face of the city's declining economic fortunes and the over-abundance of labor, many black workers had difficulty finding steady work. The seriousness of the unemployment problem among blacks was revealed by an incident that occurred in late 1869. At this time the City Inspector's Office, which was responsible for the maintenance of municipal property, announced its intention to hire fifty new workers to fill jobs as street hands. Consequently, the inspector's office became glutted with between five and six hundred men, mainly unemployed blacks, many of whom were skilled workers, and all clamoring for work. Outside city hall, "the pavement was completely blocked up, and as the crowd continued to increase, fears were entertained that the street cars would be interrupted in their trips." The crowd of unemployed job seekers became so unruly that the police had to be called to maintain order. Even city employment was not necessarily steady work, though. With so many workers unemployed, in 1871 the municipal government attempted to distribute the jobs at its disposal to the greatest number of laborers by filling a single job with a series of men who each worked only two days per week. While touring the black community that year, a white visitor reported being "struck by the number of men who appear to have no employment." Under such circumstances, some of Charleston's black workers were forced to take temporary jobs in the countryside to supplement their incomes. Several went to Aiken to help build a Catholic church, while on several occasions black workers ventured to the countryside to work on railroads then under construction.[41]

Although the building tradesmen were especially hurt by Charleston's depressed economy, all black workers were sorely affected. The wages paid to some workers actually declined from their prewar levels. One city resident rejoiced that in spite of such bad conditions, blacks were still willing to work and instructively noted, "The Negroes are very thankful for work at even the very scanty wages our friends can now afford." In another case a white cooper complained that although before the war, millers paid them fifty cents per tierce, in 1869 the price had dropped to between thirty-three and thirty-five cents per tierce, even though they were heavier. Similarly, it was a general complaint among black workers in a wide variety of skilled jobs that the wages they received were less than those paid to slave mechanics. Black workers in Charleston were not alone in lodging such complaints; skilled blacks in Edgefield County were similarly affected by declining postwar wage levels.[42]

Forced to work at low wages in a city that remained economically depressed throughout the period, black workers had great difficulty accumulating property. This problem was particularly acute among unskilled laborers. Of 184 that persisted in Charleston from 1870 to 1880, only 12, or 6.5 percent, had accumulated any real property by the latter date and three-quarters of this property was valued below five hundred dollars. Skilled workers had greater chances of obtaining property than other black workers, but even among their ranks the acquisition of real property was no mean task, as Table 9 reveals. In 1871 only 71, or just above 8 percent, of the workers in the major skilled trades owned any real property. Important variations did exist, however. While only 4 and 5 percent of the blacksmiths and coopers owned real property in 1871, 20 percent of the butchers and 14 percent of the tailors did. Several factors may have accounted for the observed variations. While certain skilled occupations were practiced by both urban and rural slaves, others were in the main urban occupations. Certainly rural slaves worked both as blacksmiths and coopers, and after migrating to Charleston during Reconstruction they continued to practice their trades. On the other hand, it is doubtful whether many rural migrants had previously worked as either slave butchers or tailors, thus these two occupations probably included fewer former rural slaves with more marginal skill levels than some other occupations. Comparison of literacy rates for these occupations is also instructive. Blacksmiths and coopers were the least literate workers of the categories surveyed. On the other hand, butchers and especially tailors showed much higher rates of literacy. While literacy in itself did not necessarily improve the workers' level of skill, it probably greatly affected their ability to make key economic decisions and successfully negotiate property transactions.[43]

TABLE 9

PROPERTY ACQUISITION AMONG BLACK MALES
IN MAJOR SKILLED OCCUPATIONS, 1870–71 AND 1880

N	Occupation	Property 1870–71		Persisting Ten Years		Persisters and Property, 1880	
		N	%	N	%	N	%
73	Blacksmith	3	4.1	32	44	3	9.4
57	Tailor	8	14.0	36	63	7	19.4
75	Brick Mason	3	4.0	39	52	3	7.7
40	Baker	3	8.0	15	38	2	13.3
93	Butcher	19	20.0	49	53	12	25.0
77	Painter	7	9.1	37	48	5	14.0
79	Cooper	4	5.1	39	49	3	7.7
246	Carpenter	17	7.0	129	52	22	17.1
54	Barber	5	9.3	31	57	6	19.4
83	Shoemaker	2	2.4	50	60	5	10.0
877		71		457		68	

Source: *Charleston Ledger of Taxpayers for 1871, 1880 CTAO, Charleston City Directories,* 1878, 1879–80, 1881.

Finally there were more former free blacks among the tailors and butchers than among coopers (most of whom had been slaves before the war) and blacksmiths. Several of these free blacks accumulated sizable amounts of property before the war that they retained during Reconstruction. In this respect the butchers represent a good example, in that at least 14 percent of those practicing the trade in 1870 were free before the war. Of this group, men like Joshua Wilson and Elias Garden had both accumulated sizeable real estate holdings as free blacks. In 1860 their properties were worth fifty-two hundred dollars and fourteen thousand dollars respectively. Although the value of their real estate declined following the war, the resumption of their trades, undoubtedly with much of their former clientele, enabled them to prosper and to continue to hold places among the black economic elite.[44]

The case of George Shrewsbury is an outstanding example of how former free persons of color could use the postwar political opportunities for their economic advantage. George Shrewsbury was a butcher during the antebellum years, and, although he began life as a poor man, by 1860 he had accumulated fifty-five hundred dollars in real estate along with twelve slaves. Following the war he did not become directly involved in politics for a number of years, preferring to concentrate on his business affairs. He benefited from both business acumen and political connections, though. Shrewsbury was a Democrat and won an appointment as a commissioner of the City Alms House under Democratic mayor John Wagener. He also served as principal meat supplier for that facility. This award was somewhat controversial in that another butcher charged that Shrewsbury's contract was granted even though his was not the lowest bid. The city council investigated but never clearly denied the implied charges of political favoritism. Later, in 1873, Shrewsbury was convinced to run for an aldermanic seat on the slate of Republican mayoral candidate George Cunningham to broaden support for the party. After winning office, he was awarded contracts to supply meat products for two additional city facilities, the Old Folks Home and the Orphan House. George Shrewsbury died in 1875, but the real property holdings in his estate were still worth fourteen thousand dollars in 1880.[45]

Those skilled craftsmen who remained in the city for ten years had a better chance to obtain property, but even among them the number of property holders remained small. Of the workers in the ten major skilled occupations that remained from 1870 until 1880, only 15 percent had acquired any real property by the latter date. Of the property accumulated by this group, three-quarters of it was valued at five hundred dollars or more. Those occupational groups that acquired the most property by 1871 continued to maintain their lead: 25 percent of all butchers and 19 percent of all barbers and tailors held real property. Brick masons, coopers, and blacksmiths continued to reflect the least amounts of property acquisition. The increases in the rate of property accumulation by occupation was not fictitious (i.e., caused by those without property migrating from the city), because in over one-half the cases, workers with property in 1880 held none in 1871. Clearly, then, if few black skilled workers were upwardly mobile to more prestigious jobs in the decade of the 1870s, a greater number did experience property mobility.[46]

Despite the manifold problems they faced, Charleston's black workers made practical use of their numerical strength, drew upon a comparatively well-informed and aggressive leadership, and successfully formulated strategies and institutions to protect their economic interests. Since they realized that the former masters' paternalism was destroyed by emancipation, and they were now confronted by the vicissitudes of life and employment in postwar Charleston, black workers took steps to fill the void. Organizations such as the Butcher's Mutual Aid and Protective Association and the Draymen's Benevolent Association were designed to provide relief for their members and families in times of sickness, death, or unemployment. Their efforts did not end with mutual aid societies, and to safeguard their immediate interests as workers, black men formed unions. Between the end of the Civil War and the mid-1880s, they founded several labor organizations, most notably among the coopers, longshoremen, cotton pressmen, carpenters, tailors, and brick masons.[47]

The common objectives of black and white workingmen sometimes led to cooperation between the two groups. To this end, integrated unions were formed. The Cigar Makers' Protective Union was one example and elected the black Sidney C. Eckhard, a former secretary of the longshoremen's union, to the position of vice president. Eckhard was known as "a man of intelligence" and exercised "considerable influence with his race." Joseph A. Galliott, another black, acted as the union's corresponding secretary. The Journeymen Mechanics' Union, which drew membership from a wide variety of skilled occupations, was also integrated. J. W. Millar acted as its vice president, Joseph P. Howard was the treasurer, and E. P. Jefferson and H. B. Noisette acted on the union's executive committee. The movement afoot in late 1869 and early 1870 to federate white workingmen into a single organization made overtures to black workers, urging them to form a similar body among themselves. Despite some initial opposition in their ranks, it seems that such an organization was formed among blacks. By mid-1870 the organization of the workingmen's movement in Charleston was completed with the election of an executive committee composed of three black and three white workingmen from each ward. No further information on the movement is available, but it seems that the organization may not have progressed beyond discussing the common problems of black and white workers.[48] Even though these initiatives were rare, they were still noteworthy for two groups that, five years earlier, had totally and diametrically opposed interests.

In other attempts to enlist aid for their cause, some black workers linked their destinies with the destiny of the nationwide labor movement of whites. Bricklayers' Union Number One of South Carolina was organized in 1881 and federated with the International Bricklayers' Union. It is not clear whether blacks were charter members of the union, but certainly by the mid 1880s it was integrated, and it acted to uphold wage levels for its members irrespective of race.[49] Although blacks already maintained a functioning carpenters' union, after receiving direct communications with the National Brotherhood of Carpenters and Joiners of the United States and Canada in 1883, they met to reorganize and to affiliate with the international carpenters' union. According to their leaders, several advantages would result from affiliation. As he chaired the meeting of approximately two-hundred-fifty union men, F. E. Rames stated that "the skilful [sic] carpenters of the city were much hampered by the large number of 'saw and hatchet' jacklegs who were constantly coming into competition with them." Once appropriate rules were adopted for membership in the union, "both incompetent and unskilled labor would be eliminated." Furthermore, Rames continued, their connection with the powerful carpenters' international "would give them a strong backing" in their just demands as workers.[50]

Unfortunately, the relations between blacks and white unions were often antagonistic. For example, the rules of the Typographical Union of

Charleston prohibited the admission of blacks and even forbade its members to work in the same room with blacks. Thus, when the *Daily Republican* hired white union printers, they had to work in separate rooms away from the paper's regular black printers. In its disposition toward blacks, the Typographical Union was typical and, more often than not, blacks were entirely excluded from the white unions of Charleston.[51]

For some blacks the conditions under which they worked were as important as their wages. Phosphate mill owners wanted their employees to work in gangs under contract; although they were never organized into a union, blacks used their collective strength to refuse. This was an endless source of frustration for owners because many rural freedmen only desired to work in the phosphate industry to supplement their farm income. At peak times in the planting or harvest season, this group could not be relied upon for long periods of time. The freedmen demanded to be paid according to the task system, which had often been used as a method of antebellum labor management in the Low Country. In this industry, one task consisted of digging down a vertical foot in a fifteen-by-six-foot pit and was paid at the rate of twenty-five to thirty cents per vertical foot. The workers were paid according to the amount of labor done, not according to the amount of mineral produced. Black workers' preference for this method ensured that they would have some control over the amount, regularity, and pace of their work.[52]

During Reconstruction, the priority of black workers focused mainly upon securing adequate wages rather than on attempting to improve the conditions under which they labored. Once they were organized, black workers used their numerical concentrations in certain occupations to their best advantage by striking to force concessions from employers. The tailors provide a prime example of working-class consciousness among black laborers. Early in October 1869, the predominantly black Journeymen Tailors' Union, led by Samuel Garrett and Nathaniel T. Spencer, began an investigation of how the wages they received compared with those paid for comparable work in other cities. After they found that their wages were inadequate, the tailors began negotiations with their employers and asked for an increase variously estimated at between 15 and 33 percent for each category of garment tailored. When the merchant tailors refused to grant the desired increases, the tailors launched a strike that was honored by most of the union's members. The strike lasted only a few days, as the merchants and journeymen reached a mutually satisfactory agreement.[53]

Strikes sometimes produced unanticipated results for those involved. In fall 1869, this became painfully clear to black laborers who were repairing the Meeting Street pavement. Their strike over wages failed because, shortly after they walked off, their places were quickly "filled by others glad of the job." Ordinary laborers such as these were usually poorly organized and were easily replaced by scabs and consequently had fewer chances of successfully striking. Replacement was not the only potential problem that could result once the decision was made to strike. Sometimes when black and white workers were equally represented in the work force of a given occupation, the blacks were left open to the duplicity of their white counterparts. The painters' strike of 1869 clearly reveals the triumph of race consciousness over class consciousness. While first-class white painters received $2.50 per day and second-class painters received $2.00, the corresponding rates of pay for blacks were $1.75 and $1.25. In late October both black and white journeymen painters struck together, demanding a uniform scale of pay for all: $2.50 for first-class work and $2.00 for second-class work. After an abortive attempt to procure New York painters as strikebreakers, the employers granted wage increases. But, while the wages of whites were raised to $2.50, the employers refused to raise the rate paid to black painters. Although it was the cooperation of blacks that made the wage increase for whites possible, the latter resumed work and deserted the cause of their darker allies.[54]

During Reconstruction and throughout the remainder of the century, the longshoremen launched the most ambitious, aggressive, and well-organized campaign to secure their interests as workingmen. After resuming business activities after the war, black longshoremen worked for seventy-five cents per day. As early as 1867 and 1868, they initiated strikes against the shipping companies and stevedores that were partially successful and in some cases raised the wages of experienced hands to between $2.00 and $2.50 per day.[55]

That such steps could be taken by this group of workers at such an early date is especially meaningful. This is because most dock workers were probably former slave laborers or porters whose wages had been fixed by city council ordinance during the antebellum years. The regulations had been specific, indicating the allowable rates for a full day, a half day, and by the hour. Slaves and also free blacks who had demanded higher wages or who even had refused to work for anyone offering the standard wage could be punished with lashes, fines, or incarceration. By adopting such an aggressive posture, these postwar workers confirmed the dawning of a new day even for common labor.[56]

Democrats were deeply disturbed by the longshoremen's demands and considered them unjustified, especially given the difficult economic times confronting the city. After chiding the 1868 strikers, the *Daily News* also warned that if blacks continued to press their demands, "young white men, natives of Charleston, would be but too glad to take their places." In its explanation of the offensive taken by black workers, the *Daily News* found the answer in the new political order that was taking shape. The February 1868 longshoremen's strike coincided with the South Carolina Constitutional Convention, which brought black and white Republicans into South Carolina government. As the editor explained, the money paid to black convention delegates "demoralized the whole race, and colored muscle now competes with colored brain" for influence. The editor contended that the strike was the result of the Union League and "designing men who have in view sinister ends." On other occasions Democrats also explained black labor activism as the result of the machinations of white Republicans or black demagogues, and they failed to recognize its real sources.[57]

The early attempts by longshoremen to advance wages were sometimes thwarted by employers who were able to replace dock hands with whites eager for any kind of work or by the lack of solidarity among the hands themselves.[58] These problems pointed to the acute need both for organization and for aggressive tactics to accomplish the longshoremen's goals. To present a more unified front in negotiations with employers, the Longshoremen's Protective Union Association was incorporated in 1869 under the leadership of Tobias Y. Clark, Charles Swinton, May Edwards, Richard Green, Anthony Grant, and others. Union membership grew rapidly, and by 1875 it was estimated at between eight hundred and one thousand "of the bone and sinew of the colored workingmen of Charleston." There were a small number of whites who also joined the union. By the mid-1870s, the longshoremen's union had accumulated two thousand dollars in its treasury, had deposited fifteen hundred dollars in the Freedmen's Bank, and by 1880 owned property on Chalmers Street downtown worth twenty-five hundred dollars.[59]

Effectively organized in a union and numerically dominant in their jobs on the docks, black longshoremen were a force to be seriously reckoned with on every wharf in Charleston. According to a local newspaper, Charleston witnessed a "heretofore unprecedented outcropping of 'strikes'" in the fall of 1869. One of the most important of these involved the city's black longshoremen. These workers presented the stevedores and shipping agents with demands, including pay increases to $2.50 per day for hands and $3.00 per day for foremen, the designation of regular working hours from 7:00 A.M. to 5:00 P.M., and pay at the rate of 40 cents per hour for overtime work. To avoid a protracted dispute, some employers quickly gave in to the workers' demands. Most employers, however, refused to do so, and the Charleston and New York Steamship Line engaged forty whites from New York, whom they substituted for the black hands who had gone out on strike October 1. Other lines also procured whites and used them as scabs. By October 4, however, the striking dock hands succeeded in disrupting most of the work that the whites had been performing, and, after taking complete possession of Adger's Wharf, they "drove off everybody, white and black, whom they suspected of a desire to go to work." Finally, on October 6, Toby Clark, president of the Longshoremen's Union, along with city officials and shipping agents, ironed out a compromise. The regular hours of work were designated as between 7:30 A.M. and 6:00 P.M. with one hour for dinner. The rate of pay agreed upon was $2.50 per day and 40 cents per hour for overtime. A very important concession was won when shipping agents and stevedores agreed to employ only union men except in cases of emergency. These provisions and rates only applied to the skilled longshoremen who worked on board ships, and dock hands could be employed by the companies at the best attainable rates regardless of the longshoremen's association. These guidelines were generally adhered to, except by the Charleston and New York Steamship Line, which dismissed union longshoremen when they refused to work for wages lower than the union scale. Furthermore, the line announced that it would never hire another union man and proceeded to hire only those who would work for the low wages. On October 9, three hundred black longshoremen and a few whites gathered at Adger's wharf, and the crowd vented its anger "in oaths and threats directed against the work-ingmen in particular, and all whites in general." At the height of the confrontation, some were heard to shout that "they would drink the blood of the white men." Finally, the police arrived and only through their intervention could the wharves be cleared.[60]

The strike was normally used to serve purely economic ends. But during Reconstruction, economic and political issues were so closely related that it was sometimes impossible to address the one without simultaneously confronting the other. On one occasion, for example, Charleston longshoremen launched a strike against their employers in which not only the economic but also the political issues involved were displayed in bold relief. In late October 1869, the cotton shippers refused to utilize the ship *A. B. Wyman* because it was being loaded by George B. Stoddard, a white Republican and a member of the Longshoremen's Union. Stoddard was subsequently dismissed. After word of his dismissal spread along the wharves, the members of the union immediately suspended work. At first they struck all wharves but later directed their work stoppage specifically against those lines shipping cotton to Europe as these made up the core of opposition against Stoddard. An emergency meeting of the men took place on October 28; approximately three hundred union members were present, along with many other workingmen who were not members of the union. After discussing Stoddard's case, the meeting resolved that the strike should continue "until the shippers withdraw all discrimination against longshoremen on account of their political sentiments, whether such members be Republicans or Democrats." According to those present, an aggressive defense was necessary because the action of the shippers was "but the first move of a determined effort to crush out the longshoremen who have demanded and received higher wages."[61]

The strike was successful, and by November 2, Stoddard was reinstated, and the workmen resumed normal activities. The strike presented the Longshoremen's Protective Union Association with a timely opportunity to further bolster its position vis-à-vis the shippers. During its course, the union resolved that none of its members "shall be allowed to work at stowing, or store any cotton, for any stevedore who is not a member of this Union, under pain of being fined in the sum of ten dollars." Their strategy must have worked because after the strike one local newspaper caustically noted, "most of the stevedores" could be seen "making overtures to join the organization."[62]

In August 1873 the cotton longshoremen announced that, beginning September 1, the rate of pay for their services would be $4.00 for hands and $4.50 for foremen. Their tasks required a degree of skill and strength, for these workers actually stowed cotton in the holds of ships, sometimes using powerful hand screws to compress the bales into the smallest possible space. Since the cotton hands provided a critical service on board the ships, the demands were readily met.[63]

In the wake of the cotton hands' wage increases, the dock hands presented a series of demands. The regular laborers were hired at a rate of $1.75 per day, which they demanded be increased to $2.50. This demand the ship captains and stevedores were willing to comply with, but as a caveat they demanded the right to select the workmen hired. The more radical members among the longshoremen believed that this infringed on the union's rights and convinced their fellows to strike on these grounds. At one wharf several of the workers refused to join the strikers after accepting the terms of the employers. When quitting time arrived, "several hundred colored men assembled at the wharf, and when the hands who had accepted the agents' terms attempted to go home, they set upon them and compelled them to flee for their lives." Only the refuge of the ship's hold saved these recalcitrant workers from the wrath of the mob. On Brown's Wharf the strikers prevented the unloading of the *Ashland,* and when it cleared from the wharf, they "congregated at the approaches to it, and indulged freely in violent and threatening language." Finally, though, the determination of the strikers at Brown's and Union wharves dwindled, and they accepted the advanced wages with the stipulation that the stevedores select their own hands.[64]

The compromise reached at both Brown's and Union wharves drew attention to the need for union intervention at Adger's Wharf. At this particular wharf, hands were employed at a rate of $10.00 per week, a rate which was lower than that proposed by the union. Furthermore, extra hands were hired at a rate of only $1.50 per day. Many of these dock hands were from the islands and countryside and, according to Charleston men, "do not belong to the union and have no business to come to the city and work for low wages." On the evening of September 3, a crowd of several hundred union men descended upon Adger's Wharf "and immediately began a violent ASSAULT UPON THE WORKMEN." According to one reporter, "The strikers set upon the few workmen against whom their rage was directed, and beat them severely, using clubs, sticks, rocks, cotton hooks, and whatever other implements they could lay their hands on." The next day the Adger Line, still refusing to ·concede the union's wage demands, had all of its work prevented by union men who blocked the entrances to the wharf and threatened any worker that dared to approach them with violence. After Democratic mayor John Wagener and the chief of police assessed the resolve of the longshoremen, they intervened in the dispute and finally persuaded the Adger Company to grant the wage increases while retaining the right to select workers.[65]

Though their union enabled longshoremen to procure just wages for their services, the problems attending longshore work remained manifold. The method by which workers were procured was extremely casual. There was no definite means of notifying workers when ships were due to arrive, nor was there any effective system for adjusting the number of men to the amount of work available at any given dock. These circumstances encouraged the oversupply of workers and engendered hostility between Charleston men and those from the surrounding countryside who were willing to work at low wages or to act as scabs. Furthermore, longshore work was irregular. Workers might alternatively experience days of work at a frenetic pace followed by days or even weeks of idleness. One longshoreman indicated that many were "idle about two or three days each week." Even when steady work could be obtained, the length of the cotton season in which longshoremen were regularly employed was estimated at only between three and five months out of a year. Such factors ensured that the longshoremen, although paid well by the day, would be one of the poorest groups among black workingmen.[66]

The longshoremen's strike of September 1873 encouraged an attempt by other black workers to increase their wages. On September 8, a crowd of approximately fifty black workingmen announced they intended "to cause a general strike among all the laborers in the city" and visited all mills and wharves along both the Ashley and Cooper Rivers. In turn, they conferred with the workers at each site and "boldly avowed their determination to allow no laborer to work, anywhere in the city, for less than two and a half dollars a day." The next day, the strikers, not content with mere words, determined to use more forceful means. Upon arriving at the mill operated by R. R. Hudgins and Co., the men "immediately took possession of the mill, drove the hands out, and made an attempt to mob the saw-filer, a white man, who was engaged at work on a flat." By the day's end, the strikers had succeeded in shutting down "most of the mills in the city," even spreading the strike to workers at the suburban phosphate mills. Mill owners either suspended their operations or, in at least one case, replaced the striking workers with white scabs. Mill labor was procured easily enough, and in the end the lack of organization and divisiveness among the workingmen led to the failure of the strike. By September 16, the men began returning to work, and the mills were resuming normal operations.[67]

In the final years of Reconstruction, the longshoremen and the Cotton Pressmen's Union launched strikes, but these were unsuccessful. The lack of worker solidarity and the resolve of employers in the face of the 1870s depression were factors that undermined their attempts. Another factor that thwarted the unions must be attributed to the policies of Republican mayor George Cunningham. He was determined to protect workers who desired to work at existing wages from union assaults and intimidation. His administration's effective use of the police to intervene in strikes to preserve order made it difficult for union men to maintain effective work stoppages.[68] The posture adopted by Mayor Cunningham was based on common middle-class assumptions that were widely shared by most political leaders, Democrat or Republican, black or white. These assumptions about labor, wages, and property were the same as those that prevented bolder steps to redistribute land following the Civil War. Ultimately, union failures were not surprising. That black workers won any successes, even temporary ones, in the face of almost insurmountable obstacles is surprising.

The Civil War and Reconstruction shattered traditional work relationships in the South, and a new order was created, in part, by those blacks who took immediate steps to redefine their roles as workers. To this end, they quickly seized upon the new opportunities that arose with the destruction of the old slave system. As many rural freedmen perceived greater economic prospects in the city, Charleston became one of the major foci for their rural-to-urban migration. In the city, the chances of obtaining and practicing a skill were greater, yet competition among workers was more keen there also. In the city, black workers competed for jobs with both native whites and immigrants. Furthermore, throughout the period, black workers indigenous to Charleston were often hostile to those freedmen that had left the plantations and had come to the city to look for work.

Despite the heightened levels of competition in Charleston, the overall skill level of the black labor force remained virtually unchanged during the period. Three factors account for this stasis. First, the sheer size of the black labor force was important. Black men made up slightly over one-half of the city's work force and were not only represented in skilled occupations but also had actually dominated many of them since the antebellum period. Their numerical preponderance made them difficult to eliminate. Second, though an immigrant community was present, Charleston—as a Lower South city—failed to attract the large populations of immigrants that continued to arrive in the cities of the Upper South and especially those in the North. In those places, the new arrivals supplanted black workers in many of the trades and services they had performed traditionally. Finally, during Reconstruction, Charleston remained primarily a commercial city and failed to undergo the kind of industrial or transportation changes with the attendant economic specialization that characterized northern cities and also those of the New South. In the context of the new or highly technical industries of the late nineteenth century, black workers were usually relegated to those occupations requiring the least skill.[69]

Continuity measured in terms of aggregate skill level should not obscure the vital changes that occurred. Individual skilled black workers experienced a pronounced downward mobility during Reconstruction, and though the data is not unequivocal, it seems that the rural migrants that came to the city may have fared worse than their urban counterparts. In large part, the apparent difference may be explained by the fact that members of the former group possessed more marginal skills, were hindered by higher rates of illiteracy, and were less familiar with the exigencies of life as independent workers than the urbanites. To strengthen their position as free men, Charleston's black workers attempted to acquire property. There was considerable variation in the degree to which certain occupations facilitated property accumulation. Some occupations simply were more remunerative than others, but also free blacks were disproportionately concentrated in certain job categories. Many had already accumulated property before the war and were more advantageously positioned to benefit from the new postwar economic opportunities. Yet, for even the most diligent, the acquisition of real property was at best tremendously difficult.

Low wages, Charleston's depressed economy, illiteracy, and sometimes poor training impeded black workers' attempts to translate skills into property holding. Only 15 percent of those black men engaged in major skilled occupations and residing in Charleston from 1870 until 1880 had any real property by the latter date. It clearly did mean something to possess a skill, since less than 7 percent of the unskilled black workers residing in Charleston for ten years had yet obtained any property.

Finally, with the decline of the paternalism that characterized the former labor system, black workers recognized that their economic well-being depended solely upon their own efforts. To this end, they organized labor unions, the most powerful of which was the Longshoremen's Protective Union Association. The unions revealed the growing class consciousness of black workers during Reconstruction by engaging in strikes primarily to improve wage levels. One of the reasons why the longshoremen were able to win even limited success was because black men virtually monopolized work on the docks. Whites were averse to performing dock work generally and weren't therefore available for use as strikebreakers. Even the longshoremen's union fell prey to the lack of worker solidarity. Its members also quickly learned not to expect special consideration from the Republican-controlled city council or Republican Mayor Cunningham when their activism ran afoul of the law. Even so, the unions and the activities of the non-unionized reflect in a very dramatic way the changed circumstances black workers had themselves helped to bring about during Reconstruction and its immediate aftermath.

Alonzo R. Ransier,
state representative,
lieutenant governor,
and congressman.

Avery Research Center
for African American
History and Culture,
College of Charleston

Robert C. DeLarge,
state representative
and congressman from
South Carolina.
Library of Congress

George Shrewsbury,
successful Afro-American
businessman and
Democratic member of
the city council.

George Mears with wife.
Mears was a Democratic
state representative after
Reconstruction.

Avery Research Center for
African American History and
Culture, College of Charleston

The Mosquito
fleet supplied
city markets
with seafood.
Caroliniana Library,
University of South
Carolina

Weighing cotton
bales before
shipping.
*Black Charleston
Photographic
Collection, College of
Charleston Library*

Drayman transporting
cotton bales on a
Charleston wharf.

Caroliniana Library,
University of South Carolina

Watermelon
market.

Caroliniana Library,
University of South
Carolina

Street vendors.

Black Charleston
Photographic Collection,
College of Charleston Library

Holloway's Harness Shop was one of the several small black businesses.

Black Charleston Photographic Collection, College of Charleston Library

Peter Lindau at
his shoemaking
establishment.

Caroliniana Library,
University of South
Carolina

Digging in the
phosphate pits.

*Caroliniana
Library,
University of
South Carolina*

Processing
phosphate
rock.
*Caroliniana
Library,
University of
South Carolina*

Members of a bricklayers' union.
Black Charleston Photographic Collection, College of Charleston Library

Lt. James H. Fordham
of the Charleston
Police Department.
Theodore D. Jervey, The
Slave Trade: Slavery and
Color *(Columbia, S.C.:
State Company, 1925)*

Members of a black fire
engine company.
*Avery Research Center for African
American History and Culture,
College of Charleston*

Members of a
black hook and
ladder company.
*Avery Research
Center for African
American History
and Culture, College
of Charleston*

CHAPTER FIVE

"THE GREAT WORK BEFORE US"

Education as the Means to Elevate a Race

Black Charlestonians had long displayed an interest in education. During the antebellum years, free blacks established schools, and some even sent their children to the North to attend schools. In the South, their educational efforts were always severely restricted by the white community and became even more limited with the increasing proscription of free black life in the decades before the Civil War. Urban life provided many informal means for slaves to acquire a knowledge of reading and writing, and some even managed to attend clandestine schools. In general, public opinion and the legal system completely opposed introducing slaves to even the most rudimentary forms of education. The outcome of the Civil War abruptly ended these proscriptions, and Reconstruction brought about the expansion of Charleston's educational facilities. By the late 1860s, the activities of the Freedmen's Bureau, the freedmen's aid societies, and black community leaders resulted in additional private and, for the first time, publicly financed schools for black Charlestonians.

Prior to Reconstruction, South Carolina could claim the dubious distinction of being the only southern state without any constitutional provisions for public education. In Charleston, however, a system of "free schools" did develop before the war. Before 1855 there were eight or nine such schools created, but unfortunately these were usually located in remote areas of the city, had poor lighting, inadequate ventilation, and had only the barest furnishings. Others were without permanent locations, and teachers had to rent accommodations for classrooms wherever they could be found. Classes were poorly attended, and the schools were stigmatized as pauper schools because the indigent were given preferential admission. As the sectional conflict over slavery widened by the early 1850s, local community leaders and politicians realized the need for educational reforms to preserve the public welfare and to harmonize potentially antagonistic class interests, among other things. To this end, in 1854 the Charleston School Board obtained a state appropriation for upgrading the standards of the city's schools. Between 1855 and 1860, public expenditures for education increased dramatically. Pupil enrollment rose accordingly, at least four public schools were erected for whites, and a thorough system of primary and normal education created.[1]

It was the Civil War that established the preconditions for the large-scale education of black Charlestonians. Early during the Union occupation, Colonel Woodford, commander of Charleston Post, appointed the abolitionist James Redpath as superintendent of public instruction for the city. He was given possession of Charleston's schools, which he reopened beginning March 4, 1865. The first school to be convened was the Morris Street School, which, according to observers, became "so crowded with colored children that it was impossible to classify them." Approximately one thousand black students enrolled almost immediately, and about two hundred whites, many of whom were the children of Irish and German immigrants, also enrolled at Morris Street School.[2] There was no attempt to combine the races in the same classrooms, and the second floor of the building was exclusively reserved for whites, while the black students occupied the first and third floors. This spatial arrangement did not carry over into the recreational periods; it was reported that "in the playground, white and black boys joined together in the same sports—as they do in the public streets." The continuous and increasing demand for instruction led to the opening of additional facilities, and by July Redpath reported that he maintained five public day schools in Charleston that enrolled approximately four thousand pupils. The city schools remained under the control of the Union army and the Freedmen's Bureau until the fall of 1866, when they began to be restored to the Charleston Board of School Commissioners.[3]

The services provided by the northern benevolent societies and the Freedmen's Bureau were essential for the survival of the schools, especially in their early stages. Originally, James Redpath used many southern whites to staff his schools, but he replaced them when other teachers, sponsored by northern benevolent societies, became available. By the summer of 1865, Redpath reported that his teachers were either northern whites, South Carolina blacks, or Union army officers. The salaries of many of the teachers, as well as books and other essential supplies, were contributed largely by the National Freedmen's Relief Association, the New England Freedmen's Aid Society, and the American Missionary Association.[4]

As a northern abolitionist organization, the American Missionary Association was the most well known of the freedmen's aid societies. It entered this area of service as an extension of its antislavery and religious activities. Officially nonsectarian, it maintained a close working relationship with the Congregational and Presbyterian churches. In the Reconstruction South, its objectives were to promote the values of evangelical Protestantism and to provide formal education to the freedmen in order to prepare them for effective participation in society and government.[5]

Aid rendered by the Freedmen's Bureau in the form of transportation and sustenance for the teachers was also indispensable. Bureau assistance was important in other ways. After Saxton School had to relinquish its accommodations at the Normal School to city officials, the Freedmen's Bureau relocated its pupils and provided desks, chairs, and other essential furnishings to Military Hall where classes resumed in fall 1866. Even when Morris Street School was restored to the Board of School Commissioners, there were not sufficient funds for the city to reopen and staff it, so the school was rented to the Freedmen's Bureau from January 1867 until July and continued to be staffed by benevolent society teachers. When Reuben Tomlinson, the state superintendent of education for the Freedmen's Bureau, requested renewal of the bureau lease of the school, the school commissioners declined to do so. Nevertheless, board members recognized their "duty to provide education for the children in . . . [the] city, of whatever race or color" and expressed a willingness to undertake their responsibilities. At their August meeting, the commissioners decided that black students would continue to be educated at Morris Street School with a curriculum similar to that of the white schools. This was the only instance in the entire state in which municipal authorities voluntarily assumed the responsibility for the education of black children.[6]

Freedmen's education was further advanced through several private schools that were created during the period. Shaw Memorial School was an important example. It was founded shortly after the Civil War through funds raised by northern philanthropists, black soldiers, and residents of the Sea Islands to commemorate the life of slain Union war hero Col. Robert G. Shaw of the Fifty-fourth Massachusetts Regiment of the U.S. Colored Troops. Until 1874, Shaw Memorial School was supported by the New England Educational Association, but by that time, perhaps due to a deepening economic depression, the organization's funds were insufficient to maintain the school effectively. Fortunately, the Charleston Board of School Commissioners had determined earlier in the year that another public school for blacks was necessary. Negotiations were initiated between the two organizations, and when the school commissioners pledged to retain Shaw's name and to maintain the school for all children regardless of race, the New England Educational Association agreed to rent the building and its furnishings for ten years. Instructional services thus continued uninterrupted for the school's approximately five hundred students, who, beginning in the fall of 1874, were educated in Charleston's second public school for blacks.[7]

Avery Institute was originally part of Saxton School, organized in October 1865 by Francis L. Cardozo, and staffed by American Missionary Association teachers. After Cardozo made a strong appeal for the creation of a normal or high school for advanced students, the A.M.A. purchased a lot on Bull Street near Smith Street and enlisted the services of the Freedmen's Bureau, which built and furnished Avery in 1868, at a cost of approximately fifteen thousand dollars. By 1880 Avery Institute had an enrollment of 448 students who were taught by an integrated staff of eight teachers, three Charlestonians, and five northerners.[8]

Despite northern missionaries' widespread belief that slavery left blacks depraved, indolent, and dependent, they often found upon arrival in the South that blacks had already established and staffed schools for themselves. Black churches were instrumental in promoting freedmen's education. When one representative of the A.M.A. arrived at Plymouth Church, he found a school already organized and operated by a black superintendent and black teachers. Wallingford Academy was organized by Rev. Jonathan C. Gibbs at Zion Presbyterian Church in 1865. Three years later the school was reorganized and moved to a building on

Nassau Street, which was jointly purchased by the Salome Presbyterian Church, the Presbyterian Committee of Missions for Freedmen, and the Freedmen's Bureau. The school flourished throughout Reconstruction and by 1880 had an enrollment of over five hundred students. Freedmen's schools were also maintained by black Baptists, the African Methodists, and the Methodist Episcopal Church.[9]

Initially the cause of freedmen's education was most vigorously championed by northerners and the black community. Among native whites, the Protestant Episcopal Church was distinguished for its early and impressive educational efforts among the freedmen. In 1866 the trustees for the church, Rev. A. Toomer Porter, George Trenholm, and Samuel L. Bennett, purchased the Marine Hospital with funds raised in the North and contributed by the Protestant Episcopal Freedmen's Commission. The following year Franklin Street School was established there with the hope that it would not only contribute to the general uplift of the freedmen but also stem the tide of blacks leaving the Protestant Episcopal Church. The teachers were all white Charleston women, and in 1867–68 the Franklin Street School's enrollment was 621.[10]

While whites in Charleston were not as violently opposed to the idea of educating blacks as were their rural counterparts (largely because they were familiar with the schools free blacks maintained before the war), a good deal of hostility existed nevertheless. In the winter of 1865, Francis Cardozo, principal of Saxton School, recalled that while many northerners frequented the school, "not a single Rebel" had ever done so, but "they pass by on the opposite side, and mutter curses as they hear the children sing." During the same time, a white woman, "very finely dressed and apparently quite lady like," came to the school door and, upon looking at the students, declared, "Oh, I wish I could put a torch to that building! *the niggers*." Such incidents were not unusual and were motivated by more than one factor. Some whites simply opposed educating former slaves. Others were chagrined that the Freedmen's Bureau would take the public school buildings originally constructed for whites to educate blacks.[11]

Given their racial predilections, white Charlestonians felt effectively excluded from public education. In articulating these sentiments, the *Daily News* editorialized that "one of the most trying persecutions of the military rule" was that "while the time of the negroes has been so taken up with going to school . . . white people, if they wished their children educated at all, have been compelled to send them to private schools at much expense." A Charleston diarist saw ominous consequences in the Freedmen's Bureau policies and sarcastically concluded that blacks would keep the school houses, "until the little nigger race shall be prepared to enter College, whilst our poorer white children are growing up in Ignorance and vice."[12]

By late 1866, most whites were becoming reconciled to the idea of freedmen's education, but they remained hostile to northern teachers, many of whom were outspoken critics of southern society. White Charlestonians were especially resentful of northerners, including Gilbert Pillsbury, the superintendent of freedmen for the New England Freedmen's Aid Society, and later the first Republican mayor of Charleston. Shortly after his arrival in the city, Pillsbury compared it to the Biblical Sodom and declared it "a city of ruins, both material and mental. There are everywhere so many awful impresses of Almighty wrath, causing such profound and solemn musings, that one is almost unfitted for duty." Although it was once a magnificent place, "Charleston had the facilities for a better civilization than it knew, or practiced . . . . I am surprised at all these strange and costly adjuncts to the 'peculiar institution.' I wish you could be here, to wonder and admire and *hate*."[13]

Although Francis L. Cardozo was a native Charlestonian, he was equally critical of his birthplace and incurred the ire of whites. In his remarks on Charleston society, he commented that "slavery has produced such corrupting and degrading influences, that it requires a generation to remedy, and the whole of the social organization must be remodelled." Men and women who viewed the South in this way taught the freedmen to pray "God bless—Abraham Lincoln—our President—and Liberator." Reuben Tomlinson also reported that though teachers generally took no active part in politics, they "feel it is their duty to assist the people in their several neighborhoods, to the means for forming correct judgments as to political affairs." No wonder that a local newspaper accused northern teachers of slandering the history and people of the South. Furthermore, its editorial continued, teachers that encouraged the freedmen to assert their civil and political rights instilled "principles and ideas totally at variance with the opinions of the community in which they are obliged to live."[14]

In 1865 housing for employees of freedmen's aid societies was in short supply and several employees from the American Missionary Association and another Boston-based society were lodged in the house of Robert Barnwell Rhett, former editor of the fire-eating *Charleston Mercury*. The ironic symbolism of this situation was readily apparent to the teachers who understood the depth of native residents' enmity. One forbodingly wrote that "this Rhett house . . . is so full of teachers . . . we should none of us be surprised if they made a bonfire of us some dark night."[15]

Given the northern teachers' attitudes toward the South, their often close relations with blacks, and the antislavery posture of their sponsoring agencies, native whites reasoned that placing such persons in charge of the delicate matter of freedmen's education was dangerous and would lead to racial integration in the schools and to social equality generally. For one Charleston woman, these trends had already become a distasteful reality when she observed one of James Redpath's schools in mid-1865 and uttered disgustedly, "The place is now an African Heaven, Redpath a John Brown desiple [*sic*] has all the Schools open and the negro and whites Pell Mell altogether." This observer certainly exaggerated the interracial contacts between students at Morris Street School, and even the initially limited amount of integration there failed to continue for even one year. In mid-1866, a local newspaper reporting on the schools found no whites in attendance at Morris Street or any of the freedmen's schools.[16]

Two years later, the white community's fears of racial integration in the schools were revived. The new state constitution, formulated in 1868, empowered the general assembly to provide for the compulsory attendance of children at either public or private schools. Even more disquieting for whites was the constitutional provision that required that all schools and colleges or universities receiving state funds "shall be free and open to all the children and youths of this State, without regard to race, color or previous condition." Generally, black delegates were unwilling to compromise on these provisions, which they hoped would create a new, more efficient, and progressive educational system.[17] For Rev. Benjamin F. Randolph, inclusion of the anti-discrimination clause raised a fundamental issue of Reconstruction. In debate over this matter, he admonished the other delegates that, "the time has come when we shall have to meet things squarely, and we must meet them now or never.

The day is coming when we must decide whether the two races shall live together or not." At the same time, many whites believed that the new constitutional provisions made the future of the school system doubtful. The *Daily News* apprehended racial mixing in the schools and predicted that the "indiscriminate huddling together of whites and blacks would, cause the ruin of the public schools, and reduce them to a condition in which they are neither honorable, serviceable nor advantageous."[18]

The dreaded scenario so feared by whites never occurred, but only in part because of their opposition to integration. Francis Cardozo and other framers of the new constitution never anticipated more than a limited integration, which *might* occur in remote locations, due to the scarcity of the school-age population. Cardozo railed against critics of the educational provisions, arguing that "we have not said there shall be no separate schools. On the contrary, there may be separate schools, and I have no doubt there will be such in most of the districts." It was important, however, that no legal barriers be created to interfere with students' access to the educational system, so that "if any colored child wishes to go to a white school, it shall have the privilege of doing so."[19]

There was another reason why integration never received serious consideration. In 1869 the editor of the Charleston *Daily Republican* probably overstated the case by claiming that blacks were "decidedly in favor of separate schools," but some recognized the unique value of such schools when they maintained high standards. This was surely the case in Charleston, where blacks remained more interested in quality education than in integration. Francis L. Cardozo, who believed Avery Institute was the best school in the city, stated with confidence that for this reason "the colored pupils in my school would not like to go to a white school." As forums for the display of talented black students and professionals, the very existence of all-black schools was considered a powerful argument against detractors of the race. The Sabbath schools maintained by black churches usually provided instruction in both academic and religious subjects and represented an important source of community pride and educational autonomy.[20]

In 1869, several blacks, including members of the upper class such as Benjamin Bosemon, Robert C. DeLarge, and Alonzo Ransier, discussed forming a grammar school to provide advanced training for black youth. After deciding that a call for integrating the Charleston High School would "only cause dissention and be productive of evil rather than good," they petitioned the city council for a grant of land for the purpose. The original petition indicated the school would be "for the sole use and benefit of the colored people—to be governed and controlled by the same." The petitioners also stipulated that the teachers "shall in all cases, be colored men, thoroughly trained and educated." After some criticism by no less a personage than Robert Purvis, the veteran Philadelphia abolitionist, and perhaps others, it was decided to admit all qualified students, regardless of race.[21] Apparently, however, the land grant was never made.

Samuel R. Cox, a former free person of color and a member of the Board of School Commissioners, may have shared the assumptions of the 1869 group. In 1876 he urged that body to create two evening schools for adults, specifying that one school would be for black students and the other for whites. Each school was to have equal appropriations, and the white school would be controlled by the white commissioners and the black school by black commissioners. The school commissioners failed to implement this plan. The foregoing examples are important in that they suggest black Charleston's upper class, including former free persons of color, may have been more race conscious than heretofore assumed.[22] Given the relatively large number of schools in Charleston and the attitudes of both the black and white communities, public education there was destined to be conducted on a segregated basis.

Since they were prohibited from learning to read or write while slaves, the freedmen displayed a good deal of enthusiasm for formal instruction. The traveler Sidney Andrews observed that, in contrast to the indifference whites showed toward education, blacks "are much interested in the matter. They all seem anxious to learn to read, many of them appearing to have a notion that thereby will come honor and happiness." But the objectives the freedmen hoped education would achieve were not always as ethereal or as vague as Andrews conceived them to be. The 1865 Charleston Colored People's Convention captured more fully the urgency with which blacks viewed good schools and a thorough education when the delegates advised their audience that "an educated and intelligent people can neither be held in nor reduced to slavery." Education provided a means to reject a painful past while taking advantage of the new opportunities created by freedom. It is no wonder that white Charlestonians noted that the former slaves had almost a literal "thirst for knowledge" and constantly discussed school and their teachers. This same alacrity did not escape the notice of Gen. Rufus Saxton of the Freedmen's Bureau, who reported, "Their desire of learning is intense. They feel that is one of the means by which they are going to be elevated [thus] all the schools established there by northern benevolence are crowded with children."[23]

Adults were equally anxious to learn, and they attended the numerous evening and Sabbath schools established for them. According to another Bureau official, adults might be seen "during the intervals of toil, when off duty as servants, on steamboats, along the railroads, and when unemployed in the streets of the city or on the plantations, with some fragment of a spelling-book in their hands earnestly at study." If no other opportunities afforded themselves, many adults enlisted the services of their own more knowledgeable children, who taught them how to read and write.[24]

Simple eagerness to learn was not always enough, and black Charlestonians found it necessary to make great sacrifices to attend school. Many of the freedmen's schools were maintained wholly or in part by the monthly tuition parents paid. Even though the Charleston Public Schools were tuition-free, children still had to purchase their own books and supplies. This presented a hardship to black families and especially to those of the lower class, whose scarce financial resources were already overburdened; many could only raise the requisite funds with the greatest difficulty. Sometimes books and slates were gratuitously distributed to students by the benevolent societies, while teachers sometimes were able to loan books to a few of their pupils. According to a correspondent for the *New York Times*, most students found it necessary to "work at odd jobs early and late, when out of school, and often go barefooted and hatless, saving their pennies for the purchase of some necessary volume." The sacrifices blacks were willing to make to secure an education for themselves amazed one white visitor, who characterized Charleston as "a city, first, of idle, ragged Negroes, who, with no visible means of support, nevertheless send an astonishing multitude to school."[25]

Despite the efforts of self-sacrificing parents and students, the freedmen's schools faced tremendous difficulties. Financing was a perpetual problem. As the resources of the northern freedmen's aid societies dwindled beginning in 1868, and the Freedmen's Bureau ended its educational efforts in 1870, many schools were thrown into dire fiscal straits. When the Protestant Episcopal Board of Missions reduced its funds for the support of Franklin Street School, Rev. A. Toomer Porter had to close it, to turn the building over to St. Mark's congregation, and to commit the students to the city's charge. Schools that were completely supported by the freedmen suffered from even greater financial woes, due to the poverty of the black community and the casual employment of many working-class blacks. The tenuous position of black workers was often exacerbated by political discrimination against them, which directly affected the freedmen's schools. Rev. Richard H. Cain's freedmen's school was no longer financially solvent by 1868, "in consequence of so many being discharged from employment" for their "political opinions and Loyalty [sic] to the Govt." This proved an ongoing problem, and in 1877 the principal of Avery Institute explained that the school's enrollment had dropped not only because of "the prevailing poverty of the colored people" but also because "many lost their places (where at best they were illy paid) last fall from political differences and as the election is not yet, officially decided, matters are no better."[26]

The freedmen's schools also faced problems of a more directly pedagogical nature. Schools often attracted more students than they could effectively enroll, which meant some had to be turned away. Others could only be accommodated in shifts; at Saxton School a teacher complained that "my schoolroom will not hold all the pupils at once and I receive the juveniles in the morning and the older or rather more advanced" students later. Overcrowding in classrooms made discipline problems inevitable. Teacher-student ratios were high by today's standards; for instance, at Saxton there were approximately forty students per teacher. When the A.M.A. queried the school principal about reducing the size of the teaching staff, he responded that whereas it was possible for a single teacher to instruct fifty northern students, "these scholars here are so undisciplined, and have never before enjoyed the advantages of a public school that a teacher cannot do the same justice to them."[27]

Northern teachers, most of whom had never encountered southern blacks before, must have found conversing with Charleston's freedmen particularly vexatious, since many freedmen were rural migrants who spoke Gullah. One who observed the freedmen's speech patterns noted that English seemed "to tumble all at once from his mouth," and the words "get sadly mixed up whenever he endeavors to speak. The phraseology is usually so odd, too, that even after the stranger has become a little accustomed to the thick tones of the voice and the enunciation, he cannot readily understand."[28]

Another frustrating problem for teachers was student retention. In his comments on the transitory school population in mid-1866, Assistant Commissioner Tomlinson reported that in January in Charleston and throughout the state, many of the schools lost their advanced students, who were replaced by those "fresh from the fields." At the same time, Arthur Sumner, principal of Morris Street School, observed that even though the school year lasted almost eight months, most of his pupils had not been enrolled quite six months because "hundreds have come and gone during the term." Teachers complained that once their students acquired the rudiments of reading and writing, they were content to forsake further schooling in order to seek employment.[29]

This was particularly the case with older students, who found it necessary to work. Even younger students of working-class backgrounds had difficulty completing a full course of study, because the income from their labor was needed by their families. For these families a trade apprenticeship offered the possibility of more immediate remuneration and was preferable to an extensive academic program. Noticeably upset by this trend, one educator sadly remarked that after much diligence, "we find we have been educating children to become barbers & shoemakers and we have to preach to them (the parents especially) over and over again, about the superiority of an education to a trade."[30]

The fiscal and pedagogical problems of the freedmen's schools were exacerbated by the difficulty of securing and maintaining adequate teaching staffs. Addressing this matter, Mr. L. B. Corey, principal of Avery wrote to the A.M.A. that unfilled vacancies among his corps of teachers made it necessary to use advanced students in their stead. Unfortunately, student enrollment had already dropped because of the shortage of teachers, and he warned his superiors that "I do not see how we can meet the pressing wants of the school without at least two more efficient teachers."[31] The inadequate supply of teachers was compounded by the general preference for northern over native teachers. Sarah Stansbury, a former New Jersey teacher, began teaching at Saxton School, and she provided special training sessions for native teachers. Her attitude reflected a broad consensus of opinion on native teachers' abilities. Her observations led her to conclude that "we cannot expect a teacher who never was taught anything but by rote to . . . wake up thought or in any way to get up any thing [sic] like enthusiasm." The native teachers "only know the beaten track. . . . It is my every day [sic] experience to find my suggestions working out anything but the end designed."[32]

Due to the short supply of trained personnel and the greater expense of employing northern teachers, Francis L. Cardozo was forced to utilize some native teachers. However, he firmly believed it best for his staff to be composed mainly of northerners because in his opinion, northern teachers were more competent. When his preference for northern teachers led the home office of the A.M.A. to conclude mistakenly that he did not want black teachers, Cardozo emphatically denied this. In reiterating the point, he expressed his indifference as to the teachers' race: "all I ask is that they be competent for their work, and when I made the request I did so because Northern Teachers are more competent than Southern ones."[33]

As most native teachers were black and most northern teachers white, preference for the latter could become a racial issue. When Mortimer A. Warren, one of Cardozo's successors at Avery, requested that the A.M.A. send additional teachers, he specified that only white teachers be sent. Warren reasoned that since several of Charleston's most prestigious schools employed white teachers only, to do otherwise would jeopardize the reputation of his school. But throughout the period under consideration, Avery did continue to maintain an integrated faculty. The foregoing perceptions of native teachers explain why they did not necessarily receive the same salaries granted to northern teachers. For instance, at Saxton School, while southern teachers were paid twenty-five dollars per month, northerners were paid thirty-five dollars per month. Even when Francis L. Cardozo appealed for the equalization of pay for qualified native teachers, increases came slowly; at least one native teacher resigned, taking a higher paying position at another school.[34]

Of the black men and women who became teachers in the freedmen's schools, a large number had been free before the Civil War. A few were northern ministers with exceptional educational qualifications. Rev. Jonathan C. Gibbs, the Presbyterian minister and founder of Wallingford Academy, was from Philadelphia, had graduated from

Dartmouth College, and had attended Princeton Theological Seminary. The Methodist Rev. Benjamin Franklin Randolph was born in Kentucky but moved to Ohio where he was educated at Oberlin College. He later relocated to Buffalo, New York, where in 1858 he was employed as the principal of a public school for blacks. During the Civil War, Randolph joined the Union army, in which he acted as chaplain for the Twenty-sixth Regiment of the U.S. Colored Troops. With the cessation of hostilities, he took a teaching position at the Morris Street School before receiving an appointment to the Freedmen's Bureau as the assistant state superintendent of education. In this capacity Randolph was instrumental in securing the services of teachers and in establishing schools for freedmen on plantations around Charleston.[35]

Most of the black teachers were Carolinians, and a disproportionate number were either members of Charleston's antebellum free black community or were their descendants. Of these, a significant number were members of the old free brown elite and had enjoyed opportunities that enabled them to become educators after the war. Amelia Shrewsbury, Harriet Holloway, Charlotte Johnson, Monomia McKinlay, Joanna Weston, and Margaret Sasportas were included among the group that attended Charleston's schools for free persons of color.[36]

During Reconstruction and the years immediately following, the teachers that staffed the schools in the city of Charleston and in rural Charleston County were distinguished from their antebellum counterparts by their increased professionalism. Now more than before, they possessed formal training, and public school teachers in Charleston County underwent a certification process. By 1880 the state superintendent of education was sponsoring a Normal Institute for Colored Teachers to promote their professional development and was "encouraging" teachers to attend. This initiative was complemented by a Normal Institute sponsored by white school administrators in Charleston. These new opportunities were especially important for black women, who made their first entry into the professions through teaching.[37]

Francis L. Cardozo was easily the most distinguished of Charleston's new educators and ranked as one of the city's most intellectually accomplished citizens, black or white. Born in Charleston in 1837, Cardozo attended one of the schools for free blacks for eight years, and at the age of twenty-one, he traveled to Glasgow, Scotland, to prepare for the ministry. He pursued a four-year course of study at the University of Glasgow where he won honors for his Latin and Greek scholarship. Cardozo also won a competitive academic scholarship and continued his studies at the Presbyterian seminaries in Edinburgh and London. After returning to the United States in 1864, he pastored a church in New Haven, Connecticut, before volunteering his services to the A.M.A. as a teacher. After coming to Charleston, he organized Saxton School and later Avery Institute.[38]

Though none of the other black teachers could duplicate Cardozo's educational achievements, some were distinguished in their own right and well suited for promoting the cause of freedmen's education. The Charlestonian Frances A. Rollins studied at the Institute for Colored Youth in Philadelphia prior to the Civil War and during Reconstruction taught in at least two of the city's freedmen's schools. Immediately following the war, Frances and her sister Charlotte obtained the assistance of James Lynch of the A.M.E. Church to establish a freedmen's school. Later, Frances joined the staff at Avery Institute. She was considered one of the best teachers in Charleston and achieved notoriety as the biographer of Dr. Martin R. Delany.[39]

Some of Charleston's native black teachers taught the children of the free black community before the Civil War. One such person was a Mrs. Stromer, who founded a school as early as 1820, maintained it until the war, and became one of the first teachers in the freedmen's schools during Reconstruction. Another outstanding case was that of Mary F. Weston, a former classmate of Francis L. Cardozo. During the antebellum years, she maintained a school and on one occasion was arrested for violating the laws regulating the instruction of blacks. After the intervention of her mother's guardian, Mary Weston was granted a special permit to maintain her school, provided that no slaves were taught and that a white person was present at all times. She complied with the stipulations, and her school remained open for the duration of the war. Cardozo hired her to teach his most advanced girls' class at Saxton School because he deemed Miss Weston "a most excellent and experienced teacher," who was quite the equal of any northern teacher. In mid-1866 blacks made up one-half of Avery's twenty-member faculty. By relying upon native Charlestonians, the A.M.A. not only was able to reduce its expenses—these teachers did not have to be boarded and their salaries were lower than those generally paid to northern teachers—it also drew upon a pool of black talent, which strengthened the identification of the school with the antebellum free brown elite. [40]

Many black teachers possessed the requisite training to become effective instructors and had a well-developed sense of race consciousness, which gave them a peculiar commitment to freedmen's education. When Benjamin F. Randolph applied for employment with the Freedmen's Bureau, he wrote that "I don't ask position. But I ask a place where I can be most useful to my race. My learning, my every experience as a Teacher North, and my faithful service as a Chaplain demand that I seek Such a place among my race." William O. Weston, a member of the old free brown elite and an A.M.A. teacher, combined a sense of noblesse oblige with devotion to his race when he rejoiced that "the slave whom it was a crime to teach, breathes the air of Liberty." Now that spelling books would replace vulgar amusements and ribald songs, "he . . . whose time or advantages admits, would be recreant to God and the race, did he not rush to the rescue and endeavour to fit them for their ransomed and elevated position."[41] Rev. Ennals J. Adams, principal of Shaw Memorial School, and other teachers reached the same conclusions for the psychological benefits that would accrue. Unfortunately, there were ex-slaves who had been so devastated by their servitude that they lacked confidence in the abilities of men and women of their own race and accepted the belief in white superiority. According to Adams, these beliefs would be destroyed "proportionately as the educated and good and those who are in the full sense of the phrase men and women . . . [are] shown to an advantage amongst the ignorant of this people."[42]

The schools operated by the Freedmen's Bureau and the various missionary societies generally maintained a uniform curriculum, and teachers devoted most of their time to instructing fundamentals. Of the twelve hundred students attending two freedmen's schools in December 1865, approximately one-third were learning the alphabet. There were significant differences between the achievement levels of students at the several schools. At Saxton, none of the student body was learning the alphabet, and all knew at least the fundamentals of spelling and reading. After mastering these subjects, the students began reading lessons taken from a series of primers, each ranked in progressive order of difficulty. During the winter of 1865–66, about two-thirds of those freedmen taking reading lessons received the lessons from the first or lowest series. The standard curriculum contained other subjects also, including geography, grammar, composition and penmanship, mental arithmetic (consisting of the most basic problems), and written arithmetic, which was more advanced and included fractions.[43]

Freedmen's education was not limited to the rudiments. All the city's major schools provided primary and intermediate levels of instruction, but a few also provided grammar or normal training for the most academically advanced and enterprising pupils. When a correspondent for the New York *Times* visited the grammar department of the Morris Street School, he found "black boys and girls, who, without a moments hesitation, can solve the most difficult problems in algebra . . . [and] little fellows, twelve and fourteen years of age [who] readily answer questions in ancient and modern history."[44]

At Wallingford Academy the academic course, in addition to the common disciplines, also included English literature, history, natural philosophy, physiology, and algebra. Wallingford had a normal department, in which courses on school management and the methods of instruction were taught. Among the schools of Charleston, Avery Institute ranked first; James Alvord, superintendent of education for the Freedmen's Bureau, believed it to be the best school for blacks in the entire state. Avery's reputation compared quite favorably with other A.M.A. schools, and one agent described it as standing "at the head of all the Colored schools of the South . . . [as] the bright consummate flower." Created from the ranks of the most promising students at the Old Saxton School and conceived primarily as a normal school, Avery was part of the A.M.A. design to promote black teacher training in the major southern cities. It offered few basic educational courses, and prospective students were required to pass an examination prior to admission. The curriculum afforded the broadest range of study, and, in addition to the advanced subjects taught in other schools, Avery offered a classical preparatory program. Its students received special attention and more intense training. On a typical day, one visitor to the school observed the most advanced boys' class intently at work, "transposing, analyzing and parsing a passage from Milton's 'L'Alegro.'" Included as part of the normal training curriculum were courses in general history, political economy, civil government, botany, geometry, bookkeeping, and rhetoric.

Teacher education became the hallmark of Avery Institute, and its normal graduates commanded top salaries and taught in schools not only in Charleston but throughout the state.[45]

Throughout Reconstruction most of the students at Avery were freedmen, and these were considered the most talented members of the group. With its reputation for academic excellence and leadership initially provided by the well-known and accomplished scholar Francis L. Cardozo, Avery Institute attracted the children of upper-class blacks and particularly those of the old free brown elite in disproportionate numbers. The children of this group more often possessed the skills necessary for completing a full course of study at Avery, and their parents could more easily afford the relatively expensive tuition (one dollar per month in 1874) charged by the school. In spite of financial straits, some parents sent their children to Avery for a few years, hoping to provide the academic challenge and cultural exposure to give them an advantage over their peers. The children of former free blacks dominated the more-challenging courses of study. A reporter observed that the more advanced classes were "composed mainly of those who were born free, and who now constitute an aristocracy of color." This is why the upper crust of black Charleston society regarded Avery as an outstanding "recherche seminary" for preparing future leaders.[46]

The school's public examinations were always special occasions and the elite family names represented in attendance included the McKinlays, O'Hears, Noisettes, Holloways, Ransiers, Shrewsburys, Spencers, and the Aspinalls, to mention only a few of the most prominent. In addition to providing the extensive academic training desired by the elite, Avery Institute was another of a host of institutions that crystalized the esprit de corps of the upper class. The school examinations and special programs were held at churches attended by the elite. Several of the teachers were Avery graduates, and the former students maintained an alumni association that held annual reunions and provided scholarships to graduates who planned to attend college. The values of the group were embodied in the Avery Motto: "Vestigia Nulla Retrorsum," which was Latin for "No stepping back again." They were generally committed to racial uplift and both community improvement and self-improvement. These attributes were not new but were deeply rooted in the antebellum heritage of the colored elite.[47]

Just as Avery symbolized the aspirations of the elite, most of its students were freedmen drawn from humble backgrounds who were also being afforded important opportunities, and for the first time. Shaw Memorial School was an important example in this regard. Its student body was primarily comprised of freedmen, but it differed from Avery because, in 1867, 80 percent of its advanced classes were made up of former slaves. The new educational opportunities represented the means by which freedmen would eventually close the cultural and economic divide separating them from Charleston's free persons of color and their descendants. A convergence of abilities between the two groups was already evident as early as 1867. That year, in reflecting on student progress in several classes at Morris Street School, the principal noted that the freedmen "rank equally well with those who were free and had received some instruction before and during the war."[48]

Charleston lacked institutions of higher education for blacks; however, some attended such facilities in other locations. Nancy Weston's sons Archibald and Francis Grimké were educated in schools for free blacks during the 1850s. So when the boys began studies at Morris Street School, their abilities were recognized by the principal Frances Pillsbury and her husband Gilbert of the Freedmen's Bureau. The Pillsburys' assistance enabled Archibald and Francis to leave Charleston in 1865 and later enroll at Lincoln University in Pennsylvania. New opportunities for advanced studies were appearing in South Carolina also. The need for trained ministers and teachers was responsible for the creation of some advanced schools. Payne Institute was founded by the African Methodists in 1871 to promote ministerial education. By 1880, the South Carolina and Columbia Annual Conferences decided to move the Institute from its original location in Cokesbury to Columbia, where it became the nucleus of the newly organized Allen University. The school contained preparatory and academic departments and provided religious education through its Ministers' Short Course. By 1882, Allen's enrollment was approximately 250, and a law department was added under the direction of D. Augustus Straker, the distinguished black barrister. Two years later, the first law class was graduated and admitted to the South Carolina bar. The Revs. Paul W. Jefferson, Norman Bascom Sterrett, Bruce H. Williams, B. F. Porter, Samuel Washington, and Augustus T. Carr, all prominent Charleston ministers, served on Allen's board of trustees.[49]

Benedict Institute in Columbia was an advanced school founded by the northern Baptist American Home Missionary Society in 1870 to train black teachers and ministers. Black Baptists in the state supported the school through contributions made to the Baptist Educational Missionary and Sunday School Convention. Throughout the 1870s, Benedict was essentially a high school with a theological department. By 1894 it had added a normal school, an industrial department, and a nurse's training program. That same year, the school was incorporated as Benedict College.[50]

Claflin University was established by the Northern Methodists in 1869, and Baker Theological Institute, which was transferred from Charleston to Columbia, became the nucleus around which the school was organized. When the South Carolina legislature created the South Carolina Agricultural College and Mechanical Institute in 1872, authority for its governance was divided between a board of trustees appointed by the legislature and the trustees of Claflin. This arrangement made the Agricultural College and Mechanical Institute essentially the industrial department of Claflin University. By the end of Reconstruction, the department operated a 250-acre experimental farm and maintained shops for training carpenters and blacksmiths. With the exception of its theological department, for most of the 1870s Claflin was in reality a high school. In 1877 a normal department was added. It offered a three-year program by 1879. The previous year, college-level courses were first offered. By 1881 a law department was established under former State Supreme Court Justice Jonathan Jasper Wright, who conducted classes at his office on Queen Street in Charleston. Wright served on the board of trustees with the distinguished Revs. Francis L. Cardozo, Joshua L. Wilson, Samuel Weston, and Joseph Sasportas. Throughout the period, prominent black Charlestonians had their children educated at Claflin and contributed funds to the university.[51]

During Reconstruction, the University of South Carolina at Columbia also afforded advanced training for black students. The newly organized university was indeed unique among institutions of higher learning in the former Confederate states because of the degree to which it was racially integrated. Prior to 1868, the issue of admitting blacks to the university had not been broached because the separation of the races in education was assumed among whites. To forestall any potential problems in this regard, white Democrats introduced legislation in 1867 that would have created a college for blacks at the Citadel in Charleston while preserving the University of South Carolina for the exclusive use of whites. This proposal, however, was never acted upon.[52]

Blacks did not ignore the important issue of equal access to the state university. In 1868 the non-discrimination clause in the new constitution's educational provisions addressed the matter of the admission of blacks to the state university in general terms. To be consistent, in early 1869, the university's articles of incorporation were reviewed and amended, making it illegal for either the trustees or the faculty to discriminate between students on account of "race, color or creed" in determining admissions. Shortly thereafter, the general assembly elected the prominent black Charlestonians Francis L. Cardozo and Dr. Benjamin A. Boseman to the university's board of trustees. Henry E. Hayne, the secretary of state, became the first black student to attend the University of South Carolina when he matriculated as a medical student in October 1873. Hayne's admission precipitated wholesale resignations among the student body and the faculty; however, the university remained open and supported by the enrollment of black students, who, by the end of Reconstruction, accounted for at least one-half of the student body.[53]

The most notable black to attend the university at this time was state treasurer Francis L. Cardozo, who enrolled in the law department. There were many black Charlestonians in attendance at the university, and these were often young men from socially prominent families of free backgrounds, who had completed preparatory training at prestigious schools such as Howard University, Howard Academy (in Columbia), or Avery Institute. According to two University of South Carolina professors, the students from Avery were deemed especially advanced, and many demonstrated their outstanding achievements by successfully competing for state scholarships, beginning in 1874.[54]

Several of those trained at the university assumed positions of importance in Charleston's black community. Cornelius C. Scott, a native Charlestonian of free background, graduated from Avery Institute in 1872 and later enrolled in the university academic program. After graduating in 1877, Scott returned to Charleston to teach languages at his alma mater. Thaddeus Saltus, the first black Episcopal priest in South Carolina and an assistant rector at St. Mark's Church, attended Avery Institute before entering the classical program of the University of South

Carolina in 1873. Rev. John L. Dart graduated from Avery, attended both the University of South Carolina and later Atlanta University, and graduated from the latter in 1879. After graduating from Newton Theological Seminary in Massachusetts, teaching at Wayland Seminary, and pastoring several churches, he returned to Charleston and took charge of Morris Street Baptist Church in 1886.[55]

Because of their exceptional educational qualifications, some black Charlestonians received national acclaim. T. McCants Stewart was one such person. Born of free parents in 1852, he began his education in one of Charleston's schools for free blacks. During Reconstruction he did preparatory work at Howard University from 1869–1873 and entered the University of South Carolina academic program in the latter year, taking his A.B. and LL.B degrees in 1876. After teaching math at the State Agricultural and Mechanical College and practicing law with Robert Brown Elliott, Stuart left South Carolina for the North. He was later ordained as an A.M.E. minister and pastored churches in Philadelphia and New York, before emigrating to Liberia in 1883 where he became Charles Sumner Professor of Belles Letters at Liberia College. Stewart eventually returned to the United States and was widely recognized as a national Afro-American leader until 1906, when he took permanent residence in Liberia.[56]

The integration of the University of South Carolina lasted until the restoration of the Democratic party's political control of the state in 1877. In June of that year, the conservative-dominated state legislature began devising plans for the creation of two racially segregated institutions of higher learning. Shortly thereafter, the State Scholarship Act, which had provided support for black students, was repealed. Finally, the 1877 university appropriation was so woefully inadequate that the school had to close its doors.[57]

While the Democrats reorganized the state university, they used the Charleston public school system as evidence of their willingness to continue providing quality education regardless of race. Black Charlestonians did enjoy a higher quality of public education compared with that available in other parts of the state. Their schools had the longest sessions of any in the state. Whereas during the 1879–80 school year, the length of the average school session in the state was three-and-a-third months, the schools in Charleston averaged ten months. But even in Charleston's public schools, blacks were not immune to problems. As late as 1880, in a state with provisions for compulsory education mandated by its constitution, only 60 percent of the school-aged whites and 55 percent of the school-aged blacks attended school. More ominous for blacks was the growing disparity in the appropriations made for black and white pupils. In 1884, the Charleston Board of School Commissioners appropriated an average of $16.53 for each of the city's white students but only an average of $9.72 for black students. Furthermore, white boys were given increased opportunity for advanced study two years earlier, when the school comissioners were empowered to grant scholarships to meritorious students who desired to attend Charleston High School. Blacks were not allowed to attend this school and thus were precluded from the competition for the scholarships.[58]

While racial discrimination in educational funding and facilities was harmful to blacks generally, its consequences were most detrimental to the middle- and lower-class families, because they couldn't afford the private schools that were available to the elite. Finally, black leaders criticized the Charleston Board of School Commissioners because of the commissioners' discriminatory practices in the hiring of teachers. In 1880 over half of the school population was made up of black students, but only six of the city's ninety-one public school teachers were blacks. All these were presumably at the Shaw School (also known as Mary Street School), where Rev. Ennals J. Adams was the principal. There was no positive change five years later, when, of the thirty to forty teachers assigned to the city's two black public schools, only four were black. Black teachers generally had no options but to work either in private schools or in the county schools located outside Charleston.[59]

For all its limitations, Reconstruction was nevertheless a period of significant educational advancement for blacks. Despite the sacrifices they were required to make to attend school, the prospect of obtaining formal education was enthusiastically received throughout the black community. Formerly barred from education, many freedmen believed that the best way to ensure their continued survival was to acquire at least the rudiments of reading and writing. The quest for education thus became another method by which the former slaves rejected the past and asserted their independence.

The alacrity blacks displayed for learning required the expansion of the educational facilities available to them. The combined educational efforts of the northern freedmen's aid societies, the Freedmen's Bureau, and the black churches were of tremendous importance and led to the creation of a number of private schools in Charleston. During Reconstruction these schools were the prototypes of Charleston's public schools for blacks. There was some initial opposition to public education for the former slaves; however, this dissipated gradually. Municipal authorities established the first public schools for black students by incorporating two of the freedmen's schools into the larger municipal school system.

Although most blacks were occupied by learning the fundamentals, the education provided by the new schools was not limited to the rudiments. Some of the schools in Charleston offered normal and college preparatory courses. Black Charlestonians pursued advanced studies at several institutions of higher learning that were established in other parts of the state, and some even attended the University of South Carolina for a brief period. While advanced studies were available to all blacks, the students most academically prepared and financially able to pursue them were from upper class, often aristocratic, families. Many were members of the antebellum free colored aristocracy or its descendants. This fact, in part, explains why the newly emerging class of professionals, which made up much of the upper class, contained a disproportionate number of persons with free black backgrounds. Even so, the new educational possibilities accompanying Reconstruction afforded the freedmen the experiences and skills that, given time, eroded the social and cultural distance between themselves and those with a heritage of freedom.

Among the professionals, black teachers were especially important, and the city and county schools, public and private, all utilized their services to varying degree. Most black teachers were native Carolinians, and some had acted as teachers in Charleston's free black community. As symbols of achievement, teachers were seen as particularly important role models for aspiring young blacks. The rise of this group was especially valuable for women, who were generally unrepresented in professional occupations until Reconstruction. Along with other members of the elite, they assumed positions of social responsibility, and their existence and activities reveal the evolving complexity of the black community.

CHAPTER SIX

CLASS, STATUS, AND SOCIAL LIFE IN THE BLACK COMMUNITY

In 1877 a journalist for the *Atlantic Monthly* was surprised to learn that South Carolina blacks had "among themselves social rank and aristocracy outrageously severe and strictly discriminated." Members of the middle class were conscious of the distinction between themselves and the mass of blacks, and, according to the same observer, "Those who have been trained up 'genteelly' in white families of the highest respectability, as waiting men, maids, drivers, and so on, of course pride themselves not a little on their polished deportment."[1]

Even during the antebellum period, black Charlestonians could hardly have been described as a homogeneous group, and considerable variation existed in the quality and character of life. Before the Civil War, the basis for the most important social distinction was legal rather than strictly sociological and divided Afro-Americans into slaves and free persons of color. Black slaves usually worked as domestics or as unskilled laborers. Some, like the slave artisans, did acquire skills and training that qualified them for positions of greater responsibility. These, along with the privileged house slaves owned by aristocratic whites, formed the upper echelons of the slave social hierarchy. Free blacks suffered legal and social disabilities but, unlike the slaves, were never completely proscribed. They were generally light complexioned, and the men worked at skilled trades. A significant number acquired real property, and some even held slaves. Among free persons of color, a well-developed class structure emerged, which was supported by group institutions. But the social structure of the antebellum black community could not withstand the forces unleashed by the Civil War and Reconstruction, which modified that structure in important ways. Certain social cleavages extant prior to the war were amplified, while others diminished in significance. Under changed circumstances, workers and others availed themselves of new opportunities as the black community assumed a firmer institutional basis. The final product was the emergence of new groups and a greatly accelerated process of social differentiation among black Charlestonians.

After the Civil War, throughout the South the freedmen hoped for a major reallocation of land, which would establish them as a class of small holders. In Charleston, as in other places, the major index of social status was wealth, which was measured primarily in real property accumulation. For most black Charlestonians, property acquisition remained an unrealized dream; even among the more successful, the process was usually slow and difficult. Sometimes, in order to surmount the difficulties facing individuals, groups of blacks pooled their financial resources and acquired land. In 1868, two hundred freedmen from Charleston formed the Freedmen's Land and Home Society for acquiring property and housing. They contracted to pay ten dollars an acre for a six-hundred-acre plantation located at Remley's Point, just opposite the city. Their first cotton crop failed to realize their expectations because of insect pests and thieves, who stole much of the harvest. They remained undaunted and vowed "to watch the crop night and day" the next year until it was safely marketed. The Charleston Land Company, organized for a similar purpose, acquired land, which its members farmed cooperatively, in the same vicinity, near the Wando River.[2] Unfortunately, though, even these collaborative efforts failed to produce a large class of black landowners.

The black working class contained approximately two-thirds of the city's entire black population and was made up of persons with little or no property who, when employed, usually worked as domestics or in unskilled or semiskilled capacities. Little concrete information is available on such persons, who, unlike the socially prominent, left few written records. It does seem likely that their characteristics and problems closely resembled those observed among working classes in general. Restricted to providing services that required minimal or no skill, such persons normally suffered from low wages, endemic unemployment, and underemployment. These disadvantages were exacerbated during Reconstruction by the twin problems of Charleston's depressed economy and its burgeoning oversupply of labor. That the very existence of such persons could be precarious was revealed in 1878, when the city council, pressed by financial exigency, considered reducing the unskilled laborers it employed. In the course of the debate on this matter, one alderman urged caution because these men and others like them were literally "starving for work." He further warned that the "conditions of the laboring classes of the city was [*sic*] actually appalling," and he predicted that if the city failed to employ them, "there would be a bread riot in less than thirty days." Work on the docks also presented problems, and, although they were often highly paid when they worked, longshoremen could depend on steady employment for only four to five months per year.[3]

Under such adverse conditions, savings were almost unknown, and property accumulation virtually impossible. It seems likely that the working class, more than any other class, was comprised of recent migrants from the countryside, many of whom existed on the very fringes of society and had greatly reduced life chances. The tenuous economic position of this class was also evident in the poor housing accommodations its members were limited to. Domestics fared better than others if they resided in the same houses with their employers. However, most members of the working class lived apart from their employers in cheap rented housing, which was often unhygenic and overcrowded. One observer of such residences reported that often there were "as many as five different families in one small building." Another noted that "a crowd of colored persons living in a house in Tradd street ... have [*sic*] made the location a perfect nuisance to the neighborhood." Less fortunate individuals were even too impoverished to obtain housing and could be found sleeping under old buildings and even on the pavement of obscure alleys.[4]

In every respect, members of the black middle class experienced a better quality of life than those below them. The middle class was composed of workers and included slightly less than 30 percent of the city's black population. Its members were primarily drawn from the ranks of skilled craftsmen but also included all persons fortunate enough to have acquired real property valued between 250 and 999 dollars. Because of the greater regularity of their employment and their ability to command higher wages than the unskilled, almost two-thirds (sixty percent) of the property holders were artisans; moreover, a diversity of occupations was represented among the propertied middle class. In addition to the craftsmen, this group most notably included laborers, farmers, draymen, drivers, porters, waiters, fishermen, shippers, and seamen.[5]

While the vast majority of middle-class black workers were employed by whites, some did open their own businesses. Several operated restaurants, groceries, and wood yards. Artisans also maintained shops of various kinds. The ability of blacks to become self-employed as craftsmen or entrepreneurs was highly valued in the black community and could further distinguish both the middle and upper class from the masses.[6] Usually entrepreneurs engaged in small-scale operations that entailed little capital investment and employed few workers. In 1880, the total capital invested in George A. Glover's saddle- and harness-making establishment was $650. Glover employed up to four hands who were collectively paid $900 and produced a product valued at $1,800 during the year. Sometimes these business ventures could be considerably smaller in scale, especially if they were operated by family members. This seems to have been the case with J. B. Dacosta's shoemaking establishment, which entailed a capital investment of only $100, employed three workers, two of whom were children, and produced products valued at $500 annually.[7]

During Reconstruction and the years thereafter, the institutional development of the black community provided opportunities for black workers that had scarcely existed before the Civil War. Shaw Memorial School, which, according to the Charleston *Courier*, compared favorably "in point of architectural construction, convenience, and elegance" with other similar buildings in the city, was built entirely under the direction of the black contractors S. W. Wigfall and William J. Brodie. When Mission Presbyterian Church was constructed, black contractors did all the bricklaying and woodwork. When Emanuel A.M.E. Church was rebuilt, an observer noted, "A significant feature of its construction is that the builder is a colored man, and all the work on the church is the labor of colored mechanics." Individual blacks, of course, also utilized each other's skills, and when George Shrewsbury, a man of considerable means, had houses constructed, he employed the services of a black contractor.[8] Even the modest success of the small shopkeepers and artisans seemed to augur well for future economic progress.

While members of the middle class often enjoyed comfortable living circumstances, economic restraints prevented most in the lower class from effectively sharing in many of the values and activities of the larger community. Among the most alienated elements of the lower class, the numerous lottery establishments, saloons, and disorderly houses provided outlets for pleasure-seeking activities of an often illicit nature. Elliott Street and the surrounding alleys, described as "the filthiest and certainly the wickedest," region of the city, were especially known for such activities. It was in these places that the frustrations of life at the bottom of society often erupted into violence. Both Elliott Street and the "notorious" Gabeau's Row around Elizabeth and Charlotte streets were frequently the scenes of brawls, robberies, and sometimes even murders.[9]

The social lives of most black Charlestonians hardly included such conduct, and their recreational pursuits were considerably more diverse and respectable. The church was the most important social institution in the black community, and several religious societies, such as Mary and Martha, Sons and Daughters of Zion Number Two, and Rising Sons and Daughters of Bethelem Star, sponsored both sacred and secular events, including picnics and concerts. There were also a large number of fraternal organizations in the city, most notably the Ancient York Masons, Odd Fellows, Good Samaritans, Good Templars, Knights of Damon, and the Catholic Knights of America. These lodges and the black fire companies held banquets, balls, and parties and organized excursions around Charleston harbor and to other cities. Charleston also contained several dance halls and the Marble Skating Rink, which was the scene of promenade concerts and skating contests.[10]

For those interested in sports, several options were available. The Washington Race Course was a favorite resort for those who enjoyed horse racing. There were also the Monrovia, Charleston Union, and Attucks regatta clubs, which sponsored boat races on the Ashley and Cooper rivers. Black Charlestonians organized several baseball teams, the most important of which were the Arlington, Catchers, Eckford, United, Pacific, Fulton, Active, and Resolute teams. By the mid-1870s citywide and statewide tournaments were organized among the black clubs, and in 1876 the Fulton team of Charleston won the state championship. The militia companies of the South Carolina National Guard and the rifle and cavalry clubs held frequent marksmanship contests.[11]

Musical entertainment was especially popular, and several black minstrel companies performed throughout the city. Benford and Mazyck's Negro Minstrel Troupe, the South Carolina Minstrels, and the Chicora Minstrels made annual tours of the southeastern and northern states. Their performances were well attended, and the South Carolina Minstrels were especially noted for the scene entitled "Ten Years of Fraud." Bands were organized, and the most well known were the Chicora Coronet and String Star Band, the Phoenix Band, and the Excelsior Band. They provided musical festivities that featured popular and operatic pieces at Military Hall as well as on the Battery, and they performed at most of the major social events in the black community.[12]

In addition to such ordinary recreations, there were occasions that called for special celebrations. At these times black Charleston bustled with festive activity. The date of Crispus Attucks' death, Liberian Independence Day, passage of the Emancipation Proclamation, the Fourth of July, and the anniversary of the Fifteenth Amendment were all events that called for special commemoration. On these occasions Charleston became the focal point for individual celebrants and groups that included fire companies and militia units from the nearby Sea Islands and other places in the region. One observer reported that black Charlestonians typically celebrated the Emancipation Proclamation with "effusive fervor and gusto." On this occasion in 1870, "the streets were crowded at an early hour by throngs of colored people, mostly in gorgeous garments, and all with smiling and expectant faces." The major attraction of the day was the militia parade, which was led by ten or twelve companies of the First Regiment of National Guards "comprising a fine body of men, from five to seven hundred strong." Its "usual full complement of mounted officers" were "wild with excitement, and went galloping hither and thither at the slightest provocation." The march, led by Gen. Robert Smalls and Samuel Dickerson, both former slaves, proceeded up King Street to rendezvous with the Union League and the Longshoremen's Association.[13]

While the middle class was distinguished from the masses of freedmen, the top of the social hierarchy revealed black Charleston's increasing social and economic differentiation most vividly. In 1880 the 356-member upper class included less than 2 percent of the black population. Of its members, at least 40 percent had been free before the war and 96 percent could read and write. A free black heritage and literacy brought advantages that, in part, provided the basis for the group's prosperity. One of the main components of the upper class included 186 individuals who had accumulated comparatively large amounts of real property, worth $1,000 or more. This group was largely composed of skilled craftsmen (54 percent), professionals (13 percent), and proprietors (9 percent). Unskilled, semiskilled, and service workers made up only 24 percent of its members.[14]

Many members of this economic elite maintained well-established businesses that relied extensively on the patronage of whites. The vegetable farmers and florists Joseph and Philip Noisette maintained twenty acres of land, including a sixteen-acre farm in the northern portion of Charleston collectively valued at $5,800. The Noisette farm was one of the regular stops made by the South Carolina Railroad; its produce brought handsome profits to its owners and provided regular employment for several black farm laborers. Among all the caterers and restaurateurs in the city, the name of Thomas R. Tully, the "famous Charleston caterer," was outstanding. His King Street establishment attracted an extensive white patronage. According to one observer, Tully was especially well known among whites "to whom he was an oracle in matters culinary." Tully's restaurant was also frequented by members of the black upper class. When Lt. Henry O. Flipper, the first black graduate of West Point, visited Charleston in 1877, it was reported that "the upper crust of colored society . . . determined to entertain him at Tully's and in that culinary artist's best style." At the high point of his career, the enterprising Tully accumulated over $4,500 in real and personal property. Tully's business operations also provided employment for other blacks, and in 1881 his catering services, restaurant, and market stalls required a staff of at least six persons.[15]

Upper-class tradesmen also enjoyed an extensive white patronage throughout Reconstruction and the years shortly thereafter. The carpenter shop maintained by Richard and Charles Holloway was widely known and patronized by the entire community. The butcher George Shrewsbury was not only prominent among blacks but was highly esteemed by whites, who patronized his market stalls regularly. During the antebellum period, Shrewsbury, a free black, cultivated a very close relationship with Rev. A. Toomer Porter, a white Episcopalian minister. When Porter founded the Holy Communion Church Institute after the war, he naturally chose Shrewsbury to provide the school with its regular supply of meat. By the end of his career, the butcher had transacted over twenty thousand dollars worth of business with the school. It was no wonder that in 1869, when little new construction was occurring in the city, Jacob Schirmer noted, "Opposite us are two buildings putting up for Shrewsbury the Butcher."[16]

Sometimes municipal government and corporations provided important commercial opportunities for black entrepreneurs and craftsmen. George Shrewsbury's established reputation served him well during Reconstruction. He benefited from the patronage of both Democratic and Republican city administrations during the era and received important contracts from each. Robert Howard was a city alderman under Republican Mayor Pillsbury. He maintained a business as a wood factor and also secured contracts from the city to supply firewood that generated approximately two thousand dollars in annual income.[17] When the Charleston Street Car Company held a reception in honor of its new streetcar system, Thomas Tully, the famous caterer, was called upon to provide the fare. George Shrewsbury, Robert Howard, and Thomas Tully were all antebellum free persons of color. The antebellum business reputations enjoyed by Shrewsbury and Howard enabled them to capitalize on postbellum opportunities fairly easily.[18]

With established reputations for skilled craftsmanship and sometimes considerable business acumen, the economic elite was able to amass considerable amounts of property. In 1880, the median value of property held by the group was $1,575, but throughout the 1870s, many members of the economic elite accumulated substantially more. John W. Hall's activities as a cotton shipper enabled him to accumulate real and personal property valued at almost $10,000. Joseph A. Robinson, known for his skill as an upholsterer and as an undertaker, accumulated a personal estate valued at $6,900. Neither man had belonged to the old Charleston free brown elite but were members of the new rising generation of Charlestonians that would eventually rival and overshadow the achievements of the formerly more privileged group. One of the most well-known members of the new group was Stephney B. Riley, a former slave carriage driver, who, after the war, owned and operated one of Charleston's most extensive hack stables and livery services. He employed several other blacks and accumulated property valued at $3,750.[19]

Although changes began to occur in the composition of the economic elite during Reconstruction, those persons who had been well-established antebellum free persons of color continued to be its most substantial members. One example was Anthony Weston, who established his reputation as an antebellum millwright and blacksmith and who continued his trade during Reconstruction. The real property in his estate was valued at almost $19,000 in 1880. Richard Dereef, another member of the former free brown elite, had a well-established reputation as a wood factor; he sold a large plot of land in Mazyckborough to the South Carolina Railroad for $17,000. He gave a mortgage on the property, and, with interest charges, the total cost to the railroad was $24,000. After such a large conveyance, Dereef continued to own at least 4 houses throughout the city valued at $7,400. The carpenter Richard Holloway owned several houses, collectively valued at $9,300, that were distributed throughout the city.[20]

The accumulation of real estate was only one of several ways members of the upper class made use of their financial assets, and several men invested considerable amounts in other aspects of the state and local economies. The case of William McKinlay Sr. is an outstanding example. A member of Charleston's free brown elite, McKinlay was a tailor by trade, and by the early 1870s he had become one of the richest black men in the city. He owned $23,000 worth of real property and invested over $13,000 in the Blue Ridge Railroad, $6,200 in State of South Carolina stock, and $500 in 6 percent stock issued by the city of Charleston. The prosperous butcher George Shrewsbury amassed a "considerable fortune" by the mid-1870s, most of which was invested in state and municipal securities and local business ventures. He was able to capitalize on the upsurge in railroad building during Reconstruction and on the new phosphate and fertilizer industry that developed during the period. Between the Northeastern Railroad, the South Carolina Railroad, and the Enterprise Railroad, Shrewsbury invested over $17,000. Shrewsbury invested $3,828 in the Charleston Fertilizer Company and in the Stono Phosphate Company.[21]

Some men, not content to invest in the businesses of others, incorporated themselves and initiated their own enterprises. The Palm Oil and Grease Company, authorized to manufacture lubricants, and the Edisto, Cawcaw and Waites Canal Company formed to engage in the phosphate and lumber business; the two companies also dug a navigable canal that linked the Ashley and Edisto rivers. Corporations were formed to assist in raising capital for business enterprises, for home improvements, and for land purchases. One such organization was the Workingmen's Building and Loan Association, which was organized and directed by such men as Charles C. Leslie, William Ingliss Jr., Francis H. Carmand, Richard Birnie, William J. Parker, Gordon M. Magrath, and A. J. Boyden, all of whom were known in elite circles. The capital raised by the Sumner Building and Loan Association was used to purchase property on Meeting Street that was later used as a community entertainment hall and a center for the meetings of fraternal societies and militia units.[22]

The most impressive commercial venture launched by members of Charleston's black elite was the establishment of the Enterprise Railroad. Incorporated in 1870 at a capital value of $250,000, the railroad was constructed in 1874 to provide transportation to both freight and passengers. Its horse-drawn coaches extended from Magnolia Avenue beyond the corporate limits of Charleston to East Battery and made connections with all the principal wharves and railroad depots. In 1870, state legislator Richard H. Cain was responsible for the legislation incorporating the railroad. He subsequently served as president of the company, William R. Jervey served as corresponding secretary, and William McKinlay served as treasurer. With the exception of Timothy Hurley, a leading white Republican, the membership of the board of directors was entirely black and included Joseph H. Rainey, Dr. Benjamin A. Boseman, William J. Brodie, J. N. Hayne, Thaddeus K. Sasportas, John Wright, Henry Maxwell, Lucius Wimbush, Robert Smalls, and William E. and Samuel Johnston. William J. Whipper of the firm Whipper, Elliott, and Allen, acted as the legal advisor and subscription agent for the railroad.[23]

The new venture was important and revealing for a number of reasons. It is clear that the elite and working classes perceived the railroad in diametrically opposing ways. Discussion of the proposed railroad represented a serious threat to the city's draymen, three-quarters of whom were black; many believed that the Enterprise Railroad would eliminate their jobs. For this reason Rev. Hezekiah H. Hunter, a black Presbyterian minister from New Jersey and a self-proclaimed spokesman for the freedmen, was highly critical of the railroad. He also criticized its president, Richard Cain, for using fraudulent means to win approval of this scheme to benefit the few at the expense of the many working men. Cain denied the charges and argued that the new railroad would not displace the present draymen but would actually provide new jobs for two or three hundred workmen. The draymen and their representatives remained unconvinced.[24]

Another equally revealing aspect of the Enterprise Railroad project was that only one of Charleston's substantial antebellum free black taxpayers was represented on the board of directors. That lone representative was William McKinlay. The reasons why the old elite failed to participate in a more active way are unclear. Most important, this new venture revealed the increasing diversity of the postbellum elite. At least two members of the board were transplanted northerners, as was the railroad president. Some had been free before the war but, with the exception of Thaddeus K. Sasportas, weren't from elite families. Finally, at least two, Robert Smalls and William Jervey, had been slaves and during Reconstruction held seats in the general assembly.[25] The Enterprise Railroad continued its operations into the 1880s, but the role of blacks as policy makers diminished considerably during the 1870s. They continued as investors during the decade, but even before the end of Reconstruction the railroad clearly passed to the control of whites.[26]

While the wealthy were highly regarded because of their economic achievements, the upper class also contained those who were influential and esteemed largely because of the prestige, social prominence, or unique responsibilities entailed by their occupations. Very few of the persons who held high status positions would have been considered materially prosperous. In 1880, of the 181 members of this group only 35 of them, or 18 percent, owned any real property in Charleston and only 10 percent owned real estate valued at $1,000 or more. Certain of the occupations in this group existed before the Civil War, but the activities of those who held them were usually severely restricted by the dictates of a slaveholding society.[27] Other important occupations found in the group were completely new to the black community. The rapid development of this high status group was at once symptomatic of the political changes occurring in the South during Reconstruction and also of the increasing institutional complexity of black Charleston.

The dominant elements in the high status group were ministers and teachers. Although there were persons who acted in these capacities prior to the Civil War, virtually none pursued these vocations on a full-time basis. For instance, while Samuel Weston was an exhorter among the black Methodists during the antebellum period, his full-time occupation was that of a tailor. Furthermore, Weston inspired the confidence of white Methodists without which even the restricted services he provided could not have been possible. With the rapid proliferation of black churches after the war, men like Weston pursued the ministry as their primary occupations, and a professional class of black ministers began to develop. Teachers were not entirely new to the black community, but there were very few before the war, and their activities were limited by the web of restraints designed to control Afro-Americans. The expansion of public and private schools during Reconstruction provided new professional opportunities, especially for women. Although teachers were not the vocal leaders the clergymen often were, the enthusiasm that blacks of all ages expressed for learning made teachers a highly esteemed group and entry into the teaching profession a common aspiration.[28]

The nature of the services provided by the high status group made basic literacy a minimal requirement, and often members of the group were quite well educated. The increasing educational levels and professionalism of the upper class was most clearly revealed by the appearance of two entirely new groups, black doctors and lawyers. Of Charleston's five black physicians, Dr. Martin R. Delany, a native of Pennsylvania, was the most famous. Well known for his activities as a black abolitionist, African ethnographer, and exponent of black nationalist ideology, and as a Union army officer, Delany also had the mind of a trained scientist. In the early 1850s, he attended Harvard Medical School where he came within four months of completing his medical degree before the racially motivated protests of white students prevented him from enrolling in the final courses. After coming to South Carolina as a major in the Union army and serving as an agent for the Freedmen's Bureau, Delany established his medical practice and became one of the most well-known doctors in Charleston's black community.[29]

Dr. Benjamin A. Boseman, a native of Troy, New York, finished his medical degree at Bowdoin College and came to Hilton Head, South Carolina, as an assistant surgeon in the United States Colored Troops. Upon moving to Charleston, he immediately began his medical practice and became the physician of the Charleston Jail. Dr. Boseman's skills were highly regarded and his reputation spread rapidly, especially among the elite. In a complimentary article, the *Daily News* observed that he "has the family practice of the most influential and respectable members of the colored population in the city." Not all of Charleston's most successful doctors were relocated northerners. Dr. Moses G. Camplin, for example, was a native Charlestonian and acquired his medical training during the war. Camplin later served as the lecturer on physiology and the laws of health at Baker Theological Institute and maintained a successful practice throughout Reconstruction. Dr. William D. Crum was another native Carolinian who entered the medical profession. Born free on the eve of the Civil War in Orangeburg, Crum attended Avery Institute in Charleston and graduated in 1875. Shortly thereafter, he entered the University of South Carolina and later enrolled at Howard University. Upon completion of his medical degree, Crum returned to Charleston, where he began his practice and became one of the city's leading black citizens.[30]

The interpretation of the law was essential for the black community's survival, and several men were attracted to the legal profession. Samuel Dickerson, a former slave, and John M. Freeman Jr., the son of a free black Charleston carpenter, both had become lawyers by late 1870. In addition to serving the needs of litigants, the services of such men were equally important in other ways to a community in which most of the residents were illiterate and unfamiliar with business and legal procedures. In several cases it was only the intervention of F. D. J. Lawrence that enabled ex-soldiers or their families to obtain their military pensions. The most outstanding black lawyers were of northern origin. Macon B. Allen of Massachusetts was admitted to the bar of that state as early as 1845, and he had been involved in the activities of the American Antislavery Society. After relocating to South Carolina, he became judge of the Charleston Inferior Court and joined with the state legislators William J. Whipper and Robert Brown Elliott to form the law firm Whipper, Elliott, and Allen. Jonathan Jasper Wright, a native of Pennsylvania, attended Lancasterian University in New York. He read law with several northern lawyers before coming to South Carolina in 1865 with the American Missionary Association to organize schools for blacks. Upon passing the Pennsylvania bar examination in 1866, he took an appointment from Major Oliver O. Howard as the special legal advisor to the freedmen at Beaufort. By 1880, Wright had moved to Charleston where he continued his practice.[31]

Due to their wealth or social prominence, some upper class blacks won the respect of leading whites, who solicited their opinions on important issues and sometimes invited them to participate in joint business ventures. In 1878 when the *News and Courier* ascertained the citizens' views on how the city debt might be funded, along with the advice of prominent whites, the newspaper sought the opinion of Samuel L. Bennett because he was well known as "a colored man of some means" and as a leading figure in his community. When white businessmen formed the Building and Loan Association, Richard Birnie, a prosperous cotton shipper, was elected as one of its officers.[32]

Often, close relations with prominent whites represented a continuation of antebellum social affinities and the desire of upper-class blacks to associate with persons they considered their social equals. Although James H. Holloway was specifically referring to politics when he declared that many former free blacks and their descendants "preferred to affiliate with the classes when they could do so without compromising their manhood," his observation also applied to other social relations. The case of George Shrewsbury is an outstanding example. Although he developed a business relationship with the prominent Episcopal minister Rev. A. Toomer Porter, their deep personal friendship stemmed more from the two men's respect for each other as representatives of the finest qualities in the southern aristocratic tradition. When early in 1865 Porter decided to evacuate the city, Shrewsbury tried to persuade him to remain in Charleson by volunteering the members of his own family to act as Porter's servants. The minister declined the offer and fled the approach of the Union troops. Shortly after the end of the war, the two men met in the city market, and Shrewsbury, delighted at seeing his old friend, "expressed his gratitude that the gentlemen were coming back for Charleston was not home without them."[33]

The vicissitudes of war left Porter impoverished, and much of his property had been confiscated by the Freedmen's Bureau. Upon learning this, Shrewsbury approached the minister, offered him a loan of one hundred dollars, and refused any payment of interest because, as he told Reverend Porter, "I have been abundantly repaid in feeling I was the means of relieving you in a sore time of need, and when ever you wish it again it is at your disposal." Later, when Porter established an endowment fund for the Holy Communion Church Institute, a school and orphanage for white boys, George Shrewsbury made a five-hundred-dollar contribution. His generosity ranked him among the largest contributors to the school.[34]

During Reconstruction most politically active blacks were Republicans and often fell prey to political discrimination as a result. Even elite status could not completely insulate them from this kind of retribution, retribution that was sufficient motivation for some to join the Democrats. This may have been a reason why elite craftsmen, such as William J. Parker, not only consistently supported the Democrats but also became much more actively involved in their campaign efforts by 1876. While actively campaigning for the Democrats and encouraging black support, Sidney C. Eckhardt identified a critical issue by simply stating he "was under no obligation to the Republican party for a single dollar that he had saved." When in 1868 Thomas Tully discovered rumors that accused him of being a Republican, he responded with a note in the *Daily Courier* denying the charges, which, according to him, were calculated to harm his business. The caterer took no chances as the critical election of 1876 approached: he published another note to "remind the general public of what his old customers all know, that he has been for years a staunch Democrat and is now a supporter of Hampton and good government."[35]

Other members of the elite, such as George Shrewsbury and Richard Dereef, shared the same financial concerns but also clearly identified with the Democratic party because of the gentlemen statesmen associated with it in South Carolina. Richard Dereef was certainly one of the most well-to-do members of Charleston's colored aristocracy but was only sporadically involved in Reconstruction politics. He was appointed an alderman in 1868 by the military authorities. Later that year, when the municipal election results were disputed, Dereef was the sole black who voted with the whites to invalidate the election and to delay the installation of the city's first elected Republican administration.[36]

Richard Dereef did not run for office, but during the period he was a consistent supporter of Democrats. In 1876 his support for Wade Hampton was not the result of political expediency, as it was for some, but grew out of his long-standing respect for South Carolina's tradition of aristocratic leadership. Dereef's adherence to these sentiments is why even early in Reconstruction the *Daily Courier* could describe him as "a fine type of the free colored man . . . who illustrated in old times our peculiar form of society, and we believe is to-day as true to the interests which have bound him to Charleston as any man in this community."[37]

Some upper-class blacks of slave background also cultivated close personal relationships with the South's "best men" and chose to affiliate with the Democrats. After the war, a black Charlestonian described Stephney Riley, the former slave who became a prosperous stable owner, as a Democrat "devoted to the South, respected by all—hated by many—a power in himself." Given his politics and success in business, Riley became "exceedingly popular with a certain class of white gentlemen of convivial habits who were in the habit of visiting . . . [his] house to enjoy his liquors and cigars." These friends were quite useful when, after the municipal election of 1868, Riley was pursued by a mob of black Republicans, who, after failing to capture him, attempted to damage his stables. Numerous white citizens offered their houses as refuge for the black Democrat and also collected over six hundred dollars, which they presented him with to repair the damage done to his business. After whites vowed to take matters into their own hands unless Riley was given protection, Mayor Clark employed his personal carriage to drive him through the city.[38]

Richard Dereef represented one example of the colored elite's politics. Members of that group, however, revealed a diversity of political sentiment. William McKinlay was one of the wealthiest colored aristocrats and became a vigorous supporter of the Republican party and an officeholder during Reconstruction. Edward P. Wall had been one of the most conservative and "exclusivist" members of the antebellum elite but became a leading organizer of the Republican party following the war and acquired the reputation of a radical in local politics.[39]

Robert C. DeLarge was from an upper-class slaveholding family and was a member of the Brown Fellowship Society. William R. Hampton, a former free person of color, was of middle-class status during Reconstruction but obtained membership in the Brown Fellowship Society also. Despite their conservative backgrounds and their sometime claims to membership in the colored aristocracy, these men were not averse to embracing racial issues. They even challenged the racial status quo during Reconstruction by advocating, or at least supporting, civil rights measures. Their willingness to forthrightly concern themselves with racial matters confirms Martin R. Delany's observations about many blacks with a heritage of freedom in Charleston. Based upon his interaction with the family of Anthony Weston and probably some of the McKinlays (since the two families were very close), he concluded that they "gave evidence of their pride in identity and appreciation of race" that equaled that of the "proudest Caucasian." Such sentiments are not often associated with Charleston's free persons of color but in fact played an important role in motivating their activism.[40]

The success of the elite in their traditional crafts, their ability to enter and succeed in new business pursuits and professions, and the acceptance of some members of the black upper class by prominent whites shaped their racial ideology and social world view. The upper class was generally integrationist in outlook. In response to those men entertaining the notion of emigration "where they can be alone, under their 'own vine and fig tree'" the black newspaper *New Era* retorted:

> We are Americans and Carolinians by birth-right, National and State pride, and feel that we can stay just where we are, and none will molest us! . . . if we are law abiding, and do all our knowledge will enable us, in bettering the general condition, and that of our own. We are satisfied that the thinking and influential element of the white race will aid us in the development of our faculties and physical forces. Then another important consideration is we very much prefer to be near a civilization in advance of ours, and our present capabilities in that direction.[41]

Many assumed that support from the better class of whites, so crucial for racial uplift, would be forthcoming only if the black masses adopted the mores of their social betters. Upper-class blacks consistently stressed this point and admonished those below them to adhere to the Protestant work ethic and other cherished values. Rev. Richard H. Cain pointed out that the largest problem facing blacks was one of education because black people had not begun to think for themselves. Too many were "fiddling away and dancing and picnicing, and some of them don't own the sand in their shoes." Others threw money away on frivolities: "[A] Negro dresses himself, puts a cigar in his mouth, and stands on the corner, arms akimbo, thinking he is a fine gentleman and perhaps has a four weeks unpaid board-bill." According to Cain and others, such wasteful behavior and attitudes had to be eliminated before the race could progress.[42]

The members of the upper class urged the masses to strive for greater respectability by learning trades, through simple virtue, and through hard work and thrift. Industry and economy were both important because, as a group of black ministers declared, "It is not so much what we make as what is saved that brings wealth." In 1883 William Holloway, editor of the Charleston *New Era,* admonished that "nothing can be accomplished, by waiting for somebody to do something for you. . . . The wisest plan is to get to work yourself." He encouraged the propertyless to "save up the odd pennies, and buy a lot, build thereon, a cabin if you can do no better." The acquisition of one's own property was of the utmost importance because the difference between rental fees and taxes on real estate could be saved. These savings, combined with "the fruit of other economies," would enable those less fortunate to improve the quality of their lives and eventually live in comfort.[43]

According to T. McCants Stewart, the sagacity and business acumen demonstrated by men like Charles C. Leslie, the prosperous Charleston wholesale and retail fish dealer, were the characteristics upon which "the success of the race in the future must largely hinge." With the demise of political Reconstruction, by the early 1880s, middle-class virtue, diligence, and commercial success became even more important as keys to racial progress. In 1885 a conference of black clergymen sounded what would soon become a familiar theme when the clergymen observed that property holders were one of the most powerful elements of every race, while the poor were always oppressed. The major task facing blacks, then, was to accumulate property because, in their view, "no man is likely to question the right of a man to act and think for himself who has by his industry and economy accumulated his $10,000 or $20,000. Wealth as well as knowledge is power." Booker T. Washington could not have expressed these sentiments more compellingly.[44]

The ability to maintain a distinctive lifestyle separated the elite from the rest of black Charleston as much as their occupations and relative prosperity did. Many lived in quite elegant housing. A. O. Jones, clerk of the state house of representatives, lived in a three-story residence, with piazzas on each story, a slate pyramidal roof, and a neat cupola on its annex. It was described as "one of the handsomest residences on Green Street." A well-to-do ship captain H. T. Graddick lived in a two-story dwelling with double piazzas and several "square rooms, dressing rooms, pantries and attics." Samuel Garrett, a minister and a popular municipal alderman, owned a home near Zion Church that contained nine large rooms all lighted by gas and erected at a cost of $2,700.[45]

In other respects, members of the black elite enjoyed lifestyles comparable to their white counterparts. Some employed servants to attend to their homes and personal drivers for their carriages. In his analysis of the "upper tendon of Colored Charleston," a local reporter observed, "Their handsome, intelligent faces, and really elegant dress" presented "a very fine appearance. In courtesy and native refinement, they are far in advance of the upper ten of many cities it has been our good fortune to visit." A visitor to the home of a prominent black Charlestonian remarked that it was "furnished with every modern improvement" and included a table that "was supplied with choice meats and rare wines." When a reporter went to the home of Rev. L. R. Nichols, he was entertained in "a well-furnished and cozy parlor, containing a large new piano and half a dozen oil paintings." The children of such families were able to attend school regularly, and many even had private music lessons. In one household there were two sisters who not only played the piano competently but also, according to a visitor, "had admirably solved the sweet mysteries of Shubert's and Bach's most difficult music." Upper-class men adhered to nineteenth-century notions about women and their role in the family. For 106 of these men (or 79 percent of the upper-class husbands) the woman's place was in the home, and in contrast to the larger black community, in which approximately one-half of the married women worked, only rarely did upper-class wives obtain employment. To provide for the ongoing care of their wives and families, several upper-class husbands secured life insurance policies.[46]

Marriage was an especially important phase of life for the elite, and the wealthiest and most aristocratic families preferred endogamous marriages. Thus, the Holloways and Browns, the Dereefs and Westons, McKinlays and Barnets, and the Plumeaus and Thornes were all intricately related by marriage. Marriages were occasions for careful planning and celebration. In elite families, brides often received dowries. When Samuel Weston's daughter was married, he provided a "marriage outfit" of $150. When Emma Rose Wilder, daughter of the black postmaster of Columbia, was married, the ceremony reception was reported to be "the society event of the season." Members of the Charleston elite attended the wedding and their presence was striking. The gifts they gave to the newlyweds were also impressive and included many silver gold-lined serving utensils, silver casters, and lace handkerchiefs. Anniversaries were no less occasions for celebration. The fifteenth wedding anniversary of Mr. and Mrs. W. S. Johnson was celebrated in "splendid style" when friends presented them with an attractive forty-two-piece china tea service. A band was hired for the occasion, "while an abundance of delicacies, and dancing in the moonlight made the scene charming."[47]

The distinctive lifestyles, world view, and esprit de corps of the black upper middle and upper classes were fostered by an amalgam of social organizations. There were mutual aid societies, such as the Charitable Union Association, whose function was as much social and recreational as benevolent. A relatively young organization, having only been founded in 1873, it was one of the most respectable associations in the city, and its 1883 banquet was described as "the most notable event, which has occurred in colored society." In attendance were guests representing "the pulpit, medical profession, legal profession and gentlemen of letters and note generally." The festivities of the evening included band music, cornet and accordion solos, formal speeches and toasts heralding the glories of "the State of South Carolina," "The City of Charleston," "Education," "The Virtues of Woman," and a superb dinner that "recalled the glory of nature's best."[48]

While the Charitable Union was open to the upper middle class, the elite maintained several exclusive benevolent societies, the most prestigious of which existed prior to the Civil War. The Humane and Friendly Society was founded in 1802. The Friendly Union, Brotherly Association, Unity and Friendship, Union Assembly, and the Friendly Moralist Society were all founded during the antebellum period and included only the most prominent members of the upper class. Although membership lists are incomplete, it seems that these organizations limited their membership to either the old free brown elite or their descendants, which preserved their status as the aristocracy among the upper class.[49]

The grand patriarch of all such associations was the Brown Fellowship Society, which was founded in 1790 and was the earliest known black organization in Charleston. Members of the society believed it to be "the Representation of the Self Respect, intelligence, and Social Status, of the Old Free Brown Men of the City of Charleston." The organization's most important function was that of transmitting the cultural heritage and social traditions of the free brown elite to succeeding generations, thus shaping their attitudes, manners, and world view. The organization maintained its own burial ground and meeting hall on Liberty Street where regular celebrations and banquets were held. The old brown elite did found new charitable societies, such as the Mutual Fellowship Association and the Live Oak Mutual Aid Association, but these also seem to have limited the membership and served to cultivate group consciousness among the aristocracy of the black community.[50]

The role of voluntary associations among Charleston's aristocrats indicates that wealth was not the sole or even most important criterion for admission into their ranks. Other more subjective criteria, including family background, associations, outstanding achievement, intelligence, and respectability were all important. Longstanding membership in the Brown Fellowship Society, dating as it did from the years immediately following the American Revolution, was a source of pride. Aristocratic families, such as the Holloways, Mushingtons, and Dereefs, could trace their family memberships for several generations. The members of the organization encouraged their children to intermarry. One member proudly recalled that his maternal and paternal relatives had been members of the Brown Fellowship, and "so from generation to generation we meet to talk of the deeds of the Fathers and enjoy the congeniality of those born to the relations of friends."[51]

Although William Rollin wasn't a member of the Brown Fellowship Society, he was economically as well off as many of its leading members and equally patrician in outlook. As a wood factor, he owned one slave and accumulated three thousand dollars in real estate by 1860. He took great pride in his descent from a French family from Santo Domingo and sent his oldest daughter, Frances, to a school in the city where she was taught by a member of a well-established French family. In the 1850s Frances went on to attend the Institute for Colored Youth in Philadelphia.[52]

Despite apparent setbacks caused by the Civil War, during Reconstruction William Rollin continued to prosper. He turned to farming and expanded the value of his real property in the upper wards of the city to $4,400 by 1880. During the same time, Frances Rollin became actively engaged in Republican politics and romantically involved with William Whipper, the black state legislator from Beaufort and law partner in the firm Whipper, Elliott, and Allen. When, after a short courtship, the two decided to marry, Frances' father objected vociferously, claiming that she was acting hastily. Frances' sister Charlotte was perhaps more forthcoming in her comments about the father's (and her) objections to the union. She said, "In fact, our family never condescended to notice such small people as Elliott and Whipper, although Whipper married our sister Frances. They are both negroes and our family is French." The two were married in 1868 despite William's and Charlotte's objections.[53] The nature of Charlotte's protests gives ample evidence that even exceptionally well-educated, politically connected men like Whipper, himself a member of the new elite, were not qualified to enter the colored aristocracy.

Other families had distinctive origins or traditions that gave them special claims to aristocratic standing in the black community. Joseph and Philip Noisette owned approximately twenty acres of farm land, valued at $5,800, in Charleston Neck on San Souci and Simon streets in the 1880s. Their wealth set them apart from other blacks; their family tradition of descent from the famous French horticulturist Philip Stanislaus through his slave Celestine was even more distinctive. Their successful vegetable farm and nursery represented the continuation of a long family horticultural tradition extending at least as far back as the eighteenth century.[54]

The Weston family could claim a unique tradition also. Two of its earliest members, Lydia and Anthony, were owned by Plowden Weston the wealthy Low Country rice planter, before he emancipated them. Anthony, a highly trained slave millwright, developed a widespread reputation and an extensive patronage throughout the Low Country, which was the source of his wealth. The Westons took pride in Anthony's standing in both black and white communities. It was this family background, along with the accomplishments of other members, that won places for the Westons in the Brown Fellowship Society.[55]

There were several organizations dedicated to serious intellectual and cultural pursuits. The Charleston Dramatic Club and other black drama troupes produced plays, including "The Lady of Lyone," "Othello," "Above the Clouds," and "The Last Loaf" at St. Mark's Hall and the Academy of Music. The Reading Association, organized by members of Centenary Church, established a public reading room on King Street. The St. Mark's Association was founded by members of St. Mark's elite congregation for the moral and intellectual advancement of the church and the black community at large. The association maintained its own building with a library, drawing room, lecture hall, and meeting rooms open to all the respectable societies of the city.[56]

Several of the major black churches initiated lecture series, often featuring local speakers on topics of popular interest. Martin R. Delany's series of lectures on Africa was extremely popular and explored such specific topics as the "Moral and Social Relations of Africans in Central Africa" and the "Commercial Advantages of Africa." Overall, the lectures were many and diverse and included such topics as "Temperance," "the condition, duty and dangers of the colored man in the United States," "Popular Superstition," and "The Influence of Christian Females."[57]

Members of the elite believed that literary associations and debating societies facilitated intellectual development and the spread of "race culture." Several such associations and societies were formed, and the oldest and most aristocratic was the Amateur Literary and Fraternal Association, originally founded in 1855. Formed for the purpose of "mutual improvement in elocution, composition, debate and the thorough cultivation of fraternal feelings," some of its outstanding members were Alonzo J. Ransier, William J. McKinlay, Dr. Benjamin Boseman, Edward M. Brawley, and Richard Birnie. Younger and less aristocratic but thoroughly elitist were the other two major literary societies, the Douglass Literary Association and the Sumner Debating Club. These associations maintained libraries and held regular meetings at which it was the duty of previously designated members to entertain the group with debates, lectures, or some other form of literary exercise. The forum they provided led to many evenings of lively discussion. Sometimes the topics under consideration were also major concerns of contemporary interest, such as whether the intellectual capacities of the sexes were equal or whether the progress of science and the arts had corrupted or purified morals.[58]

On other occasions the issues broached related more directly to the affairs of the black community. This was the case when in 1884 the members of the Douglass Literary Association debated the question "Ought the America [*sic*] Negro to abstain from politics, at the present time?" This issue was hotly contested, with those on the affirmative contending that "the Negro had nothing to gain, at the present by politics; but should look after his industrial and educational interests." The negative side argued that blacks were citizens and should utilize politics to determine who should represent them. This debate was decided in favor of the negative.[59]

Some members of Charleston's black upper class had nationally recognized reputations for their literary achievement. When Martin Delany came to Charleston he had already written *Blake: or The Huts of America*, a novel about a conspiracy of slave insurrectionists. In 1882 he was elected as an honorary member of the Philoephian Literary Association of Lincoln University and was scheduled as the speaker at the organization's upcoming anniversary.[60]

Frances A. Rollin provided another important example. She was an exceptionally well-educated woman who hoped to pursue a literary career. After meeting Martin Delany, she was duly impressed with his achievements and decided to write his biography. To complete the project, she spent several months between the fall of 1867 and the summer of 1868 in Boston. While there, she met important activists, including William Lloyd Garrison and Wendell Phillips, and collaborated with Richard Greener, who would soon become Harvard's first black graduate. In her free moments, Frances thrilled at the opportunity to attend lectures and readings by such literary figures as Ralph Waldo Emerson and Charles Dickens. Her biography, *The Life and Public Services of Martin R. Delany,* was published in 1868, unfortunately under the pseudonym "Frank" to enhance its sale. Even so, her authorship was known, and Frances Rollin received national recognition for this important literary achievement.[61]

For purely social occasions, the elite relied on the Attucks Social Club, the Terpsichorean Club, and the Social Seaside Circle. Although the membership of the fraternal societies drew largely upon the masses of the black community, the elite participated in them and were especially attracted to Freemasonry. The Masonic Order was organized among blacks in Boston as early as 1775, but it only spread to Charleston with the coming of black troops during the Civil War. One of the earliest Masonic lodges was located on Morris Island and was organized by members of the Fifty-fourth Massachusetts Regiment. In 1866 at least one representative of the national Masonic fraternity was dispatched to Charleston to organize additional local lodges. Finally, in 1871, a Royal Arch chapter was formed, and in 1872 the Grand Lodge of Free and Accepted Ancient York Masons of South Carolina was incorporated. Most of the cooperators were representatives of Charleston's black upper class and included George E. Johnson, William H. Berney, T. B. Maxwell, William B. Nash, Benjamin A. Boseman, Henry J. Maxwell, Henry E. Hayne, William Ingliss Jr., William C. Young, H. L. Bell, Robert B. Elliott, Richard E. Dereef, James A. Bowley, Richard H. Gleaves, and William H. Jones Jr. Several of these men served as officers for both the state Grand Lodge and its subordinate local lodges in Charleston.[62]

By the early 1880s, there were at least eight Masonic Lodges in Charleston, two of which, the Drayton Lodge Number Four and the Union Lodge Number One, were popular among the elite. Included among their officers were many local notables who were members of other upper-class social organizations. Together with the social clubs and several Odd Fellows Lodges, the Masonic Lodges provided many recreational activities for the upper class, including parties, dances, picnics, fairs, and excursions to the seaside resorts on Sullivan's Island.[63]

In Charleston, as in other major southern cities, a longstanding historical relationship existed between social status, occupation, color, and wealth. The vast majority of the slaves were black, illiterate, unskilled, and prohibited from owning property. In contrast, Charleston's free persons of color were mainly light complexioned, literate, skilled workers who sometimes owned real estate and personal property, including slaves. According to contemporaries, some even "sympathized (or professed to sympathize) with the rebellion" and took steps to distinguish themselves from the larger slave population. Tendencies such as these resulted in a certain amount of tension between slaves and members of the free brown elite.[64]

The distinct advantages enjoyed by those with a heritage of freedom translated into social privilege during Reconstruction. But the background of freedom was esteemed for more than the socioeconomic advantages it conferred; it acquired social value in and of itself. After emancipation destroyed the special status enjoyed by free persons of color, many in the group, especially members of the elite, distinguished the mass of freedmen from themselves and referred to one another as "free issues" or "bona fide free." On one occasion, Jane Van Allen, an American Missionary Association employee, found this tendency pronounced among the elite and observed that "many of the 'brown people' here, think they are a great deal better than those who were slaves; and wherever you meet them, they are sure to tell you, that they were free; but they think the Northern people must think the colored people are just as good as they are."[65]

Along with the dichotomy between free persons of color and freedmen, the legacy left by the antebellum system of racial slavery made complexional differences the basis for additional divisions within the black community. Just as before the war, mulattoes often valued their light complexion because it revealed their white ancestry. In its most crass form, the worshiping of fair complexions led some to view their darker brothers and sisters contemptuously. On one occasion, a newspaper reporter observed "two showily dressed colored girls, attended by a black servant woman, who got into the street railway cars, and upon entering, one of the girls ordered the 'mauma' to stay on the platform." When the conductor requested that she find a seat, the servant refused, saying, "Oh Lor' bless you massa, no missus wouldn't 'low it." After the conductor made it clear that riding on the outside of the car was a violation of the law, the woman took a seat by her mistress, "who appeared quite indignant that black folks should be allowed to ride side by side with 'ladies.'" On another occasion, a visitor to Charleston remarked that "on the walk outside my window, a couple of ebony damsels and a mulatto boy are belaboring one another in terms more vigorous than select as to each others claims to 'respectability' on the ground of color."[66]

Complexional considerations could influence the pattern of institutional development. While the Phoenix Band was "a full blooded organization," the Chicora Band was composed of mulattoes. This was even more graphically revealed at Avery Institute, a private school for Afro-Americans. A large segment of the school's students were the fair-skinned children of the elite, and since the teachers were either white or mulattoes, the arrival of a black teacher created dissension among some students. According to the principal, "some said they should leave the School rather than be taught by a black teacher." Such sentiments were not rare. "The light *colored* people in this city are . . . quite as much prejudiced against the *negro* as many of the whites. And Mrs. Shaw being undoubtedly a pure negro had this prejudice to contend with."[67]

While the mulatto valued the admixture of white blood, darker blacks often reveled in their unadulterated African ancestry. One ex-slave recalled that "after freedom I got mannish. Wid not a drop of blood in me but de pure African, I sets out to find a mate of the pure breed." Some darker blacks were even scornful of the mulattoes, whom they viewed as enigmas. After two mulatto boys began to argue over the shade of complexional difference between them, a "jet black" youth contemptuously remarked, "You ain't white people, an' you never kin be niggers. You'se just nuffin at all. As foh me, I'se pure blooded black nigger . . . lemme tell you. It makes me tired to hear two mulatto niggers talking like dat." According to a New York *Times* correspondent, "it is a common thing to hear an ebony rice-field hand say of some cream-colored city dandy; Dat white washed nigger am just like a mule. He ain't got no country and no ancestor."[68]

Northern blacks were highly critical of the degree of color prejudice among black Charlestonians, and Martin R. Delany attempted to show its destructive force by explaining its origins as part of a ploy by the slaveholders to divide and control the disunited black population. But it seems that even northern blacks may not have been oblivious to gradients of color because, as one upper-class mulatto noted, "It is a singular fact that the black men from the North prate so much about the distinction we, the 'browns' make between ourselves and the 'black,' and yet every black man who comes here from the North brings with him a mulatto wife, and those who get married here look for the 'brownest' woman they can find."[69]

With the destruction of the status of free blacks, the forces of racism impinged on Charleston's entire black population more uniformly than ever before. Within this context, complexion did become less relevant as an index of status, and one contemporary observer reported that "the old jealousy between blacks and mulattoes is disappearing." However, complexional differences continued to influence the interpersonal relations of black Charlestonians, and in the early 1880s, the *New Era* lamented what it described as this "GREAT EVIL" by which "the blackman is prejudiced against the brown man, and—vice versa; the 'dark brown' against the 'light brown,' and so on, from the deepest dark to faintest tint of color."[70]

The era of Reconstruction and the years shortly thereafter represent a critical period for the evolution of social structure in black Charleston. Emancipation destroyed the quasi-caste system of the antebellum years that had divided blacks into slave and free. Consequently, a more viable community was created. Social cleavages continued to exist but were now formed more clearly along class lines. The process of social stratification was enhanced and accelerated by the relative fluidity of the period. Although all black workers were presented with new employment possibilities, those without skills were least able to benefit from these opportunities and were relegated to the ranks of the lower class. The middle class fared better. Many of its members were skilled workers; others, as a result of their sheer industriousness and frugality, were able to accumulate modest amounts of real and personal property. The most accomplished members of this group even established small-scale businesses.

Some of the changes occurring during the period were most evident among the members of the upper class. Many such persons were skilled tradesmen who accumulated relatively large amounts of property. Some established substantial businesses. The upper class also included new groups that were esteemed because of their professional standing and influence within the community. These were typically ministers and teachers, but doctors, lawyers, and government officials were also included among this group. Even at this early date, the existence of the professionals was dependent entirely upon black constituencies, and the appearance of this group demonstrates how rapidly the black community was becoming institutionally complete. Members of the economic elite also benefited, as their community became increasingly developed, but unlike the professionals, their services were not usually limited to the black community. Members of the upper class remained fundamentally integrationist and generally shared the class values of their white counterparts.

Patterns established during the antebellum period greatly influenced the form of postbellum social structure. This was most apparent among the upper class, which was disproportionately comprised of former free blacks. The superior educational attainments, skills, and property accumulation of this group easily translated into positions of privilege and influence after the war. Many of the most affluent members of this group were native Charlestonians who possessed a well-developed espirit de corps and who largely constituted the aristocracy among the upper class. Complexional consciousness remained important in black Charleston and especially so among members of the aristocracy, who often valued light complexions as symbols of their privileged positions.

Finally, Charleston's black community was the scene of a vibrant social life, and while many of its social organizations and activities were new, others had origins in the antebellum period. The latter organizations were usually created by the elite; while they provided pleasurable activity, they also enhanced its exclusivity and group consciousness, reinforcing the established social hierarchy.

An early
school for
freedmen in
the basement
of Zion
Presbyterian
Church.

*Avery Research
Center for African
American History
and Culture,
College of
Charleston*

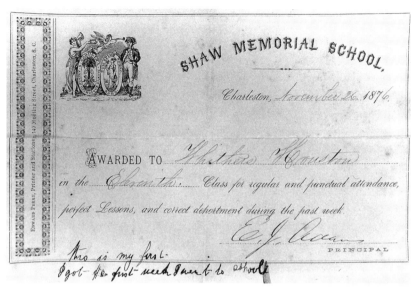

Certificate of exemplary attendance from Shaw
Memorial School issued by Rev. Ennals J. Adams.

*Avery Research Center for African American History and
Culture, College of Charleston*

Avery Institute offered an advanced curriculum
and prepared many future black educators.

*Avery Research Center for African American History and
Culture, College of Charleston*

Avery
Institute
graduating
class, 1880s.
*Avery Research
Center for
African American
History and
Culture, College
of Charleston*

Francis L. Cardozo organized Avery
Institute; he was later elected state
treasurer and secretary of state.

*Avery Research Center for African American
History and Culture, College of Charleston*

Rev. Norman B. Sterrett and
Emanuel A.M.E. Church.

*Black Charleston Photographic
Collection, College of Charleston Library*

Zion Presbyterian Church (ca. 1930s) was the scene for freedmen's political meetings. *Caroliniana Library, University of South Carolina*

St. Mark's Protestant
Episcopal Church
(ca. 1990) had an
elite congregation.

Caroliniana Library,
University of South Carolina

The Centenary
Methodist
Episcopal Church
Steward Board
(ca. 1900).

Caroliniana Library,
University of South
Carolina

Rev. Moses B. Salter of
Morris Brown A.M.E. Church.

*Avery Research Center for African American
History and Culture, College of Charleston*

Rev. John L. Dart of Morris Street Baptist Church.

Avery Research Center for African American History and Culture, College of Charleston

Dr. William D. Crum, a
distinguished Avery Institute
student, later graduated from
Howard University.

Avery Research Center for African
American History and Culture,
College of Charleston

The Unity
and Friendship
Society.

*Black Charleston
Photographic
Collection, College of
Charleston Library*

CHAPTER SEVEN

"BEHOLD A NEW ZION"

The Black Church

No set of antebellum social arrangements was more profoundly affected by emancipation and Reconstruction than that set associated with religion and the church in Charleston's black community. Antebellum blacks sometimes attended churches established specifically for them, and within those confines, acted as leaders among their peers. These activities existed at the sufferance of whites, who regulated them and hoped to add sacred legitimacy to their secular position as masters. But with the end of the Civil War, black Charlestonians rejected many of the old churches, created a well-ordered religious life that served their own interests, and provided a firm basis for the expansion of black religious leadership.

For most black Charlestonians, the decision to desert their former houses of worship was dictated by the imperatives of a well-developed slave religion. One of the most widely adhered-to features of the slaves' eschatology was the powerful Biblical story of the Israelites' deliverance from their Egyptian bondage. Slaves related this Exodus story to their own experience in word and song, which strengthened their resolve to endure the day-to-day hardships of their plight while maintaining a hopeful vision for the future. Their expectation was for a divine redemption no less concrete than that provided to the children of Israel and other Old Testament characters and for delivery to a new promised land.[1] The destruction of the slaveholders' regime in the Civil War fulfilled their most secret yet apocalyptic visions; it now only remained for them to bring order out of the chaos, to give structure and new meaning to their spiritual lives.

A mass exodus of black congregants occurred in the final days of the war and proceeded most rapidly and extensively among the Baptists and Methodists, which evoked a good deal of comment from contemporary observers. In mid-1865, one writer, noting the transformation of religious life in Charleston, remarked that "in fact the colours are Seperated [*sic*] now as to churches. The Blacks, now have Calhoun St. Zion, Old Bethel in Calhoun St. also I believe another Methodist church—Morris St. Baptist and perhaps some other old churches to themselves." A year later the First Baptist Church of Charleston reported that "great changes have taken place, both in the number and constituency of membership; most of the colored members [have] withdrawn for the purpose of forming Churches under the pastoral charge of persons of their own race." In 1859 there were 4,246 blacks in the four Methodist Episcopal South churches in Charleston; yet, by 1866 these same churches failed to report a single black member. The visual impact of the desertions was considerable, and one observer at Trinity M.E. Church South recalled, "some 2,000 colored people used to hold their membership there, and the galleries were always crowded," but now "everything changed [and] the galleries were empty."[2]

For most, severing old church affiliations was an absolute necessity because the southern churches and clerics were tainted as bulwarks of the slave system and as ideologues of secession. One reporter noted that freedmen generally "have had no sympathy with the southern clergy" and "left the societies where white people occupied the best seats and formed societies of their own recognizing no man as master, and no man as slave." In 1865 black Methodists in Charleston held two meetings at Zion Church to consider "their best interests as a religious community." In their reflection on the past, those assembled stated that "we formerly were by force of circumstances, members of the M.E. Church, South, [and] subject to religious bondage, with no rights but to obey orders." With the dawning of religious liberty, the decision was made to "sever forever our relations to the M.E. Church, South, and from its acts of disloyalty to the Government." Given these widespread sentiments, most of those present followed the urgings of their leaders and joined the

African Methodist Episcopal Church. Unfortunately, sometimes there were no denominational alternatives. Margaret Sasportas, who was raised as an Episcopalian and wanted to join that church, reported that she simply "could not under a Rebel Minister."[3]

Initially, most southern churches desired to maintain their black membership. According to delegates at the Southern Baptist Convention of 1866, this was the only way to blunt the influence of the northern churches, to prevent blacks from being educated by Rome "in the vestments of Popery," and to develop a trained group of missionaries to evangelize Africa. Southern whites were generally opposed to receiving the freedmen as equals within the church, however. After leaders of the First Baptist Church discussed how the status of its black members might be affected by emancipation, they concluded that "we are prepared cordially to welcome them to all the ecclesiastical privileges with us which they have heretofore been accustomed to enjoy." That nothing had changed was revealed in the recommendation for "the appointment of a joint committee upon the colored membership of our United Churches, so that Church care and Gospel discipline may be extended to them as formerly."[4]

Black Baptists, enamored of their new freedom, were unwilling to accept a subordinate position and became a discomfiting presence to southern churchmen. One church wrote to the Charleston Baptist Association and complained "that their colored members are in disorder" and requested advice. The South Carolina Baptist Convention revealed that while whites were interested in the spiritual welfare of their black co-religionists, most were unsure how to proceed "at a time when a marked alienation of feeling has been created by fanatical or mercenary interferences from abroad." The problems of interracial adjustment within the Baptist church reached intolerable proportions for the whites, and the Charleston Baptist Association was forced to concede the inevitable. In an 1867 directive, it suggested that "the best course for the Church to pursue, would be to advise the colored members in a friendly way to withdraw and form a separate interest, if they cannot harmoniously co-operate with this church."[5]

The secession of Charleston blacks from the white Baptist church and the establishment of independent Baptist organizations began shortly after the city's occupation by federal troops. Facilitated by the denomination's congregational form of organization, black Baptist churches proliferated rapidly in and around the city. The premier black Baptist church in Charleston was organized in May–June 1865 when several black members of Citadel Square, Wentworth Street, and First Baptist Churches met to consider "the propagation [*sic*] of a Free Baptist Church." Rev. John Bolles and a Reverend Waring, chaplains of the 55th Massachusetts and 102d Michigan Regiments of the U.S. Colored Troops respectively, were invited to attend. In the ensuing discussion over the best organizational strategy, Reverend Bolles observed that "there was only one Church" and advised emulating the "firm unbroken unity of the Nation," which secession had failed to destroy. The assembled leaders decided against forming three separate churches, voting instead to consolidate into a single congregation. The result was the creation of Morris Street Baptist Church under the leadership of Rev. Jacob Legare as pastor; he was assisted by Revs. Edward Lawrence and Charles Smalls.[6]

Both Reverends Legare and Lawrence had been ordained before the war and were leaders, among black members, of the First Baptist Church, while Charles Smalls had been a leader at Citadel Square. The church began with seventy-three persons, but its popularity increased rapidly, and by the mid-1880s, the congregation of Morris Street Baptist Church contained approximately 2,700 members. As the leading black Baptist church in the state, its clergymen were instrumental in establishing Baptist congregations in Charleston and in the surrounding countryside. When the Summerville Baptist Church was created, for example, its members unanimously decided to "place themselves under the watch care of the Morris Street Baptist Church." Clergymen from Morris Street also acted as supply pastors for the Summerville church. Shortly after the organization of Morris Street Church, Rev. Charles Smalls was called upon to organize another group of blacks who left Charleston's white Baptist churches, and in October 1865, under his auspices, Calvary Baptist Church was established. By 1868 its members purchased a lot at the corner of Morris and Smith Streets and, by using the services of their own skilled tradesmen, erected a building. The other two major Baptist churches in the black community, Salem Baptist and the Fourth Baptist Church, were organized from Calvary in 1867 and 1875 respectively.[7]

The diffusion of Baptist churches in black communities throughout the state led many churchmen to call for the coordination of denominational activities. Ministers such as Jacob Legare, Edward Lawrence, and J. C. Pawley of Morris Street Church and Charles Smalls and William Carr of Calvary Church were the avant-garde of this group. Together with representatives from fourteen other churches, these men formed the Gethsemane Baptist Association in November 1867. This was the first black Baptist Association in South Carolina. Although the formation of regional associations would continue, there remained the need for more collaboration at the statewide level. It was the initiatives of Rev. Edward M. Brawley, a native Charlestonian and member of Morris Street Baptist Church, that were largely responsible for addressing this matter. Brawley was representative of the new, rising generation of professionally trained clergymen who became influential in Charleston for the first time during Reconstruction. Born of free black parents, he obtained the rudiments of formal education in Charleston and continued his college preparatory studies in Philadelphia at the Institute for Colored Youth. In 1870 he briefly studied theology at Howard University before entering Bucknell University in Lewisburg, Pennsylvania, in 1871 to continue his theological studies. As a sophomore he was licensed to preach by the local Baptist church and was ordained after graduating in 1875.[8]

After his ordination Brawley was commissioned by the American Baptist Publication Society as a missionary to South Carolina. Once in the state, he began work by establishing additional regional associations and by reorganizing many of those already extant. Brawley's most important accomplishment was the creation of the Baptist Educational Missionary and Sunday School Convention of South Carolina in 1877. The convention drew support from the major associations throughout the state, and several Charleston ministers were prominent among its leadership. Brawley became the organization's secretary and financial agent, while Revs. John C. Butler, J. A. Chase, and Jacob Legare were all members of the board of managers. Two of the objectives of the convention were to assist aspiring ministers to further their theological education and to improve the efficiency of the Baptist Sunday Schools. One of the most important accomplishments of the convention occurred in the field of state missions. In certain areas of the state, there were no qualified Baptist ministers, while in other areas there were only a few.

To coordinate missionary activity, the convention managed a fund generated by the contributions of the regional associations and sponsored missionaries in the areas where their services were most needed. Rev. Edward M. Brawley continued to work with the convention until 1883, when it had 350 ordained ministers and 550 affiliated churches serving the spiritual needs of approximately 100,000 members.[9]

Unlike the Baptist denomination, which expanded almost entirely through the efforts of local leaders, the spirit of Northern Methodism was assisted by representatives dispatched from the national church organization. Rev. Theodore W. Lewis, a Northern Methodist missionary from Massachusetts, was sent to South Carolina and entered Charleston with the Union army in February 1865. Later that year, the Rev. Alonzo Webster, a Methodist missionary from Vermont, arrived and both men began organizing churches throughout the state. Prior to Charleston's collapse, many whites had fled, and there were no Methodist Episcopal Church South ministers present in the city. Consequently, Union army officials gave authority over the Methodist churches to Reverend Lewis. By this time, three congregations of black Methodists were assembled, and, through the efforts of their leaders along with those of Reverend Lewis, all three affiliated with the Northern Methodist church.[10]

Old Bethel M.E. Church was the only one of the three black Methodist churches with origins in the antebellum period. In 1852, when the white members of Bethel Church constructed a new edifice, they allowed the black congregants to use the old frame building. During the war, when all black Methodists were organized into a separate charge known as the City Colored Mission, Bethel was designated as one of its two official meeting places. After Charleston's occupation, the congregation continued worshiping in the old building under the auspices of the Northern Methodists, and in 1880 the congregation was given ownership of the building.[11]

The other two black Methodist congregations were organized during and after the Civil War. St. James, also known as Spring Street M.E. Church South, was used as a military storehouse, but with the city's occupation, blacks began holding regular worship services there, and these continued while the church remained under the authority of Reverend Lewis. By the fall of 1865, the M.E. Church South was allowed to repossess its churches with the exception of Spring Street. Much to the disappointment of Southern Methodists, this church remained under the control of black Methodists until early 1868. By 1873 the Wesley Methodist Episcopal Church, as the congregation came to be known, purchased property located at Meeting and Spring streets and two years later erected its own church building.[12]

When whites reclaimed Trinity M.E. Church from the Northern Methodists in October 1865, native white ministers expressed the hope that "white and colored members might worship according to the plan of the old regime." While meeting with leaders of the black membership, the white pastors "appealed to the old associations" and asked them to "stay with us in your old places in the galleries." In response, Reverend Lewis, who was in the audience, arose and said, "Brethren and sisters, there will be no galleries in heaven. Those who are willing to go with a church that makes no distinction as to race or color, follow me to the Normal School on the corner of Beaufain and St. Phillips Streets." Although some blacks had strong attachments to the southern church, leaders, such as Samuel Weston, only joined with it because, as he recalled, "to have done otherwise would have been insurrection." These persons responded to the irresistible image of the "Old Mother Church" portrayed by Reverend Lewis, "rose to a man," and enthusiastically departed from Trinity. This congregation purchased a building formerly owned by Wentworth Street Baptist Church in 1866, and there established Centenary M.E. Church (the name was chosen because 1866 was the centenary of American Methodism). By 1880–81, Centenary had a membership of almost 1,700 and was the largest and most prominent Northern Methodist church in Charleston.[13]

In Charleston, and generally throughout South Carolina, the Methodist Episcopal Church failed to attract white members. By 1881, of thirty-six thousand Northern Methodists in the state, only sixty-nine were white. Furthermore, the church often met with the overt hostility of southern whites. The remembrance of the bitter controversy in the church during the 1840s, which led to its bifurcation along sectional lines, and the subsequent histories of the factions left wounds that were not easily healed. After the war, the Northern Methodist presence became another symbol of southern defeat. Conversely, for Northern Methodists, the military outcome of the Civil War revealed the essential bankruptcy of southern society. The southern churches and ministers were singled out for special criticism by Northern Methodists, who questioned southerners' spiritual integrity and capacity to effect the will of God. Shortly after the South's defeat, a conference of New England Methodists expressed the belief that the southern church "had been so completely leagured with detestable sin that its representative ministers . . . [were] incapacitated for the work of social and religious regeneration." At the same time, a Northern Methodist bishop believed that "the very conscience of the professedly religious portion of the South was debauched." The ministers were considered especially guilty, and "both preachers and people were backslidden into a depth out of which even the mercy of God might fail to lift them."[14]

These beliefs were quite persistent, and as late as 1870 Rev. Theodore W. Lewis, as chairman of a Methodist committee investigating the religious condition of the country, lamented that "the religious institutions of the South are corrupted, and her garments are moth eaten." This increased the importance and responsibility of the Northern Methodists for the religious transformation of the South. According to Lewis, they were "called upon as faithful watchmen in Zion, to lift up our Voice like a trumpet, and show unto the people their sins, whether they will hear or forbear." It was such attitudes that in part explain the alienation of most white Charlestonians from the Northern Church.[15]

Another source of hostility between Northern and Southern Methodists stemmed from the disputed claims to church property. In Charleston the most bitter dispute of this kind involved the estate of John McKee. McKee was a wealthy Charleston Methodist, who, upon his death in 1831, bequeathed a large portion of his estate to his heirs and stipulated the circumstances under which part of the land must be ceded to the Methodist Church. During the Civil War, these conditions were met, and the M.E. Church South appointed trustees to administer the McKee estate. With the Union occupation of Charleston and the reestablishment of the original Methodist Episcopal Church, that body appointed George Shrewsbury and Charles Holloway, both former free persons of color, as guardians of the McKee property. In 1866 these men, along with the other trustees of the Church, brought a suit against their rivals that charged John R. Mood, the M.E. South administrator, with "conniving, and fraudulently conniving, craftily and subtly, to deceive and defraud" their church of its right to the property.[16]

In the case of *Trustees of the Methodist Episcopal Church v. Dr. J. R. Mood*, tried before the Superior Provost Court for the Military District of Charleston, the plaintiffs argued two basic points. First, they charged that the M.E. South had seceded from the Methodist Episcopal church and that the secessionists did not have the right to take property which was the possession of the general conference. Second, they argued that it was impossible for the secessionists to claim the right to property not possessed by the original church at the time of the secession. In the face of such persuasive arguments, the judge concluded that since the M.E. Church South was not extant at the time of McKee's death, the testator could hardly have desired his property to go anywhere but to the original church. The property was turned over to the Northern Methodists and retained. By the mid-1880s, one of the buildings was used as the Centenary parsonage, while the others were rented and the receipts equitably divided between Charleston's three black Methodist churches.[17]

This particular dispute over church property is important because it also reveals that the attitudes and behavior of former free persons of color were more complex than has been recognized. Both George Shrewsbury and Charles Holloway had been important representatives of the antebellum free brown aristocracy and both were generally regarded as respectable and conservative during the period following the war. Yet, both were still willing to take the considerable personal and financial risk to their own businesses to challenge leading whites over this very important matter. In this regard the action they took was little different from the challenges mounted by less well-established black Charlestonians to white authority in its various forms during the period.[18]

The comparatively egalitarian racial policies of the M.E. Church in South Carolina also precluded the possibility of attracting church support from whites. In 1871 the South Carolina State Conference affirmed its "solemn conviction that the true basis of organization in State or Church is without distinction of race or color." Again, in 1880, when white Methodists from the Southern Central Conference of North Carolina planned to begin the organization of whites in South Carolina, the South Carolina Conference opposed such a step as "a thing inconsistent with the gospel of Christ and the principles of our Church." Furthermore, South Carolina delegates to the general conference were instructed "to inform that body that we do not desire separate work, on the ground of color."[19]

While the professed racial egalitarianism of the Northern Methodists repulsed whites, it stimulated enthusiastic support among blacks. James Holloway, who was called upon to rationalize his Methodism, explained that "I stand on an equal footing with every layman in the Church and is eligible [sic] to any Position my education, training and experience qualify me to fill, and if my sons qualify themselves, and are called of God, there is nothing to bar them from the Bishopric other than votes." Such views were reinforced by the fact that most Northern Methodist ministers in Charleston were black. One of the most impressive Methodist ministers was Rev. Benjamin Franklin Randolph. He was a college-educated northerner who served as a chaplain for a black regiment during the war. Randolph was instrumental in furthering the Northern Methodist cause in Charleston, especially through the columns of the *Charleston Advocate,* a denominational paper that he helped establish and operate.[20]

Most of Charleston's Methodist ministers were from the city and its environs, and several had been important religious leaders during the antebellum period. Indeed, it was in this cadre of experienced men with long-established ties in the community that the northern missionaries found their greatest strength. Without them, it would have been considerably more difficult for any northern denomination to mount an effective missionary campaign because the northern missionaries were inadequately staffed for the purpose.[21]

In reflecting on the growth of the church during the era, one white Methodist clergyman recalled that as an exhorter and class leader at Trinity M.E. Church South, the free black Samuel Weston was "highly respected under the old regime." A black colleague described him as one of "the old veterans of the Cross," who, along with Bishop Whightman, was considered amongst the "mighty men in their day." Weston was a central figure at important religious revivals, and several men who received their early religious training in his class were later called into the ministry. Of this number, the most prominent was Daniel Alexander Payne, the African Methodist minister.[22] During Reconstruction Samuel Weston assisted the Reverends Lewis and Webster in the reorganization of Charleston's churches and ministered to a church in Camden, as well as to Wesley Methodist Church in Charleston, until his death in 1882. Rev. Joseph A. Sasportas, another former free black, had been a local preacher in the M.E. Church South before the war and had ministered to both black and white congregations. During Reconstruction he became the minister for the Summerville Church and also became the first black presiding elder over Summerville District, before accepting an appointment to Old Bethel in 1874.[23]

The Holloway family produced several men who were notable Methodist preachers in Charleston. Richard Holloway established the family tradition in the early nineteenth century, when he began his ministry among blacks in the city. Charles Holloway furthered the tradition with his ordination in 1853 as an exhorter at Trinity and continued his ministry at Centenary Church, where he served as a local preacher, class leader, and superintendent of the Sunday School. During Reconstruction, Mitchell and James H. Holloway were also ordained as Methodist ministers. The leadership of such men made the growth of the Methodist Episcopal church possible, and in Charleston the church included almost three thousand full members and probationers by 1881.[24]

Former slaves also made important contributions to the Northern Methodist missionary campaign, and Abraham Middleton was an outstanding example. As a member of Old Bethel, he was considered an especially devoted Methodist. During the antebellum years, Middleton acquired literacy in a school operated by a free black woman; then he obtained some formal ministerial training after the war and was admitted to the ministry in 1867. He used all his manifold talents in the cause of Methodism and was considered an enthusiastic preacher. According to Rev. W. H. Lawrence, he "organized whole sections of the State into Methodist parishes." As a skilled carpenter, Middleton was literally responsible for constructing twenty-eight churches and for remodeling others, including Centenary, where he refurbished the pulpit and constructed the alter. Reverend Middleton was especially well known in the Pee Dee and Summerville areas, and eventually he was appointed presiding elder for the Port Royal District.[25]

The missionary zeal of the Northern Methodists met with the equal ardor of African Methodism, which eventually became the most popular Methodist denomination among the freedmen. The diffusion of African Methodism in South Carolina began during the Civil War when Rev. James Lynch of Baltimore was dispatched to the state by the general conference. He arrived with the fall of Charleston and began the church's missionary effort. After a series of religious meetings at which Bishop Wayman preached a sermon entitled "I seek my brethren" and Lynch appealed to the black population for support, a group of exhorters, class leaders, and stewards representing Bethel, Trinity, and Cumberland Street M.E. Churches South resolved to join the African Methodists. By mid-May, the former Charlestonian Bishop Daniel A. Payne reentered Charleston for the first time in over thirty years to establish the African Methodist Episcopal church officially. After preaching at several churches, Payne organized the South Carolina Conference on May 16, 1865, with sixteen ministers, among whom were Revs. Richard H. Cain, Theophilus G. Steward, and Augustus T. Carr. All these men took places in the advance guard of the African Methodist missionary effort. Because of these talented men, A.M.E. church leaders hoped South Carolina would become the centerpiece of the church missionary effort in the Southeast.[26]

Amiable relations developed between the A.M.E. and the M.E. Church South, even though the former attracted most of the southern church's black membership. A surprised observer for the *Christian Recorder* noted that "we have the cordial welcome and cooperation, of all Southern [Methodist] clergymen . . . bidding us God Speed, and a hearty good will . . . although in so doing, they give, in some cases, nearly their entire congregations, upon whom they have depended for support." In 1867, a committee of Southern Methodist churchmen that discussed the relations between themselves and the new black churches declared "that we are ready to render them any service, even in their new Church relations, which may be desired, and which may consist with other claims upon us."[27] Southerners preferred the African Methodists because they were less powerful than their Northern Methodist counterparts. The African Methodists were also perceived as being less threatening because their all-black congregations and clergy eliminated the possibility of breaches of the accepted racial etiquette and the establishment of social equality.[28]

Before the construction of the city's largest A.M.E. church building was completed, the Charleston Quarterly Conference of the M.E. Church South granted blacks permission to worship at Trinity Church until they were ready to use their new church. Representatives of the Southern Methodists sometimes attended the conferences of their African counterparts, made speeches that addressed their common concerns, and welcomed them as fellow warriors in Christ. Spokesmen for the Southern Methodist Church captured the spirit of cooperation when they declared that "the best of feelings should be cultivated between the A.M.E. Church and the M.E. Church South [because] . . . we must occupy the Southern field as allies till the colored people become one church." The cordiality that developed early between the two denominations was quickened by the embittered relations between Northern and Southern Methodists. In fact, by 1866 and perhaps earlier, the Southern Methodist Conference directed those blacks who desired to leave their church to join with the African Methodists. Encouraged by this turn of events, Rev. Richard H. Cain could joyously proclaim before a conference of black ministers and laymen that "the kindest feelings exist between the white and colored people of South Carolina; and between the M.E. Church South and the African Methodist Episcopal Church."[29]

Compared with the magnanimity displayed by the Southern Methodists, the encounter between the African Methodists and the Northern Methodists was marked by considerable acrimony. A.M.E. ministers charged that Rev. Theodore W. Lewis and others frequently portrayed their church as "incendiary and insurrectionary in its instructions, and efforts" while publishing articles in the Charleston *Advocate* that were "loaded with a tirade of scandal and abuse of our Church." Matters worsened when Reverend Lewis urged black Methodists to have nothing to do with the A.M.E. Church because it was theologically different and threatened defectors with the loss of their church property. No wonder Reverend Cain observed that the expansion of the A.M.E. Church assumed the character of a "battle" and a "mighty contest." African Methodist ministers criticized the Northern Methodists for contending that their church "was based on the distinction of color" and for creating the impression that whites and mulattoes were barred from membership. Reverend Cain categorically denied that such discriminations existed, because they would retard "the cause of our elevation as a race" and the prosperity of the church.[30]

While African Methodist churchmen denied that their denomination made invidious distinctions based on race, they reaffirmed the continued need for complexional institutions. While Reverend Lewis called for all Methodists to join a single denomination, Daniel Payne argued that "circumstances indicated" it would be a long time before blacks and whites could worship at the same altar in the Methodist Episcopal church. Further, he forcefully pointed out that any "colored man ignored half his own manhood who consented to sit in a gallery or 'negro pew,' and submit to a distinction in the House of God." The larger issue in contention was that of community autonomy and of racial self-esteem.[31] According to one writer, there had always been those, both black and white, who disparaged the idea of separate churches for blacks. Such persons "always want the negro to surrender" his independence. If he had a church, they urged him to "disband it and rush with haste into the bosom of the white brethren. Regardless of terms, which equals are ever wont to consider." In the view of this writer, most blacks thought too much of themselves, their communities, and leaders to barter them away. He thought "they esteem the simple gospel from the lips of their own untutored brethren, better than philosophy from the cultured lips of Saxon cures [sic]." Their own churches were far better than the galleries and back seats preferred by their so-called friends.[32]

The appeals made by the Northern Methodists and especially their criticism of the African Methodist Church exacerbated social cleavages that already existed within the religious community. Although free blacks and slaves had different interests at times, many hoped "freedom's bright rays would dispel the mists of ignorance and prejudice, and that a common interest in churches would have united Christians in their efforts for good among themselves." However, this was failing to occur because of the deception of the Methodist Episcopal ministers, who, according to one man, were "seeking to divide us, and foster and encourage strife and unkindness among us, by keeping up those distinctions which have been our ruin."[33]

Richard H. Cain also noted that "the name of the African M.E. Church was pronounced, by a certain class in this city, to be a disgrace; and one went so far as to say, that if Bishop Payne would return North he would pay his passage back." This animosity resulted from the misconception of those "who had established caste distinctions in society on a false basis—a basis which existed under the old regime, but which is repugnant to every instinct of a high minded freeman and incompatible with the genius of liberty." The ambivalence and hostility between darker- and lighter-complexioned blacks had "been fanned and kept alive by the ill advice of their leader [who] counsels them to a continued separation and antagonism among themselves, and a warfare with those with whom they were formerly identified, in church relations, as pastors and flocks." The counsel of Northern Methodist leaders did not go unheeded. According to another who witnessed the enmity between rival Methodists, the seeds of discord had been so thoroughly planted by the M.E. Church that its members "who are under T.W. Lewis jurisdiction, are as bitter (some of them) against their former classmates as if they were enemies."[34]

For some African Methodists, the integrity of the Methodist Episcopal church had yet to be demonstrated, and, for them, its history of racism belied any professions of Christian brotherhood. After much searching, one black critic found it was impossible to determine what the Northern Methodists had done to benefit blacks during the antebellum years. On the other hand, the same man charged that "their ministers generally lent their influence to the oppressor," excluded blacks from their annual conferences, and forced proslavery ministers on black congregations. These pastors "would preach over a deceased member's remains and refuse to speak of him as a 'Brother' and also refuse to take a colored child in their arms to baptize it." Moreover, black elders and deacons had been required to accept the rite of ordination in private. According to this critic, Northern Methodists certainly were not in a position to lecture to their southern counterparts. This was because "if they have gotten rid of their ANTI-Negroism disease, they certainly have not been rid of it long, for we do not yet behold in their organization the healthful glow of the spirit of liberty."[35]

The same considerations led a correspondent for the *Christian Recorder* to ask rhetorically what Northern Methodists expected to gain by "opposing the establishing of a church, by black men among black men?" Why would representatives of that church "seek to tear down the work of colored men among colored men, the very people whom they profess to come to benefit. . . . Cannot a colored man be just as good a Christian worshipping under a black bishop as under a white one, who has no interest in his race[?]" For these and other reasons, many African Methodists concluded that the Northern Methodist ministers were unscrupulous in their methods and paternalistic if not racist in their attitudes toward blacks. The activities of Rev. Theodore Lewis and his supporters seemed to confirm these beliefs and led one A.M.E. minister to describe him as "this Judas who comes here to rule over our people with his Yankee rod of iron."[36]

In spite of denominational contention, the banner of African Methodism advanced steadily, propelled by the activities of a corps of ably trained and aggressive clergymen. One of the most outstanding members of this group was Richard Harvey Cain. Born in Ohio in 1825, Cain was originally licensed to preach in the Methodist Episcopal Church; after becoming dissatisfied with it, he later joined the African Methodists. Cain studied at Wilberforce University for a year, later took charge of a church in Brooklyn, New York, and was ordained as an elder by Bishop Payne in 1862. He remained in New York until the organization of the South Carolina Conference, which he joined in 1865. Once in South Carolina, Cain succeeded James Lynch as the missionary responsible for ministering to the Sea Islands and the lower part of the conference as far south as Savannah. Reverend Cain was the living embodiment of the church militant, and under his auspices churches were established in Summerville, Lincolnville, Georgetown, Marion, and Sumter besides in Charleston, which became the focal point of his efforts. By 1871 he was appointed the presiding elder for Charleston District.[37]

In and around the city, Cain found ample support among black pre-war religious leaders. In fact, Rev. Theophilus Steward believed that the A.M.E. church succeeded as a result of its "policy of ordaining the 'old leaders' and sending them out to preach as best they could." One such person was Augustus Thomas Carr. Born a slave, Carr purchased his freedom and that of his family and before the war operated a lucrative livery stable business in Georgetown. Carr became a member and class leader in the M.E. Church South; Cain met him at Georgetown and received him into the A.M.E. Church along with approximately three thousand of his followers. Carr was ordained as an itinerant minister in 1866 and later served in the A.M.E. churches in Charleston; by the time of his death in 1882, he had been the presiding elder over the Edisto District of the South Carolina Conference for four years. As one of the early founders of African Methodism in the state, Bishop Payne described Carr as Reverend Cain's "most efficient assistant in putting tens of thousands . . . within the jurisdiction of the A.M.E. Church."[38]

Richard Vanderhorst was another notable antebellum religious leader who continued to act in that capacity under the auspices of the A.M.E. church. Born a slave in Charleston, he obtained his freedom before the Civil War. Vanderhorst had been a leader among the Southern Methodists, but in 1865 joined the A.M.E. church as a local preacher. Eventually he left it to become one of the first bishops in the Colored Methodist church.[39]

The previous history of the African Methodist church in Charleston was especially important for its success during Reconstruction. Its new representatives, such as Richard H. Cain, viewed themselves not as creating African Methodism anew, but as reestablishing a broken tradition. Rev. Augustus T. Carr was fond of pointing out that African Methodism began as early as 1822 in Charleston (it actually began earlier), and although the original church was destroyed, "from that Church we have our strength." Carr was alluding to much more than the psychological symbolism the earlier church represented. The legacy of the original African Methodist church was kept alive in the memories of some who lived during that era and then became active in the church when it was reestablished.[40]

The first African Methodist church constructed in Charleston during Reconstruction was built by the architect and contractor Robert Vesey, the son of the famous Denmark Vesey, and perhaps himself a member of the church. More important were the activities of John Graham. Born a slave on John's Island in 1803, he came to Charleston, where he seems to have been associated with the ill-fated African church and later became a class leader and preacher in the Southern Methodist church. With the cessation of war hostilities, Graham organized meetings to effect secession from the M.E. Church South, so that when Bishop Payne entered Charleston, he found "that no small number were packed up and ready to move here . . . for some in this Conference had been well informed of the A.M.E. Church." John Graham was ordained in 1865 and during the remainder of his life was assigned to the Mission of James and John's Islands and to the churches on Mt. Pleasant, where he acted as presiding elder.[41]

With such dedicated leadership, the African Methodist Episcopal church flourished in Charleston. African Methodists under Reverend Cain's charge originally worshiped in Zion Presbyterian Church. When this was no longer possible, despite "the unsettled state of affairs, and the exceedingly high prices of all kinds of building materials," Cain raised enough money from his congregation to purchase a lot and began constructing a church. Emanuel A.M.E. Church, as the edifice was known, was located on Calhoun Street, east of Meeting, and was built at a cost of approximately twenty-two thousand dollars. Emanuel, which seems to have been the largest church in the connection, was known as "the mother church of African Methodism in the State" and by 1883 had a membership of almost four thousand. Charleston's two other major A.M.E. churches were spawned by Emanuel.[42]

During Richard H. Cain's three-year pastorate, the congregation purchased a building from the Lutheran church in Morris Street, and in 1867 the Morris Brown A.M.E. Church was organized there. Emanuel's membership continued to grow, and the ministerial responsibilities became too great for one person. Rev. Norman Bascom Sterrett, a later pastor, devised a plan to divide the congregation, and his members purchased the old Glebe Street Presbyterian Church property (also known as Zion Presbyterian Church on Glebe Street), and in 1882 the Mt. Zion A.M.E. Church was organized. By the early 1880s, with approximately five thousand members, African Methodism was the largest Methodist denomination among blacks in Charleston and the second largest denomination in the state.[43]

While the postwar expansion of African Methodism was impressive, by the mid-1880s the denomination was facing serious internal problems. In an article entitled "The Dangers of the Hour," Rev. Paul E. Jefferson, presiding elder for Charleston District, was highly critical of dissidents among the laiety and clergy, who at this time demanded changes in the structure and operation of church government. While the radical nature of some of the proposals was unsettling to conservative leaders (i.e., selection of ministers by election rather than by appointment), Jefferson was especially dismayed by those leaders who defied the law of the church to accomplish their goals.[44] The city of Charleston was not immune to these influences, and several of the local A.M.E. churches were the scenes of militant dissension.

Beginning as early as 1874, many members of the South Carolina Conference objected to the distribution of the conference claims and charged that the funds raised in the South were used almost exclusively to benefit northern clergymen and the northern interests of the church.

Dissatisfaction over this issue continued during the early 1880s, as southern African Methodists decried the disproportionate influence northerners exercised within the church at large.[45]

In South Carolina, one of the major critics of A.M.E. officialdom was a native Charlestonian, Rev. William E. Johnson. So highly critical was Johnson of northern influence in the church that in 1884 he "denounced the pastors of the A.M.E. Church as 'carpet-baggers and mushrooms'" and declared his intention of organizing an Independent A.M.E. church of the South. Johnson was suspended for insubordination at the annual conference that year and became the second minister suspended in as many years. A year earlier Rev. J. E. Hayne, another Charlestonian, had been suspended. Disciplinary measures taken against these two well-known men led many to conclude that northern interests, intent on dominating the church, were committed to dismissing southern preachers "who have any independence of character or of speech." Reverend Johnson was undaunted, and in April he took possession of a meeting held at Graham's Chapel from Rev. J. E. McKnight, the presiding minister, in order to dramatize his cause. As a result, many members left the church, joining the entire congregation of Trinity Chapel (which McKnight also had charge of), to worship with Johnson in a new location.[46]

The most dramatic confrontation occurred at Morris Brown Church, where Rev. Samuel Washington, a native of Nevis, had been the pastor for approximately one year. The suspensions of Reverends Hayne and Johnson brought Reverend Washington into conflict with Samuel B. Garrett, a local preacher, a member of Morris Brown, and now one of Johnson's staunchest adherents. In addressing the congregation, Garrett told his listeners that they were being oppressed and announced that rather than endure continued abuse, he and his supporters would withdraw from the denomination and form another church. Consequently, Garrett was also suspended for insubordination.[47]

The event that precipitated near violence at Morris Brown was a disputed church election in which Garrett's sympathizers accused Reverend Washington of, among other things, extreme partisanship, of interference with the responsibilities of the trustees, and of procedures that were contrary to the church Discipline. Shortly after the disputed election, a mob of approximately three hundred persons led by Samuel

Garrett came to the church to shut it down. After placing locks on the doors, they ordered Washington to leave. When he refused, a crowd armed with sticks gathered around him threateningly, while Garrett and another man forcibly carried him out of the building. After another confrontation, Reverend Washington and his loyalists managed to regain possession of the parsonage. But the rebels retained control of the church and vowed to remain there until the courts decided the lawful owners of the property. The dissidents then chose the suspended Rev. J. E. Hayne as their interim minister.[48]

At least five churches in and around Charleston were rent by similar rebellions. Along with Morris Brown and Trinity Chapel in the city, St. Peter's on John's Island, Payne's Chapel on James Island, and the Lincolnville Mission were embroiled in the controversy. The problems of African Methodism in Charleston understandably attracted the attention of the 1884 general conference. During the course of discussion, Presiding Elder Paul W. Jefferson addressed the delegates on the effects that recent events in Charleston would have on the future of African Methodism both regionally and nationally. He admonished the conference to make no concessions to the rebels lest dissatisfaction be encouraged throughout the South. He charged that an influential group of men had planned to secede from the A.M.E. church and that these persons had done everything within their power to bring calumny upon the church to further their own interests.[49]

The seriousness of the Charleston dispute required the general conference to dispatch Bishop Henry M. Turner there in hopes of resolving the controversy. Although tempers flared in the course of a very heated meeting, the participants generally expressed a willingness to remain in the church. Bishop Turner then announced that Reverend Washington would be restored for twenty-four hours as pastor of Morris Brown and would afterwards be transferred to a church in Louisville, Kentucky. Turner terminated the suspension of Rev. J. E. Hayne, who was thus virtually assured of receiving the appointment at Morris Brown because of his tremendous support among its members. By effecting this compromise, Turner was able to keep the Morris Brown congregation in the A.M.E. church. Although the breach was repaired at Morris Brown, Rev. William E. Johnson remained outside the African Methodist church, and in 1885 he created and assumed leadership of the Independent African

Methodist Episcopal church, which derived some of its support from recalcitrant dissenters in Charleston.[50]

In contrast to the enthusiasm black Methodists and Baptists evinced for establishing separate churches, many of the Presbyterians were extremely reluctant to sever the ties with their original churches. One man told Rev. Thomas D. Smyth, the prominent Presbyterian divine, that blacks initially refrained from joining an independent church while they waited to see the course of events, "hoping on your return with nucleus retained to build up [the] congregation . . . As their Shepherd it was only for you to hold forth crook and they would have flocked to your standard." Rev. John L. Girardeau of Zion Presbyterian Church fled Charleston, served as chaplain to a Confederate regiment, and was imprisoned during the war. Despite this, he recalled "one of the first invitations, in writing, which I received . . . to resume labor, was from this colored membership, entreating me to come back and preach to them as of old." After Girardeau returned and obtained possession of his church, it merged with Glebe Street Presbyterian Church while retaining its original name. Most of the churches' black members attended the original Zion Church, while the whites attended the Glebe Street branch. This plan of organization allowed black Presbyterians to elect their own deacons and elders, but they could only be represented in the upper courts of the church by their pastor and by the elders of the white church.[51]

In 1873 the work of the Presbyterian church among blacks was reported as "languishing," and the status of those already within the fold of the Southern Presbyterian church had become increasingly problematic. The South Carolina Synod of that year hotly debated the issue of effecting an ecclesiastical separation from the blacks and the establishment of an Independent African Presbyterian Church. This same matter was broached at the general assembly of the church in 1874, and the delegates overwhelmingly voted in favor of separation between black and white Presbyterians. When Girardeau convened the black members of Zion and explained that they might withdraw from the church, he found that while the elderly members vigorously opposed the idea of separation, "Young Africa," which was in the majority, favored it. Over 350 of Girardeau's black members left under these circumstances, and by 1879 Zion Presbyterian Church on Calhoun Street was itself affiliated with the Atlantic Presbytery of the Northern Presbyterian Church.[52]

Actually, the erosion of Southern Presbyterian influence among black Charlestonians antedated the events of 1873–74. As early as August 1865, Jonathan C. Gibbs, a black minister and missionary of the Northern Presbyterian Church, was dispatched from Philadelphia to Charleston to oversee the church's interests. Reverend Gibbs occupied Zion Church and later brought suit under the Civil Rights Act to retain possession. He unsuccessfully contested the legal title to the property, arguing that since the church had been built for blacks it should belong to the Northern Presbyterians. The restoration of the church property to the Southern Presbyterians provided additional reasons for blacks to desert Zion for other congregations, including Siloam Church (later known as Wallingford United Presbyterian Church), organized by Reverend Gibbs and Elias Gardner in 1867.[53]

Rev. Ennals J. Adams was the most influential of the black Presbyterian ministers. A college-trained pastor from Newark, New Jersey, Adams was well suited for missionary activity, having served the American Missionary Association at the Mendi Mission in Sierra Leone during the Civil War. By May 1865 Adams had relocated to Beaufort where he preached to the freedmen, and by June he had arrived in Charleston. After preaching at Zion Church briefly, he received authorization from the military to take charge of the Glebe Street Church, where on July 30 he began services for the city's freedmen and for the black troops of the Fifty-fourth Massachusetts Regiment. Shortly thereafter, the Glebe Street property was returned to the Southern Presbyterians, and Adams decided to establish a New School Presbyterian Church. In early October 1865, he, along with newly elected elders Robert Howard, William Ford, and Robert Morrison and a congregation of fourteen full members, held services at the New School Mission Presbyterian Church.[54]

After the creation of this church, a representative of the black congregation at Second Presbyterian Church criticized the white membership and its minister, Rev. Thomas D. Smyth. At issue was the white membership's "deprecating spirit of exclusiveness" that excluded blacks from the "rights due to all church members in good standing regardless of majority or caste." Consequently, the black congregants found it necessary to form "separate organizations . . . to attest to Whites . . . [their] desire to worship God unmolested under [their] own vine and fig tree."

These men and women joined Reverend Adams' church. Black members of the Scot's Presbyterian and the First Presbyterian churches also united with Mission Presbyterian Church, and by 1867 its congregation consisted of between three hundred and four hundred persons. That same year, under Adams' leadership, plans were laid and construction begun on the church's first building, located on George Street between King and St. Philip streets.[55]

While the Protestant Episcopal church experienced losses similar to those of its competitors, its leaders conceded such defections unwillingly. In 1866 the Committee on Diocesan Relations to the Colored People declared that "duty, interest, humanity and religion, all urge us to prompt and vigorous exertion, to keep or to reclaim, to the wholesome teaching of the Church, this numerous and important class of our population." The Diocesan Council hoped that by establishing missions and congregations "consisting in whole or in part of Colored People" (as had already been done around Beaufort), those who had taken flight to the exclusively black churches might be induced to return to their former denominational affiliation.[56]

Charleston was one of the few places in the entire state where separate Episcopal churches for blacks existed prior to the Civil War. Calvary Church was originally established for slaves in 1849, and as an Episcopal mission station, it continued to attract a small congregation of freedmen throughout Reconstruction. Initially, though, the Union occupation of Charleston had led to the closing of all the Episcopal churches. When a few of the white churches did reopen, many blacks who had previously attended them found that there was little or no room, even in the galleries where they had previously worshiped. Because of this, a group of prominent former free black Episcopalians reluctantly left their churches. Motivated by "an ardent desire to avail ourselves again of the instruction of the Church in which we were reared," they began temporary services at the Orphan House Chapel. There they organized St. Mark's Protestant Episcopal Church. The most prominent members were unwilling to completely reject the past and elected Rev. Joseph Seabrook, a white minister, as rector because he had been a long-time friend and spiritual mentor.[57]

Bishop Thomas Davis rejoiced at the emergence of St. Mark's congregation, an event which seemed to bode well for the future of the church among blacks. In writing to the church vestrymen, he stated, "I have been very anxious to know whether they [the blacks] would all hold on to the Church or not. I do not know and cannot know yet of all the rest, but it is cheering and encouraging to see you all stepping out so soon and so boldly for your old faith." In 1866 St. Mark's congregation purchased a building and by 1876 began the erection of a new edifice, located at Warren and Thomas Streets, at a cost of $15,000. By this time, St. Mark's had grown to 187 communicants and had a total membership of 506. Its members raised over $2,300 for the diocese during the convention year of 1875, which made their church one of the largest in terms of its contributions. The members also contributed disproportionate amounts to the University of the South and to the relief fund for the widows of deceased clergymen, despite the fact that blacks could not attend the university nor were there any black clergymen in the diocese at this time.[58]

Despite the singularity of its congregation, which was "composed of the thriftiest and most respectable class of colored people" in Charleston, and its exemplary contributions to the larger church, St. Mark's failed to receive full acceptance by its white brethren. Shortly after its organization, St. Mark's leaders consulted Bishop Davis regarding the wisest course to follow in seeking admission to the diocese. They were counseled to wait until a later date when whites had better adjusted to the momentous changes that had occurred in the South. Ten years later, in 1876, St. Mark's congregation applied for admission, and this matter became a focal point of debate at the Diocesan Convention of 1876.[59]

Some of those in favor of admission appealed to the delegates' sense of Christian duty, maintaining that St. Mark's met all the requirements established by the diocesan constitution and canons, and argued that any other course would abridge the church's ecclesiastical rights. Others emphasized the unique qualities of this congregation, the respectability and prominence of its members as well as their historically intimate relations with whites. In fact, one delegate firmly believed that although St. Mark's congregation was "not of our race," they were "yet closely allied to it, and more in sympathy with us than with the blacks." The admission of such a congregation would more completely bind them to the Episcopal church and "may make them a link between us and the scattered members of our former charge [while] their refusal would repel them from our doors, and weaken our hold upon them, and upon the colored race in South Carolina."[60]

Those opposed to St. Mark's admission believed its entry would establish a precedent for the admission of other black congregations and would thus diminish the influence of the white laity. Others argued that representatives of St. Mark's need not be admitted to enjoy their rights as Christians, while some questioned the ability of the church to send qualified delegates. Finally, it was feared that the presence of a congregation such as St. Mark's, comprised as it was of so many former free persons of color, would be dangerous because "it is this class in which miscegenation is seen, and which tempts to miscegenation." Such persons would demand social equality, and this would alienate many of the white parishes, which were already drifting away. Because of the nonconcurrence of orders when the vote was taken—the clergy voted favorably and the lay delegates voted negatively—the application of St. Mark's for admission was rejected. This controversial subject led many white Episcopalians to call for the organization of blacks into missionary episcopates that would allow them to establish a separate convention.[61]

The Protestant Episcopal church was as opposed to the abridgment of racial etiquette in the acceptance of clergymen as it was to the seating of black laymen at Diocesan conventions. Rev. Thaddeus Saltus, the first black assistant minister at St. Mark's, was ordained to the diaconate in 1881 and a year later to the priesthood. He was the first black to be admitted to the holy orders of the Protestant Episcopal church in South Carolina.[62]

So vocal was the opposition to Saltus's ordination that the Standing Committee of the Diocese appended resolutions to their report that reaffirmed their commitment to white supremacy in the church. That body declared that "the race in possession of the higher gifts" was responsible for remedying the spiritual deficiencies of the black population. Anything contrary to this position "would reverse the order of missionary operations and even of nature itself." The committee was certain that neither race could gain if "the race having the lesser Christian knowledge and culture should be advanced to the position of teachers of the other race." It was only the exceptional nature of Saltus's case and the realization that his activities would be limited to St. Mark's and other "similiar" congregations that allowed his credentials to be approved. In the Diocesan Conventions of 1882 and 1883, Saltus was admitted with all the privileges of the convention. Nevertheless, at the Diocesan Convention of 1885 the laity vigorously protested the seating of black clergymen and unsuccessfully attempted to have black clergymen's names excluded from the list of clergy.[63]

The number of black Congregationalists in Charleston had never been large. During the antebellum years, most attended the Circular Congregational church, but when this edifice was destroyed during the Great Fire of 1861 and a smaller building was subsequently erected, many of the black congregants left the church. Some, mainly the younger former members, joined other denominations; others began separate services in an old chapel owned by the Circular church. In 1867 the latter established Plymouth Congregational Church with Reverend Merritt, an American Missionary Association missionary, as their pastor. Despite support from the A.M.A., Plymouth never flourished during Reconstruction. Plagued by financial problems, factionalism among its membership, and Congregationalism's apparent lack of appeal, its membership was only 198 by 1876.[64]

The church, like so many other institutions, reflected the socioeconomic differentiation of the black community; even so, the lines of social distinction separating denominations were not rigidly drawn. Generally, the Baptist and Methodist churches drew their congregations not only from Charleston proper but from the surrounding countryside and the nearby Sea Islands as well. By the mid-1880s, Morris Street Baptist Church, with a membership of approximately 2,700, maintained ten mission stations outside the city. The congregations of the Baptist and Methodist churches were generally made up of freedmen similar to the members of Emanuel A.M.E. Church, who were described as "common laborers, and have nothing to depend upon for a living but their hard earned daily wages." Nor were the officers of these churches prominent. Of the stewards and trustees of Emanuel and Morris Brown A.M.E. churches, only two of twenty-six could be classified as members of the upper class in 1880.[65]

While Plymouth Congregational church and Mission Presbyterian church attracted some members of the elite,[66] Centenary Methodist and St. Mark's Protestant Episcopal churches were, more than any others, the favorite churches of the black upper class. Centenary was in many ways quite different from all the other Methodist churches. The vast majority of its congregation resided in the city of Charleston proper, and a large number of its leaders and members had been free persons of color before the war. Among the most socially prominent families at Centenary were the Westons, Wilsons, Johnsons, Millses, Browns, Sasportases, Hamptons, McKinlays, Ransiers, Holloways, Ryans, and Wigfalls. These and other black families were among the wealthiest in Charleston. Of the stewards and trustees listed for 1881, nine of twenty-one were included among the upper class. Of the first twelve pastors at Centenary, nine were white, and when black ministers were selected for the church, the congregation (even until the mid-twentieth century) was always concerned with the physical characteristics of the pastor and his wife, the preference being for those of light complexion.[67]

Many upper-class churchgoers who did not attend Centenary worshiped at St. Marks. Of the original eight vestrymen and wardens, seven have been identified, all of whom had been free persons of color before the war. In describing the congregation, the *News and Courier* stated that it was "well known" that St. Mark's was "composed of a most intelligent and respectable portion of the colored citizens of Charleston"; the most socially prominent families that held memberships there were the Walls, Maxwells, Mushingtons, Kinlochs, Elfes, Leslies, Dacosters, Montgomerys, Inglisses, Dereefs, Bennetts, McKinlays, O'Hears, Greggs, Houstons, and Bosemans. Of the wardens and vestrymen in 1880, six of nine were included in the upper class. St. Mark's congregation was overwhelmingly composed of mulattoes, many of whom were as color conscious as they were class conscious. Ed Barber, a light complexioned ex-slave, recalled "tramping" about Charleston and attending St. Mark's, where, according to his testimony, "all de society folks of my color went to." He explained that were it not for his "bright" complexion he would not have been admitted because, "no black nigger welcom [*sic*] dere, they told me."[68]

The exclusivity of St. Mark's was living testimony of the ambivalence and even aversion some members of the old free brown elite continued to show to their darker complexioned brethren of slave ancestry. Furthermore, the congregation's selection of a prominent minister from the old regime as its rector and the struggle for admission to the

Diocesan Convention reveals the brown elite's continued attempt to ingratiate itself with leading southern whites.

Cultural differences between black Charlestonians were also reflected in their denominational affiliations. Such distinctions were seen most graphically in the different characteristics of the religious services of the upper class, and those held by working class blacks. Many of the upper class, especially former free persons of color and their descendants, found the liturgical, formal services and deliberative sermons of the Presbyterian, Congregational, Episcopal, and some Methodist churches appealing. Rev. Benjamin F. Jackson of Plymouth Congregational Church delightfully explained that shortly after his arrival, the congregation requested him to preach a series of doctrinal sermons that covered an array of major theological ideas. In mid-1865 Thomas Cardozo, an American Missionary Association teacher and brother to Francis Cardozo, was frustrated because he did not feel comfortable with the form of worship found in most of Charleston's black churches. The religious services offered by the black Episcopalians were the exception, however, because according to him these congregations "worship intelligently."[69]

Working class blacks that belonged to churches were generally more at home in the Baptist and Methodist churches. The freedman Ed Barber found the worship service at St. Mark's distressing, and he recounted "how they did carry on, bow and scrape and ape de white folks. I see some pretty feathers, pretty fans, and pretty women dere! I was uncomfortable all de time though . . . cause they was too 'hifalootin' in de ways, in de singin' and all sorts of carrin' ons." The services in the pietistic churches were devoid of the sacerdotalism and ritualism found in the liturgical churches attended by the upper class. The characteristic form of worship was more informal, and the ministers' sermons were more emotional and invited a high level of ecstatic lay participation. The members of these churches believed in a highly personal God who revealed himself as he had in Biblical times.[70]

The demonstrative religion practiced in the services and prayer meetings of these churches was characterized by the outpouring of the Holy Spirit among those who "got glory" and the shouts, visions, and bodily gyrations that sometimes accompanied the process. Meetings such as these evoked much comment among whites, and one observer was amazed at the religious fervor witnessed among a large group of black worshipers, "who spent the entire night in singing, praying and mutual exhortations, with an enthusiasm that would have put to the blush the religious zeal of many a white devotee."[71]

Without question, the church was the most important institution in the black community. Even during the antebellum years, the black congregations of white churches constituted an important touchstone of black life. A leading sociologist of the black church attributes its signal importance among Reconstruction black communities to two related factors. First, it was the single institution with the most inclusive membership; second, so many non-church organizations and activities were dependent upon its physical, organizational, or financial resources.[72] The black church became the arbiter of both public and private morality while it attended to the spiritual needs of the faithful. The black church also served as a place of refuge from the racism and hostility of the white community.[73] Within its confines, it was possible for black men and women to meet on the basis of equality, to determine policy, and to act as leaders and members of a local, regional, and perhaps national organization.

The activities of the church were not limited to the sacred realm. Its presence and activities were especially important in the years immediately following the Civil War. This was because during a time when much of the familiar order was disintegrating because of migration and the breakup of plantation life, the church provided stability and a means to reestablish a sense of community. The church fostered economic cooperation by pooling the resources of individual members for the construction of buildings and for other purposes. Many benevolent societies and mutual aid societies were based on church groups and were also dependent upon pooled resources. Other secular activities were also important. By 1869 some of the city's black churches were cooperating to sustain an orphanage for black youth. Emanuel African Methodist Church maintained a home for the aged on a plantation not far from the city limits. The congregation of Morris Street Baptist Church organized a relief society to assist a large number of destitute blacks who migrated to Charleston in hopes of emigrating to Africa. In 1878, when yellow fever epidemics broke out in Memphis and New Orleans, Charleston's various black churches took up collections for the afflicted in those cities.[74] The social welfare functions of the church were especially important for those in the lower classes, because such persons had few economic resources and experienced considerably diminished life chances.

Although women were relegated to subordinate roles in the church, their services were essential for fulfilling both its sacred and secular mission. Women made up the majority of the membership and played supportive roles when denominational associations met, by making arrangements and securing accommodations for visitors. The missionary effort of the church, care for the sick and indigent, and staffing the Sabbath schools were all important areas of the women's endeavor. Women also played a crucial role as fundraisers; the numerous bake sales, raffles, fairs, and special collections they organized generated the funds for acquiring real estate and constructing new church buildings, as well as for other special projects.[75]

In view of the peculiar significance of the church for the black community and the distinctive identity and problems faced by blacks, many believed that ministers of their own race were best qualified to articulate their concerns. When considering this matter, an editorial in the *Christian Recorder* observed that, just as Irishmen were most suited to preach to Irish congregations and Germans to Germans, black clergymen could best serve the needs of blacks. Rev. Ennals J. Adams implied as much when, shortly after his arrival in Charleston, he lamented that many blacks were reluctant to take bold initiatives and were "in a stand-still condition, for want of master workmen of their own color." The main problem, according to Adams, was that blacks had not been afforded enough opportunities to lead themselves. Rev. Richard H. Cain was of a similar mind and in early 1865 proclaimed that "we know how to serve others . . . but, have not learned how to serve ourselves. We have always been *directed by others* in all the affairs of life: they have furnished the thoughts while we have been passive instruments, acting as we were acted upon, mere automatons." According to Cain, even the abolitionists, who were ostensibly fighting for the interests of the blacks, never placed them in positions of authority or trust.[76] Black churches provided forums for the recruitment and emergence of much-needed leadership skills.

As a national racial enterprise, the leadership and local missionaries of the A.M.E. church articulated a special sense of responsibility and mission for labor amongst the freedmen. Its efforts won special praise, because it provided unique opportunities for leadership and collective action that produced a salutary effect upon the entire black community. Timothy Hurley, a white Republican newspaper editor, declared that the accomplishments of the African Methodist church were testaments to the black community's ability to prosper, to choose competent leaders, and to determine its own destiny. The organization and progress of African Methodism challenged the fundamental assumptions held by racist whites, as it began to efface both the self-doubt and hatred that too many had internalized while slaves, replacing those assumptions with confidence and racial pride. This was no mean task because, as Rev. Richard H. Cain warned: "The people are emancipated but not free! they [sic] are still slaves to their old ideas, as well as to their masters." This was because most had been taught that the whites were superior and "they believe it still." To combat self-contempt, blacks had "to be taught manly dignity, and the value of a name and position."[77]

The work of racial uplift was the special responsibility of black missionaries, according to Reverend Cain, because talented and devoted whites could "teach ever so well, yet it has not the effect to exhalt the black man's opinion of his own race, because they have always been in the habit of seeing white men in honored positions, and respected." When black men were given the opportunity to exhibit "the same great comprehension of facts, this ocular proof of the mind of that class, is tenfold more convincing, and gives an exhalted opinion of the race to which they belong, and enables them to feel that they have a claim to equal manhood with others." In African Methodism, blacks recognized what Cain referred to as "the idea of Nationality of Manhood," which stressed not only religious liberty but self-government and held that the time had arrived for the black man to take his rightful position in the world through such avenues.[78]

Charged with such important responsibilities, as the black church grew, some of its leading ministers called for a more highly educated clergy. All were not immediately convinced of this need, and some questioned displacing the traditional religious leaders with persons who, although theoretically more qualified, might not have the sensitivity and experience of the older generation. This was why the leaders at Morris Street Baptist Church agreed with Deacon Edward Carter in 1865 when he "spoke of the old ministers as, being preferable" to new ones and urged "the rising members [to] get theologians" later, if they chose to. Some among the older generation of religious leaders were apprehensive about the call for more sophisticated clergymen because they were conservative and feared change. As a representative of the educated clergy, Rev. Edward M. Brawley initially met with bitter opposition from the old leaders, who pronounced his innovative proposals for unifying and reorganizing South Carolina's black Baptists radical and unfeasible.[79]

Fortunately, opposition to innovation and to the call for educational improvement diminished, and most concerned persons understood the urgency of developing a formally educated group of clerics. One such person was Rev. James C. Waters. He was encouraged at the prospect that future generations of Methodist pastors would "be a very different something from the characters who now bear that name." Waters was concerned with the all-too-widely-held belief that "if God calls a man to the work he will fit him for it, and [all] that is necessary is merely to 'open your mouth and God will fill it.'" Against this line of reasoning, he concluded that "if God is to be held responsible for what we often hear dropped from the pulpit, he is decidedly a very different character from what the Bible represents him." A committee of Baptist ministers indicated that as increased numbers of blacks completed their training in public schools, they would demand a more educated ministry. In urging their listeners to take heed, the clergymen rhetorically asked, "Are not ministers public teachers? and [sic] how can they teach the people unless they stand intellectually on a higher plane?"[80]

Institutions devoted partially or wholly to the goal of ministerial education were created. In addition to its missionary work, the Baptist Educational Missionary and Sunday School Convention held Ministers' Institutes at its annual conventions. During the course of these sessions, lectures and practical demonstrations were given on topics such as "How to Construct a Sermon and Preach It" and "How to Study and Interpret the Scriptures." Doctrinal sermons that treated an array of theological and scriptural issues were a required part of the convention's annual meetings. The convention also maintained scholarship funds to defray the educational expenses of aspiring ministers. The first educational grant was created by the congregation of Morris Street Baptist Church and was known as the Jacob Legare Annual Scholarship in honor of the church's revered first minister. In the first eight years after its organization, the Baptist Educational Missionary and Sunday School Convention provided financial assistance for sixteen ministerial students.[81]

The Northern Methodists established Baker Theological Institute, which was devoted to the training of ministers and teachers, in 1865. Rev. Samuel Weston, the patriarch among Charleston's black Methodist Episcopal ministers, acted as a trustee for the school. Local African Methodist ministers held theological training sessions at the Charleston Mission and Classical Theological Institute, while in 1871 Payne Institute was established in Cokesbury for the education of the denomination's ministers. Revs. Richard H. Cain and Augustus T. Carr served as trustees for the institute.[82] The establishment of scholarship funds, training conferences, and permanent institutes by the churches enabled many who would have otherwise been unable to do so to pursue a ministerial education. This support ensured a continuous supply of trained clergymen and also ensured that ministers would be an esteemed group in the community, in part because of their educational achievements.

The problem of pastoral education is important to fully comprehend the denominational preferences of black Charlestonians. Of the major denominations surveyed, the Protestant Episcopal and Presbyterian churches required the most comprehensive and rigorous theological education for their ministers. During the antebellum period, such stringent requirements made it difficult to secure enough qualified men in these denominations even to supply the white congregations adequately. At the same time, fearing damage to the "peculiar institution," these denominations were reluctant to utilize blacks as lay preachers to minister to their black members. The stringent educational requirements and the absence of a tradition of utilizing blacks in responsible positions ensured that there would be few black leaders among these churches during Reconstruction. Without men of their own race to act as ministers and lay preachers, most blacks remained unwilling to join churches in which they had no more influence than they had under the old regime.[83]

Bishop Howe of the Protestant Episcopal church realized the problem in 1874, when he urged the annual convention to develop a trained group of black clergymen, "otherwise without their aid, and relying wholly upon a white ministry, I do not see how this Church, which we believe to be Catholic is to make herself felt among the colored people." Nor was the seriousness of this problem lost on the Congregationalists.

When Plymouth Congregational Church was about to be dedicated, the pastor James T. Ford expressed the hope that a prominent black Congregational minister could attend and speak at the dedicatory service. According to Ford, this "would have great influence for good" because "it would help remove the thought too common among colored men here that our church brings them under white domination." The congregation went further and called for the ordination of blacks from among its membership, and it argued "that the church may find more favor in the eyes of the people, by this public recognition of the fitness of colored men to exercise in full the functions of the ministry."[84]

The Baptist and Methodist denominations enjoyed a distinct advantage over the aforementioned churches. Historically, the Baptist and Methodist churches had not required the same degree of rigorous theological training for entrance into the ministry, and pious laymen, who were examined and approved by the association or conference, could become eligible to preach.[85] Even during the antebellum years, a small but influential group of black exhorters emerged to minister to the black congregations. Less stringent formal educational requirements and a tradition of utilizing blacks, many of whom continued their activities after the war, made the Baptist and Methodist denominations particularly attractive to black Charlestonians that strove to create a community of their own design.

Given the influence of the church and the relatively high educational attainments of black ministers, many naturally assumed secular leadership roles along with their strictly pastoral responsibilities. Even before arriving in Charleston, some of these men had established records of leadership. Rev. Ennals J. Adams participated in the northern Colored Convention movement during the 1850s and was also active with Rev. Richard Cain in the African Civilization Society. Rev. Jonathan Gibbs was involved with the Pennsylvania Equal Rights League, several had served in the Union army as regulars or as chaplains.[86] Their interest and involvement in community affairs led some to participate in the politics of Reconstruction. Ministers were able to build support for their leadership as they fulfilled their routine pastoral duties. They also had a relatively secure income and the financial support of their congregations. These factors insulated them somewhat from economic retribution and afforded the opportunity to enter the field of politics. Some attended the Colored People's Convention in 1865 and played a major role in organizing the Republican party. Richard H. Cain, Benjamin F. Randolph, Francis L. Cardozo all served as delegates to the 1868 Constitutional Convention where they promoted the educational, civil rights, and economic interests of their community. The ranks of Randolph, Cain, and Cardozo were joined by Revs. Bruce Williams, William E. Johnston, and William R. Jervey, all Charleston clergymen who also held seats in the state general assembly during Reconstruction.[87]

In 1868 Reverend Ennals J. Adams, the Presbyterian cleric, served as an alderman appointed under military authority. During Reconstruction Rev. Samuel Garrett, a former free person of color from Charleston, became an A.M.E. minister associated with Morris Brown Church. He was exceedingly popular during the period, serving as chaplain of one of the black fire companies, as a member of the Colored Firemen's Union, and as a local labor leader. Such an extensive base of support within the community no doubt assisted him in winning three terms as a municipal alderman during the years 1871–77. In 1872 he was responsible for winning a significant increase in the city appropriation to the Old Folks Home for aged and infirm blacks.[88]

Richard H. Cain was one of the most outstanding examples of the preacher-politicians during Reconstruction. Even while leading the A.M.E. campaign to reestablish the church, Cain was becoming extensively involved in the secular affairs of black Charleston. After the summary arrest, without a hearing or trial, and incarceration of Jefferson Williams, a black youth, for allegedly assaulting a white child, Cain protested immediately to Robert K. Scott of the Freedmen's Bureau. He charged that such travesties occurred all too frequently and that redress was usually not possible. Thanks to his timely intervention, the youth was released.[89]

Cain also had an involved political career. In addition to having served in the constitutional convention of 1868, he was also a member of the state senate from 1868 to 1870 and a member of Congress for two terms, 1873–75 and 1877–79. Throughout his career as a preacher-politician, Reverend Cain showed great concern for the plight of the working class. In the constitutional convention and later in the senate, he was one of the leading advocates of the South Carolina Land Commission and of policies to assist the freedmen to acquire land. Cain also purchased over five hundred acres of land north of the city near Summerville on which he created a new suburban town, known as Lincolnville. During Reconstruction he sold plots to black families and intended it to become an all-black town. Although he encountered ongoing legal difficulties in implementing his plan, by the mid-1880s the town consisted of about one hundred homes, almost wholly owned by blacks.[90]

Reverend Cain supported civil rights legislation and took the lead in demanding that white Republicans share power and offices more equitably with blacks. Through the columns of his newspaper, the *Missionary Record,* he showed himself to be an outspoken critic of Republican corruption and, much to the chagrin of his colleagues, sometimes supported Democrats if he considered them to be more honest and capable.[91]

As a highly articulate group, black clergymen were often called upon to act as spokesmen for the community's general concerns. The abrupt overthrow of political Reconstruction in 1876 led many blacks to contemplate emigration to Africa. In Charleston, emigrationist sentiment was galvanized by the formation of the Liberia Exodus Joint Steamship Company. Several of the organization's most dynamic members were ministers, most notably Rev. Benjamin F. Porter, who served as its president. By mid-1885, after several incidents of racial violence, including the murder of the prominent black Stephney Riley by a wealthy white man, the black citizenry was so outraged that many expected a race riot to ensue on the day of Riley's funeral. It was perhaps only due to the influence of black ministers through their churches that violence was averted. When it became apparent that Riley's assailant might escape conviction by legal maneuvering, meetings were organized by black clergymen to express the community's indignation. At one meeting, several ministers remonstrated that unless blacks were accorded equal justice, "it may not be long before the revolution of St. Domingo in the times of Toussaint L'Overture will be repeated in the South." According to a prominent white clergyman, the speech of Rev. J. E. Hayne was so fiery and "sweeping in its denunciations of recent deeds of wickedness" that it was largely responsible for the grand jury's return of a true bill against the accused murderer.[92] A deteriorating climate of race relations was only one of many issues black ministers were routinely expected to confront as they fulfilled a multiplicitly of roles in their increasingly complex community.

Reconstruction brought about the reordering of religious life in Charleston. At this time most blacks were as unwilling to accept positions of subservience in their spiritual lives as they were in their secular lives. They therefore deserted the white churches with which they had been affiliated to form independent ones under their own authority. Although they faced numerous problems that stemmed from the racism of southern whites, denominational rivalries, internal dissensions, and from the poverty of most of their members, the expansion of black churches in Charleston was phenomenal. Sometimes the work of missionaries from the North and the Upper South facilitated the spread of particular denominations. However, the proliferation of black churches and denominations did not represent a complete break with the past because their expansion was usually made possible by reliance upon a corps of men, both ex-slaves and prewar free blacks, who had gained acceptance as religious leaders during the antebellum years. Without their involvement the postwar missionary efforts would have been far less successful.

The church and its leaders became especially influential in black Charleston for several reasons. In addition to their sacred authority, black ministers who were relatively and sometimes exceptionally well educated naturally assumed important secular leadership roles. Black churches were important because their existence was a physical testament to black Charlestonians' changed status and their determination to establish an autonomous community life. In most cases the church was more completely controlled by blacks than any other major institution in their community and within its confines the members could exercise authority, make independent decisions, and seek refuge from the oppression of the white world without.

Finally, the church, like many other institutions, reflected the prevailing social structure of the black community, and specific denominational affiliation served as an index of social preferment. This was most clearly evident among the aristocratic members of the upper class, whose church preferences demonstrated an attempt to cultivate group consciousness and exclusivity and to preserve their privileged antebellum heritage.

CHAPTER EIGHT

"AN EQUAL CHANCE
IN THE RACE OF LIFE"

Postbellum Race Relations

Slavery in the Old South was more than a mere system of labor exploitation, and in this setting, in which black people were owned by whites,
the system also regulated race relations. The intricately detailed body of
ordinances associated with slavery established the social subordination
of all blacks. Intellectually, this subordination was justified by practical
security concerns but also by a thoroughgoing and widespread belief
in the blacks' racial inferiority. The slaves' emancipation and the rise
of Radical Reconstruction challenged assumptions about hierarchy and
place in the postbellum South. As Charleston's black community became
institutionally more complete and its leaders and members more self
assured in this period, they simultaneously fought the myriad of white
attempts to treat them as social inferiors. They sometimes struggled
against racial segregation and claimed many of the rights and privileges
enjoyed by other citizens. Local activism was sometimes assisted by
black and white Republican leaders, who sponsored important governmental policy changes and civil rights legislation. The results of black
Charlestonians' collective efforts yielded a new era in race relations
which differed radically from its antebellum predecessor as well as from
the rigid system of Jim Crow that characterized the late nineteenth- and
twentieth-century South.

The resounding defeat suffered by the South in the Civil War left
whites angry, while emancipation and the disintegration of the old order

exasperated and bewildered them. Rev. R. W. Memminger wrote that "the old regime understood slavery and its relationships; under the new dispensation we shall have to learn the meaning of a new state of affairs. It is almost impossible that the men of the old regime should be able to comprehend the meaning of such a changed status." Furthermore, there was not only an inability but also, according to him, "in most cases, an unwillingness to adapt oneself to the changes effected by a radical social revolution."[1] This unwillingness was rooted in the racist perceptions whites held of blacks. Most believed blacks were innately inferior. Many even accepted the racist theories of white supremacists, such as "Ariel," who contended that blacks were neither descendants of Adam nor Ham but were related to the "higher orders of the monkey." As such, blacks were often described as possessing infantile mentalities and as being naturally credulous, superstitious, vicious, absurdly pretentious, excessively sensual, sexually depraved, indolent, and improvident. Since they were so poorly constituted to successfully live as free men and women, it was expected that most would either drift into an utterly barbaric state or die out entirely due to natural causes. This would bring a welcome solution to the race problem for many, and a Charleston woman of this opinion considered it a "blessing . . . that the race will not last long for they are dying at 95 per week in the city."[2] No such easy solution to the problems of race relations would occur though, and Charleston's black population not only failed to disappear but even increased.

Because of their racist perceptions and their inability to conceive of interacting with blacks outside the master-slave relationship, many whites attempted to avoid demeaning contacts with freedmen. Shortly after the war, a Charleston woman wrote, "We very rarely go out, the streets are so niggery and Yankees so numerous." Charleston's July Fourth festivities were dominated by blacks, and whites scrupulously avoided appearing on the streets. In 1869 a local newspaper reported that "nobody participated in the celebration but the colored people and the four white men who were in the procession." Crowds of black celebrants "appropriated the national festivity" and "to judge BY THE PROCESSION and the appearance of the streets, one would almost imagine oneself in Liberia."[3] The aristocratic William Heyward refused to dine at the Charleston Hotel because, according to him, "the negro waiters [were] so defiant and so familiar in their attentions." Withdrawal produced psychological benefits, and Heyward rejoiced that "I am perfectly independent of having negroes about me; if I cannot have them as they used to be, I have no desire to see them except in the field." Another contemporary believed it "revolting" to reside "in a Land where Free Negroes make the majority of the inhabitants." This was especially galling because "every mulattoe [*sic*] is your equal & every 'Nigger' is your superior." In the most extreme cases, whites sometimes left the country to avoid contact with the former slaves. One refugee was the prosperous landowner Dr. Arthur G. Rose, who emigrated to England because he "couldn't stay in a country with so many free negroes."[4] Most whites did not seriously entertain emigration as a solution to the race problem, and their withdrawal from disquieting interracial contacts provided only the most ephemeral of remedies.

White control over the black population disintegrated rapidly following the end of the war; the advent of Radical Reconstruction and the entry of blacks into political life accelerated the process. Any lingering hopes whites maintained of regaining control over the freedmen in the near future were quickly shattered. When the special legislative session of the of summer 1868 convened, black men made up 75 of 124 members of the state house of representatives and 10 of the 31 senators. Throughout the period, blacks formed a majority in the lower house. In the Senate they constituted a significant minority bloc. This and subsequent legislatures rewrote the legal code and revolutionized the judiciary by opening all judicial offices to blacks. Further, these legislatures ordered that blacks be represented on all juries of the state courts. Charleston had black men seated in the city council beginning in the spring of 1868. During Reconstruction, except for the years 1871–73, they filled one-half of the eighteen city council seats.[5]

The horror and demoralization created over the prospect of black officials was so great that Alfred Huger marveled that this "cruelty & oppression have not doomed us to madness or driven us on to suicide!" To white Charlestonians, the social and political equalitarianism of Reconstruction degraded their once glorious city to the depths of Paris gripped in the throes of the French Revolution. Chagrined at the unfolding scenes of Reconstruction, Eliza Holmes told a friend, "We are being made however, day by day, to realize, the . . . equalities of all things." This "brings to my mind the scenes I have read of, during the Revolution in France of the hundred days, when the Nobility were so terribly treated, surely our humiliation has been great where, a Black Postmaster is established here at Headquarters and our Gentlemens Son's [*sic*] to work under his biddings." An editorial in the *Daily News* expressed the same revulsion: "We see among us a modified Jacobinism . . . with its ferocity tamed and its grotesqueness heightened but still the same coarse demagogue who proclaims 'liberty, equality, fraternity, in our streets, and whose proclamation means precisely what it meant eighty years ago—' Down with the gentry 'and up with the canaille!'" When in 1868 blacks were appointed as aldermen for Charleston, one prominent Charlestonian wrote in disgust and disbelief, "We actually have negroes in Council. It is the hardest thing we have yet had done to us." In expressing his fear that racial integration of the city's major facilities would be next, the writer continued, "Where it will all end I do not Know. It does not seem possible in the dispensation of Providence that the negro can rule over the white man & yet I am sometimes staggered by the turn events are taking."[6]

Political participation further polarized the estranged races as specific party affiliation became a surrogate for racial loyalty. Whites largely identified with the Democratic party, while blacks affiliated with the Republican party, the party of Lincoln and emancipation. These tensions were further exacerbated by the militia units blacks organized to protect themselves. Incorporation into the state militia in 1869 gave them legitimacy while heightening the physical threat they posed to whites. In warning of eminent danger in the summer of 1868, a local newspaper pointed out that black militia units had been stealthily drilling in several places in the city, "working patiently and steadily to make themselves trained and disciplined armed associations." This was occurring throughout the state, and the organization of these battalions had but a single objective. In the editor's view, "It is their avowed purpose to overawe the white man, to keep him down by force of arms." Rev. Richard H. Cain rejoined that malevolent purposes had not led blacks to organize militia units; instead, the units were organized to protect their rights. According to him, black men and women would respect the law, but they were also "prepared to stand by their liberties . . . and see that the liberties of their children are guarded with sleepless vigilance. Let their foes be aware!"[7]

It is no wonder that violence often resulted from the electoral competition of the contending political parties; throughout South Carolina black politicians lived perilous lives, especially in the countryside. There were several political assassinations of Republicans in the South Carolina upcountry during the election campaign of the fall of 1868. The most prominent was that of Benjamin F. Randolph, chairman of the Republican State Executive Committee and state senator from Orangeburg County. Randolph was murdered on October 16 in Abbeville County, where he had gone to lead a rally for the Republicans. Even though acts of political terrorism usually occurred in the isolated rural areas, they alarmed black Charleston and placed its members on the defensive. Randolph's murder convinced state representatives Alonzo Ransier and Robert C. DeLarge that the Democrats intended to precipitate a war of the races. Days after the dastardly act, black Charlestonians organized indignation meetings, and Richard H. Cain warned the governor that the "state of excitement" in Charleston was "intense." He believed such a brazen act by the Democrats "emboldened these of this city and the lives of the leading men of our party are threatened." Several "have been marked out as victims before election." Since he was quite familiar with black Charlestonians' determination to protect their leaders, Cain wrote, "I tremble for this city if any unwise Step be taken by the Democracy, to murder any prominent man in this Community, the people have sworne, [*sic*] to burn this city to ashes and have no mercy on the Democrats."[8]

While there were no political assassinations in Charleston, violent encounters between black Republicans and white Democrats were not unusual. Henry W. Ravenel observed that in the summer of 1868, blacks became so "riotous" that at "the late Democratic meeting in Charleston . . . the whites found it prudent to go armed; and a threatened violent interruption of the meeting was only averted by the appeal and interference of the more prudent colored Radicals." In preparation for the fall elections, Mayor Clark thought it prudent to appoint one hundred special police to assist the regular force to maintain order. Although incidents occurred on election day, the polls and the city were relatively calm, especially compared with some of the later elections.[9]

The 1871 municipal campaign was particularly exciting, and numerous violent confrontations occurred between blacks, the city police, and U.S. troops at the polls. In the aftermath of John Wagener's Conservative victory in the mayoral contest, riots broke out. According to the *Courier*, some black Republicans sought retribution for their political defeat by attacking German merchants, who were Wagener's ethnic kinsmen, and blacks who had voted for the Conservative ticket. Political tumult punctuated the Reconstruction years and reached its apogee before the fall elections of 1876; the tumult only added recurring tensions to Charleston's uneasy black-white relations.[10]

Republican control of the state legislature beginning in 1868 provided the legal impetus for the transformation of race relations in Charleston. The bill of rights in the new constitution of 1868 outlawed all distinctions between persons based on race or color. To fulfill this provision and to ensure that all statutes provided impartial legal remedies for both races, state representative Alonzo Ransier of Charleston secured passage of "An Act to Secure Equal Civil Rights" in 1870.[11]

The issue of legal remedies for the practice of racial segregation in public places took the question of civil rights into a realm wholly foreign to American jurisprudence at the time. The attempt to outlaw racial discrimination in public accommodations began in the legislature at its very first session in 1868. Benjamin Boseman of Charleston introduced a wide-ranging anti-discrimination bill, the discussion of which opened a serious rift between black and white Republicans on the issue of civil rights. Although passed by the House, the bill's provisions were so radically altered in the Senate that the result did little more than confirm the most basic civil rights already established in previous state and federal legislation. J. H. Ferriter, a native Sumter Republican and one of the bill's most strident critics, expressed the reason for white opposition when he described it as "the first entering wedge towards social equality." He then went on to advise blacks against antagonizing their former masters because blacks only enjoyed any rights "by the *sufferance* of the white race." Daniel Corbin, a senator from Charleston, warned supporters of the original bill that "they were treading on dangerous ground" by demanding "for the negro rights which were neither claimed nor expected by the white man." The amended bill was considered a victory for the most conservative Republicans and Democrats, and most blacks refused to support it. The result was that this legislative session failed to pass any civil rights legislation.[12]

In 1869 black legislators were finally able to pass a public accommodations act, but its rather limited and vague scope failed to placate many. The issue of equal access to public places reemerged with a vengeance in the spring of 1870, and the resulting debate again revealed the ongoing and acrimonious rift between black and white Republicans in this matter. The precipitant was a more comprehensive and punitive public accommodations bill that was introduced by Robert Smalls, the former Civil War hero who had become a state representative from Beaufort. The bill made it unlawful for corporations or businesses for which a charter or license was required to refuse admission or service or otherwise discriminate between patrons because of race. The penalties for violators were stiff and included forfeiture of license or charter, a fine of one thousand dollars, and possible imprisonment for up to three years.[13] After passing the House, the "Bill to Enforce the Civil Rights Bill of the United States" was forwarded to the Senate, where some of its provisions were again vigorously opposed by white Republican senators who were led by Daniel T. Corbin, chairman of the judiciary committee. The bill's opponents amended it to drastically reduce its penalties, to modify the section on burden of proof, and to delay implementation until May 1, 1870. In the acrid debate that followed, black politicians from Charleston labored assiduously to protect the original bill. Rev. Richard H. Cain was a leading opponent of amendment in the Senate. One of the leading speakers at a public indignation meeting, state representative Robert C. DeLarge, denounced the amendments as an attempt to deny equal rights to people who fought, bled, and died for the Republican cause in the recent Civil War.[14] When it became known that Senator Corbin's desire to delay implementation was a concession to Charleston's Academy of Music, black representatives were outraged. The reaction of Representative Alonzo Ransier of Charleston was typical, when he exclaimed that the pecuniary interests of businesses weren't matters of public concern. Furthermore, he "was not willing that his wife should be insulted till the first of May to oblige anybody." Representative Ransier's objections reflected a larger concern, though, a concern that was rooted in the issue of black-white relations within the Republican party. There were many blacks who distrusted their white Republican compatriots. The debate over the civil rights bill demonstrated why. In Ransier's view, Senator Corbin and whites with similar views "disregarded those who had elevated" them, and their actions "marked the palpable determination to give only back seats to the colored man." Despite the acrimony and internal Republican divisions surrounding the civil rights bill in the state legislature, the measure passed with little modification of its original provisions.[15]

The passage of the new civil rights act outraged whites, and the *Daily News* editorialized that legislators decreed "that colored men shall have a legal right to force themselves upon those who do not desire their company, [and] that they shall thrust themselves into the beds which were not made for them, and sit at tables which were not spread for them." In the name of justice, the editor fulminated, all associations that did not "huddle together unlikes and dislikes" were prohibited. Proprietors and their supporters argued that all persons had the right to operate their businesses as they saw fit. They believed the indiscriminate mixing of the races would make it impossible to maintain successful business enterprises because whites would rather stay home than patronize integrated facilities.[16]

In calling on whites to forswear prejudice and concede them legal equality, blacks vociferously denied they were demanding social equality. William Whipper scoffed at the idea of legally enforced social equality and explained, "We only ask an equal chance in the race of life." When a black clergyman was interviewed by a northern reporter on this matter, he said it was preposterous to force the "respectable negroes of any community into social relations with any class whose society is not desired or desirable." He only desired "to make honesty, integrity, intelligence and virtue the only standard of excellence." If this were done, he believed matters of social equality would take care of themselves. After likening society to a kaleidoscope in the diversity of its hues, William Holloway likewise scoffed at the suggestion that blacks desired social equality with whites. His experience convinced him that "the colored people have in their own circles, all the polish, refinement and education they need, hence they have no cause to go abroad, and especially in alleged interdicted spheres."[17]

The earliest major challenge blacks made to their exclusion from public facilities occurred before the passage of the first public accommodation acts and focused on Charleston's streetcars. Prior to the Civil War, Charleston had no public transportation, but by December 1866 the city's first street railway system was constructed. Few whites doubted the right of freedmen to patronize the streetcars, but during the first few months of its operation no decision was made on how the black ridership could best be accommodated. Some whites suggested that separate cars be provided exclusively for them, while others proposed that certain sections of all cars be assigned for their use. Both these proposed schemes were rejected by the black community, and its leaders stood firm in their demand for equal access to the railway system. The result was their de facto exclusion unless they chose to ride on the platforms outside the cars. Before the railway company resolved this problem, blacks made several attempts to ride inside the streetcars, and each time they were forcibly ejected and sometimes jailed by the city police. The most dramatic encounter between the railway company and demonstrators occurred on the afternoon of March 26, 1867. After the adjournment of a freedmen's mass political meeting held earlier, several seized a streetcar on Meeting Street

> and a large crowd of negroes rushed into it, to the great discomfort of the white passengers, and although remonstrated with and appealed to by the Conductor, declined to go out. Mr. Faber then stepped to the front platform and requested the driver to run the car off the track, as this was his only alternative. The effort to comply with his request failed, and the driver at the suggestion of Mr. Faber unhitched his horse, and leaving the car on the track went up to the company's stable. Finding themselves disappointed the rioters endeavored to push the car forward, when Mr. Faber put down the brake and stuck to his post, although he was threatened by one of the number who had stolen the iron by which the switches are turned, and held it in a striking attitude over his head, whilst others strove to pull Mr. Faber away from the brake. At this juncture the timely arrival of the police relieved him from his embarrassing situation. In the meanwhile, the cars of Messrs. Roumillat, Rives and St. Amand had been invaded in the same way, and in some instances the lady passengers were compelled to leave them for fear of personal insult and injury. When the rioters found that the Conductors could not be awed into acquiescence with their demands to be permitted to ride on an equality with the white passengers, they tried to interrupt the travel of the cars by placing stones in the track.[18]

In April black Charlestonians continued their acts of civil disobedience, which led to further confrontations with the police and the U.S.

military. Finally, on one occasion that month, Mary Bowers, intent on exercising her rights, occupied a seat inside one of the cars and had to be forcibly removed. This incident prompted her to lodge a formal complaint with Assistant Commissioner Robert Scott of the Freedmen's Bureau. In the resulting discussions with company president Jonathan Riggs, Scott urged quiet concessions to black demands. It was Bureau intervention, and the possibility of court action, along with militant community activism, that forced the company to end its racial discrimination at this time. Beginning in May 1867, all persons were granted free access to all seats in the cars. One month later, Major General Sickles, the military commander, issued an order prohibiting racial discrimination on street railways, railroads, and steamboats. Because of this, the editor of the Charleston *Mercury* predicted the company would lose much of its white patronage. However, exactly two months later, the paper reported that the streetcars were more heavily patronized than before. At first, whites were reluctant to mix with black riders, and in early May one observer noted, "It was common during the day to see the inside [of the cars] occupied by a few freedmen, while white people stood on the platform." Extensive separation of this kind did not endure long, and there were numerous examples of black and white passengers seated together aboard the cars.[19]

In 1883 in his comments on the general transformation of white attitudes on this matter, the editor of the *New Era* recalled that not long after the streetcar company began service, a white man changed his seat because a black sat next to him. In doing so, the white passenger remarked "that he didn't have New England olfactories." Eventually that same "gentleman" was seen "riding in the street-cars right next to a fat black 'mauma' and didn't seem to mind it a bit." With biting sarcasm, the editor explained, "He has either got New England olfactories, or else, he has accepted the situation as a sensible man." Racial incidents sometimes did occur. But blacks continued to ride on the city railroad unrestricted, and it seemed that whites became less openly hostile when encountering blacks in the same cars.[20]

Many steamboat companies were initially bastions of segregation. In 1865 Richard Cain described the treatment blacks received on the coastal steamers as "shameful" because "no accommodations are afforded to colored people, as a general thing." Rev. Francis L. Cardozo referred to the discriminatory practices of a northern line when he wrote to his superiors. He explained that a black teacher had to be transported "on the Peoples Line as they do not take *colored* persons on the Leeary Line, except as *Steerage* Passengers. I think such pandering to Southern prejudices . . . is worse now than it was before the war." In 1867 the regular Fourth of July steamboat excursion continued to be offered on a segregated basis. Sometimes the local ferry companies provided entirely segregated ships for the use of each race. Even when blacks and whites were admitted aboard the same boat, they were kept segregated; the advertisement for the steamer *Fannie* announced that its upper decks and saloons were "reserved exclusively for WHITE PERSONS."[21]

Reconstruction did witness important changes, however. Shortly after military rule commenced, Commander Sickles abolished discrimination on public conveyances, and recalcitrant shipmasters who discriminated between the races were sometimes arrested as a result. An important example occurred in late 1867. At this time, Frances Rollin, a prominent black teacher in the city freedmen's schools, was denied first-class steamer accommodations while traveling between Charleston and Beaufort. Miss Rollin soon filed charges in the provost court against Capt. W. T. McNelty of the Pilot Boy for violating General Sickles' orders. In the legal proceedings that followed, she was advised by Maj. Martin R. Delany, the former army officer and Freedmen's Bureau agent. Frances Rollins' complaint was upheld, and the ship captain was fined $250.[22]

The discriminatory policies of steamboat companies came under additional pressure due to the new state constitution and after the legislature passed the first civil rights legislation. By then, Elizabeth Hyde Botume, a Freedmen's Bureau teacher who was returning to South Carolina from the North, noticed several important changes when she took a steamer from Charleston to Beaufort. Before this time, she remarked, "No colored person was allowed on the upper deck, now there were no restrictions . . . [and] they were everywhere, choosing the best staterooms and best seats at the table." Southerners remained generally reluctant to mix freely with black passengers; consequently, at dinner time the blacks were served first, and the whites waited until a later time. There is evidence that some steamers continued to admit black passengers without discrimination in the mid-1880s. In 1884 when irate whites demanded that the Sullivan's Island Ferry Company exclude or segregate blacks, company representatives refused and explained that such a policy violated the law.[23]

Racial discrimination on railroads was also prohibited by law. Railroad companies provided both first- and second-class accommodations, and while most blacks preferred the less expensive seats, there were many cases of blacks riding first class among the whites. According to a South Carolinian, even in the late 1870s, this was "so common as hardly to provoke remark." Even so, "if a negro enters a car in which all the other travelers are white the latter, if they do nothing else, yet plainly evince aversion, and, if practicable a wide space is left around such intruders." It wasn't always possible to avoid blacks on trains, and on one occasion a white passenger was so astonished to find that all the double seats in the first-class car were "occupied by some one of the lately ostracized class" that he exclaimed, "Can't I sit down even here without being beside a nigger?" Upon looking around the car, he found a group of men from Charleston engaged in conversation. On the seat opposite sat the light-complexioned Robert C. DeLarge, the land commissioner, who was also participating in the conversation. The white passenger supposed that he had finally found a seat beside a white man, and "the discriminating scion of chivalrous stock took a seat beside him." But DeLarge, who did not wish to be disturbed, turned to him and declared, "Look, here . . . I'm a nigger too." This was too much to bear, and the exasperated intruder was forced to retreat.[24]

Free access to first-class cars did not end abruptly with the ouster of the final Republican government in 1877. In fact, certain political decisions unwittingly led to even greater racial mixing on trains in the early 1880s. In its attempt to eliminate unfair rate discrimination by railroads, the state legislature and the state railroad commission either directly eliminated all second-class fares in 1882 or fixed the fares so low that second-class seats could not economically be offered. One white Carolinian was of the opinion that the sale of second-class tickets "did prevent a certain portion of the passengers, white as well as colored, from riding in first class cars." But further, "the abolition of the sale of second class tickets did . . . to a certain extent, increase the number of colored people riding on first class cars." An editorial in the *News and Courier* also pointed out that "as long as there were two rates of fare for passengers the colored people usually took second class tickets and rode in the second class carriages," but now "the colored people sometimes crowd into the first class carriages." Whites were usually offended by the presence of blacks in the first-class cars, but in the early 1880s the demand for their complete segregation was not yet universal. Whites' lack of unanimity on the question of complete segregation was revealed when some demanded the repeal of the state Civil Rights Act (reenacted in 1882). According to the *News and Courier,* such a step was unnecessary since all judges and jurors were Democrats. Furthermore, the editors of the paper believed it unwise to segregate all blacks, "whatever their respectability and means, to travel in second-class cars."[25] The presence of blacks in first-class cars with whites was "not always or necessarily an evil" because "it has been the rule, also for well to-do colored persons, particularly women to travel first class. No trouble or discomfort has been complained of heretofore, on this score." In the estimation of the paper's editors, many of the complaints stemmed from the change in the character and number of blacks who rode first class in 1883. Even at this time, race seemed not to have completely overshadowed class as a factor in determining black-white relations on the trains. By the end of the year, at least two railroads had filed a joint tariff for first- and second-class passenger rates with the state railroad commission. The *News and Courier* expected that other railroads would soon do likewise and predicted that "there is no probability that the present mixed condition of passengers will long continue." Nevertheless, as late as 1885, T. McCants Stewart could report that black ladies and gentlemen traveled first class in South Carolina and could even be seen dining with whites in railroad saloons.[26]

In their quest for full public equality, blacks sometimes found small businesses among their most intractable opponents. During the period under consideration, blacks were completely excluded from hotels and were generally refused service at white-owned barber salons. Soda shops and ice cream parlors rebuffed black patrons. In the summer of 1866, when a black Union army sergeant visited a soda shop operated by Mr. E. E. Bedford and Co., his request for service was refused. No succor was obtained from the provost court to which the soldier had applied because, according to the judge, merchants had the authority to regulate their businesses as they saw fit.[27]

Black politicians were active on the local level and took action to protect their constituents' civil rights. In September 1869 Edward P. Wall and William R. Hampton, who were both city alderman, visited Wulburn's Saloon and called for refreshments. After having to wait for a "considerable time," the drinks finally arrived but cost twice the rate usually charged. Later, while engaged in conversation, "they attempted to open a window in order to get air, but it was closed as often as it was opened" because as the proprietor told others, he "did not wish any one [*sic*] to see that there were colored men on his premises." The outraged aldermen discussed the incident in the city council, which was considering a petition made by Mr. Wulburn for the transfer of a tavern license into his name. After a heated debate, all the black aldermen, with the exception of one, and their white supporters voted to deny Wulburn's request for a license because of his discrimination.[28]

When such blatantly discriminatory acts continued, some aldermen attempted to write an anti-discrimination provision into the municipal code. Although the initial attempts failed, black aldermen such as Edward P. Wall and William R. Hampton remained committed to this purpose. By mid-1870, Alderman Wall had organized enough support to amend the municipal licensing law to include prohibitions against racial discrimination and to establish suitable penalties for violators.[29]

In March 1870, a group of blacks, including Alonzo J. Ransier, the state representative, William R. Hampton, and others, visited several white restaurants and saloons to investigate their treatment of blacks. At some of the establishments, they received drinks gratis, but several proprietors refused their patronage and were subsequently arrested for violating the civil rights acts. In reaction, white restaurateurs and saloon keepers resolved to band together and raise moneys to test the constitutionality of the civil rights legislation. By the summer, though, true bills had been returned against the accused. But nine months later, the civil rights cases were struck from the court of general sessions docket, because the litigants had reached a settlement. According to one of the solicitors, "all parties had long since complied with the requirement of the law—persons were admitted to all public places without discrimination."[30]

Controversy also developed at the Academy of Music over the unrestricted admission of blacks. When the academy, Charleston's major performing arts facility, was under construction in 1869, plans had already been established for the segregation of black patrons. While whites enjoyed full access to the dress circle on the main floor, blacks were consigned to accommodations in the upper tiers, including the balconies, and one-half of the seats in the family circle. Many blacks despised such arrangements not so much because the facilities were segregated but because the accommodations were inferior to those of the whites. Other blacks, especially members of the elite, felt uncomfortable in the presence of their social inferiors and the unsavory characters who were sometimes admitted to the upper tiers. According to a local paper, such persons "wished that black as well as white 'aristocracy' should be provided for." In January 1870 blacks attempted to obtain admission to the dress circle, but in each case were refused. After the second unsuccessful attempt, J. C. Claussen and Joseph P. Howard swore affidavits and had the proprietor John T. Ford arrested for violation of the Civil Rights Act. In February the grand jury returned a true bill against Ford, but the following month the plaintiffs dropped their charges since by this time blacks won free access to all seating at the academy.[31]

This policy change was anathema to white theater patrons, and in 1873 a woman despaired that "even the Theatre is an uncertain pleasure," because "you know that you may have a negro next to you." In another case, as late as 1883 one white patron complained about the great "evil" of allowing unescorted black and white women previously restricted to the family circle to take seats in other parts of the theater. It is not clear how long such racial mixing continued; on at least one occasion in 1883, seating arrangements segregated the races, but there is also evidence that suggests that some blacks continued to be admitted to the academy on an equal basis with whites through the 1890s.[32]

Although most businesses that excluded black patrons were white owned, black proprietors were, ironically enough, sometimes guilty of discriminating against their brethren. This was the case among several exclusive black barber shops that tried to maintain the patronage of whites by excluding blacks. A local newspaper reported that an unidentified but well-known black restaurateur also adhered to this practice. On one occasion when blacks visited his establishment and requested drinks, they were refused and "the reason alleged being that his custom was white, and miscegenation would ruin him." Finally, the would-be patrons were encouraged to leave by the proprietor and the police, who threatened the intruders with two months in the guardhouse.[33]

Charleston's municipal institutions reflected the prevailing sentiment among whites for separation of the races. De facto racial segregation was practiced in the public schools. During Reconstruction and throughout the 1880s, white paupers were supported in the Charleston Alms House while aged, infirm, or indigent blacks were cared for at the Ashley River Asylum. In 1868 Charleston maintained separate hospitals for each race in different parts of the city, but by the early 1870s the patients in these facilities were relocated to the newly organized City Hospital on Queen and Magazine streets. The buildings of the old workhouse (now incorporated into the City Hospital) were used as an insane asylum and hospital for blacks. Although part of the same complex, the buildings of the old Roper Hospital were exclusively used for the care of white patients. During the 1870s certain of the hospital's insane wards contained both black and white inmates in adjacent rooms, but by 1880 the entire facility was strictly organized into racially exclusive wards. Black and white orphans were also placed in separate facilities. White children without parents became the charges of the Charleston Orphan House. Black orphans were cared for in the Freedmen's Bureau's Shaw Orphan Asylum, which became the State Orphan Asylum after 1868. Shortly after the Democrats regained control of the state government in 1877, the modest appropriation for the State Orphan Asylum was decreased and eliminated entirely by the 1879–80 fiscal year. Black orphans were forced to rely on the beneficence of private citizens or the Ashley River Asylum. In addition to the burial grounds owned by black and white churches, the city maintained separate cemeteries for the dead of each race.[34]

Black men joined the municipal police force during Reconstruction. The first appointment was made under mayor George Clark in the summer of 1868. The new appointee to the position of station house door keeper was the son of Richard Holloway and represented one of the first families of black Charleston. Clark's successor, Republican Gilbert Pillsbury, and other local Republican leaders became increasingly concerned about the concentration of Democrats on the force. They also desired to reward their supporters, who were clamoring for jobs. Based on these concerns, Mayor Pillsbury decided to begin to reduce the Democratic policemen. That fall thirty Democrats were dismissed and replaced with equal numbers of blacks and whites.[35] Racial and political tensions mounted further when Mayor Pillsbury ordered the discharge of three white roundsmen (inspectors responsible for supervising the beat patrolmen) and replaced them with blacks. In mid-October when a squad of police was ordered to the scene of a disturbance under the command of a black roundsman, one white policeman refused to go and later resigned, vowing that "he would not be placed under the command of a negro." *The Daily News*, which reported the incident, gleefully noted that white Republican policemen also "fumed and fretted" over the appointment of blacks to such sensitive positions and sent a delegation to the mayor in protest.[36] The orders were not rescinded, and blacks continued to hold positions of authority. H. C. Minott was appointed as a sergeant and James H. Fordham, a former free person of color, served as a lieutenant from 1874 until at least 1896 and was highly regarded. Lt. George Shrewsbury, another former free black and son of the prominent alderman George Shrewsbury Sr., headed the city's detective force during the mid-1870s. The size of the police force varied during the 1870s, fluctuating around one hundred men. In 1873 about one-half of Charleston's policemen were black, and as late as 1878 they still formed about one-third of the force. That year, the city council agreed that future appointments should conform to that ratio.[37]

Slaves had rendered service to Charleston's municipal fire department during the antebellum years. Several such black companies, including the Ashley, founded in 1846 (formerly known as Number Nine), and the Comet Stars, founded in 1851 (formerly known as Number Five), survived and continued to serve the city during Reconstruction. They were joined by the free black fire companies instituted during the Civil War and those established by the freedmen afterwards. Despite the efficiency of many of the black firemen, their companies were initially viewed only as auxiliary units and were not considered an official part of the fire department. In mid-1865 some white firemen were entirely opposed to the continued reliance on blacks and called for the complete disbandment of their units.[38] This would have violated a longstanding tradition and failed to win much support.

As early as September 1865, a group of civic-minded blacks volunteered to create a fire company to man the city's hook-and-ladder truck but were rebuffed. The board of firemasters desired to create such a unit but formally resolved that it should be composed of white men. Later, in 1867 and 1868, black fire companies petitioned the Democratically controlled city council for full admission to the fire department; their requests were denied.[39]

With the advent of the Pillsbury administration in 1869, black firemen renewed their efforts to win admission to the fire department. To assist them, white Republican alderman Thomas J. Mackey introduced an ordinance that would have admitted the black fire companies on a separate but equal basis. Specifically, its provisions were to create a board of colored firemasters that would consist of the presidents of the black companies and would have responsibility for administering the operations of the black unit. The whites would be controlled by a separate board. Both divisions of the department would have been responsible to a single chief. The response of the white community was predictably indignant on this matter. A petition signed by three thousand taxpayers argued that such a step would introduce "an element of discord and dissatisfaction to its [the fire department's] members."[40] The *Daily News* denounced "the attempt to make the negro firemen the equal of the white firemen" and predicted that this attempt, "if persevered in," would cause "ill feeling, if not tumult and bloodshed and it may lead to a practical disbanding of the white Fire Department." Full admission would not only elevate the black companies' status but would also equalize their pay scale with the whites. In the course of the discussions about the fire department, Alderman Mackey also decried the fact that these highly qualified men continued to be paid only on the same hourly basis as antebellum hired slaves had been, while the official companies were paid on a monthly basis.[41]

When the presidents of the black fire companies learned the details of the Mackey bill, they requested that the racially exclusive boards be eliminated, which was agreed to. Despite the protests and dire predictions of the whites, the United, Comet Star, Niagara, Prudence, Ashley, and Union companies were incorporated into the department on an equal basis with the existing companies of their class in August 1869.[42]

In the spring of 1870, white firemen displayed their displeasure over the admission of the black companies. In April the board of firemasters decided to abandon the usual custom of having a parade followed by an inspection of the fire companies in favor of having an inspection only.

This course was chosen to avoid the appearance of social equality between black and white firemen. In response, a special session of black and white city councilmen called the firemasters' decision a violation of the law and instructed Mayor Pillsbury to order the white firemen to participate in the customary parade or have their companies dissolved. The order of the city council created quite a sensation. An irate white citizen caustically wrote, "This day for many Years has been a gala day for the citizens, but its glories are gone and gone forever. Our infernal rulers having incorporated the 'Niggers' into the Fire department." Now they would all have to parade "by his most Royal Majesty the Mayor with his White and black Colleagues." With no other recourse, the white fire companies complied. In addition to the annual departmental parade, black and white firemen usually paraded their units separately. Throughout the period black and white fire companies also maintained separate equipment handling tournaments to demonstrate their skills.[43] There never was any attempt to create integrated fire companies at this time, but the inclusion of blacks as an official part of the department was an important departure from antebellum practice.

By mid-1870 most of the black fire companies used hand-operated engines while the white fire companies almost universally operated the larger and more powerful steam engines. However, by August 1872, the black Comet Star company had acquired a steamer and petitioned the board of firemasters for admission to the steamer division. An upgrade in status would increase the unit's salary from eight hundred to eighteen hundred dollars per annum. One of the problems at this time was that the city council was controlled by Democrats—this was during the administration of John Wagener, from 1871 to 1873—and the board of firemasters believed the department already had excess steamer capacity and deemed admission of another unit inexpedient.[44]

Samuel Garrett, a black alderman and a political independent who had introduced the bill to admit the Comet Stars, charged that in reality the council opposition "lay on the ground of color." He recalled that almost a year earlier, when the same council desired to admit two white companies, it had raised the limit on the number of steamers permitted and had accomplished its purpose. Alderman Frank Brown, a black Democratic alderman, also spoke in favor of admitting the unit. In his admonition to his colleagues, he pointed out that blacks had been promised equal protection by the Democratic administration that was now in control of the city and that blacks had asked for very little until now. In December 1872 the matter was still being debated, and, although some white aldermen favored admission, there weren't enough votes to prevent Garrett's bill from being indefinitely postponed. Ultimately, political change would bring victory to the Comet Stars: when Republican mayor George Cunningham's administration assumed office in late 1873, one of the first items of business was to admit the company into the steam division.[45]

By 1878 the eight black fire companies in the Charleston Fire Department included five hand-operated engine companies, two steamers, and one hook-and-ladder truck collectively manned by over five hundred men. The number of black firemen decreased considerably during the next four years, however, as retrenchment occurred and as the fire department was reorganized from its volunteer basis into a smaller paid department. These changes eliminated several white engine companies and all black firemen except those attached to a single hook-and-ladder truck. Many whites had great praise for the efficiency of the black steam fire engine companies and attempted to dissuade the city council from its reorganization plans. The *News and Courier* soundly criticized the board of firemasters for forcing black firemen to bear a disproportionate burden of Charleston's retrenchment policies. The paper pointed out that the black steamers were efficient and were entitled to be represented among the other companies, even if that meant dismissing more whites. In conclusion, the *News and Courier* warned that the "political and industrial future will be dark indeed, when the color line is sharply drawn in this community."[46]

The absence of a rigid color line helps explain the hodgepodge of both racial separation and interaction observed among those that attended public recreational activities. Visitors to Charleston often observed that blacks were usually reluctant to "intrude themselves" into places or areas frequented by whites. One Carolinian also observed that at circuses, "there are always placed two series of seats on opposite sides of the tent; the whites occupy one of these, the negroes the other." In all such public gatherings, he continued, "each race contrives, by a process of elective affinity, to congregate by itself." But separation was not complete, and there were public recreations at which blacks and whites interacted. According to a local paper, when Charleston's German citizens held their Schutzenfest in 1868, "the Teutons made no distinction in class color or previous condition" and admitted blacks to the shooting tournament and picnic. Black and white citizens attended the race course, and it seems were seated indiscriminately, as both races frequented the integrated Club House Saloon. Whites also attended the affairs of black churches, and when the New Orleans Jubilee Singers performed at Morris Brown, the *News and Courier* reporter noticed "a number of white persons" in the audience.[47]

Despite whites' desire for separation of the races, complete physical isolation was impossible. Furthermore, interracial contacts were facilitated in Charleston because the city maintained significant features of its antebellum residential pattern. Before the war, Charleston (as was typical of the older commercial cities of the South) failed to develop a sharply differentiated housing pattern based on socioeconomic status. Nor did such a pattern develop during the 1870s and 1880s, because Charleston remained a commercial city with a stagnant economy. In the absence of an industrial transformation, and even though a streetcar system was created during Reconstruction, Charleston remained essentially a walking city. In describing its neighborhoods in 1874, one writer noticed that "the magnificent and the mean jostle each other very closely in all quarters of the city; tumble down rookeries are side by side with superb houses." Before the war it was typical for slaves to live in outbuildings in the masters' backyards. This pattern continued in the postbellum years, and freedmen often rented the same accommodations from whites, or in the case of domestics lived in the same houses with their white employers.[48] This not only ensured that high and low status individuals often resided close together but also ensured that blacks and whites would have regular contacts. The postwar intermingling of different classes and races is evident on a section of Church Street in the first ward. By the Battery at its southern end, house number one was occupied by Bruce Philips, a black laborer. Whites occupied the next several residences on both sides of the street along with either the black or immigrant domestics in their employ. Of the white male residents, several were employed as cotton merchants, and one was an accountant. The white minister William B. Yates lived on the east side at number ten, along with his family and black servants, and across the street was John Meyer, a white retail grocer. Richard Birnie, the black cotton shipper, and his family resided at number thirteen near Lightwood Alley and owned another adjacent residence both valued at $2,100. At number fourteen on the east side, William Heyward, a white rice planter, resided along with several black families, the members of which worked as laborers, wood sawyers, and servants. The white lawyer George D. Bryan lived at number twenty-seven, and W. T. McDonald lived along with her relations at number thirty, where she operated a boarding house for black travelers.[49]

Although the housing pattern was not sharply drawn along class lines, residential differentiation did exist. In general, declining gradients of status were discernible from west to east and from south to north. By 1880 two-thirds of Charleston's professionals (i.e., lawyers, merchants, physicians, and brokers) lived south of Calhoun Street in the lower four of the city's eight wards. Furthermore, almost 57 percent of the professionals lived in the westernmost wards (wards two, four, six, and eight). White Point Gardens was located at the extreme southern tip of the city on the Battery. With its tree- and shrub-lined walkways amid the colorful gardens, this was the favorite resort of those who desired to take a leisurely stroll or to attend musical concerts, which were regularly performed here. Historically, the lower two wards were the sites of the Low Country planters' summer residences, and the largest, most elegant homes—often constructed of brick—were located in this part of the city. Meeting Street was a major north-south thoroughfare in these wards and traversed the city; south of Broad Street, it contained the property and residences of many of Charleston's most prominent white families, including the Smyth, DeSaussure, Adger, Ravenel, Jervey, and Trenholm families. Several of the city's major institutions were located at the intersection of Meeting and Broad. Here could be found city hall, the county courthouse, the municipal guardhouse, and the famed St. Michael's Church. Broad Street, which ran east and west, was lined with legal and other professional offices, and Charleston's banks and brokerage houses were located near the intersection with East Bay. To the northwest in ward four, north of Beaufain, another highly desirable residential community had developed. The lower four wards did contain industrial and commercial areas; for instance, in wards two and four there were several mills located on the banks of the Ashley River. But the heart of Charleston's mercantile district lay in the eastern wards between East Bay Street and the Cooper River. The area included the site of a continuous array of piers, shipyards, wharves, warehouses, and cotton presses along the waterfront portion of ward one north of the Battery and ward three.[50]

Calhoun Street, which extended east and west, divided the upper from the lower wards. In the upper city, there were two especially desirable residential neighborhoods. One was located northeast in ward seven around Hempstead Mall between Meeting Street and East Bay. The area known as the West End, however, was the most pleasant section of the upper city. Located between Calhoun and Spring, west of Rutledge, this area was sufficiently removed from the hustle and bustle of the industrial and commercial districts of the city. Rutledge Avenue, which ran through this neighborhood, was a broad tree-lined street with handsome residences with large yards and elegant gardens. These scenes were typical of several streets nearby, where many of the city's prosperous businessmen resided.[51]

Although certain sections of the upper wards were especially attractive, only about one-third of Charleston's professionals lived in this part of the city, which was generally identified with the working class. In 1880 about one-third of the employed males in wards one and two were professionals, compared with slightly more than one-fourth in wards five and six. The contrast is even more pronounced in the northernmost wards, and in numbers seven and eight, only 14 percent of the employed males worked as professionals. The houses in this area were generally smaller than those in the lower city and were usually constructed of wood (because the upper wards were excluded from the restrictions on the construction of wooden buildings until 1869). The easternmost portion of the upper city (wards five and seven) contained a few wharves, at least one shipyard, the depot of the Northeastern Railroad, and the municipal gas works, all along the Cooper River and Town Creek. The center of the upper city, north of Calhoun beginning at John between Meeting and King streets, was the location for the depot and roundhouse of the South Carolina Railroad. The railroad workshops were located further north at Spring Street. According to a local newspaper report, King and other adjacent streets north of Vanderhorst have "long been a disgrace to Charleston." Parts of this area were burned by fires during

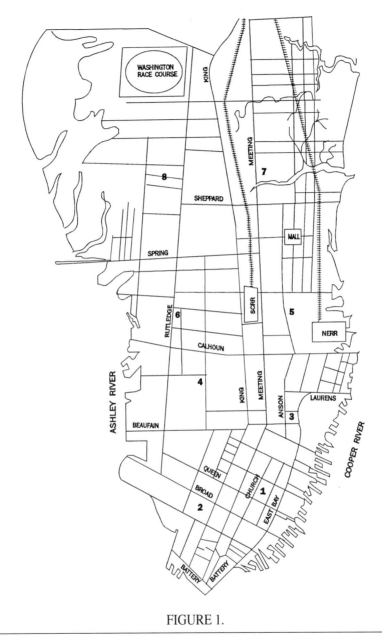

FIGURE 1.

MAP OF CHARLESTON 1879

Adapted from Walker, Evans, and Cogswell Map of Charleston Revised 1879

the Confederate evacuation in 1865, and many of the wooden houses here remained dilapidated. Below Calhoun, King Street was the site of the city's major retail trade, and many fashionable shops were located there. But the upper part of King Street was sometimes pejoratively referred to as "New Jerusalem" because of its numerous small clothing, dry goods, fruit, drug, and second-hand furniture stores that displayed their wares on the sidewalk or in the windows. The depot for the street railway and additional depots for the South Carolina Railroad and the Northeastern Railroad were located further north of Shepard. North of Shepard, there were also several farms, including the one owned by the Noisette family. To the west lay Potter's field, and by the mid-1880s the butcher pens were constructed in this northwestern part of the city. The phosphate works were located in the Neck outside the city and along the shores of the Ashley and Cooper rivers.[52]

In 1880 blacks continued to be widely distributed through every part of the city and nothing resembling the modern urban ghetto existed. Certain closely settled enclaves of black population had begun to emerge, however. The descriptive popular names sometimes applied to certain streets with large numbers of black residents provide illustrative testimony to this fact. For instance, Beresford Alley was commonly known as Mulatto Alley, and a section of Philadelphia Street was pejoratively referred to as Coon Alley. A contemporary pamphlet described the area of King Street between the Battery and Queen Street (in ward two) as "infested by" negroes. Part of this area was destroyed by the disastrous fire of 1861 and still remained "one of the most disagreeable and dirty portions of the city." In this vicinity, Smith's Lane, Wimm's Court, and Price's Alley, which ran perpendicular to King Street just north of the Battery, were overwhelmingly inhabited by black residents. Generally, clusters of black population tended to be east or west of the north-south corridor formed by Meeting and King streets. Princess, Beresford, Clifford's Alley, Simon's Row, and several other streets in ward two west of King Street between Beaufain and Queen were also heavily populated by blacks. In the lower wards, the black population gravitated toward the numerous alleyways, lanes, and courts that bisected the larger streets. This was especially the case in the eastern portion of wards one and three where blacks were concentrated in residences behind the wharves. Stoll's Alley, St. Michael's Alley, and

Cordes Court were typical, and the residences here were inhabited largely by blacks employed as domestics, laborers, cotton hands, fishermen, pilots, sailors, and longshoremen.[53]

The sections of the city where blacks concentrated were not only unaesthetic but also quite often unhealthy. This was certainly the case in the northeastern portion of ward three, which was bounded by Calhoun, Anson, and Laurens. This area was known as Gadsdenboro or, more descriptively, as Rottenborough. Largely inhabited by working class blacks, according to the board of health, this part of the city had long been regarded "with indignant disgust" by the community. The area was almost entirely comprised of low land and marsh land. Attempts were made to fill this low-lying district with street sweepings, sawdust, rice chaff, offal, and dirt, but decomposition ensued, and the land sank down again. During periods of heavy rain, the land flooded, and stagnant pools collected under the houses, which caused the board of health to describe this area as a "dangerous and unhealthy region" that served as a breeding ground for infectious diseases. The conditions that obtained here occurred in many places on the east side and were avoided by all who could afford residences in more salubrious locations.[54]

The upper wards were generally less healthy than the lower part of the city. The land along the Ashley and Cooper rivers was quite low and especially so in ward seven, which was crisscrossed with rivulets. During high tides and periods of heavy rain, the land became inundated. The drainage network was inadequate in many places, which made it difficult to maintain sanitary conditions. Garbage was formerly dumped in Charleston Neck and used to reclaim land, and human excrement continued to be deposited at the northern end of King and Meeting streets. Many residents believed that the poor sanitary conditions in the upper wards were responsible for the incidence of malarial fevers and a related ailment popularly known as Neck Fever.[55]

A major trend occurring during Reconstruction and the years thereafter was the gradual shift of the black population northward. In 1860 9,728, or 58.6 percent, of all Charleston's blacks resided in the lower four wards, but by 1880, although their absolute number had increased to 11,848, only 45.6 percent of all blacks continued to reside there. Seven of the city's eight wards reflected increased black populations during the twenty-year period, but the black population was expanding much more rapidly in the upper wards. While the percent increase in wards five through eight varied between 75 and 187 percent, a growth rate of 55 percent was the greatest registered by any of the lower four wards. The northwestern part of the upper city was growing quite rapidly as low-lying lots were filled in, and farm land was sold for building sites. By 1880 blacks made up 60 and 62 percent of wards six and eight respectively, and these two wards became the site for one of the largest concentrations of blacks in the city. At this time, the area west and north of the railroad yards and workshops between Vanderhorst and Congress, including Warren, Radcliffe, Morris, Bogard, Race, Chestnut, Fludd, and a number of nearby streets were heavily settled by blacks. Quite often, the male workers of this area were employed as laborers, farm hands, mill hands, and to a lesser extent as craftsmen.[56] Though concentrations of blacks are discernible, they were not confined to these areas, and most lived in other locations. At this time, class was as important a determinant of residential pattern as race was.

The close proximity in which blacks and whites lived and worked in Charleston not only led to interracial contacts but also sometimes led even to miscegenation. Interracial sexual encounters were the concomitant of slavery, and although whites publicly expressed a revulsion against this kind of intimacy, these contacts continued after the Civil War. Among many, however, the aversion to interracial sexual relations reached phobic proportions. Such persons warned that emancipation logically led to miscegenation, which was contrary to Holy Scriptures and injurious to the white race. A year after the war, a South Carolinian then in New York warned her relative in Charleston, "It will not do to keep those lovely girls of yours in S. C. for negro men to Court them; for in Congress they intend to give the negroes Great power over the whites." Whites were usually incensed at the display of intimacy between men and women of different races. In her correspondence with a friend shortly after the war, one outraged white woman discussed a "yankee" ball in Charleston, "at which the colored, Miss Susan Alston Pringle, Miss Adele Alston, etc., were the bells [*sic*] of the evening." She then rhetorically inquired "how does that make you feel . . . Belle?" Another Charlestonian wrote of walking on the Battery until a carriage drove past "with two negro women on the back seat with a white man *between* them and a black woman & white man on the front seat." Such

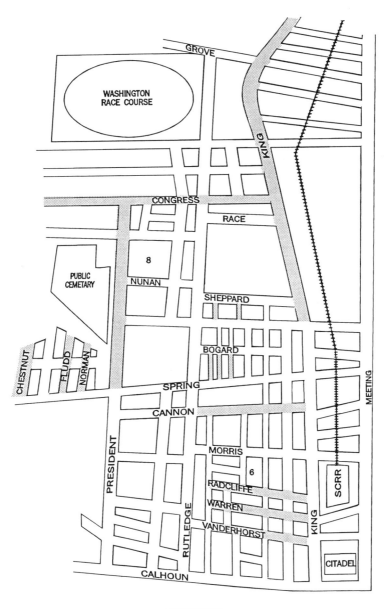

FIGURE 2.

MAP OF WARDS SIX AND EIGHT SHOWING SEVERAL AREAS
OF CONCENTRATED BLACK POPULATION 1879-1880

Adapted from Walker, Evans, and Cogswell Map of Charleston Revised 1879

scenes were intolerable to this observer, who was forced to abruptly end the stroll as a result.[57]

In the attempt to forestall miscegenation, in 1865 the new state legislature prohibited interracial marriages, but this legislation was overturned once the Republicans gained control of the state government in 1868. After the overthrow of the Radical government in South Carolina, the Conservatives reenacted the ban against interracial marriages in 1879, but this probably had no effect on sexual intimacy between the races. During the twenty years after the war, there were numerous instances of interracial marriages, and these were usually excoriated by the white community. In 1870 a local paper reported the case of a white man who had recently married a black woman and had "promenaded" his new bride down Meeting Street, "which occasioned considerable disgust." Romance did not always lead to marriage, and there were numerous instances of interracial couples cohabiting. Sometimes the fact of interracial sexual contacts came to public attention only because the persons involved ran afoul of the law. This was certainly the case in 1869 when a black Charleston woman named a white man in a paternity suit. As a major port city, Charleston contained several brothels, and when disturbances occurred at these locations, the police blotter revealed them to have been among the most integrated places in the city. In 1880 John Page, a black man, maintained a barroom on Elliott Street tenanted entirely by white prostitutes. Many of the houses of ill fame were staffed by both black and white women and drew upon an integrated clientele.[58] The psychological distortions of racism led some blacks to identify with whites and to court their romantic and sexual favors pathologically, but most refused to disparage their race in this way. Many prided themselves on their unadulterated racial backgrounds. Others, such as Martin R. Delany, warned that the males of a race never attained greater levels of civilization than their women. He therefore urged black men to do as white men did and give their women special attention and respect while watching them "with jealous care."[59]

One of the ways in which blacks demonstrated their racial pride was through expressions of interest in Africa and in the possibility of emigrating there. In the 1870s there were several Charlestonians who were familiar with Africa and with the idea of African emigration. In 1861 Rev. Richard H. Cain served as a director of the African Civilization

Society and as a member of the organization's general committee along with Rev. Ennals J. Adams. Its purpose was to encourage the spread of western civilization in Africa and to assist in the formation of an "African Nationality" where blacks could govern their own affairs. Reverend Adams later went to Sierra Leone, where he spent approximately two years as a missionary under the auspices of the American Missionary Association. Dr. Martin R. Delany was an exponent of emigration in the 1850s and journeyed to Yorubaland in 1859 to explore the region and to query African rulers about allowing Afro-American emigrants to settle there. Upon his return Delany also cooperated with the African Civilization Society. The average black Charlestonian learned about Africa through a variety of means. Some heard stories from relatives passed down from the slave era. Some corresponded with persons who had emigrated. Other emigrants left relatives in Charleston with whom they visited and imparted information. Informed blacks often gave lectures on the land and people of Africa. One of the most notable lecturers was Professor Jacob C. Hazeley, a Sierra Leonean graduate of Cambridge University, who gave accounts of the Ashanti people, of the prolific gold mines of West Africa, of the Niger River, and of the activities of the famous Yoruba missionary, Bishop Samuel Crowther.[60]

The interest blacks expressed in emigration was quickened after the violent overthrow of Reconstruction in 1876–77 undermined their political strength. At this time Rev. Benjamin F. Porter lamented that within months, blacks had been "hurled from the pinnacle of fame to the depths of degradation." This was convincing evidence that they now had no prospect of becoming the equals of whites in America. As life in South Carolina promised to become more precarious for blacks during the post-Reconstruction era, many contemplated emigration.[61]

While the overthrow of Reconstruction forced blacks to reevaluate their prospects for becoming full and equal American citizens, the impetus for emigration was not wholly negative. Many blacks were drawn by the positive attractions of Africa. Martin R. Delany tirelessly discussed the ancient Egyptian and Ethiopian origins of western civilization and hoped to help reestablish the African continent's lost grandeur by emigrating. T. McCants Stewart, the Charlestonian who later emigrated to Liberia to accept a professorship at Liberia College, also spoke of the "Regeneration of Africa." Like Delany, Stewart believed that "Africa had already played an important part in the ancient history of the world and that . . . she will yet act [*sic*] an important role in its modern history." All that was necessary was redemption and "hers will be the finest civilization of the world." Delany, Stewart, and several other black Charlestonians understood the great economic potential of the African continent and therefore encouraged black men with skills and capital to emigrate and contribute to its industrial and commercial development. In addition, black Charlestonians often articulated the belief that Africa was a special place in the world set aside by God wherein all African peoples could reach their fullest human potential. Dr. Moses G. Camplin, who described himself as "an old friend of Liberia," wrote: "Africa is the land of promise & rest to the Colored man a land of pure liberty & freedome. I only would to God that I could go there—but it is out of my power so to do—But O Lord Our God hasten the day when every Color'd Soul in America—or in any other part of the world may return to Africa—a land of rest—a land of peace—a land of happiness—a land [of] glory—a land of exceeding great Joy—which Thee Lord our God has given to the Sons of Ham as an inheritance for ever. . . ." Though it seems Camplin never emigrated, his interest in Africa continued into the late nineteenth century.[62]

By the mid to late 1870s, several of Charleston's black churches had become interested in Africa as a field of missionary endeavor. Many black clergymen believed that as the most advanced group of African descendants, Afro-Americans had a special responsibility in their missionary work. According to their view, the emigration of Afro-Americans to Africa and proselytizing the Christian faith among the indigenous people represented the fulfillment of divine will. At the South Carolina Annual Convention of the A.M.E. church in 1874, the pastor's address declared, "Africa now in her benighted, pagan condition, must and will become enlightened and Christianized through the labor and instrumentality of her own sons and descendants, providentially educated and trained for that purpose by the grace of God." The spread of Christianity was an essential feature in the total process of "African Redemption," the end result of which would be an advanced civilization in which blacks throughout the diaspora would desire to participate. Mr. A. Weston wrote that the first thing the black churches should do was to organize missionaries and to "send them two by two through

Africa, to enlighten those who need enlightening and to inform the enlightened we should like to come home." Weston believed that Africa was a "goodly land" and that it was God's providential design for Afro-Americans "to go [there] and enlighten their fathers."[63]

Many in the black community looked unfavorably on emigration because the loss of population would further undercut the political strength of the black electorate. Others feared that many trained men would be attracted to Africa and their leaving would thus deplete the pool of potential black leaders, leaders who were critical to the progress of the race in America. Rev. Ennals J. Adams argued that black Americans needed to make more progress here before going to Africa. While contrasting the freedmen's degraded condition immediately after the Civil War with the tremendous progress they had made since, Adams rhetorically asked that if blacks were resigned to life in America then, why couldn't they continue living in the country now? He further warned of Africa's unhygienic environment and of the "superstitions" of the inhabitants. In Adams' view, black Americans enjoyed the benefits of western civilization and Christianity "to an extent which could not be hoped for in Africa for generations," and if they couldn't progress here, he doubted they could do so where such advantages were absent. While Jonathan J. Wright conceded that some blacks with education and skills might usefully go to Africa, he feared that the exponents of emigration were encouraging a mass exodus of ill-prepared and ignorant persons, the end result of which would "only be to take darkness into darkness."[64]

Despite opposition, the enthusiasm for emigration did not wane immediately following the demise of Reconstruction. In the spring of 1877, a correspondent for the *Missionary Record* reported that pro-emigration sentiment was greater than it had been for six years. All along the routes of the major railroads, people were inquiring how they could arrange to go to Liberia. Whites recognized the enthusiasm in the black community over the emigration issue and feared losing their workers. One contemporary noted, "The papers are very careful not to offend the colored people just now, as they fear an emigration by the wholesale."[65]

To encourage emigrationist sentiment, the Rev. Benjamin F. Porter organized the Liberia Exodus Association in the summer of 1877. By August the emigration enthusiasts decided to sell stock to finance the movement, and the Liberian Exodus Joint Stock Steamship Company of Charleston was organized with Rev. Porter as president, J. C. Hazeley as vice president, Rev. Harrison N. Bouey as recording secretary, and Rev. George Curtis as corresponding secretary. Later, Martin R. Delany and his son St. Cyprian became officials in the company. The Liberian Exodus Association and its subsidiary company hoped to establish a niche in West Africa where black men and women with education "can maintain a position equivalent to their attainments and talents." Unless this were done, black people would be confined "to a subordinate and menial position" in America.[66]

The response to the Liberia Exodus Association was widespread. A New Orleans organization of eighteen hundred black women and their families was formed to assist the emigrationists; they sent a representative to Charleston and contributed to the Liberia Joint Stock Steamship Company. Letters inquiring about the prospects of emigration were received from blacks as far away as Nebraska. Communications were established with the Liberian government, which agreed to accept Afro-American settlers and provide each family with twenty-five acres of land gratis, with the option of purchasing more if desired. By January 1878 the Association raised six thousand dollars through the sale of stock and ten months later acquired the steamship *Azor*. The ship soon docked in Charleston and was consecrated on March 21 amid an enthusiastic crowd of approximately five thousand spectators.[67]

On April 21, 1878, the *Azor* set sail for Liberia filled to capacity with two hundred and six passengers. Some of them were from Charleston, but many were from other places in South Carolina and out of state. All of the emigrants that had converged on Charleston during the months before the *Azor*'s departure were unable to emigrate at this time, though, and approximately two hundred were forced to wait for a later voyage. Two congregations were organized among the first group of emigrants. The one was created four days before the *Azor*'s departure when Bishop John M. Brown and Rev. Augustus T. Carr organized the African Methodist Liberian Mission Church. The Rev. Santania F. Flegler was appointed pastor of the one-hundred-one-member church. The Baptist emigrants were organized into Shiloh Church, with a congregation of approximately one hundred members, through the efforts of Revs. Jacob Legare, Harrison N. Bouey, Edward M. Brawley, J. A. Chase, and others.

A collection was taken up to raise funds for building a church edifice in Liberia, the American Baptist Publication Society sent twenty-five dollars' worth of Sunday School literature, and the American and Foreign Bible Society contributed one hundred Bibles. At the time of departure, no pastor had been chosen. One year later, though, the Baptist Educational Missionary and Sunday School Convention sent Rev. Harrison N. Bouey to Monrovia as their missionary agent. Bouey remained in Liberia for three years and established two mission stations, one at Barnsville and the other at Roysville. These were the areas where the *Azor* emigrants were located. Later, the missions were organized into full churches. Reverend Bouey also organized two associations, a National Baptist Convention, and, upon his return to South Carolina, he became the general agent of the Liberian Convention.[68]

By the fall of 1877, an estimated sixty thousand persons were sympathetic to the idea of emigration, and one year later the American Colonization Society estimated that easily five hundred thousand blacks had expressed an interest in returning to Africa. Nevertheless, the Liberia Exodus Association failed. Beset by rising debts, by inadequate operating capital, and by the gullibility of its own leadership, the association went bankrupt, and finally unscrupulous whites gained control over the *Azor*. No more passengers were taken to Africa by the Liberia Exodus Association after the initial 1878 voyage.[69]

Despite the enthusiasm many expressed for African emigration, in 1878 most black Charlestonians remained decidedly in favor of continued life in America. Critical to the understanding of that commitment were the dramatic and positive changes in race relations that characterized the years of Reconstruction. Blacks were not satisfied with the mere extinction of their former servitude, and they strove for a full measure of freedom. To this end, they aggressively fought against many forms of racial discrimination as vestiges of slavery and products of racism. Black politicians codified the demands of their constituents by passing civil rights legislation. Success in the legislative halls was translated into social reality as some blacks took seats on streetcars, obtained first-class accommodations on trains and steamers, and attended the theater, the race track, and restaurants, and also frequented public parks on an equal basis with whites. These instances of racial integration caused consternation among whites, who generally demanded segregation wherever possible. Unrestricted racial mixing was far from universal. Determined whites continued to discriminate between the races, and certain facilities, such as hotels and barber shops, remained interdicted areas. Segregation was also widespread in the administration of Charleston's municipal services. More important than the existence of segregation, though, is the fact that at the same time, substantial examples of racial integration could also be found. The overthrow of political Reconstruction paved the way for increased attacks on blacks' civil rights. Nevertheless, many instances of unrestricted access to public accommodations continued into the 1880s. Reconstruction represented an important time of transition in race relations. De facto segregation can certainly be found during the period; however, the fact that blacks won access to many facilities from which they had heretofore been excluded is an important advance over antebellum racial policy. Even when evidence of Jim Crow can be found, the system was neither as rigid nor as pervasive as it later became by the turn of the century.[70]

THE LEGACY OF RECONSTRUCTION

Reconstruction was a period of optimism for black Charlestonians. The Thirteenth, Fourteenth, and Fifteenth Amendments brought emancipation to the slaves and conferred political rights on the men. For the first time, black Charlestonians voted and elected members of their own race as state representatives, senators, and congressmen, and black men were elected and appointed to a variety of lesser positions, including municipal aldermen. They also sat on juries and testified against whites in court. The existence of this new leadership group gave its constituents the feeling that they indeed had some influence over governmental affairs and that their interests would be served. Black political leaders enlisted the support of sympathetic whites to pass civil rights legislation designed to protect their rights as citizens and to prevent racial discrimination. As a result they gained unprecedented access to public facilities and conveyances. Cases of discrimination and de facto segregation occurred, but the amount of interracial mingling that existed is sufficient to identify race relations during the Reconstruction years as relatively fluid compared to what had gone before and what later developed.

Long before their first ballots were ever cast or they asserted their rights in public places, black Charlestonians had engaged in activities that gave meaning to their new status as free men and women. They created labor unions to fight for their interests as workers. They also established schools for the education of their children. Later, the most aggressive and ambitious students insisted upon attending the University of South Carolina, which was integrated for a short time. Black churches that were spiritually responsive to their members were also created at this time. Their congregations and pastors played important secular roles as well.

Unique opportunities developed during the era as new employment possibilities were created as the black community moved toward greater institutional complexity. Black craftsmen were primarily employed by whites, but more than ever before a market developed for their skills within their community. Most workers held no property, but the possibility of its acquisition existed where it had not before. Some blacks availed themselves of the new educational opportunities to become teachers, ministers, doctors, and lawyers. These were the first professionals in black Charleston, and, along with the businessmen and politicians, they significantly broadened the composition of the upper class. The existence of professional groups was almost entirely attributable to the black community's need for their services. A disproportionate number of those in the upper class had been free before the war, but the freedmen also ascended to prestigious positions and often accumulated property. The emerging professional groups were a physical testament to the intellectual capacity of the race, and the community's property holders, though small in number, demonstrated its diligence and industriousness.

These developments were part of the enduring legacy of Reconstruction, and they seemed to indicate that, given time, black Americans could make substantial progress and even be accepted as full partners in the American Dream. These hopes were soon shattered, though. While the nascent form of important and lasting changes can be discerned during the Reconstruction years, black Charlestonians' attempt to win complete and equitable participation in American society remained the era's greatest unfulfilled striving.

The extreme hostility of whites to black political participation was another part of Reconstruction's legacy. White Carolinians were especially hostile to the political advances made by black men during Reconstruction and did everything conceivable to impede them. By 1876, in South Carolina the Republicans were divided among themselves, and the Democrats were more determined than ever before to "redeem" the state from what they incessantly denounced as "negro supremacy." In the election of that year, the Democrats took two approaches to the black electorate. Wade Hampton, their gubernatorial candidate, made overtures to blacks by calling for honest government and by pledging to uphold their civil and political rights. Hampton's rhetoric called for the obliteration of the race issue from politics, and he envisioned moderates of both parties cooperating to bring about responsible government under white Democratic leadership.[1]

But another tendency also emerged in the Democratic party. The more militant white supremacists were not interested in biracial and bipartisan cooperation. They found the idea of appealing to black voters with the promise of moderate progress intolerable. For them, the only way to eliminate the race issue from politics was to destroy the black electorate. The campaign of fraud, violence, and intimidation they launched during the election was designed to accomplish this purpose. The Hamburg Massacre, which occurred in July 1876, marked the Democrats' determination to carry the election. In the Upland county of Aiken, a dispute between a black state militia unit and local white rifle clubs left several black men either dead or severely wounded, signaling the violent days to come. The resulting Democratic victory in 1876 was but a single phase in the counterrevolution to establish white supremacy. During his short administration as governor—he was elected to the Senate and assumed his seat early in 1879—Hampton continued his moderate appeal, warned leaders of both races against drawing the color line in politics, and even appointed blacks to minor bureaucratic positions to create a greater base of interracial support. Nevertheless, violence, fraud, and the intimidation of blacks continued as endemic features of South Carolina elections.[2]

While they feared the evil effects that these distasteful methods might have on the political system, white Carolinians were equally concerned that even these measures might not be sufficient to maintain their political power, and they searched for an ultimate solution. In 1882 the state's congressional districts were gerrymandered to allow the Democrats to carry six of the seven congressional seats. The new election law of that year made registration and voting procedures more complicated and was aimed at destroying Republican influence in the state. Once instituted, this measure decreased South Carolina's Republican vote by two-thirds and the black vote by one-half. Those still eligible continued to vote during the 1880s, and they sometimes succeeded in electing other blacks to the state legislature. At this time, though, black

Republicans had almost no hope of winning elections outside the three counties with the greatest black populations (Beaufort, Berkeley, and Georgetown). A small number of blacks sometimes ran on the Democratic ticket, and throughout the 1880s and 1890s the only black state legislators elected from Charleston and Orangeburg Districts were Democrats.[3]

By 1890 the most rabidly racist elements gained the ascendancy in the Democratic party, and the campaign to eliminate the remaining portion of the black electorate reached a new intensity when led by Gov. Benjamin Tillman. The constitution of the Democratic party was revised in 1890 to require statewide primaries beginning in 1892, and requiring any blacks who wanted to vote in them to produce evidence that they had consistently voted Democratic since the 1876 election. Finally, to preclude any possibility of a regular Democratic defeat by a coalition of blacks and groups of dissident whites, the state constitution was revised in 1895 to include a poll tax, literacy test, and an understanding clause. The combined effect of these measures was to rob blacks of any effective access to the political system while allowing enough flexibility for loyal Democratic whites to continue exercising the franchise. Where these methods proved ineffective, vote fraud still provided the ultimate solution. Shortly after the turn of the century, a group of Charleston blacks told an English visitor that their major grievance was the inequitable administration of the election laws and the fraudulent reporting of electoral results. One man recalled an election "in which he himself, and others of his people to his certain knowledge, cast Republican ballots; but the result, as announced, showed not a single Republican vote."[4]

A second phase in the counterrevolution to establish white supremacy occurred when its advocates enacted laws to enforce the social subordination of blacks and to codify the etiquette of race relations. In 1889 South Carolina's civil rights law was repealed, and this fateful step ushered in an era when the comparatively fluid interracial contacts of earlier years were completely replaced by a rigid, pervasive, and legally enforced racial segregation. Late nineteenth-century laws governing interracial contact on various modes of transportation reveal changing white sentiments in South Carolina. In 1898 the first law requiring Jim Crow facilities on first-class railroad cars was passed, and two years later the law was revised to require separate coaches for each race on trains with multiple cars. In 1904 steamboats and ferries were segregated, in 1906 segregated dining facilities were required in train stations, and in 1917 the State Railroad Commision even prohibited railroad companies from unloading blacks and whites in the same locations. In the early years of the twentieth century, there is evidence that suggests that blacks continued to ride the Charleston streetcars freely, but in 1912 a new law relegated them to the back seats.[5]

In other ways the deteriorating climate of race relations was readily apparent. In early 1882 the city switched over to a paid fire department from the old voluntary form, and in the retrenchment that accompanied the reform, black fire companies were disbanded with a single exception. By the final years of the nineteenth century, the number of black policemen was also reduced as they increasingly fell victim to what one white resident described as a growing "caste feeling."[6] The testimony of long-time black residents who grew up at the turn of the century is also revealing. By then, the municipal parks that had once been routinely frequented by throngs of black revelers were now interdicted zones. Mamie G. Fields recalled that custom required blacks to walk around Hampton Park rather than through it. Access was granted to the Battery Park on the Fourth of July, a holiday that apparently many older white Charlestonians still considered a "Yankee holiday."[7]

By 1915 the South Carolina legal code was prescribing the acceptable boundaries of interracial contact between employees on their jobs. By this time, even the *News and Courier,* which had once ridiculed the idea of Jim Crow facilities, suggested that the legal segregation of the races was an insufficient remedy for the "negro problem." According to the editor, there was "no room" for blacks in America, and a lasting solution to the race problem could only be found in their deportation.[8]

In her reflections on the differences between Reconstruction race relations and the early twentieth century race relations, Frances Rollin described the latter as "these days of bitter hostility and proscription upon which we have fallen." In the earlier period, there was greater tolerance, which had vanished. With regard to public conveyances, she said, "Colored passengers, no matter how cultured, refined or able to pay, whether on land or sea in the Southland, are subjected to the most humiliating and degrading treatment."[9]

By the early years of the twentieth century, the counterrevolution of white supremacy was consolidated, and the political legacy of Reconstruction had been destroyed. From this point, it would take over half a century and a second Reconstruction to begin to fulfill the promises made by the first. The successes that were eventually won in the later years were made possible in part because of Black Charleston's institutional growth during the original Reconstruction. One only has to remember the vital roles black ministers and their congregations played in that later struggle. There is also the example of Avery Institute. Septima P. Clark graduated from there and went on to become an important Low Country educator and nationally known civil rights activist. Such twentieth-century legacies of Reconstruction confirm that enduring intimacy that ever links past and present.

APPENDIX

TABLE 10

POPULATION OF CHARLESTON, 1790–1860

	Slave	Free Black	White	Total
1790	7694	586	8089	16359
1800	9819	1024	9630	20473
1810	11671	1472	11568	24711
1820	12652	1475	10743	24780
1830	15294	2107	12888	30289
1840	14673	1558	13030	29261
1850	19532	3441	20012	42985
1860	13909	3237	23376	40522

Source: U.S. Bureau of the Census, *Population of the United States Compiled from the Fifth Census* (Washington: Government Printing Office, 1832), 14–15, 94–95; *Population of the United States Compiled from the Sixth Census* (Washington: Government Printing Office, 1841), 44–45; *Population of the United Stated Compiled from the Seventh Census, Statistics of Population, Tables 1–8* (Washington: Government Printing Office, 1853), 339; *Population of the United States Compiled from the Eighth Census* (Washington: Government Printing Office, 1864), 452.

TABLE 11

POPULATION OF CHARLESTON, 1860, 1880, 1900

Wards	1860[a]		1880[b]		1900	
	Black	White	Black	White	Black	White
1	1199	2397	1674	2236	1759	1533
2	2824	2048	2716	2516	917	1542
3	1726	3816	2692	3214	1293	1926
4	3979	4687	4766	6006	2847	2032
5	2078	2591	3702	2354	2417	2533
6	2781	3371	4875	3185	1982	2431
7	690	1852	1595	2119	2373	1808
8	1383	2448	3974	2375	3273	2102
9	N.A.	N.A.	N.A.	N.A.	1779	2170
10	N.A.	N.A.	N.A.	N.A.	3456	2354
11	N.A.	N.A.	N.A.	N.A.	5921	2591
12	N.A.	N.A.	N.A.	N.A.	3505	1216
Totals	16660	23210	25994	24005	31522	24238

Source: U.S. Bureau of the Census, *Population of the United States Compiled from the Eight Census* (Washington: Government Printing Office, 1864), 452; *Twelfth Census of the United States in 1900, Population*, vol. 1 (Washington: Government Printing Office 1901), p. 642; *Charleston News and Courier*, July 28, 1880.

[a]Not including Charleston Neck.

[b]This data is compiled from the 1880 census manuscripts as published in the *News and Courier,* July 28, 1880. The *Compendium of the Tenth Census 1880* does not report ward populations by race, but the total ward and city figures reported in the paper are reasonably close to the census totals.

TABLE 12

POPULATION AND LITERACY OF FREE BLACKS
IN SELECTED CITIES, 1850

County	City	City Free Black Population	County Free Black Population	Adults Neither Reading Nor Writing	
				N	%
Charleston	Charleston	3441	3849	45	1.1
Chatham	Savannah	686	731	183	25.0
Mobile	Mobile	715	941	12	1.3
Orleans	New Orleans	9905	9961	2279	22.8
Jefferson	Louisville	1538	1637	567	34.6
Baltimore	Baltimore	25442	29075	9318	32.0
Washington	Washington	8158	8158	2674	32.7
Henrico	Richmond	2369	3637	1594	43.8
Norfolk	Norfolk	956	2307	780	33.8
Davidson	Nashville	511	854	147	17.2

Source: U.S. Bureau of the Census, *Population of the United States Compiled from the Seventh Census, Statistics of Population, Tables 1–8* (Washington: Government Printing Office, 1853).

TABLE 13

SELECTED OCCUPATIONS OF MALES ACCORDING TO RACE AND NATIVITY, 1870[a]

Occupation	Black		Irish		German		Native White		City Totals[b]
	N	%	N	%	N	%	N	%	
Domestics	661	97.7	2	.3	1	.1	12	1.7	676
Laborers	1826	78.1	268	11.4	39	1.6	189	8.0	2336
Seamen	127	51.2	25	10.0	5	2.0	57	22.9	248
Fishermen	265	96.3	0	0.0	3	1.0	3	1.0	275
Carpenters	495	73.0	36	5.2	14	2.0	121	17.7	681
Brick masons	163	78.3	8	3.8	1	.5	36	17.3	208
Draymen	250	77.1	51	15.7	8	2.4	14	4.3	324
Tailors	119	73.4	6	3.7	23	14.1	11	6.7	162
Wood sawyers	41	95.3	0	0.0	0	0.0	1	2.3	43
Bakers	46	42.5	2	1.8	41	37.9	15	13.8	108
Coopers	82	82.8	4	4.0	1	1.0	10	10.1	99
Blacksmiths	73	54.4	11	8.0	6	4.4	39	28.6	136
Shoemakers	90	60.0	15	10.0	27	18.0	12	8.0	149
Pilots	14	18.4	4	5.2	2	2.6	43	56.5	76
Painters	79	54.1	15	9.8	7	4.5	45	29.4	146
Barbers	58	92.0	1	1.5	0	0.0	2	3.1	63
Stone masons	14	51.8	3	11.1	0	0.0	9	33.3	27
Clerks	22	2.1	37	3.5	127	12.2	824	79.7	1033
Constables	16	76.1	3	14.2	0	0.0	2	9.5	21
Longshoremen & Stevedores	18	46.1	4	10.0	2	5.0	14	35.0	31

Occupation									
Carters	87	82.8	14	13.3	2	1.9	2	1.9	105
Porters	126	82.3	10	6.5	1	.6	10	6.5	153
Sail makers	10	66.6	1	6.6	0	0.0	4	26.6	15
Metal smiths	19	27.9	3	4.4	5	7.3	38	55.8	68
Plasterers	12	54.5	1	4.5	0	0.0	9	40.9	22
Millers	25	43.1	0	0.0	17	29.3	15	25.8	58
Cabinet makers	8	23.5	0	0.0	10	29.4	11	32.3	34
Millwrights	25	75.7	1	3.0	0	0.0	6	18.1	33
Engineers	17	18.6	5	5.4	2	2.1	63	69.2	91
Butchers	97	77.6	2	1.6	4	3.2	21	16.8	125
Gardeners	29	64.4	5	11.1	4	8.8	4	8.8	45
Cigar makers	20	48.7	0	0.0	3	7.3	10	24.3	41
Machinists	7	7.3	3	3.1	1	1.0	77	81.0	95
Firemen (All)	8	44.4	0	0.0	0	0.0	10	55.5	18
Apprentices	89	38.5	1	.4	0	0.0	139	60.1	231
Farmers & Farm Laborers	130	69.5	9	4.8	10	5.3	38	20.3	187
Teachers	13	27.0	0	0.0	9	18.7	21	43.7	48
Merchants	6	1.1	41	8.1	90	17.9	319	63.6	501
Ministers	20	34.4	5	8.6	0	0.0	28	48.2	58
Printers	11	14.8	6	8.1	1	1.3	53	71.6	74
Confectioners	7	43.7	0	0.0	2	12.5	4	25.0	16
Grocers	2	.7	15	5.5	211	77.8	37	13.6	271
Policemen	33	42.3	24	30.7	2	2.5	17	21.7	78
Cotton menders	8	80.0	0	0.0	0	0.0	2	20.0	10

TABLE 13 *continued*

Occupation	Black		Irish		German		Native White		City Totals[b]
	N	%	N	%	N	%	N	%	
Shipwrights & Builders	6	25.0	2	8.3	1	4.1	14	58.3	24
Wheelwrights	12	50.0	5	20.8	2	8.3	5	20.8	24
Boatmen	26	96.2	0	0.0	1	3.7	0	0.0	27
Planters	8	10.1	2	2.5	2	2.5	64	81.0	79
Shop & Storekeepers	11	6.8	48	30.0	60	37.5	20	12.5	160
Hucksters	66	67.3	14	14.2	4	4.0	6	6.1	98
Coachmen	57	98.2	1	1.7	0	0.0	0	0.0	58
Factors	13	19.6	0	0.0	1	1.5	51	77.2	66
Upholsterers	4	22.2	1	5.5	3	16.6	7	38.8	18
Saddlers	5	50.0	2	20.0	0	0.0	2	20.0	10
White washers	25	100.0	0	0.0	0	0.0	0	0.0	25
Mattress makers	6	100.0	0	0.0	0	0.0	0	0.0	6
Railroad hands	11	27.5	6	15.0	5	12.5	18	45.0	40
Wharf builders	3	60.0	0	0.0	0	0.0	2	40.0	5
Mill hands	22	70.9	2	6.4	1	3.2	6	19.3	31
Cotton pressmen	3	25.0	2	16.6	0	0.0	6	50.0	12
Cotton samplers	7	100.0	0	0.0	0	0.0	0	0.0	7

Source: *U.S. Manuscript Census of Population*, 1870, City of Charleston

[a]Males aged fifteen and above.

[b]Totals include other foreign workers.

TABLE 14

SELECTED OCCUPATIONS OF MALES ACCORDING TO RACE AND NATIVITY, 1880[A]

Occupation	Black		Irish		German		Native White		City Totals[b]
	N	%	N	%	N	%	N	%	
Domestics	560	98.0	4	.7	3	.5	4	.7	571
Laborers	1977	83.4	140	5.9	30	1.2	210	8.8	2370
Seamen	84	38.0	20	9.0	7	3.1	80	36.1	221
Fishermen	252	97.6	0	0.0	0	0.0	1	.4	258
Carpenters	472	65.9	21	2.9	22	3.0	196	27.3	716
Brick masons	123	66.1	15	8.0	1	.5	45	24.1	186
Draymen	259	80.6	28	8.6	8	2.4	24	7.4	321
Tailors	107	69.0	6	3.8	19	12.2	16	10.3	155
Wood sawyers	66	94.2	0	0.0	0	0.0	4	5.7	70
Bakers	50	40.6	1	.8	32	26.0	35	28.4	123
Coopers	110	93.2	2	1.7	0	0.0	5	4.2	118
Blacksmiths	76	51.3	9	6.0	4	2.7	53	35.8	148
Shoemakers	112	73.6	8	5.2	18	11.8	6	3.9	152
Pilots	22	27.5	3	3.8	1	1.2	44	54.3	81
Painters	98	57.3	7	4.0	3	1.7	57	33.3	171
Barbers	104	96.2	0	0.0	1	.9	2	1.8	108
Stone masons	12	34.2	5	14.2	1	2.8	16	45.7	35
Clerks	24	1.8	29	2.2	86	6.6	1126	86.4	1302
Constables	3	37.5	3	37.5	0	0.0	1	12.5	8
Longshoremen & Stevedores	133	70.0	8	4.2	3	1.5	37	19.4	190

TABLE 14 *continued*

Occupation	Black		Irish		German		Native White		City Totals[b]
	N	%	N	%	N	%	N	%	
Carters	176	88.4	9	4.5	2	1.0	11	5.5	199
Porters	195	88.6	9	4.0	1	.4	14	6.3	220
Sail makers	6	42.8	1	7.1	1	7.1	4	28.5	14
Metal smiths	35	36.4	1	1.0	2	2.0	56	58.3	96
Plasterers	20	71.4	2	7.1	0	0.0	6	21.4	28
Millers	5	27.7	0	0.0	3	16.6	9	50.0	18
Cabinet makers	11	33.3	1	3.0	8	24.2	9	27.2	33
Millwrights	6	75.0	0	0.0	0	0.0	2	25.0	8
Engineers	18	12.6	5	3.5	5	3.5	109	76.7	142
Butchers	126	77.3	3	1.8	5	3.0	29	17.7	163
Gardeners	30	68.1	7	15.9	2	4.5	3	6.8	44
Cigar makers	10	40.0	0	0.0	3	12.0	10	40.0	25
Machinists	4	4.4	6	6.6	1	1.1	72	80.0	90
Firemen (All)	20	45.4	3	6.8	1	2.2	19	43.1	44
Apprentices	120	55.5	0	0.0	1	.4	93	43.0	216
Farmers & Farm Laborers	159	66.2	2	.8	12	5.0	65	27.0	240
Teachers	27	36.0	2	2.6	5	6.6	38	50.6	75
Merchants	11	4.0	30	9.4	64	18.2	189	54.0	350
Ministers	33	47.1	4	5.7	2	2.8	30	42.8	70
Printers	8	8.5	2	2.1	0	0.0	84	89.3	94
Confectioners	2	11.7	1	5.8	6	35.2	6	35.2	17

Occupation								
Grocers	3	1.0	18	6.4	187	67.2	61	21.9	278
Policemen	19	21.1	27	30.0	3	3.3	39	43.3	90
Cotton menders	3	75.0	0	0.0	0	0.0	1	25.0	4
Shipwrights & Builders	1	5.8	0	0.0	1	5.8	14	82.3	17
Wheelwrights	14	41.1	4	11.7	3	8.8	13	38.2	34
Boatmen	88	92.6	1	1.0	1	1.0	3	3.1	95
Planters	8	12.9	1	1.6	0	0.0	50	80.6	62
Shop & Storekeepers	8	9.0	9	10.2	37	42.0	21	23.8	88
Hucksters	75	84.2	4	4.4	0	0.0	6	6.7	89
Coachmen	26	96.2	1	3.7	0	0.0	0	0.0	27
Factors	2	4.7	0	0.0	2	4.7	38	90.4	42
Upholsterers	6	31.5	1	5.2	1	5.2	9	47.3	19
Saddlers	4	26.6	2	13.3	1	6.6	7	46.6	15
White washers	25	100.0	0	0.0	0	0.0	0	0.0	25
Mattress makers	9	100.0	0	0.0	0	0.0	0	0.0	9
Railroad hands	43	34.1	11	8.7	4	3.1	67	53.1	126
Wharf builders	14	87.5	2	12.5	0	0.0	0	0.0	16
Mill hands	161	86.0	1	.5	0	0.0	24	12.8	187
Cotton pressmen	18	52.9	0	0.0	0	0.0	15	44.1	34
Cotton samplers	18	85.7	0	0.0	0	0.0	3	14.2	21

Source: *Manuscript Census of Population 1880*, City of Charleston

[a]Males aged fifteen and above.

[b]Totals include other foreign workers.

TABLE 15

SELECTED OCCUPATIONS OF MALES ACCORDING TO RACE AND NATIVITY, 1900

Occupation	Black N	Black %	Native White N	Native White %	Foreign N	Foreign %	Total
Farm Labor	199	94.3	11	5.2	1	.5	211
Domestic & Personal Service	3809	84.0	560	12.3	164	3.6	4533
Barbers & Hair Dressers	154	97.4	3	1.9	1	.6	158
Laborers	2774	87.0	339	10.6	73	2.3	3186
Draymen, Hackmen & Teamsters	574	90.2	42	6.6	20	3.1	636
Hucksters & Peddlers	148	89.1	2	1.2	16	9.6	166
Bakers	102	59.3	42	24.4	28	16.2	172
Blacksmiths	101	60.8	57	34.3	8	4.8	166
Boot & Shoemakers & Repairers	90	73.7	3	2.4	29	23.7	122
Butchers	108	77.1	27	19.2	5	3.5	140
Carpenters & Joiners	616	76.0	163	20.1	31	3.8	810
Coopers	82	88.1	8	8.6	3	3.2	93
Cotton Mill Operatives	35	41.1	50	58.8	0	0.0	85
Fishermen & Oystermen	249	97.2	4	1.0	3	1.1	256
Machinists	5	2.6	164	86.3	21	11.0	190
Brick & Stone Masons	163	84.8	22	11.4	7	3.6	192
Painters, Glazeers & Varnishers	186	74.4	54	21.6	10	4.0	250
Saw & Planing Mill Employees	60	60.6	39	39.3	0	0.0	99
Tailors	89	64.0	15	10.7	35	25.1	139

Source: U.S. Bureau of the Census, *Twelfth Census of the United States in 1900,*
Special Reports: Occupations (Washington: Government Printing Office, 1904), 514–17.

NOTES

ABBREVIATIONS

SOURCE LOCATIONS

SCDAH	South Carolina Department of Archives and History
SCHS	South Carolina Historical Society
USCCL	University of South Carolina Caroliniana Library
SHSW	State Historical Society of Wisconsin
CCLSC	College of Charleston Library Special Collections
RMC	Charleston County Register of Mesne Conveyance
CTAO	Charleston County Tax Assessor's Office
CCL	Charleston County Library
CCC	Charleston County Courthouse
CLS	Charleston Library Society
CCARC	College of Charleston Avery Research Center

SOURCE ABBREVIATIONS

FBP	Freedmen's Bureau Papers
CCRW	Charleston County Record of Wills
CCWI	Charleston County Wills and Inventories
AMAP	American Missionary Association Papers

INTRODUCTION

1. Hollis R. Lynch, *The Black Urban Condition* (New York: Thomas Y. Crowell, 1973), xi; John H. Franklin and Alfred A. Moss, *From Slavery to Freedom: A History of Negro Americans* (New York: McGraw-Hill, 1988), 420.

2. Alan Spear, *Black Chicago: The Making of a Negro Ghetto 1890–1920* (Chicago: University of Chicago Press, 1967); Gilbert Osofsky,

Harlem: The Making of a Negro Ghetto, New York, 1890–1930 (New York: Harper & Row, 1968); St. Clair Drake and Horace R. Cayton, *Black Metropolis: A Study of Negro Life in a Northern City,* 2 vols. (New York: Harcourt Brace & World, 1970); Thomas Philpott, *The Slum and the Ghetto: Neighborhood Deterioration and Middle-Class Reform, Chicago, 1880–1930* (New York: Oxford University Press, 1978).

3. For three excellent pioneering studies of northern black urbanites that give significant attention to the nineteenth century, see Kenneth L. Kusmer, *A Ghetto Takes Shape: Black Cleveland, 1870–1930* (Urbana, Ill.: University of Illinois Press, 1976); David Katzman, *Before the Ghetto: Black Detroit in the Nineteenth Century* (Urbana, Ill.: University of Illinois Press, 1973); Elizabeth L. Pleck, *Black Migration and Poverty: Boston 1865–1900* (New York: Academic Press, 1979). One of the early important works on blacks in a western city is Douglas H. Daniels, *Pioneer Urbanites: A Social and Cultural History of Black San Francisco* (Philadelphia: Temple University Press, 1980). Examples of studies that stimulated interest in examining the black urban experience in the South are John Blassingame, *Black New Orleans 1860–1880* (Chicago: University of Chicago Press, 1973); Robert Purdue, *The Negro in Savannah, 1865–1900* (New York: Exposition Press, 1973); Robert Engs, *Freedom's First Generation: Black Hampton Virginia, 1861–1890* (Philadelphia: University of Pennsylvania Press, 1979); James Borchert, *Alley Life in Washington: Family, Community, Religion, and Folklife in the City, 1850–1970* (Urbana: University of Illinois Press, 1980).

4. Clement Eaton, *The Growth of Southern Civilization 1790–1860* (New York: Harper & Row, 1961), 6–7, 198, 248–49.

5. William W. Freehling, *Prelude to Civil War: The Nullification Controversy in South Carolina 1816–1836* (New York: Harper & Row, 1966), 11.

6. Robert Starobin, ed., *Denmark Vesey: The Slave Conspiracy of 1822* (Englewood Cliffs, N.J.: Prentice Hall Inc., 1970), 133–37, 149–51.

7. Martin Abbott, *The Freedmen's Bureau in South Carolina 1865–1872* (Chapel Hill: University of North Carolina Press, 1967); Carol Bleser, *The Promised Land: The History of the South Carolina Land Commission, 1869–1890* (Columbia, S.C.: University of South Carolina Press, 1969); Peggy Lamson, *The Glorious Failure: Robert Brown Elliott and the Reconstruction in South Carolina* (New York: W. W. Norton, 1973); Joel Williamson, *After Slavery: The Negro in South Carolina During Reconstruction, 1861–1877* (Chapel Hill: University of North Carolina Press, 1965).

8. Lamson, *Glorious Failure,* 121–22, 289–90; Abbott, *The Freedmen's Bureau,* 135; Bleser, *Promised Land,* 155–56.

9. Thomas Holt, *Black Over White: Negro Political Leadership in*

South Carolina During Reconstruction (Urbana, Ill.: University of Illinois Press, 1977), 4–5.

10. John Blassingame, *The Slave Community: Plantation Life in the Antebellum South* (New York: Oxford University Press, 1972); Thomas L. Webber, *Deep Like the Rivers: Education in the Slave Quarters 1831–1865* (New York: W. W. Norton, 1978); Herbert G. Gutman, *The Black Family in Slavery and Freedom 1750–1925* (New York: Pantheon Books, 1976).

11. Williamson, *After Slavery,* 298–99.

CHAPTER 1

SLAVERY IN ANTEBELLUM CHARLESTON

1. According to Richard C. Wade, in cities "both white and Negro communities included many different parts, and in the larger places a highly sophisticated system evolved with almost endless groupings and distinctions." The distance between master and slave was "filled with all kinds of diverse elements, inevitably disturbing the institution's ordinary relationships." Richard C. Wade, *Slavery in the Cities: The South 1820–1860* (London: Oxford University Press, 1964), 246–48.

2. See the Appendix, Table 10; Fredrika Bremer, *The Homes of the New World: Impressions of America,* 2 vols. (New York: Harper & Bros., 1853), 1: 264; John B. Adger, *My Life and Times 1810–1899* (Richmond: Presbyterian Committee of Publications, 1899), 167.

3. Claudia D. Goldin, *Urban Slavery in the American South 1820–1860: A Quantitative History* (Chicago: University of Chicago Press, 1976), 25. When Goldin examines urban slave owners and hirers as a percentage of urban white males aged twenty and above the following is the result for 1850:

City	Percentage
Baltimore	4
Charleston	59
Louisville	15
Mobile	35
New Orleans	16
Norfolk	43
Richmond	40
Savannah	30
St. Louis	4
Washington	12

J. L. Dawson and H. W. DeSaussure, *Census of the City of Charleston, South Carolina, for the Year 1848* (Charleston: J. B. Nixon, 1849), 34.

4. John A. Eisterhold, "Charleston: Lumber and Trade in a Declining Southern Port," *South Carolina Historical Magazine* 74 (April 1973): 64–65, 67; Frederick A. Ford, *Census of the City of Charleston, South Carolina for the Year 1861* (Charleston: Evans & Cogswell, 1861), 16, 18; *Charleston Daily Courier,* February 2, 1860; Ernest Lander, "Ante-Bellum Rice Milling in South Carolina," *South Carolina Historical Magazine* 52 (July 1951): 130–31; Ernest M. Lander, "Charleston: Manufacturing Center of the Old South," *Journal of Southern History* 26 (August 1960): 341, 344.

5. Helen T. Catterall, ed., *Judicial Cases Concerning American Slavery and the Negro,* 5 vols. (Washington: Carnegie Institution, 1926–37), 2: 279, 368, 370; Petition of John Strohecker, et al., 1844, Petitions Relating to Slavery, South Carolina Department of Archives and History (hereafter referred to as SCDAH); James Stirling, *Letters from the Slave States* (London: John W. Parker, 1857), 230; Okon Edet Uya, *From Slavery to Public Service, Robert Smalls 1839–1915* (New York: Oxford University Press, 1971), 6–7; Ford, *Census of the City of Charleston.*

6. *Charleston Daily Courier,* May 5, 1817, March 9, 1832; Robert S. Starobin, *Industrial Slavery in the Old South* (New York: Oxford University Press, 1970), 123; Samuel M. Derrick, *Centennial History of the South Carolina Railroad* (Columbia, S.C.: State Co., 1930), 124, 232; Dale Rosengarten, et al., "Between the Tracks: Charleston's East Side During The Ninenteenth Century," *Charleston Museum*, Archaeological Contributions, No. 17 (Charleston: Charleston Museum, 1987), 129.

7. U. B. Phillips, *American Negro Slavery* (New York: Appleton, 1918; reprint ed., Baton Rouge: Louisiana State University Press, 1969), 405 ; John M. Vlach, *Charleston Blacksmith: The Work of Philip Simmons Revised Edition* (Columbia, S.C.: University of South Carolina Press, 1992), 14; *Charleston Daily Courier*, January 1, 1839, July 14, 1859.

8. Rosengarten, et al., "Between the Tracks," 129; Louisa Lord to Martha Riggs, November 8, 1854, February 10, 1861, Samuel Robertson to Louisa Lord, April 15, 1857, Letters of Louisa Lord, South Carolina Historical Society (hereafter referred to as SCHS); James Hamilton Jr., *An Account of the Late Intended Insurrection Among a Portion of the Blacks of This City Published By the Authority of the Corporation of Charleston* (Charleston: A. E. Miller, 1822), 21; Thomas Cooper and David J. McCord, eds., *The Statutes at Large of South Carolina; Edited, Under Authority of the Legislature,* 10 vols. (Columbia, S.C.: State Co., 1930), 7: 363; Loren Schweninger, "Slave Independence and Enterprise in South Carolina, 1780–1865," *South Carolina Historical Magazine* 93 (April 1992): 107–108.

9. Cooper and McCord, eds., *Statutes at Large of South Carolina,* 7: 363; *Charleston Daily Courier,* December 15, 1858; A Bill To Provide A More Summary Remedy For The Offence of Permitting Slaves to Hire

Their Own Time, December 10, 1864, Petitions Relating to Slavery, SCDAH; Presentment of the Grand Jury of Charleston, October Term 1857, Fall Term 1858, SCDAH; Catherine Weyman to Edward, May 28, 1817, Weyman Family Papers, University of South Carolina Caroliniana Library (hereafter referred to as USCCL).

10. Wade, *Slavery in the Cities,* 45; Minutes of the Board of Fire-masters, September 18, October 16, 1848, June 5, 1849, November 25, 1850, January 24, 1851, SCHS.

11. Minutes of the Board of Firemasters, June 5, November 19, 1849, SCHS; *Ordinances of the City of Charleston from the 19th of August 1844 to the 14th of September 1854 And the Acts of the General Assembly* (Charleston: A. E. Miller, 1854), 131; Daniel E. Huger Smith, *A Charlestonian's Recollections 1846–1913* (Charleston: Walker, Evans, Cogswell, 1950), 67.

12. Alexander Edwards, ed., *Ordinances of the City Council of Charleston From In the State of South Carolina Passed Since the Incorporation of the City* (Charleston: n.p., 1802), 409. Minutes of the Board of Firemasters, June 5, 1849, SCHS.

13. Minutes of the Board of Firemasters, June 5, November 19, 1849, April 10, May 30, 1850, January 24, 1851, SCHS. The sale of badges by the city is one rough estimate of how extensively slave hiring was practiced. In 1849 the city authorities issued 4,480 badges for this purpose. The cost of these badges varied depending on the occupations for which they were issued. In 1860 an artisan's badge cost seven dollars, and a house servant's badge cost two dollars. Michael P. Johnson and James L. Roark, eds., *No Chariot Let Down: Charleston's Free People of Color on the Eve of the Civil War* (Chapel Hill, N.C.: University of North Carolina Press, 1984), 90–91; Rosengarten, et al., "Between the Tracks," 70.

14. *A Digest of the Ordinances of the City Council of Charleston From the Year 1783 to October 1844 To Which are Annexed the Acts of the Legislature which Relate Exclusively to the City of Charleston* (Charleston: n.p.; 1844), 171; Petition of the Coopers of Charleston, 1793, General Assembly Petitions, SCDAH.

15. Schweninger, "Slave Independence," 108.

16. Edward R. Laurens, *An Address Delivered in Charleston Before the Agricultural Society of South Carolina* (Charleston: A. E. Miller, 1832), 7–8; Petition of G. B. Stoddard, et al., 1859, Petitions Relating to Slavery, SCDAH. The South's dread of northern emissaries and infiltrators increased to incredible proportions by the eve of the Civil War. For an extended treatment of this theme, see Steven A. Channing, *Crisis of Fear: Secession in South Carolina* (New York: W. W. Norton, 1974), 41–42.

17. Presentment of the Grand Jury of Charleston, 1826, SCDAH; Abiel Abbott Journal, November 22, 1818, Papers of Abiel Abbott, SCDAH.

18. Carter G. Woodson, *The Education of the Negro Prior to 1861: A History of the Education of the Colored People of the United States from the Beginning of Slavery to the Civil War* (New York: G. P. Putnam's Sons, 1915; reprint ed., New York: Arno Press, 1968), 123–25; Holloway Papers, College of Charleston Library Special Collections (hereafter referred to as CCLSC); Janet D. Cornelius, *When I Can Read My Title Clear: Literacy, Slavery, and Religion in the Antebellum South* (Columbia, S.C.: University of South Carolina Press, 1991), 109, 116; Brian Waters, ed., *Mr. Vessey of England Being the Incidents and Reminiscences of Travel in a Twelve Weeks Tour Through The United States and Canada in the Year 1859* (New York: G. P. Putnam's Sons, 1956), 60.

19. Daniel A. Payne, *Recollections of Seventy Years* (Nashville: African Methodist Episcopal Sunday School Union, 1888; reprint ed., New York: Arno Press, 1968), 19; C. W. Birnie, "Education of the Negro in Charleston, South Carolina, Prior to the Civil War," *Journal of Negro History* 12 (January 1927): 20; John Blassingame, *Slave Testimony: Two Centuries of Letters, Speeches, Interviews and Autobiographies* (Baton Rouge: Louisiana State University Press, 1977), 618.

20. Documents Relative to the Denmark Vesey Insurrection, Document B, SCDAH; Bremer, *Homes of the New World*, 1: 305, 2: 499; Channing, *Crisis of Fear,* 39.

21. Robert Starobin, "Disciplining Industrial Slaves in the Old South," *Journal of Negro History* 53 (April 1968): 116; Woodson, *Education of the Negro,* 84; Omar ibn Said, "Autobiography of Omar ibn Said," *American Historical Review* 30 (July 1925): 789–94; Documents Relative to the Denmark Vesey Insurrection, Document B, SCDAH; George P. Rawick, ed., *The American Slave: A Composite Autobiography,* 19 vols. (Westport, Conn.: Greenwood Press, 1972), 3: 215; Mamie G. Fields, *Lemon Swamp and Other Places: A Carolina Memoir* (New York: The Free Press, 1983), 1–3.

22. Robert F. Durden, "The Establishment of Calvary Protestant Episcopal Church for Negroes in Charleston," *South Carolina Historical Magazine* 65 (April 1964): 67, 69; George A. Blackburn, ed., *The Life Work of John L. Girardeau* (Columbia, S.C.: State Co., 1916), 44; J. H. Thornwell, *The Rights and Duties of Masters: A Sermon Preached at the Dedication of a Church Erected in Charleston, S. C. For the Benefit and Instruction of the Colored Population* (Charleston: Walker & James, 1850), 6–7; *Public Proceedings Relating to Calvary Church and the Religious Instruction of Slaves* (Charleston: Miller & Browne, 1850), 5, 32.

23. *Charleston Mercury,* July 14, 1849; Thomas D. Smyth, *Autobiographical Notes, Letters and Reflections* (Charleston: Walker, Evans and Cogswell, 1914), 695; Durden, "Establishment of Calvary Protestant Episcopal Church," 70, 72, 82–83; George W. Williams, ed. *Incidents In*

My Life: The Autobiography of the Rev. Paul Trapier, STD With Some of His Letters (Charleston: Dalcho Historical Society, 1954), 27–28; Blackburn, ed., *The Life Work of John L. Girardeau,* 32, 44; Adger, *My Life and Times,* 174–75, 178; *Public Proceedings Relating to Calvary Church,* 9.

24. *Public Proceedings Relating to Calvary Church,* 9; Thornwell, *The Rights and Duties of Masters,* 7; Reverend Dr. Thornwell, *A Review of Reverend J. B. Adger's Sermon on the Religious Instruction of The Coloured Population* (Charleston: Burgess, James & Paxton, 1847), 12–13.

25. Gullah is a term which refers to the culture developed by African people brought to coastal South Carolina from the Upper Guinea Coast in West Africa (primarily Sierra Leone) and from the Kongo-Angola region in south central Africa. The Gullah language is one of the most recognizable aspects of the creolized culture they developed in the New World and is based on the fusion of various African languages and English. Charles Joyner, *Down by the Riverside: A South Carolina Slave Community* (Chicago: University of Illinois Press, 1984), 160; Margaret Washington Creel, *A Peculiar People: Slave Religion and Community Culture Among the Gullahs* (New York: New York University Press, 1988), 15–20, 260.

26. Paul Trapier, *The Religious Instruction of the Black Population: The Gospel to be Given to Our Servants* (Charleston: Miller & Brown, 1847), 4–5; Joyner, *Down by the Riverside,* 160; quoted in Creel, *A Peculiar People,* 260; Documents Relative to the Denmark Vesey Insurrection, Document B, SCDAH; quoted in Norrece T. Jones Jr., *Born A Child of Freedom Yet A Slave: Mechanisms of Control and Strategies of Resistence in Antebellum South Carolina* (Middletown, Conn.: Wesleyan Press, 1990), 139.

27. Blackburn, ed., *Life Work of John L. Girardeau,* 62–63; Jones, *Born A Child of Freedom,* 137–38; Charles Joyner, "'If You Ain't Got Education': Slave Language and Slave Thought in Antebellum Charleston," in *Intellectual Life in Antebellum Charleston,* ed. Michael O'Brien and David Moltke-Hansen (Knoxville, Tenn.: University of Tennessee Press, 1986), 271, 274–75; Edward Pollard, *Black Diamonds Gathered in the Darkey Homes of the South* (New York: Pudney & Russell, 1859; reprint ed., New York: Negro Universities Press, 1968), 58; Documents Relative to the Denmark Vesey Insurrection, Document B, SCDAH; Trapier, *The Religious Instruction,* 23–24.

28. Minutes and Register of the First Baptist Church, Charleston County, April 15, 1850, October 29, 1852, January 15, 1855, USCCL; Blackburn, *Life Work,* 36; J. R. Puckett (in behalf of St. James Colored Missionary Society) to Revs. Bishop and Gentlemen, December 1851, Methodist Archives, Wofford College; Blassingame, *Slave Testimony,* 377; *Public Proceedings Relating to Calvary Church,* 203; unidentified

newspaper clipping in possession of Mrs. Mae H. Purcell, Charleston; Albert D. Betts, *History of South Carolina Methodism* (Columbia, S.C.: Advocate Press, 1952), 237–38; *Charleston Mercury,* October 26, 1859.

29. Thornwell, *A Review,* 14; Record of Colored Members of the Methodist Episcopal Church, Charleston, South Carolina, 16, 27–28, 68, College of Charleston Avery Research Center (hereafter abbreviated as CCARC); Rules, Permit and Regulations of the Coloured Ministers, Elders and Members of the Baptist Church in Charleston, South Carolina, July 1819, USCCL; *Public Proceedings Relating to Calvary Church,* 32, 34.

30. *Public Proceedings Relating to Calvary Church,* 32, 34.

31. F. A. Mood, *Methodism in Charleston* (Nashville: E. Stevenson & J. E. Evans, 1856), 130–31; unidentified newspaper clipping in possession of Mrs. Mae H. Purcell, Charleston; Betts, *South Carolina Methodism,* 237–38.

32. Mood, *Methodism,* 131–32; RMC Book A–9, Mortgages and Miscellaneous Records 1719–1910, RMC, 236–38; Documents Relative to the Denmark Vesey Insurrection, Document B, SCDAH; Daniel Payne, *History of the A.M.E. Church* (Nashville: A.M.E. Sunday School Union, 1891; reprint ed., New York: Johnston Reprint Co., 1968), 27. An African Methodist church existed in Charleston as early as 1810, but its precise relationship to the A.M.E. church established in 1818 is unclear. See Daniel Coker, "A Dialogue between a Virginian and an African Minister," in *Negro Protest Pamphlets: A Compendium,* comp. Dorothy Porter (New York: Arno Press, 1969), 41.

33. Recognizing the significance of the formation of the African Church in Charleston, Vincent Harding cogently argues: "At this juncture it is of critical importance . . . to see that organized rebellion on another level had already been built deeply into the structure of black church life in Charleston. The agitation from 1815 to 1818, and the concerted withdrawal from the white congregations in the latter year took significant courage for the slaves. The raising of an independent house of worship implied not only the gathering of financial resources, but it was clearly an act of defiance for all to see." Vincent Harding, "Religion and Resistance Among Antebellum Negroes, 1800–1860," in *The Making of Black America: Essays in Negro Life and History*, 2 vols. August Meier and Elliott Rudwick, eds. (New York: Atheneum, 1969), 1: 184–85.

34. *Charleston Daily Courier,* June 8, 1818; Documents Relative to the Denmark Vesey Insurrection, Document B, SCDAH; Hamilton, *An Account of the Late Intended Insurrection,* 30; Carter G. Woodson and Charles H. Wesley, *The Negro in Our History* (Washington: Associated Publishers, 1962), 150; Mood, *Methodism,* 133.

35. Rawick, *The American Slave,* 3: 51–52, 95–96; John Lambert, *Travels Through Lower Canada and the United States of North America*

in the years 1806, 1807, 1808, 3 vols. (London: Richard Phillips, 1810), 2:404; Pollard, *Black Diamonds*, 57–58; Abiel Abbott Journal, November 22, 1818, Papers of Abiel Abbott, SCHS; Channing, *Crisis of Fear*, 49.

36. Presentment of the Grand Jury of Charleston, October 11, 1822, SCDAH; Pollard, *Black Diamonds,* 61.

37. Sir Charles Lyell, *A Second Visit to the United States of North America,* 2 vols. (London: John Murray, 1849), 1: 309; Phillips, *American Negro Slavery,* 417. Very often, in Charleston masters chose to take troublesome slaves to the city workhouse, also euphemistically known as the sugar house. Here they would be whipped in a specially constructed soundproof room, removed from public view. In 1825 a treadmill for grinding corn was installed that slave inmates were required to operate continuously for eight hours as part of their punishment. While this method of correction was physically exhausting, some masters considered it less brutal and thus were more apt to use it. Jones, *Born A Child of Freedom,* 77; Robert Mills, *Statistics of South Carolina Including A View of its Natural, Civil, And Military History, General and Particular* (Charleston: Hurlbut and Lloyd, 1826), 420–21.

38. Charleston Scrapbook: Clippings Chiefly From Charleston Newspapers, 1800–10, USCCL.

39. *Charleston Daily Courier*, September 23, 1845.

40. *Charleston Daily Courier*, September 22, 23, 1845; Rosengarten, et al., "Between The Tracks," 61.

41. F. C. Adams, *Manuel Pereira, Or the Sovereign Rule of South Carolina* (Washington: Buell & Blanchard, 1853), 108–09, 121; *Charleston Daily Courier,* April 2, 22, 23, 1834; Presentment of the Grand Jury of Charleston, May Term, 1846, SCDAH.

42. Presentment of the Grand Jury of Charleston, January Term, 1859, SCDAH; Catterall, *Judicial Cases,* 2: 362; Eyre Crowe, *With Thackeray in America* (London: Cassell & Co., 1893), 148; Rawick, *The American Slave,* 2: 242; James Stuart, *Three Years in North America,* 2 vols. (New York: J. J. Harper, 1833), 2: 68; Lambert, *Travels,* 2: 390.

43. Smith, *A Charlestonian's Recollections,* 63; Goldin, *Urban Slavery*, 40; *Charleston Daily Courier*, April 9, 1860; H. P. Archer, *Local Reminiscences: A Lecture Delivered by Mr. H. P. Archer* (Charleston: Daggett Printing Co., 1893), 10.

44. Ford, *Census of the City of Charleston,* 16–17; Presentment of the Grand Jury of Charleston, Spring Term, 1856, SCDAH.

45. Ford, *Census of the City of Charleston,* 16–17.

46. Abiel Abbott Journal, November 22, 1818, Papers of Abiel Abbott, SCHS; Adam Hodgson, *Letters from North America,* 2 vols. (London: Hurst & Robinson, 1824), 1: 97–98.

47. Elise Pinckney, ed., *Register of St. Philip's Parish Church*

Charleston, South Carolina, 1810 Through 1822 (Charleston: National Society of the Colonial Dames of America in the State of South Carolina, 1973), 90–91; Minutes and Register of the First Baptist Church, Charleston County, October 16, 1848, January 16, 1849, USCCL.

48. Ford, *Census of the City of Charleston.*

49. Catterall, *Judicial Cases,* 2: 358, 375, 469–70.

50. Ibid., 2:281, 375, 469–70; For a sustained treatment of how long-term romantic liaisons with female slaves could evolve into close and protective relationships with white families, see Adele Logan Alexander, *Ambiguous Lives: Free Women of Color in Rural Georgia, 1789–1879* (Fayetteville, Ark: University of Arkansas Press, 1991), chaps. 1–3.

51. Phillips, *American Negro Slavery,* 418; Rawick, *The American Slave,* 3: 130–31.

52. Catterall, *Judicial Cases,* 2: 421; Petition of John Holmes, July 10, 1849, Petition of Edward Tash, 1801, Petitions Relating to Slavery, SCDAH; Jacob Schirmer Diary, September 1861, SCHS.

53. Harvey Wish, "American Slave Insurrections Before 1861," *Journal of Negro History* 22 (July 1937): 316; William W. Freehling, *Prelude to Civil War: The Nulification Controversy in South Carolina 1816–1836* (New York: Harper & Row, 1965), 61.

54. Letter of June 20, 1794, letters of Rusticus, SCHS.

55. Ibid., letter of August 7, 1794.

56. Jefferson firmly believed this to be one incident in the execution of a general plan organized by the Brissotine party in Paris, the first part of which had already been carried out in St. Domingue. Albert E. Bergh, ed., *The Writings of Thomas Jefferson* (Washington: Thomas Jefferson Memorial Association, 1905), 275–76. Jefferson was not the only American statesman who feared that French intrigues emanating from St. Domingue were intended to arouse the slave populations. In 1799, Robert G. Harper, a South Carolina Congressman, learned of another conspiracy. According to the testimony of Haitian military men, Hedouville, special agent for the Directory, had been "preparing to invade the southern states from St. Domingo, with an army of blacks; which was to be landed with a large supply of officers arms and ammunition, to excite an insurrection among the negroes by means of missionaries previously sent and first to subjugate the country by their assistance, and then plunder and lay it waste." Elizabeth Donnan, ed., "Papers of James A. Bayard 1796–1815," in *Annual Report of the American Historical Association,* 2 vols. (Washington: Government Printing Office, 1913), 2: 11; C. L. R. James, *Black Jacobins* (New York: Vintage, 1963), 202.

57. Marina Wikramanayake, *A World in Shadow: The Free Black in Antebellum South Carolina* (Columbia, S.C.: University of South Carolina Press, 1973), 160; Slave Conspiracy in Charleston Manuscript, USCCL.

58. Hamilton, *An Account*, 17; Documents Relative to the Denmark Vesey Insurrection, Document B, SCDAH.

59. Ibid.

60. In recalling an encounter with Vesey, one slave said: "I was one day on horseback when I met him on foot, he asked me if I was satisfied in my present situation—if I remembered the fable of Hercules' waggon [*sic*] that was stalled, when he began to pray & God said you fool, put your shoulders to the wheel whip up the horses & your waggon will be pulled out, that if we did not put our hand to the work, & deliver ourselves, we would never come out of Slavery." Documents Relative to the Denmark Vesey Insurrection, Document B, SCDAH.

61. Documents Relative to the Denmark Vesey Insurrection, Document A, Executive Department of Charleston, Document B, SCDAH.

62. Achates, *Reflection Occasioned By the Late Disturbances in Charleston 1822* (Charleston: A. E. Miller, 1822), 6–7.

63. Documents Relative to the Denmark Vesey Insurrection, Document A, Executive Department of Charleston, Document B, SCDAH; Harding, "Religion and Resistance," 85.

64. Documents Relative to the Denmark Vesey Insurrection, Document B, SCDAH. Elements of traditional African belief systems figured into the revolutionary activities of slaves in St. Domingo as well. How similar must Gullah Jack have been to Macandal, the Haitian fugitive slave insurrectionist who predicted the future, persuaded his fellows of his immortality, and "instilled in them such terror and such respect that they considered it an honor to serve him on bended knee." Even by the end of the eighteenth century, Haitian slaves were only "presumably Catholics" and continued to rely on their traditional African beliefs to satisfy their innermost spiritual strivings. With the advent of the Haitian Revolution, black leaders like Boukman the vodun high priest "utilized nocturnal rites to dramatize their cause" and to solidify diverse slave groups. As C. L. R. James argues, once the Haitian slaves learned the doubtful benefits of their isolated efforts, vodun became the medium by which the conspiracy took hold. George E. Simpson, "Belief System of Haitian Voudoun," *American Anthropologist* 47 (January 1945): 36, 38; James, *Black Jacobins*, 86–87.

65. The ethnic consciousness of the slaves was heightened by the fact that the slaveholders themselves had decided preferences for certain ethnic groups and aversion to others. Such preferences are clearly visible in data from the Charleston slave market. For the period 1733–1807, the most preferred slaves came from Senegambia and were Bambara and Malinke. Gold Coast slaves were a second choice, and Angolan slaves were always desired by South Carolina slaveholders. By contrast, Africans from Whydah were rarely desired, and traders were often urged to avoid bringing Calabar

slaves to this market. Below is the distribution of Africans arriving at Charleston according to their geographical origins for the period 1733–1807.

Origin	Percent
Senegambia	19.5
Sierra Leone	6.8
Windward Coast	16.3
Gold Coast	13.3
Bight of Benin	1.6
Bight of Biafra	2.1
Angola	39.6
Mozambique-Madagascar	0.7

See Melville Herskovits, *The Myth of the Negro Past* (Boston: Beacon Press, 1958), 48; Philip D. Curtin, *The Atlantic Slave Trade: A Census* (Madison: University of Wisconsin Press, 1969), 145, 156–57; Marguerite B. Hamer, "A Century Before Manumission," *North Carolina Historical Review* 18 (July 1940): 232; Elizabeth Donnan, "The Slave Trade into South Carolina Before the Revolution," *American Historical Review* 33 (July 1928): 816–17.

66. Documents Relative to the Denmark Vesey Insurrection, Document B, SCDAH. Sterling Stuckey's pioneering research reveals that throughout the slave era, Afro-American culture, particularly its music, folktales, and religion, retained its essentially African qualities. Among the slaves such cultural retentions were reinforced by the continued importation of Africans from the West Indies and from the Continent. The cultural dimension of the Vesey conspiracy certainly supports this contention. For an exploration of these and other related issues, see Sterling Stuckey, *The Ideological Origins of Black Nationalism* (Boston: Beacon Press, 1972), 1–2, "Through the Prism of Folklore: The Black Ethos in Slavery," *The Massachusetts Review* 9 (Summer 1968), *Slave Culture: Nationalist Theory & The Foundations of Black Nationalism* (New York: Oxford University Press, 1987), 43–58. For a different view of the relationship between slaves' acculturation and the complexity of their resistance activities, see Gerald W. Mullin, *Flight and Rebellion: Slave Resistance in Eighteenth Century Virginia* (New York: Oxford University Press, 1972), 159–63.

67. Stuckey, *Ideological Origins,* 5; Documents Relative to the Denmark Vesey Insurrection, Document B, SCDAH; See also Monroe Fordham, "Nineteenth-Century Black Thought in the United States: Some Influences of the Santo Domingo Revolution," *Journal of Black Studies* 6 (December 1975).

68. Robert Starobin, ed., *Denmark Vesey: The Slave Conspiracy of 1822* (Englewood Cliffs, N.J.: Prentice Hall, 1970), 8; Larry Koger, *Black Slaveowners: Free Black Slave Masters in South Carolina 1790–1860,* (Jefferson, N.C.: McFarland, 1985), 176, 178–79.

69. *An Account of the Late Intended Insurrection,* 17; Documents Relative to the Denmark Vesey Insurrection, Document A, Executive Department of Charleston, SCDAH. In 1793 a Charleston free black wrote the governor of South Carolina and urged him to beware of dangerous groups besides Frenchmen because "we also have enemies to the Northward." The writer conveyed his apprehensions about insurrection because he was "contented with his Situation" and had no other desire "than saving the blood of his fellow creatures." Herbert Aptheker, *A Documentary History of the Negro People in the United States,* 2 vols. (New York: Citadel Press, 1969), 1: 29. The 1797 conspiracy cited earlier in this chapter was informed on by mulatto slaves. For a detailed treatment of the class and color implications of the Vesey Plot, see Koger, *Black Slaveowners,* chap. 9.

70. Catherine McBeth to Her Brother, October 4, 1822, Malcolm MacBeth Collection, SCHS; Starobin, *Vesey,* 149–51; Walter J. Fraser Jr., *Charleston! Charleston!: The History of a Southern City* (Columbia, S.C.: University of South Carolina Press, 1989), 203; Alan January, "The South Carolina Association: An Agency for Race Control in Antebellum Charleston," *South Carolina Historical Magazine* 78 (July 1977): 192–93, 196–97.

71. Fraser, *Charleston! Charleston!* 203, 219–20, 238; Mills, *Statistics of South Carolina,* 421.

72. Francis A. Kemble, *Journal of a Residence on a Georgia Plantation in 1838-1839* (London: Longman, Green, et al., 1863; reprint ed., New York: Alfred A. Knopf, 1961), 39; William H. Russell, *My Diary North and South* (Boston: T. O. H. P. Burnham, 1863), 132.

73. *Charleston Daily Courier,* January 13, 1860, *Charleston Mercury,* October 26, 27, November 3, 15, 1859.

74. *Charleston Mercury,* October 26, 1859. For other examples of slaveholders who expressed concerns about slave behavior and the need for more stringent control in the context of Harper's Ferry, see *Charleston Mercury,* November 11, 22, 1859.

CHAPTER 2

FREE BLACK LIFE IN ANTEBELLUM
AND CIVIL WAR CHARLESTON

1. Will of John Cottingham, Vol. 1, Book A, 1671–1724, 15, Will of Thomas Bolton, Vol. 1, Book A, 1671–1724, 60, Charleston County Record of Wills (hereafter referred to as CCRW), Charleston County Library (hereafter referred to as CCL); *U.S. Bureau of the Census, Population of the United States in 1850 Compiled from the Seventh Census* (Washington: Government Printing Office, 1853), 339; U. S. Bureau of the Census, *Population of the United States in 1860 Compiled from the*

Eighth Census (Washington: Government Printing Office, 1864), 195, 214, 452, 598. Throughout the entire antebellum period, free blacks remained the most urbanized group in the United States. By 1860 in excess of one-third of the free black population lived in urban areas compared with one-fifth of the white population and one-twenty-fifth of the slave populations. Jane R. Wilkie, "Urbanization and Deurbanization of the Black Population Before the Civil War," *Demography* 13 (August 1976): 314.

2. Documents Relative to the Denmark Vesey Insurrection, Document B, South Carolina Department of Archives and History (hereafter referred to as SCDAH); Holloway Family Papers, College of Charleston Library Special Collections (hereafter referred to as CCLSC); Helen T. Catterall, ed., *Judicial Cases Concerning American Slavery and the Negro,* 5 vols. (Washington: Carnegie Institution, 1926–37), 2: 415; E. Horace Fitchett, "The Free Negro in Charleston, South Carolina," (Ph.D. diss., University of Chicago, 1950), 39; Petition of Moses Irvin, 1829, Petitions Relating to Slavery, SCDAH; *Charleston Daily News,* October 31, 1872.

3. Will of John Harleston, Vol. 20, Book A, 1783–93, 224–29, Will of Joseph Bixby, Vol. 35, Book B, 1818–26, 511–13, Will of Philip Stanislas Noisette, Vol. 40, Book A, 1834–39, 203–04, CCRW, CCL; "Odd Facts Concerning Phillipe Stanislaus Noisette Horticulturalist and Botanist of Charleston, S.C. 1795–1835," Philippe Stanislaus Noisette Papers, South Carolina Historical Society (hereafter referred to as SCHS).

4. U. S. Bureau of the Census, *Population of the United States in 1860 Compiled From the Eighth Census,* 452; U.S. Bureau of the Census, *Negro Population of the United States 1790-1915* (Washington: Government Printing Office, 1918), 220; *Charleston Mercury,* August 16, 1823. The pioneering research of Ira Berlin reveals that while free Negroes in the Lower South were three-quarters mulatto, only one-third of those in the Upper South were of mixed blood. Differences in the method of manumission largely account for the distinct demographic types produced by the two regions. In the Upper South after the American Revolution, ideological manumission occurred whereby black as well as brown slaves were emancipated. The states of the Lower South resisted ideological manumissions, only emancipating favorite slaves and particularly those who were the result of illicit sexual relations between slave women and white masters. The free Negroes in the Lower South became an even lighter group as their numbers were increased by West Indian free persons of color who arrived at the turn of the eighteenth century. In the Upper South, the early nineteenth century saw the wane of ideological emancipation, which was replaced by the more selective pattern of the Lower South. This occurred too late to overturn the former's free black majority. Ira Berlin, *Slaves Without Masters: The Free Negro in the Antebellum South* (New York: Pantheon Press, 1974), 179–80.

5. Catterall, *Judicial Cases*, 2: 326–27; Will of William Turpin, Vol. 40, Book A, 1834–39, 224–25, 229; Will of Joseph Bixby, Vol. 35, Book B, 1818–26, 511–13, CCRW, CCL.

6. Marina Wikramanayake, *A World in Shadow, The Free Black in Antebellum South Carolina* (Columbia: University of South Carolina Press, 1973), 34–36.

7. Petition of James Patterson, 1838, Petitions Relating to Slavery, SCDAH; Holloway Family Papers, CCLSC; Larry Koger, *Black Slave-owners*, 54–55, 64.

8. Berlin, *Slaves Without Masters,* 144; Catterall, *Judicial Cases*, 2: 375, 452.

9. *The Statutes at Large of South Carolina; Acts from 1838 Exclusive*, 22 vols. (Columbia, S.C.: Republican Printing Co., 1873), 11: 168–69.

10. J. D. B. DeBow, ed., *Compendium of the Seventh Census of the United States* (Washington: Government Printing Office, 1851), 64; Wikramanayake, *A World in Shadow*, 44; Berlin, *Slaves Without Masters,* 45; List of the Taxpayers of the City of Charleston for 1859, 1860, SCHS.

11. Holloway Family Papers, CCLSC; Fitchett, "The Free Negro, " 48, 162–63; Frederick A. Ford, *Census of the City of Charleston, South Carolina for the Year 1861* (Charleston: Evans & Cogswell, 1861), 10, 14; Berlin, *Slaves Without Masters,* 177; Herbert G. Gutman, "Persistent Myths About the Afro-American Family," *Journal of Interdisciplinary History* 6 (Autumn 1975): 192–93.

12. U.S. Manuscript Census of Population 1860, City of Charleston. The discussion of male workers in this chapter refers to those aged fifteen and above. J. L. Dawson and H. W. DeSaussure, *Census of the City of Charleston, South Carolina, for the Year 1848* (Charleston: J. B. Nixon, 1849), 35.

13. Abiel Abbott Journal, November 22, 1818, Papers of Abiel Abbott, SCHS; Will of Plowden Weston, Vol. 37, Book A, 1826–34, 184–85, CCRW, CCL; Siegling to Horlbeck, January 9, 1859, Bill for Partition and Relief, February 7, 1867, Noisette Family Papers, USCCL.

14. Holloway Family Papers, CCLSC; Fitchett, "The Free Negro," 108–09; Daniel A. Payne, *Recollections of Seventy Years* (Nashville: African Methodist Episcopal Sunday School Union, 1888; reprint ed., New York: Arno Press, 1968), 15, 18.

15. Samuel D. Smith, *The Negro in Congress 1870–1901* (Chapel Hill: University of North Carolina Press, 1940), 61; Martin R. Delany, *The Condition, Elevation, Emigration and Destiny of the Colored People of the United States* (n.p.: Martin R. Delany, 1852; reprint ed., New York: Arno Press, 1969), 108–09.

16. F. C. Adams, *Manuel Pereira, Or the Sovereign Rule of South Carolina* (Washington: Buell & Blanchard, 1853), 88–89; Rosser H.

Taylor, *Antebellum South Carolina: A Social and Cultural History* (New York: Da Capo Press, 1970), 82; Karl Bernhard, Duke of Saxe-Weimar-Eisenach, *Travels Through North America During the Years 1825 and 1826,* 2 vols. (Philadelphia: Carey, Lea & Carey, 1828), 2: 5; Thomas Hamilton, *Men and Manners in America* (Philadelphia: Carey, Lea & Blanchard, 1833), 347–48; Tyrone Power, *Impressions of America During the Years 1833, 1834 and 1835,* 2 vols. (London: Richard Bentley, 1836), 2: 93; Stuart, *Three Years in North America,* 2: 66.

17. Wikramanayake, *A World in Shadow,* 110; Mrs. St. Julien Ravenel, *Charleston: The Place and the People* (New York: Macmillan Co., 1927), 461.

18. Berlin, *Slaves Without Masters,* 255; W. H. Gilliland to Francis St. Mark, January 27, 1856, William H. Gilliland Papers, USCCL.

19. *A Digest of the Ordinances of the City Council from the Year 1783,* 176–77; Aptheker, ed., *A Documentary History of the Negro People,* 1: 27.

20. U.S. Manuscript Census of Population 1850, City of Charleston.

21. Edward R. Laurens, *An Address Delivered in Charleston, Before the Agricultural Society of South Carolina on September 18, 1832* (Charleston: A. E. Miller, 1832), 11.

22. Edward R. Laurens, *A Letter to the Hon. Whitemarsh B. Seabrook of St. John's Colleton; in Explanation and Defence of An Act to Amend the Law in Relation to Slaves and Free Persons of Color* (Charleston: Observor Press, 1835), 9–10.

23. Berlin, *Slaves Without Masters,* 238; U.S. Manuscript Census of Population 1860, City of Charleston.

24. List of the Taxpayers of the City of Charleston for 1860, SCHS; Wikramanayake, *A World in Shadow,* 79–80, 100.

25. Wikramanayake, *A World in Shadow,* 106–07; Fitchett, "The Free Negro," 100; Will of Thomas Bonneau, Vol. 39, Book C, 1826–34, 905–07, CCRW, CCL; Papers Relating to Peter Desverneys, Free Person of Color, SCHS.

26. U.S. Manuscript Census of Population 1850, 1860, City of Charleston; Papers Relating to Peter Desverneys, Free Person of Color, SCHS; Inventory of the Estate of Captain Williamson, Box 87, No. 21, Charleston County Wills and Inventories, Charleston County Courthouse. (Hereafter referred to as CCWI, CCC).

27. Holloway Family Papers, CCLSC; James B. Browning, "Beginnings of Insurance Enterprise Among Negroes," *Journal of Negro History* 22 (October 1937): 426.

28. List of the Taxpayers of the City of Charleston for 1860, SCHS; Koger, *Black Slaveowners,* 23–25.

29. Will of Richmond Kinloch, Vol. 46, Book A, 1851–1856, 46–49.

30. Will of Peter Desverneys, Vol. 49, Book B, 1856–62, 867–68; Will

of Richmond Kinloch, Vol. 46, Book A, 1851–56, 46–49, CCRW, CCL; Deed of Trusteeship, September 1852, John Thiegling to Dr. Horlbeck, January 9, 1859, Noisette Family Papers, USCCL.

31. Koger, *Black Slaveowners,* 25–27, 39, 146, 158.

32. Ibid., 36–37, 44; List of the Taxpayers of the City of Charleston for 1860, 332, SCHS; "Anthony Weston" in Biographical Notes for an "Encyclopedia of the Colored Race," Daniel Murray Papers, (microfilm reel 22), State Historical Society of Wisconsin (hereafter referred to as SHSW).

33. Koger, *Black Slaveowners,* 171.

34. Fitchett, "The Free Negro," 1–2; Edmund L. Drago, *Initiative, Paternalism, and Race Relations: Charleston's Avery Normal Institute* (Athens, Ga.: University of Georgia Press, 1990), 8, 23–24.

35. Fitchett, "The Free Negro," 1–2; Wikramanayake, *A World in Shadow,* 87; Inventory of the Estate of Captain Williamson, Box 87, No. 21, CCWI, CCC; Carter G. Woodson, *Free Negro Heads of Families in the United States in 1830* (Washington: Association For the Study of Negro Life and History, Inc., 1925), xxxv.

36. Barbara Bellows, *Benevolence Among Slaveholders: Assisting the Poor in Charleston 1670–1860* (Baton Rouge: Louisiana State University Press, 1993), 48; Payne, *Recollections,* 14; *Seventeenth Annual Report of the Executive Committee of the Christian Benevolent Society,* March 1856, Holloway Family Papers, CCLSC.

37. W.P.A. Notes on the Brown Fellowship Society, SCHS; *Rules and Regulations of the Brown Fellowship Society Established at Charleston, S.C.* (Charleston: J. B. Nixon, 1844), 3, 9–11, 14–15, 19; Holloway Family Papers, CCLSC.

38. Browning, "Insurance Enterprise," 426; Petition of the Brotherly Association, November 25, 1856, Petitions Relating to Slavery, SCDAH; Fitchett, "The Free Negro," 122.

39. Will of Richmond Kinlock, Vol. 46, Book A, 1851–56, 48, CCRW, CCL; William T. Catto to Richard Holloway, September 6, 1833, Holloway Family Papers, CCLSC; Drago, *Initiative, Paternalism, and Race Relations,* 27–28; *Constitution, By Laws and Rules of the Amateur Literary and Fraternal Association* (Charleston: Edward Perry, 1873).

40. Holloway Family Papers, CCLSC; C. W. Birnie, "Education of the Negro in Charleston, South Carolina, Prior to the Civil War," *Journal of Negro History* 12 (January 1927): 18; Friendly Moralist Society Minutes, "Absences," August 2, 1848, CCLSC.

41. Payne, *Recollections,* 15, 19–25, 35. Payne, although a member of the brown elite, was one of its less exclusivist representatives. Edmund Drago argues that in many cases religious affiliation served to embellish or mitigate the exclusivist tendencies within the elite. Therefore,

Methodists, such as Payne and the Holloways, tended to embrace a more inclusive view of "community." Episcopalians, such as Edward P. Wall and Michael Eggart, took a much more insular and elitist view of "community." Drago, *Initiative, Paternalism, and Race Relations,* 32–34.

42. Birnie, "Education of the Negro," 19–20; "The Autobiography of Francis Asbury Mood," 17–18 (Typescript), USCCL.

43. Fredrika Bremer, *The Homes of the New World: Impressions of America,* 2 vols. (New York: Harper & Bros., 1853), 2: 499; Birnie, "Education of the Negro," 17; Carter G. Woodson, *The Mind of the Negro as Reflected in Letters Written During the Crisis 1800–1860* (Washington: Association for the Study of Negro Life and History, 1926; reprint ed., New York: Negro Universities Press, 1969), 74; Albert W. Pegues, *Our Baptist Ministers and Schools* (Springfield, Mass.: Willey & Co., 1892), 79–80.

44. Cooper and McCord, *Statutes at Large,* 7: 468; Payne, *Recollections,* 20, 34–35; *Charleston Mercury,* October 25, 1859; See Appendix, Table 12. The campaign against slave and free black literacy escalated in the wake of the nullification crisis and the rise of an aggressive abolitionist movement in the North. Whitemarsh Seabrook, a state senator and leading nullifier, was architect of the 1834 restrictive legislation. In playing upon popular fears of rebellion, he stressed that education for blacks reduced the master's authority and jeopardized the state. In summer 1835 a mob seized abolitionists mailings from the Charleston post office and burned them. Almost simultaneously, a lynch mob sought out the proslavery Catholic Bishop John England because he had recently begun a school for free blacks. Cooler heads eventually prevailed but only after Bishop England agreed to close his school. Cornelius, *When I Can Read My Title Clear,* 39–44.

45. James H. Holloway, *Why I Am A Methodist: A Historical Sketch Of What The Church Has Done For the Colored Children Educationally As Early As 1790 At Charleston, S.C.* (n.p.: R. Wainwright, 1909), 7–8, 11, 13.

46. Payne, *Recollections,* 17.

47. Minutes and Register of the First Baptist Church, Charleston County, January 14, 1851, USCCL.

48. William M. Wightman, *Life of William Capers D. D.* (Nashville: Publishing House of the Methodist Episcopal Church South, 1896), 138–40; Fitchett, "The Free Negro," 170; Wikramanayake, *A World in Shadow,* 125.

49. Payne, *Recollections,* 11–12; Aptheker, *Documentary History,* 1:79; James Redpath, *The Roving Editor: Or Talks With Slaves in the Southern States* (New York: A. B. Burdick, 1859; reprint ed., New York: Negro Universities Press, 1968), 67–68; Taylor, *Antebellum South Carolina,* 184–85.

50. Catterall, *Judicial Cases,* 2: 335.

51. Ibid., 2: 358–59.

52. Ibid., 2: 358–359, 386, 400–01.

53. Berlin, *Slaves Without Masters,* 271; Documents Relative to the Denmark Vesey Insurrection, Document B, SCDAH; *An Exposition of the Late Schism in The Methodist Episcopal Church in Charleston In the Year 1833 Up To November 28 of That Year* (Charleston: J. S. Burges, 1834), 16, 35; *Public Proceedings Relating to Calvary Church and the Religious Instruction of Slaves* (Charleston: Miller & Browne, 1850), 53; Adams, *Manuel Pereira,* 88.

54. Friendly Moralist Society Minutes, May 19, 1843, June 11, 14, 1848, CCLSC.

55. Holloway Family Papers, CCLSC; Rules and Regulations of the Brown Fellowship Society, 12; Friendly Moralist Society Minutes, June 13, 1842, CCLSC.

56. Berlin, *Slaves Without Masters,* 198–99; Joel Williamson, *New People: Miscegenation and Mulattoes in the United States* (New York: New York University Press, 1984), 19–20, 42.

57. Quoted in Michael P. Johnson and James L. Roark, *Black Masters: A Free Family of Color in the Old South* (New York: W. W. Norton, 1984), 192; Holloway Family Papers, CCLSC; *Charleston Daily Courier,* April 25, 1834, December 9, 1835. When additional restrictions and even banishment of all free blacks was considered in the 1830s, Edwin C. Holland, a Charleston newspaper editor, counseled against treating all free persons of color the same. He believed that the "blacks" were lazy and profligate and represented a danger to the slave population. This was because "when [slaves] look around them and see persons of their *own color* enjoying a *comparative* degree of *freedom,* and assuming privileges beyond their own condition, [they] naturally become dissatisfied" and insurrection resulted. Free "blacks" should be removed, he argued. Holland opposed the removal of free mulattoes, though. They represented a *"barrier* between our own color and that of the black—and, in cases of *insurrection,* are more likely to enlist themselves under the banner of the whites." Their loyalty could be counted on because so many owned slaves and would be vigilant against any possible threat to "this species of property." Robert Starobin, ed., *Denmark Vesey: The Slave Conspiracy of 1822* (Englewood Cliffs, N.J.: Prentice Hall Inc., 1970), 133–37; Robert Harris questions whether free persons of color and mulattoes enjoyed any special treatment in Charleston. See his "Charleston's Free Afro-American Elite: The Brown Fellowship Society and the Humane Brotherhood," *South Carolina Historical Magazine,* 82 (October 1981): 304, 309. For more detailed studies of the special status of mulattoes and the three tiered system of race relations, see Robert B. Toplin, "Between Black and White: Attitudes Toward Southern Mulattoes, 1830–1861," *Journal of Southern*

History 45 (May 1979): 185–201; "Reinterpreting Comparative Race Relations: The United States and Brazil," *Journal of Black Studies* 2 (December 1971): 135–55; Laura Foner, "The Free People of Color in Louisiana and St. Domingue: A Comparative Portrait of Two Three-Caste Societies," *Journal of Social History* 3 (Summer 1970): 406–30.

58. Quoted in Koger, *Black Slaveowners,* 15–16; "Frances A. Rollin Whipper," Daniel Murray Papers (microfilm reel 8), 8–9, SHSW. For cases similar to that of William Rollin, see Michael P. Johnson and James L. Roark, *No Chariot Let Down: Charleston's Free People of Color on the Eve of the Civil War* (Chapel Hill: University of North Carolina Press, 1984), 92, 122–23.

59. Rules and Regulations of the Brown Fellowship Society, 12; Payne, *Recollections,* 24, 34–35; Holloway Family Papers, CCLSC.

60. John Siegling to Elias Horlbeck, January 9, 1859, Noisette Family Papers, USCCL; Manuscript Census of Population 1860, City of Charleston. For another example of the Noisettes' ability to enlist the support of influential whites to protect a family member from legal prosecution, see Johnson and Roark, *No Chariot Let Down,* 111, 114–15.

61. Elise Pinckney, ed., *Register of St. Philip's Parish Church Charleston, South Carolina, 1810 Through 1822* (Charleston: National Society of the Colonial Dames of America in the State of South Carolina, 1973), 7, 11; Berlin, *Slaves Without Masters,* 299; Holloway Family Papers, CCLSC; Laurens, *An Address,* 12.

62. Howell M. Henry, "Police Control of the Slave in South Carolina" (Ph.D. diss., Vanderbilt University, 1914), 29–43, 47; *Report on the Free Colored Poor of the City of Charleston* (Charleston: Burgess & James, 1842), 10–12; Bellows, *Benevolence Among Slaveholders,* 87–88, 178; Berlin, *Slaves Without Masters,* 322; Harriet Martineau, *Retrospect of Western Travel,* 2 vols. (London: Sanders & Otley, 1838), 1: 234; Lambert, *Travels,* 2: 374.

63. *Public Proceedings Relating to Calvary Church,* 9; *Report on the Free Colored Poor of the City of Charleston,* 10–12; Bellows, *Benevolence Among Slaveholders,* 179–80.

64. *A Digest of the Ordinances of the City Council of Charleston from the Year 1783,* 21–22; *Charleston Mercury,* December 11, 1822; Laurens, *An Address,* 9–10; Laurens, *Letter to the Honorable Whitemarsh B. Seabrook,* 8; Catterall, *Judicial Cases,* 2: 421. Viewed in such terms, justice under the law was a rarity for free blacks, who were tried in slave courts made up of magistrates and freeholders. Free blacks residing in Charleston did have advantages over other free persons of color, though. In capital cases Charleston's slave courts required a unanimous vote for conviction. This standard was more rigorous than that of any other place in the state. Free blacks in the rural areas were harassed and continually

found themselves accused and tried for serious crimes. One study indicates that in the upcountry, free persons of color were prosecuted at six times the rate of slaves. It is doubtful that such a disparity can be accounted for by plantation justice entirely. See Michael S. Hindus, "Black Justice Under White Law: Criminal Prosecutions of Blacks in Antebellum South Carolina," *Journal of American History* 63 (December 1976): 577, 584, 592.

65. *Charleston Mercury*, December 15, 1858, December 6, 1860; *Charleston Daily Courier*, November 15, 1858, January 19, March 1, 1860.

66. Wikramanayake, *A World in Shadow,* 169; Steven A. Channing, *Crisis of Fear: Secession in South Carolina* (New York: W. W. Norton, 1974), 47, 49.

67. Wikramanayake, *A World in Shadow,* 169–70; Channing, *Crisis of Fear,* 47, 49; *Charleston Mercury,* October 25, 1859.

68. *Charleston Daily Courier,* October 26, 1859, August 9, 1860; Johnson and Roark, *Black Masters,* 239, 249, 258–59.

69. *Charleston Daily Courier,* December 15, 16, 1859; *Charleston Mercury,* November 24, December 6, 1860; Johnson and Roark, *Black Masters,* 239, 249, 258–59.

70. Wikramanayake, *A World in Shadow,* 176, 179, 183; *Charleston Mercury,* November 24, 1860; Johnson and Roark, *Black Masters,* 279–81, 292–93; *Charleston Daily Courier,* December 16, 1859.

71. Quoted in Leon Litwack, *Been in the Storm So Long: The Aftermath of Slavery* (New York: Alfred A. Knopf, 1979), 17; Johnson and Roark, *Black Masters,* 293.

72. Henry Raymond to Mother, July 30, 1863, Henry Raymond Family Papers, USCCL; Jacob Schirmer Diary, August 25, 1862, SCHS; Minutes of the Board of Firemasters, May 12, 1862, SCHS; A.M.E. *Christian Recorder,* August 25, 1866.

73. Minutes of the Board of Firemasters, May 12, October 15, 1862, October 3, 12, 1863, SCHS; A.M.E. *Christian Recorder,* August 25, 1866; Walter J. Fraser Jr., *Charleston! Charleston!: The History of a Southern City* (Columbia, S.C.: University of South Carolina Press, 1989), 255; *Charleston Mercury,* January 3, 1861; *Charleston Daily News,* August 10, 1870; Mother to Sarah Anne, June 7, 1862, Augustine Smyth Papers, SCHS.

74. Drago, *Initiative, Paternalism, and Race Relations,* 100; *Charleston Mercury,* September 5, 1861; *Charleston Daily News,* August 10, 1870; A.M.E. *Christian Recorder,* August 25, 1866; Deposition, April 6, 1867, William H. Gilliland Papers, USCCL; Holloway Family Papers, USCCL; Benjamin Quarles, *The Negro In The Civil War* (Boston: Little Brown & Co., 1969), 264.

75. John Blassingame, *Slave Testimony: Two Centuries of Letters, Speeches, Interviews and Autobiographies* (Baton Rouge: Louisiana State University Press, 1977), 360, 699–702.

76. Quarles, *The Negro In The Civil War*, 72–74; Uya, *From Slavery to Public Service*, 20; *Charleston Mercury*, September 5, 1861.

77. E. Milby Burton, *The Siege of Charleston 1861–1865* (Columbia, S. C.: University of South Carolina Press, 1970), 252; Viola C. Floyd, "The Fall of Charleston," *South Carolina Historical Magazine* 66 (January 1965): 3; *Charleston Daily Courier,* February 20, March 1, April 19, 1865; Luis Emilo, *A Brave Black Regiment: History of the Fifty-Fourth Regiment of Massachusetts Volunteer Infantry 1863–1865* (Boston: Boston Book Company, 1894), 282–85.

78. Charles B. Fox, *Record of the Service of the Fifty-Fifth Regiment of Massachusetts Volunteer Infantry* (Cambridge, Mass: John Wilson & Son, 1868), 57–58.

79. Ibid.

80. *Charleston Daily Courier,* March 22, 1865.

81. *Charleston Daily Courier,* February 20, 1865; Frank [Frances] A. Rollin, *Life and Public Services of Martin R. Delany* (Boston: Lee and Shepard, 1883), 180, 187, 194, 202; Victor Ullman, *Martin R. Delany: The Beginnings of Black Nationalism* (Boston: Beacon Press, 1971), chaps. 4–10; "Orindatus Simon Bolivar Wall," Daniel Murray Papers (microfilm reel 22), SHSW; Joseph T. Glatthaar, *Forged in Battle: The Civil War Alliance of Black Soldiers and White Officers* (New York: Free Press, 1990), 179.

82. *Charleston Daily Courier,* March 1, April 19, 1865; Rollin, *Life and Public Services*, 200–01, 209–13.

83. Shelby Foote, *The Civil War Era: A Narrative, Red River to Appomattox*, 3 vols. (New York: Random House, 1974), 3: 970–73; Rollin, *Life and Public Services,* 193–94; A.M.E. *Christian Recorder,* October 14, 1865; *Charleston Daily Courier,* April 15, 1865.

84. Rollin, *Life and Public Services,* 194–96; *Charleston Daily Courier,* April 17, 1865; Foote, *The Civil War,* 3: 970, 972–73.

CHAPTER 3

"AN EARNEST ASSERTION OF MANHOOD":
The Quest for Civic and Political Equality

1. Joel Williamson, *The Crucible of Race: Black-White Relations in the American South Since Emancipation* (New York: Oxford University Press, 1984), 24, 28, 29.

2. Steven A. Channing, *Crisis of Fear: Secession in South Carolina* (New York: W. W. Norton, 1974), 58–59; Dan T. Carter, "The Anatomy of Fear: The Christmas Day Insurrection Scare of 1865," *Journal of Southern History* 42 (August 1976): 346.

3. Sidney Andrews, *The South Since the War* (Boston: Ticknor and Fields, 1866), 27; Isabella Middleton Leland, "Middleton Correspondence 1861–1865," *South Carolina Historical Magazine* 65 (April 1964): 108; Cousin M to Celia, June 11, 1865, Family Papers of Frederick A. Porcher, South Carolina Historical Society (hereafter referred to as SCHS); John Dennett, *The South As It Is 1865–1866* (New York: Viking Press, 1865), 193.

4. W. L. M. Burger (Assistant Adjutant General) to District Commanders, December 16, 1865, Assistant Commissioner Letters Received, Freedmen's Bureau Papers (hereafter referred to as FBP), South Carolina Department of Archives and History (hereafter referred to as SCDAH).

5. Henry Raymond to Mother, July 1, 30, 1865, Henry Raymond Family Papers, University of South Carolina Caroliniana Library (hereafter referred to as USCCL); Arney R. Childs, ed., *The Private Journal of Henry William Ravenel* (Columbia, S.C.: University of South Carolina Press, 1947), 251.

6. Henry Raymond to Mother, July 30, 1865, Henry Raymond Family Papers, USCCL; Jacob Schirmer Diary, June 1865, SCHS; Daniel E. Huger Smith, et al., eds., *Mason Smith Family Letters 1860–1868* (Columbia, S.C.: University of South Carolina Press, 1950), 231.

7. A.M.E. *Christian Recorder*, August 5, 1865, September 22, 1866; Reuben Tomlinson to Lt. Gen. C. Burger, September 12, 1865; Shole's *Charleston City Directory* 1879–80 (hereafter city directories will be cited by title and year only), 114.

8. Sarah Jenkins to Major Crawford, July 8, 1867, Assistant Commissioner Letters Received, FBP, SCDAH; A.M.E. *Christian Recorder*, September 22, 1866.

9. *Charleston Daily Courier,* June 25, 1866.

10. *Charleston Daily Courier,* July 30, 1866; Childs, *Private Journal,* 287.

11. R. H. Cain to R. K. Scott, November 11, 1867, Assistant Commissioner Letters Received, FBP, SCDAH; A.M.E. *Christian Recorder,* July 10, August 5, 1865, July 21, 1866; *New York Times,* June 11, 1865, 3.

12. *Charleston Daily News,* February 26, 1866; *Charleston Daily Courier,* July 3, 10, 11, 18, 1865.

13. Smith, *Mason Smith Family Letters*, 227; Raymond to Mother, July 30, 1865, Henry Raymond Family Letters, USCCL.

14. Caroline Gilman to Eliza, September 17, 1865, Letters of Caroline Gilman, SCHS; from ———— to Celia (name not given), May 25, 1865, Cousin M to Celia, June 11, 1865, Family Papers of Frederick A. Porcher, SCHS; Henry Raymond to Mother, June 1865, Henry Raymond Family Letters, USCCL.

15. Mrs. Gilman to Eliza, ———— 10, 1865 (month not given), Letters of Caroline Gilman, SCHS.

16. Smith, *Mason Smith Family Letters,* 236; *Atlantic Monthly,* June 1877, 675; *Charleston Daily News,* October 9, 1869.

17. *Charleston Daily Courier,* April 17, May 13, 1865.

18. Alrutheus A. Taylor, *The Negro in South Carolina During the Reconstruction* (Washington: Association for the Study of Negro Life and History, 1924), 40–41; Francis B. Simkins and Robert H. Woody, *South Carolina During Reconstruction* (Chapel Hill: University of North Carolina Press, 1932; reprint ed., Gloucester, Mass.: Peter Smith, 1966), 37–39; Herbert Aptheker, "South Carolina Negro Conventions 1865," *Journal of Negro History* 31 (January 1946): 91.

19. *Journal of the Convention of the People of South Carolina Held in Columbia, S.C. September 1865 Together with the Ordinances Reports Resolutions, Etc.* (Columbia, S.C.: J. A. Selby, 1865), 14–15, 41, 103, 121–23, 148.

20. Taylor, *The Negro in South Carolina,* 21, 50; *Journal of the Convention of the People of South Carolina,* 41, 103, 121–23, 148; *Charleston Daily Courier,* September 29, 1865.

21. Edward McPherson, *The Political History of the United States of America During the Period of Reconstruction* (Washington: Solomon & Chapman, 1875; reprint ed., New York: Negro Universities Press, 1969), 34–36; Simkins and Woody, *South Carolina During Reconstruction,* 48; Joel Williamson, *After Slavery: The Negro in South Carolina During Reconstruction, 1861–1877* (Chapel Hill: University of North Carolina Press, 1965), 72–73.

22. Ibid.

23. *Charleston Daily News,* September 14, 1865, September 15, 1868; quoted in Williamson, *After Slavery,* 72–73, 245.

24. Aptheker, "South Carolina Negro Conventions," 94–95; William C. Hine, "Frustration, Factionalism and Failure: Black Political Leadership and the Republican Party in Reconstruction Charleston, 1865–1877," (Ph.D diss., Kent State University, 1979), 35–36; *Charleston Daily Courier,* September 26, 1865.

25. Ibid.

26. *Proceedings of the Colored People's Convention of the State of South Carolina Held in Zion Church Charleston* (Charleston: South Carolina Leader, 1865), 5; U.S. Manuscript Census of Population 1860, City of Charleston, 1860; Hine, "Frustration, Factionalism and Failure," 39; State Free Negro Capitation Tax Book Charleston 1855; Will of Peter Desverneys, Vol. 49, Book B, 1856–62, 867–68, Charleston County Record of Wills (hereafter referred to as CCRW), Charleston County Library (hereafter referred to as CCL).

27. *Proceedings of the Colored People's Convention,* 7; Emma Lou Thornbrough, ed., *Black Reconstructionists* (Englewood Cliffs, N.J.:

Prentice Hall, 1972), 8; *Charleston Daily News,* October 5, 1872); T. W. Cardozo to Rev. S. Hunt, July 1, 1865, American Missionary Association Papers (hereafter referred to as AMAP), SCDAH; William J. Simmons, *Men of Mark: Eminent Progressive and Rising* (Cleveland: George M. Rewell and Co., 1887; reprint ed., New York: Arno Press, 1968), 281, 866–68.

28. *Proceedings of the Colored People's Convention,* 13, 17.

29. *Proceedings of the Colored People's Convention,* 13, 17, 19; *Charleston Mercury,* February 24, 1868.

30. *Proceedings of the Colored People's Convention,* 9–10, 23–25; *Charleston Daily Courier,* December 14, 1865; Aptheker, "South Carolina Negro Conventions," 97.

31. *Proceedings of the Colored People's Convention,* 23–25; *Charleston Daily Courier,* December 14, 1865; Aptheker, "South Carolina Negro Conventions," 97.

32. Leon Litwack, *Been in the Storm So Long: The Aftermath of Slavery* (New York: Alfred A. Knopf, 1979), 507; *Proceedings of the Colored People's Convention,* 15.

33. Samuel L. Bennett to Jas. L. Orr, January 26, Samuel L. Bennett to Gov. Orr, April 26, 1866, Governor James Orr Papers, Letters Received, SCDAH.

34. *Charleston Daily Courier,* February 15, 1867.

35. Ibid., October 23, November 4, 1865, January 23, 1866, November 28, December 10, 1866; Williamson, *After Slavery,* 328. In subsequent orders, Commander Sickles increased the likelihood blacks would serve on juries by decreeing that potential jurors be qualified under the Reconstruction Acts (March 1867) and that the names be drawn from the tax lists with no minimum property qualification for serving. Later, during Governor Scott's administration, the basis for the jury list would be changed to the voter registration rolls. An act passed in the state legislature in 1869 effecting the change also required that the racial composition of empaneled juries be reflective of the communities they represented. *Charleston Daily Courier,* June 26, October 3, 1867, April 3, 1869.

36. Simkins and Woody, *South Carolina During Reconstruction,* 60–62; Samuel L. Bennett to James L. Orr, April 26, 1866, James Orr Papers, Letters Received, SCDAH.

37. Simkins and Woody, *South Carolina During Reconstruction,* 64.

38. Hine, "Frustration, Factionalism and Failure," 57–58; *Proceedings of the Colored People's Convention,* 6–7, 18. The following are the names of the Committee of Thirteen: M. G. Camplin, E. J. Adams, Peter Miller, J. N. Hayne, Jno. B. Morris, J. D. Price, Ben J. Reils, J. P. M. Epping, B. F. Randolph, R. C. DeLarge, F. L. Cardozo, Samuel L. Bennett, W. J. Brodie, *Charleston Daily Courier,* March 22, 1867.

39. *Charleston Daily Courier,* March 22, 1867.

40. Two years earlier, Martin R. Delany also identified color consciousness as a divisive vestige of slavery that needed to be overcome. He associated its origins with the Vesey conspiracy and the fact that the chief informant was a mulatto. Black hostility to mulattoes resulted. In a speech, Delany reportedly charged that slaveholders used the conflict to their advantage, having concluded, "that their only safety was to make confidents of the mulattoes and cut off so much strength of the blacks." *Charleston Daily Courier,* May 13, 1865, March 22, 27, 1867. For another example in which invidious class and color distinctions were criticized, see *Charleston News and Courier,* November 30, 1885.

41. *Proceedings of the Colored People's Convention,* 11; *Charleston Advocate,* February 23, 1867; *Charleston Daily Courier,* March 27, May 4, 1867.

42. Eric Foner, *Freedom's Lawmakers: A Directory of Black Officeholders During Reconstruction* (New York: Oxford University Press, 1993), 87; *Charleston Daily Courier,* May 8, July 26, 29, 1867; *Charleston Daily News,* November 5, 1869.

43. *Charleston Daily Courier,* May 8, July 26, 29, 1867, August 19, 1868; *Charleston News and Courier,* September 24, 1873; *Charleston Daily News,* August 13, 1869, October 4, 1872; Williamson, *After Slavery,* 372, 375; Aptheker, "South Carolina Negro Conventions," 95; Tax List for the City of Charleston, 1871, Charleston Library Society (hereafter referred to as CLS). According to the tax list for 1869, William J. McKinlay owned $2,480 in real estate. Simpkins and Woody, *South Carolina During Reconstruction,* 117–18; Minutes of the South Carolina Conference of the Methodist Episcopal Church (North), 1869, (n.p.:n.d.), 6, 16; B. F. Randolph to Pvt. Major Reuben. R. Saxton, August 31, 1865, Assistant Commissioner Letters Received, FBP, SCDAH.

44. *Charleston Daily News,* November 8–9, 1867; Simpkins and Woody, *South Carolina During Reconstruction,* 64–65, 87, 109–10. Southerners believed it especially unfair and hypocritical for their region to be forced to accept enfranchisement of the freedmen while northern whites simultaneously denied this right to blacks. The *Courier* editorialized on this subject in 1865, and Governor James Orr also raised this issue in 1867. See *Charleston Daily Courier,* October 10, 1865, April 3, 1867.

45. *Charleston Daily Courier,* June 21, August 17, November 20, 21, 1867; Simpkins and Woody, *South Carolina During Reconstruction,* 89.

46. Thomas Holt, *Black Over White: Negro Political Leadership in South Carolina During Reconstruction* (Urbana, Ill.: University of Illinois Press, 1977), 35, 46, 116; *Proceedings of the Constitutional Convention of South Carolina* (Charleston, S.C.: Denny and Perry, 1868; reprint ed., New York: Arno Press, 1968), 7. The Charleston delegation originally consisted of nine members, but Frederick Sawyer resigned without

serving. Hine, "Frustration, Factionalism and Failure," 103. The influence of black Charlestonians wasn't limited to the city delegation because a number had ventured to other locations; they were attracted by new employment opportunities or were seeking stronger sources of political support. They were subsequently elected to the constitutional convention from their adopted counties. Henry L. Shrewsbury, Thaddeus. K. Sasportas, and William J. McKinlay became teachers for the Freedmen's Bureau in Cheraw and Orangeburg counties and were elected delegates from these places. All were from well-known free black families. Rev. Benjamin F. Randolph represented Orangeburg at the July Republican State Convention. While active in Charleston also, he may have had a larger base of political support in Orangeburg and was elected to the convention from there. *Charleston Mercury,* January 24, 27, February 24, 1868; *Charleston Daily Courier,* July 29, 1867, June 19, 1868; Williamson, *After Slavery,* 372; *Charleston Daily News,* August 13, September 18, November 5, 1869, February 9, 1871, September 27, 1872.

47. Williamson, *After Slavery,* 370; U.S. Manuscript Census of Population, City of Charleston, 1860. In 1869 William McKinlay Sr. owned over thirty thousand dollars in real estate and debt instruments, which made him one of the wealthiest men in Charleston. Tax list for the City of Charleston, 1871 CLS; Simmons, *Men of Mark,* 281, 866–68; T. W. Cardozo to T. W. Whiting, September 14, 1865, Rev. F. L. Cardozo to Rev. M. E. Strieby, August 13, 1866, AMAP, SCDAH; *American Missionary Magazine* (May 1866): 109–10.

48. *Proceedings of the Constitutional Convention,* 111, 417–23; Holt, *Black Over White,* 128.

49. *Proceedings of the Constitutional Convention,* 381, 391–94, 421, 424.

50. Ibid., 439; Carol Bleser, *The Promised Land: The History of the South Carolina Land Commission, 1869–1890* (Columbia, S.C.: University of South Carolina Press 1969), 22–24, 28; *The Constitution of South Carolina, Adopted April 16, 1868, and the Acts and Joint Resolutions of the General Assembly Passed at the Special Session of 1868* (Columbia, S.C.: John W. Denny, 1868), 33–34.

51. *Proceedings of the Constitutional Convention,* 41–43, 109–10, 113–18, 136–37.

52. Ibid., 41–43, 113–18, 140, 148, 506; *The Constitution of South Carolina, Adopted April 16, 1868,* 5; Hine, "Frustration, Factionalism and Failure," 110.

53. *Proceedings of the Constitutional Convention,* 56, 824–26, 829–30, 833–35; *The Constituion of South Carolina, Adopted April 16, 1868,* 19–20.

54. *Proceedings of the Constitutional Convention,* 828–29, 833–35. Jonathan J. Wright of Beaufort adopted the most radical position of all at

the convention by introducing an amendment that eliminated the word "male" from the voting qualifications, thereby enfranchising women. In his speech he hoped to educate men on the subject of women's suffrage and made two points. First, he argued that women were as intelligent as men and in some ways superior, yet they remained oppressed. Second, he pointed out that governments suffered because of women's exclusion from the body politic. The convention predictably refused to accept the proposed amendment.

55. *Proceedings of the Constitutional Convention,* 56, 709, 711–13, 720, 728–29, 732–33, 736–38; *Charleston Daily Courier,* October 26, 1859, October 13, 1865; *Constitution of South Carolina, Adopted Arpil 16, 1868,* 23.

56. *Proceedings of the Constitutional Convention,* 654–55, 687, 691–693, 703, 708–09; *Constitution of South Carolina, Adopted April 16, 1868,* 22.

57. *Proceedings of the Constitutional Convention,* 353–57; *Constitution of South Carolina, Adopted April 16, 1868,* 6.

58. *Charleston Daily Courier,* February 25, March 7, 12, 14, April 14, July 16, 1868; *Charleston News and Courier,* February 24, 1881; *Charleston Daily News,* May 14, 1868.

59. *Charleston Daily News,* March 9, 12, 21, 1868.

60. *Charleston Daily Courier,* March 28, July 10, 1868.

61. Simpkins and Woody, *South Carolina During Reconstruction,* 109–10.

62. *Charleston Daily Courier,* February 21, March 9, July 7, 1868; *Charleston Daily News,* May 27, June 1, 1868. Richard Cain was not sworn in as an alderman with the others and did not serve. This may have resulted from the demands of his other commitments. He had recently begun to serve in the state senate.

63. *Charleston Daily Courier,* April 29, July 24, 25, September 30, 1868; *Charleston Daily News,* May 19, 1868.

64. *Charleston Daily Courier,* April 23, May 16, November 5, 1868; *Charleston Daily News,* November 6, 1868; Walter J. Fraser Jr., *Charleston! Charleston!: The History of a Southern City* (Columbia, S.C.: University of South Carolina Press, 1989), 287.

65. *Charleston Daily Courier,* November 4, 12, 1868; Hine, "Frustration, Factionalism and Failure," 138. The names of the black aldermen elected in 1868 were William McKinlay, Robert Howard Sr., Richard Holloway, William R. Hampton, Launcelot F. Wall, Philip Thorne, Malcolm Brown, Edward P. Wall, and Thomas Small.

66. *Charleston Daily Courier,* November 12, 30, 1868, January 26, March 2, 3, 1869.

67. See Table 8, Literacy Rates of Blacks in Major Skilled Occupa-

tions, 1870, in chap. 4. Only one of Charleston's Reconstruction aldermen was a slave and those assemblymen elected from the city were former free blacks. Freedmen were more apt to represent rural Charleston County. William C. Hine, "Black Politicians in Reconstruction Charleston, South Carolina: A Collective Study," *Journal of Southern History* 49 (November 1983): 558–59.

68. Hine, "Black Politicians," 562. In Holt's profile of Reconstruction officials, at least 25 percent had been free before the war. Just over half of the black Reconstruction officials in Eric Foner's recent biographical encyclopedia of the period were free before the war. See Holt, *Black Over White*, 38; Foner, *Freedom's Lawmakers,* xv, xviii.

69. Hine, "Black Politicians," 563, 569–70. Richard E. Dereef was a successful wood factor who accumulated twenty-three thousand dollars in real estate and fourteen slaves by 1860. His real estate holdings were reduced to seven thousand dollars in 1869. In a revealing encounter initiated by Rev. Henry Ward Beecher, the abolitionist divine was entertained by Dereef in his home. Afterwards, Reverend Beecher confided his "disappointment" to a friend that Dereef, while tactful, showed no real enthusiasm or "intimacy" for "one who had done so much to bring about emancipation of the negroes." The friend who presumably knew Dereef better explained that Beecher was "treated with admirable and uncomplaining hospitality, by one whom he had relieved of considerable property." After brief service on a politically mixed board of aldermen, Richard Dereef did become involved in politics again, later in Reconstruction, he joined with the Democrats. Tax List for the City of Charleston, 1860, 1869, CLS; Theodore D. Jervey, *The Slave Trade: Slavery and Color* (Columbia, S.C.: The State Company, 1925; reprint ed., Northbrook, Ill.: Metro Books, 1972), 220–21; *Charleston Daily News,* May 20, 1868, September 22, 1870; *Charleston News and Courier,* October 14, 1876.

70. Berlin, *Slave Without Masters,* 392–93.

CHAPTER 4

THE SEARCH FOR ECONOMIC SECURITY:
Labor and Work in Reconstruction Charleston

1. William E. B. DuBois, *Black Reconstruction in America 1860–1880* (New York: Russell & Russell, 1935; reprint ed., New York: Atheneum Press, 1971), 346–47, 351. Traditional scholarship on black urban workers tended to focus on national or regional developments and on the activities of national unions and devoted comparatively little attention to Reconstruction. Examples are Sterling D. Spero and Abram L. Harris, *The Black Worker* (New York: Columbia University Press, 1931; reprint ed., New York: Atheneum Press, 1974); William H. Harris, *The*

Harder We Run: Black Workers Since the Civil War (New York: Oxford University Press, 1982). More recently, scholars have begun to focus more thoroughly on experiences of the black urban working class during the era. Examples are: Peter Rachleff, *Black Labor in Richmond, 1865–1890* (Urbana, IL: University of Illinois Press, 1989); and Eric Arnesen, *Waterfront Workers of New Orleans: Race, Class and Politics 1863–1923* (New York: Oxford University Press, 1991); Jonathan W. McLeod, *Workers and Workplace Dynamics in Reconstruction-Era Atlanta: A Case Study* (Los Angeles: University of California, Los Angeles Center for Afro-American Studies, 1989).

2. Wilbert S. Jenkins, "Chaos, Conflict and Control: The Responses of the Newly-Freed Slaves in Charleston, South Carolina to Emancipation and Reconstruction 1865–1877" (Ph.D. diss., Michigan State Universty, 1991), 102; U.S. Bureau of the Census, *Population of the United States in 1860 Compiled From the Eighth Census,* 452; *Charleston News and Courier,* July 28, 1880; Sidney Andrews, *The South Since the War* (Boston: Ticknor and Fields, 1866), 24–25; Elias Horry Deas to ———, August 12, 1865, Elias Horry Deas Papers, University of South Carolina Caroliniana Library (hereafter referred to as USCCL); Caroline Gilman to Eliza, September 17, 1865, Letters of Caroline Gilman, South Carolina Historical Society (hereafter referred to as SCHS); John Head to General Sickles, January 22, 1866, P. Rector to Brvt. Lt. Col. A. K. Smith, January 23, 1866, Assistant Commissioner Letters Received, Freedmen's Bureau Papers (hereafter referred to as FBP), South Carolina Department of Archives and History (hereafter referred to as SCDAH).

3. Abbott, *The Freedmen's Bureau in South Carolina,* 38, 41; Jane Van Allen to Mr. Whipple, April 13, 1867, American Missionary Association Papers (hereafter referred to as AMAP), SCDAH; E. Merton Coulter, *George W. Williams: The Life of a Southern Merchant and Banker 1820–1903* (Athens, Ga.: Hibriten Press, 1976), 91–92; J. P. Rutherford to Maj. Gen. Rufus Saxton, January 10, 1866, Assistant Commissioner Letters Received, FBP, SCDAH; Herbert G. Gutman, *The Black Family in Slavery and Freedom 1750–1925* (New York: Pantheon Books, 1976), 228; *South Carolina Leader,* December 16, 1865; *Charleston Daily Courier,* May 2, 1865; *Charleston Daily Republican,* December 20, 1869.

4. R. K. Scott to Circular, January 24, 1866, Assistant Commissioner Letters Received, FBP, SCDAH; Andrews, *The South,* 97–98; *Report of the Joint Committee on Reconstruction* (Washington: Government Printing Office, 1866), pt. 2, 224, 247.

5. *Report of the Joint Committee on Reconstruction,* pt. 2, 224, 247; Andrews, *The South,* 97–98.

6. *Nation,* August 15, 1872, 105–06; Jacob Schirmer Diary Index, February 8–9, December 1865, SCHS; Cousin M to Celia, June 11, 1865,

Family Papers of Frederick A. Porcher, SCHS; Caroline Gilman to Eliza, September 17, 1865, Letters of Caroline Gilman, SCHS; Andrews, *The South,* 25–26.

7. *Charleston Daily News,* January 4, 1868; Jacob Schirmer Diary Index, October 1866, SCHS; Asa H. Gordon, *Sketches of Negro Life and History in South Carolina* (Columbia, S.C.: University of South Carolina Press, 1971), 76; *Two Diaries From Middle St. Johns Berkeley South Carolina, February–May, 1865: Journals Kept By Miss Susan R. Jervey & Miss Charlotte St. J. Ravenel* (n.p.: St. John Hunting Club, 1921), 8, 10; Henry Raymond to Mother, July 5, 1865, Henry Raymond Family Letters, USCCL.

8. Jacob Schirmer Diary Index, "Our Domestic Trials with Freed-men and Others," November 15, 1866, January 11, 1873, SCHS; *Atlantic Monthly* (June 1877): 675–79; Daniel E. Huger Smith, et al., eds., *Mason Smith Family Letters, 1860–1868* (Columbia, SC: University of South Carolina Press, 1950), 213; Henry Raymond to Mother, June 1865, Henry Raymond Family Letters, USCCL.

9. *New York Times,* July 4, 1874, 5; *Report of the Attorney General to the General Assembly of South Carolina Concerning the Phosphate Interests of the State* (Columbia, S.C.: Calvo & Patton, 1877), 40; *Charleston Daily News,* July 2, 1868, January 7, 1869; U.S. Manuscript Census of Population 1870, City of Charleston; *Charleston News and Courier,* September 10, 1873.

10. U.S. Manuscript Census of Population 1870, City of Charleston.

11. Ibid.; Walter Hill, "Family Life and Work Culture: Black Charleston, South Carolina, 1880 to 1910" (Ph.D. diss., University of Maryland, 1989), 95–98.

12. Ibid.; Jacqueline Jones, *Labor of Love, Labor of Sorrow: Black Women, Work, and the Family from Slavery to the Present* (New York: Basic Books, 1985), 143.

13. Ibid.; the discussion of workers in Charleston refers to those aged fifteen years and above with the exception of the 1900 census data, which includes those aged ten and above. Native whites, who made up 29.9 percent of the work force, controlled 27.9 percent of the skilled occupations, and German and Irish workers, who composed 7.4 and 7.1 percent of the work force, controlled 6.9 and 5.5 percent of the city's skilled occupations respectively. U.S. Manuscript Census of Population 1870, City of Charleston.

14. U.S. Manuscript Census of Population 1860, 1870, City of Charleston. Former free blacks were represented among Charleston's skilled workers but not in large numbers. By 1870 those former free black males that continued to practice their antebellum trades constituted the following proportions of these selected occupations:

	N	%		N	%
Carpenters	24	4.8	Tailors	8	6.7
Butchers	13	13.7	Blacksmiths	1	1.4
Coopers	2	2.4	Bakers	0	0.0
Shoemakers	6	6.7	Painters	4	5.0
Barbers	4	6.9	Brickmasons	4	2.4

This group of workers accounts for only 4.8 percent of the black men practicing these trades in 1870. Thus, the majority of Charleston's skilled workers were former slaves. Such evidence contrasts sharply with the origins of the skilled group in New Orleans. John Blassingame's study of that city suggests that large numbers of skilled workers during Reconstruction had previously acquired their trades as antebellum free blacks. See Blassingame, *Black New Orleans,* 59–60.

15. U.S. Manuscript Census of Population 1870, City of Charleston.

16. D. E. Huger Smith, *A Charlestonian's Recollections 1846–1913* (Charleston: Walker, Evans, Cogswell, 1950), 64; *Charleston News and Courier,* September 19, 1973; clipping, Untitled Typescript in Negro Fisherman File, SCHS; Harriette Kershaw Leiding, "Street Cries of an Old Southern City," (Charleston: n.p., 1910), 1.

17. U.S. Manuscript Census of Population 1870, City of Charleston.

18. *Charleston Daily News,* February 15, 1868, November 19, 1869; Robert G. Rhett, *Charleston: An Epic of Carolina* (Richmond: Garrett & Massie, 1940), 308; *Charleston Daily Republican,* September 17, 1869.

19. *Charleston Daily News,* February 15, 1868; South Carolina *Leader,* October 21, 1865.

20. *Acts and Joint Resolutions of the General Assembly of the State of South Carolina,* 1865 (Columbia: J. A. Selby, 1865), 279; Joel Williamson, *The Crucible of Race: Black-White Relations in the American South Since Emancipation* (New York: Oxford University Press, 1984), 77.

21. *Charleston Mercury,* August 10, November 30, 1867; U.S. Manuscript Census of Population 1870, 1880, City of Charleston; Samuel L. Bennett to F. J. Moses, April 26, 1873, York Moultrie to F. J. Moses, October 1, 1873, Franklin J. Moses Papers, SCDAH.

22. U.S. Manuscript Census of Population 1870, 1880, City of Charleston. The following chart reveals labor force changes in eighteen selected skilled occupations from 1870 to 1880.

Occupation	Native White	German	Irish	Black
Wood Sawyers (Increased 62.7 percent)[1]	+3.4	0.0	0.0	-1.1
Bakers (Increased 13.8 percent)	+14.6	-11.9	-1.0	-1.9
Carpenters (Increased 5.1 percent)	+8.7	+1.0	-2.3	-7.1

Tailors (Declined)	+3.6	-1.9	+0.1	-4.4
Blacksmiths (Increased 8.8 percent)	+7.2	-1.7	-2.0	-3.1
Engineers (Increased 51 percent)	+7.5	+1.4	-1.9	-6.6
Cigar Makers (Declined)	+15.7	+4.7	0.0	-8.7
Machinists (Declined)	-1.0	+0.1	+3.5	-2.9
Printers (Increased 27 percent)	+17.7	0.0	-6.0	-6.3
Cotton Menders (Declined)	+5.0	0.0	0.0	-5.0
Wheelwrights (Increased 41.6 percent)	17.4	+0.5	-9.1	-8.9
Brick Masons (Declined)	+6.8	0.0	+4.2	-12.2
Stone Masons (Increased 29.6 percent)	+12.4	+2.8	+3.1	-17.6
Sailmakers (Declined)	+1.9	+7.1	+0.5	-23.8
Millers (Declined)	+24.2	-12.7	0.0	-15.4
Shipwrights (Declined)	+24.0	+1.7	-8.3	-19.2
Saddlers (Increased 50 percent)	+26.6	+6.6	-6.7	-23.4
Cotton Samplers (Increased 200 percent)	+14.2	0.0	0.0	-14.3

[1]Indicates whether the number employed in the occupation expanded or fell during the decade.

23. Ibid.

24. *Charleston Daily News,* November 30, 1868, August 27, 29, 1869, February 18, 1873; *Charleston Daily Courier,* August 19, 1865, July 16, August 11, September 10, October 15, 1867; July 8, 1868; *Charleston News and Courier,* January 24, 1874.

25. *Charleston Daily News,* November 30, 1868, February 18, 1873; *South Carolina Leader,* December 9, 1865; U.S. Manuscript Census of Population, 1870, 1880, City of Charleston.

26. U.S. Manuscript Census of Population 1870, 1880, City of Charleston; *Charleston News and Courier*, September 15, 1876.

27. Lady Duffus Hardy, *Down South* (London: Chapman & Hall,

1883), 51; *Charleston Daily News,* November 14, 1866, November 14, 1870, July 22, 1872; *Charleston Mercury,* December 14, 1867; *Charleston News and Courier,* May 17, 1873, October 28, 1876.

28. *Charleston Daily Republican,* August 17, 1871; Edward P. Wall to Bvt. Maj. Gen. R. K. Scott, June 22, 1868, Assistant Commissioner Letters Received; FBP, SCDAH; *Charleston News and Courier,* September 21, 1876; W. G. Marts to Rev. Dr. Strieby, July 7, 1877, AMAP, SCDAH.

29. U.S. Manuscript Census of Population 1870, 1880, City of Charleston; U. S. Bureau of the Census, *Twelfth Census of 1900, Special Reports: Occupations* (Washington: Government Printing Office, 1904), 514. Analysis of the skill composition of Charleston's black male labor force in 1870 and 1880 yields results that are consistent with research on the city's antebellum black work force. Herbert Gutman estimates that the combined labor force of both free blacks and slaves in 1860 had 26 percent of its workers engaged in skilled occupations. My analysis reveals that in 1870 and 1880, 28 and 26 percent of all black males were engaged in skilled occupations. The Civil War, emancipation, and Reconstruction, then, did little to alter the *fundamental* skill level of Charleston's black workers. Important continuities also exist between the occupational structure of blacks during Reconstruction and the characteristic occupations they performed in the early twentieth century. When the ten most important skilled occupations for black workers in 1880 are reexamined in 1900 the results indicate their continued domination by Afro-Americans during the entire period. Black workers not only failed to decline but actually increased their percentages in five of these occupations. These findings are contrary to those of Fogel and Engerman, who assert that in the period after the Civil War the freedmen were driven from the occupations they had traditionally dominated as slaves. As a result, so their argument went, a general deterioration in the skill level of black workers ensued. The Charleston data points out the more important fact that many of the skilled occupations with high concentrations of black workers were decreasing in importance as a result of the new technology and merchandising methods of the late nineteenth century. By 1900, the total number of workers in the coopering and shoemaking trades had declined by 20 percent. While black workers continued to be concentrated in such jobs, they were unable to gain access to more highly skilled trades. By 1900, blacks represented only 14 percent of Charleston's iron and steel workers. Although the number of machinists increased by 111 percent from 1880 to 1900, the number of black machinists actually declined during the period. It is the failure on this level, exacerbated by the discriminatory practices of white labor unions as they became increasingly powerful, that produced dire consequences for the twentieth-century black laborer. See Herbert Gutman, "The World Two

Cliometricians Made," *Journal of Negro History* 60 (January 1975): 111; Robert Fogel and Stanley Engerman, *Time On The Cross: The Economics of American Negro Slavery* (Boston: Little, Brown and Co., 1974), 260–61.

30. U.S. Manuscript Census of Population 1870, 1880, City of Charleston; *Charleston City Directories*, 1878, 1879–80, 1881.

31. Eric Foner, *Freedom's Lawmakers: A Directory of Black Office-holders During Reconstruction* (New York: Oxford University Press, 1993), 398; William C. Hine, "Frustration, Factionalism and Failure: Black Political Leadership and the Republican Party in Reconstruction Charleston, 1865–1877" (Ph.D diss., Kent State University, 1979), 96, 99–100; *Charleston Daily Republican*, July 5, 1870.

32. Eric Foner, *Reconstruction: America's Unfinished Revolution 1863–1877* (New York: Harper and Row, 1988), 398; Hine, "Frustration, Factionalism and Failure," 96, 99–100; *Charleston Daily Republican*, July 5, 1870; *Charleston Daily News*, October 10, 12, 1869; February 9, March 3, November 2, 8, 1870, January 24, 1872, April 2, 1873; *Charleston Daily Courier*, April 25, November 12, 1868; *Charleston News and Courier*, February 16, 1874; U.S. Manuscript Census of Population 1870, 1880, City of Charleston; *Charleston City Directories*, 1878, 1879–80, 1881.

33. U.S. Manuscript Census of Population 1880, City of Charleston; *Charleston Daily Courier*, November 3, 1868.

34. U.S. Manuscript Census of Population 1870, 1880, City of Charleston; *Charleston City Directories*, 1878, 1879–1880, 1881. A sample of skilled male workers drawn from the 1870 census (N = 896) was traced to the year 1880. Appearance in one of the 1878–81 city directories or the census of 1880 was considered persistence for the decade.

35. William E. B. DuBois, ed., *The Negro Artisan* (Atlanta: Atlanta University Press, 1902; reprint ed., New York: Arno Press, 1969), 21–22; Michael P. Johnson and James L. Roark, *Black Masters: A Free Family of Color in the Old South* (New York: W. W. Norton, 1984), 11. There certainly were those skilled black Charlestonians who viewed the rural migrants to the city as less highly trained than themselves. See p. 119.

36. DuBois, ed., *The Negro Artisan*, 21–22. Loren Schweninger has found important examples of independent entrepreneurship among Charleston's slave artisans. For example, when masters traveled north in the summer, their domestics sometimes supervised repair work performed by "virtually free slaves and free blacks as carpenters, builders, and masons, who in turn maintained small work gangs of nearly free bondsmen." See his *Black Property Owners in the South 1790–1915* (Urbana: University of Illinois Press, 1990), 48–49; and "Slave Independence and Enterprise in South Carolina, 1780–1865," *South Carolina Historical Magazine* 93 (April 1992): 113–14.

37. Ibid.; U.S. Manuscript Census of Population 1870, City of Charleston.

38. *Charleston Daily News,* December 6, 1870, June 10, 1871; *Charleston News and Courier,* September 15, 1886.

39. *Charleston Daily News,* October 4, 1869, October 19, 1870; *Charleston News and Courier,* September 29, October 6, 1869; *Charleston Daily Republican,* October 19, 1870.

40. Richard C. Wade, *Slavery in the Cities: The South 1820–1860* (London: Oxford University Press, 1964), 11–12; Roger Ransom and Richard Sutch, *One Kind of Freedom: The Economic Consequences of Emancipation* (London: Cambridge University Press, 1977), 116–117; *Charleston Daily News,* July 10, 1871, 1872; C. Van Woodward, *The Origins of the New South 1877–1913* (Baton Rouge: Louisiana State University Press, 1971), 107, 125–126; Jamie W. Moore, "The Lowcountry in Econmomic Transition: Charleston Since 1865," *South Carolina Historical Magazine* 80 (April 1979): 157, 159–61; Don Doyle, *New Men, New Cities, New South: Atlanta, Nashville, Charleston, Mobile, 1850–1910* (Chapel Hill: University of North Carolina, 1990), 5, 8–9, 72, 75, 79.

41. *Charleston Daily Republican,* June 9, 1871; *Charleston Daily Courier,* June 9, July 15, 19, September 8, 1869; *Charleston Daily News,* July 16, 1869, June 10, 1871; *New York Times,* January 19, 1884, 1.

42. *Charleston Daily News,* November 16, 1869; E. Mc. R. to Aunt Rosa, April 23, 1865, William Ravenel Family Papers, "Civil War Letter Book," SCHS; *Charleston Daily Republican,* November 24, 27, 30, 1869.

43. This information was obtained by using the manuscript census of 1870 from which samples were drawn. Unfortunately, the 1870 Charleston city tax list could not be located, and the list for 1871 was used along with the census to determine property holding. Workers were then traced through the city directories for the years 1879–80 and 1881. The appearance of a person in one of these was considered persistence. Then the 1880 tax list was used to determine the property holding of the persisters. Manuscript Census of Population 1860, City of Charleston; List of the Taxpayers of the City of Charleston for 1860, SCHS; Charleston Ledger of Taxpayers for 1871, 1880, Charleston County Tax Assessor's Office (hereafter referred to as CTAO); *Charleston City Directories,* 1878, 1879–80, 1881.

44. Ibid.

45. List of the Taxpayers of the City of Charleston for 1860, SCHS; *Charleston Daily News,* January 19, 24, 25, 1872; *Charleston News and Courier,* November 12, 1873, January 24, 1874, March 9, September 30, 1875; Charleston Ledger of Taxpayers for 1880, CTAO.

46. Charleston Ledger of Taxpayers for 1871, 1880, CTAO. Below is the dollar value and distribution of real estate held by black workers persisting 1870–1880 in selected occupations.

---

	499 or below	500–999	1000+
Blacksmith	0	2	1
Tailor	1	4	2
Brick Mason	2	1	0
Baker	0	1	1
Butcher	2	6	4
Painter	1	3	1
Cooper	2	1	0
Carpenter	5	8	9
Barber	1	2	3
Shoemaker	1	3	1
TOTALS	15	31	22
	22%	45%	32%

The concept of property mobility is extensively explored in Thernstrom's study of Irish workers in Newburyport, Massachusetts, during the nineteenth century. See Stephan Thernstrom, *Poverty and Progress: Social Mobility in a Nineteenth Century City* (New York: Atheneum, 1971).

47. *Charleston News and Courier,* October 2, 17, 1874, May 19, 1876, September 5, 1883; *Charleston Daily Republican,* November 24, December 8, 1869; *Acts and Joint Resolutions,* 1869, (Columbia: John Denny, 1869), 231; *Charleston Daily News,* October 14, 1869.

48. *Charleston Daily News,* June 28, 1872; *Charleston News and Courier,* October 6, 1876; *Charleston City Directory,* 1872–1873, 316, 1881, 224; *Charleston Daily Republican,* November 30, 1869, January 20, 25, June 10, 1870.

49. *Charleston News and Courier,* September 17, 1886. As early as 1869, black bricklayers banded together to organize a union; however, it is not clear whether this organization still existed in 1881 or whether it merged with Union Number One. See *Charleston Daily Republican,* December 8, 1869.

50. *Charleston News and Courier,* September 5, 1883. As of 1886 the National Brotherhood of Carpenters and Joiners had several black locals in southern cities, some as far away as New Orleans and Galveston. It would be 1902 before a black organizer was appointed for the international, and between 1902 and 1912 twenty-five additional locals were organized in the South on the basis of parity between black and white locals. Spero and Harris, *The Black Worker,* 66.

51. *Charleston Daily Republican,* January 25, August 4, 1870.

52. Tom W. Shick and Don H. Doyle, "The South Carolina Phosphate Boom and the Still Birth of the New South, 1867–1920," *South Carolina Historical Magazine* 86 (January 1985): 11–12.

53. *Charleston Daily Republican,* September 27, October 14, 1869; *Charleston Daily News,* October 14, 1869; *Charleston Daily Courier,* October 16, 1869.

54. *Charleston Mercury,* March 23, 1868; *Charleston Daily Republican,* October 27, November 5, 1869; *Charleston Daily Courier,* November 4, 1869.

55. *Charleston Mercury,* January 6, 1867, February 25–26, 1868; *Charleston Daily News,* February 26, 1868.

56. *A Digest of the Ordinances of the City Council of Charleston From the Year 1783 to Oct. 1844,* 173, 177, 188–89.

57. *Charleston Daily News,* February 25, 1868, October 8, 1869.

58. *Charleston Mercury,* January 6, 1867, February 25–26, 1868, 231; *Charleston Daily News,* February 26, 1868.

59. *Acts and Joint Resolutions,* 1869 (Columbia: John Denny, 1869), 231; *Charleston News and Courier,* January 26, 1875; Charleston Ledger of Taxpayers for 1880, CTAO.

60. *Charleston Daily News,* October 2, 5, 7, 11, 30, 1869; *Charleston Daily Courier,* October 5, 7, 1869.

61. *Charleston Daily Republican,* October 27, 29, 1869; *Charleston Daily News,* October 29, 1869.

62. *Charleston Daily Republican,* November 2, 1869; *Charleston Daily News,* November 1, 3, 1869.

63. Herbert Northrup, "The New Orleans Longshoremen," *Political Science Quarterly* 47 (December 1942): 526–27; *Charleston News and Courier,* September 2, 4, 1873; William C. Hine, "Black Organized Labor in Reconstruction Charleston," *Labor History* 25 (Fall 1984): 514.

64. *Charleston News and Courier,* September 2, 4, 1873.

65. *Charleston News and Courier,* September 4, 5, 24, 1873.

66. By 1898 the Longshoremen's Protective Union Association of Charleston had succeeded in obtaining higher wages for its members than were paid to similar workers in Brunswick, Savannah, and Port Royal. Longshoremen worked in gangs of five each with ordinary workers being paid four dollars and fifty cents per day and the foreman five dollars per day; the whole gang was paid twenty-three dollars. The same number of workers were only paid thirteen dollars per gang in Port Royal. Furthermore, while the Charleston rate was for eight hours, the Port Royal rate was for ten hours of work. For any fraction of the day Charleston men worked, they received pay for at least one–fourth day, while men in Port Royal could be paid for one–eighth day. Charleston men received double-time on Sundays. The Port Royal longshoremen organized their union in 1874, but they were unable to exert the same influence among the shippers that their counterparts in Charleston did. Boris Stern, U.S. Bureau of Labor, *Cargo Handling and Longshore Labor Conditions,* Bulletin of the U.S. Bureau of Labor Statistics, No. 550 (Washington: Government Printing Office, 1932), 70–71, 73; *Charleston News and Courier,* November 16, 18, 1898; *Charleston Daily Republican,* October 5, 1869; *Acts and Joint Resolutions,* 1873–74 (Columbia: Calvo and Patton), 586.

67. *Charleston News and Courier,* September 9–12, 16, 1873.

68. Hine, "Black Organized Labor," 516–17. For an example of the effective use of police power by Mayor George Cunningham against the Press Union Association see *Charleston News and Courier,* October 2, 3, 1874.

69. Paul B. Worthman, "Working Class Mobility in Birmingham, Alabama, 1880–1914," in *Anonymous Americans: Explorations in Nineteenth-Century Social History,* ed. Tamara Hareven (Englewood Cliffs, N.J.: Prentice Hall, 1971), 178–79, 197; Richard J. Hopkins, "Status, Mobility and the Dimensions of Change in a Southern City: Atlanta, 1870–1910," in *Cities in American History,* ed. Kenneth T. Jackson and Stanley K. Schultz (New York: Alfred A. Knopf, 1972), 220–21; McLeod, *Workers and Workplace Dynamics,* 24, 33, 45.

CHAPTER 5

"THE GREAT WORK BEFORE US":

Education as the Means to Elevate a Race

1. William P. Vaughn, *Schools for All: The Blacks and Public Education in The South 1865–1877* (Lexington, Ky.: University Press of Kentucky, 1974), 51–52; *Charleston Daily News,* March 30, 1868; Edgar W. Knight, *The Influence of Reconstruction on Education in the South* (New York: Columbia University, 1913; reprint ed., New York: Arno Press, 1969), 59; Laylon W. Jordan, "Education for Community: C. G. Memminger and the Origination of Common Schools in Antebellum Charleston," *South Carolina Historical Magazine* 83 (April 1982): 110–12.

2. Alrutheus A. Taylor, *The Negro in South Carolina During Reconstruction* (Washington: Association for the Study of Negro Life and History, 1924), 86; *American Missionary Magazine* 9 (May 1865): 104.

3. Ibid.; *American Missionary Magazine* 9 (July 1865): 153; F. L. Cardozo to Rev. E. P. Smith, November 21, 1866, American Missionary Association Papers (hereafter referred to as AMAP), South Carolina Department of Archives and History (hereater referred to as SCDAH); Reuben Tomlinson to Bvt. Maj. Gen. R. K. Scott, July 31, 1866, Assistant Comissioner Letters Received, Freedmen's Bureau Papers (hereafter referred to as FBP), SCDAH.

4. T. W. Cardozo to Rev. M. E. Strieby, April 29, 1865, T. W. Cardozo to Mr. Strieby, May 10, 1865, AMAP, SCDAH; *American Missionary Magazine* 9 (July 1865): 153.

5. Edmund L. Drago, *Initiative, Paternalism, and Race Relations: Charleston's Avery Normal Institute* (Athens, Ga.: University of Georgia Press, 1990), 44–45; Joe Richardson, *Christian Reconstruction: The*

American Missionary Association and Southern Blacks, 1861–1890 (Athens, Ga.: University of Georgia Press, 1986), 41–42.

6. T. W. Cardozo to Mr. Strieby, May 10, 1865, T. W. Cardozo to Rev. M. E. Strieby, April 29, 1865, Rev. F. L. Cardozo to Rev. S. Hunt, September 31, 1866, F. L. Cardozo to Rev. E. P. Smith, November 21, 1866, AMAP, SCDAH; *American Missionary Magazine* 9 (July 1865): 153; *Charleston Daily Courier,* April 11, 1865; Reuben Tomlinson to Bvt. Maj. Gen. R. K. Scott, July 31, 1866, A. B. Eaton to O. O. Howard, February 23, 1867, C. G. Memminger to Maj. Gen. R. K. Scott, July 10, 1867, Reuben Tomlinson to C. G. Memminger, July 10, 1867, R. K. Scott to Reuben Tomlinson, July 15, 1867, Assistant Commissioner Letters Received, FBP, SCDAH; Burchill R. Moore, "A History of The Negro Public Schools of Charleston, South Carolina 1867–1942" (M.A. thesis, University of South Carolina, 1942), 8–9; Edward L. Deane to Maj. Genl. O. O. Howard, January 20, 1870, Monthly and Other School Reports, FBP, SCDAH.

7. Col. Robert G. Shaw led the Fifty–fourth Regiment of the U.S. Colored Troops in an unsuccessful assault on the Confederate fortifications at Battery Wagner on Morris Island. In this battle, one of the most intrepid and bloody engagements of the war, Colonel Shaw was killed along with many of his troops. Benjamin Quarles, *The Negro in the Civil War* (Boston: Little, Brown & Co., 1969), 13–17; F. L. Cardozo to M. E. Strieby, August 13, 1866, AMAP, SCDAH; *Charleston Yearbook,* 1880, 122–23; *Charleston News and Courier,* May 19, 1882; Minutes from the Commissioners of Free Schools, March 4, April 22, May 6, December 2, 1874, South Carolina Historical Society (hereafter referred to as SCHS).

8. *Charleston Yearbook,* 1880, 125–26; F. L. Cardozo to Rev. E. P. Smith, October 25, 1866, C. Thurston Chase to Rev. Edward P. Smith, March 29, May 20, May 24, 1867, AMAP, SCDAH.

9. James D. Anderson, *The Education of Blacks in the South, 1860–1935* (Chapel Hill: University of North Carolina Press, 1991), 6–7; F. L. Cardozo to Mr. Smith, December 28, 1866, W. D. Harris to Rev. George Whipple, November 7, 1868, James T. Ford to Rev. E. P. Smith, December 21, 1869, AMAP, SCDAH; *Charleston Yearbook,* 1880, 122; District Superintendent's Monthly School Report, December 1867, FBP, SCDAH.

10. A. Toomer Porter, *The History of a Work of Faith and Love In Charleston, South Carolina* (New York: D. Appleton & Co., 1882), 6; *Charleston Daily News,* July 20, 1866, March 4, May 15, 1868, January 20, 1869; Francis B. Simkins and Robert H. Woody, *South Carolina During Reconstruction* (Chapel Hill: University of North Carolina Press, 1932; reprint ed., Gloucester, Mass.: Peter Smith, 1966), 424.

11. *Report of the Joint Committee on Reconstruction* (Washington: Government Printing Office, 1866), pt. 2, 231, 233, 251; F. L. Cardozo to

Rev. S. Hunt, December 13, 1865, F. L. Cardozo to Rev. George Whipple, January 27, 1866, AMAP, SCDAH; *Charleston Daily News,* August 30, 1866.

12. *Charleston Daily News,* August 30, 1866; Jacob Schirmer Diary, June 19, 1866, SCHS.

13. F. L. Cardozo to Rev. S. Hunt, March 10, 1866, AMAP, SCDAH; Josephine Walker Martin, "The Educational Efforts of The Major Freedmen's Aid Societies and The Freedmen's Bureau in South Carolina 1862–1870" (Ph.D. diss., University of South Carolina, 1972), 122.

14. F. L. Cardozo to Rev. S. Hunt, March 10, 1866, F. L. Cardozo to Rev. M. E. Strieby, September 12, 1866, AMAP, SCDAH; William C. Bee to James L. Orr, December 14, 1866, James L. Orr Papers, SCDAH; *American Missionary Magazine* 9 (May 1865): 104; Reuben Tomlinson to Bvt. Maj. Gen. R. K. Scott, May 1, 1867, Monthly and Other School Reports, FBP, SCDAH; *Charleston Mercury,* February 4, 1867; Vaughn, *Schools For All,* 31; *Charleston Daily News,* August 30, 1866.

15. P. A. Alcott to Mr. Hunt, November 29, 1865, AMAP, SCDAH.

16. Joel Williamson, *After Slavery: The Negro in South Carolina During Reconstruction, 1861–1877* (Chapel Hill: University of North Carolina Press, 1965), 216; *Charleston Daily News,* June 4, 1866.

17. *Proceedings of the Constitutional Convention of South Carolina* (Charleston, S.C.: Denny and Perry, 1868; reprint ed., New York: Arno Press, 1968), 690, 747, 783, 889, 901–02; *The Constitution of South Carolina, Adopted April 16, 1868, and the Acts and Joint Resolutions of the General Assembly Passed at the Special Session of 1868* (Columbia, S.C.: John W. Denny, 1868), 28.

18. *Proceedings of The Constitutional Convention of South Carolina,* 747; *Charleston Daily News,* March 30, 1868.

19. *Proceedings of The Constitutional Convention of South Carolina,* 706, 901.

20. *Charleston Daily Republican,* September 24, 27, 1869; *Proceedings of The Constitutional Convention of South Carolina,* 894, 901; Anderson, *The Education of Blacks,* 5, 12–13.

21. *Charleston Daily Republican,* September 18, 24, 27, 1869.

22. U.S. Manuscript Census of Population 1860, City of Charleston; Minutes from the Commissioners of Free Schools, June 7, 1876, SCHS. One of the challenges the A.M.A. faced was how to accommodate southern blacks who desired to exercise control over their educational lives and often demanded black principals and even all black teaching faculty. See Richardson, *Christian Reconstruction,* 190–91, 245–49.

23. Sidney Andrews, *The South Since the War* (Boston: Ticknor and Fields, 1866), 227; Simkins and Woody, *South Carolina During Reconstruction,* 426; *New York Times,* July 3, 1874, 2; *American Missionary*

Magazine 10 (February 1866): 124; Report of the Joint Comittee on Reconstruction, pt. 2, 220.

24. *American Missionary Magazine* 9 (July 1865): 153; *Report of the Joint Committee on Reconstruction,* pt. 2, 250; *New York Times,* July 31, 1874, 1.

25. F. L. Cardozo to Rev. S. Hunt, December 2, 1865, November 3, 1866, AMAP, SCDAH; J. W. Alvord, *Letters From The South Relating To The Condition of The Freedmen Addressed To Major General O. O. Howard* (Washington: Howard University Press, 1870), 7; *New York Times,* July 3, 1874, 2; Simkins and Woody, *South Carolina During Reconstruction,* 316.

26. Ellen M. Pierce to Rev. E. P. Smith, October 15, 1868, W. D. Harris to Rev. George Whipple, November 7, 1868, A. W. Farnham to M. E. Strieby, January 23, 1877, AMAP, SCDAH; Martin Abbott, "The Freedmen's Bureau and Negro Schooling in South Carolina,"*South Carolina Historical Magazine* 57 (April 1956): 79; A. T. Porter, *Led On Step By Step: Scenes From Clerical, Military, Educational, And Plantation Life In The South 1828–1898 An Autobiography* (New York: Arno Press, 1967), 224.

27. F. L. Cardozo to Rev. S. Hunt, March 2, 1866, School Report For January 1868, Benjamin F. Jackson to Rev. George Whipple, February 18, 1868, AMAP, SCDAH.

28. *American Missionary Magazine* 18 (July 1874): 147. Whites frequently commented on the Low Country blacks' unique and often unintelligible speech patterns. A white Charlestonian who toured black sections of the city recalled, "Chatter in various dialects is incessant. We do not understand what they say, unless we are bred among them." Another Charleston observer reported that "the jargon" of the James Island blacks "is simply unintelligible to one not used to it from infancy; and all this makes the street cries of Charleston unique as a philological study." Sidney Andrews, who traveled to Charleston, noted that he "met many negroes whose jargon was so utterly unintelligible that I could scarcely comprehend the ideas they tried to convey." Such difficulties existed because, as Andrews explained, the language spoken by many blacks (and some whites) was a "curious mixture of English and African." A major center of African importation and redistribution and located in a region noted for its isolated plantations that were worked by large gangs of slaves, Charleston and the Low Country generally were areas replete with African cultural retentions. Gullah has been the object of extensive research, begun originally by Dr. Lorenzo D. Turner. His work, which investigated the dialectic patterns of blacks on the Sea Islands of South Carolina and Georgia, revealed approximately four thousand West African words, as well as African patterns of syntax, inflection, and

intonation, in the Gullah dialect. Isaac Dubose Seabrook, *Before and After Or: The Relations of The Races at The South* (Baton Rouge: Louisiana State University Press, 1967), 98; *Lippincott's Magazine* 2 (July 1881): 46–58; Andrews, *The South,* 227. See especially Lorenzo Dow Turner, *Africanisms In The Gullah Dialect* (Ann Arbor, Michigan: University of Michigan Press, 1974).

29. Reuben Tomlinson to Bvt. Maj. Gen. R. K. Scott, July 7, 1866, Monthly and Other School Reports, FBP, SCDAH; *Atlantic Monthly,* June 1877, 677; M. A. Warren to Mr. Smith, October 18, 1869, AMAP, SCDAH.

30. Reuben Tomlinson to Bvt. Maj. Gen. R. K. Scott, July 7, 1866, Monthly and Other School Reports, FBP, SCDAH; M. A. Warren to Mr. Smith, October 18, 1869, AMAP, SCDAH.

31. L. B. Corey to Dear Sir, October 22, 1868, AMAP, SCDAH.

32. Sarah W. Stansbury to Rev. Mr. Hunt, November 29, 1866, AMAP, SCDAH; Henry L. Swint, *The Northern Teacher in The South 1862-1870* (New York: Octagon Books, 1967), 196.

33. F. L. Cardozo to Rev. S. Hunt, October 10, December 2, 1865, AMAP, SCDAH.

34. F. L. Cardozo to Rev. W. E. Whiting, December 14, 1865, January 31, 1866, M. A. Warren to Mr. Smith, August 20, 1870, September 3, 1872, AMAP, SCDAH; *Charleston News and Courier,* July 9, 1878.

35. U.S Manuscript Census of Population 1860, 1880, City of Charleston; Emma L. Thornbrough, ed., *Black Reconstructionists* (Englewood Cliffs, N.J.: Prentice Hall, 1972), 8; Minutes of the South Carolina Annual Conference of the Methodist Episcopal Church 1869 (n.p.:n.d.), 6; A.M.E. *Christian Recorder,* December 5, 1868; B. F. Randolph to Bvt. Maj. Gen. R. Saxton, August 31, 1865, B. F. Randolph to Bvt. Gen. R. K. Scott, March 15, 1867, R. K. Scott to Gen. O. O. Howard, March 16, 1867, Assistant Commissioner Letters Received, FBP, SCDAH; A. B. Frothingham to Tomlinson, 1 November 1865, State Superintendent of Education Letters Received, FBP, SCDAH.

36. Thomas W. Cardozo to Reverend Strieby, June 16, 1865, Rev. F. L. Cardozo to Rev. M. E. Strieby, July 18, 1865, F. L. Cardozo to Wm. E. Whiting, February 1, 1867, F. to Rev. M. E. Strieby, November 1, 1875, AMAP, SCDAH; U.S. Manuscript Census of Population 1860, City of Charleston.

37. *Reports and Resolutions,* 1875–76, (Columbia: Republican Printing Co., 1876), 419, 1880, 343; *Charleston News and Courier,* October 24, 1879, October 23, 1880, June 21, 1881.

38. William J. Simmons, *Men of Mark: Eminent Progressive and Rising* (Cleveland: George M. Rewell and Co., 1887; reprint ed., New York: Arno Press, 1968), 281; Rev. F. L. Cardozo to Rev. M. E. Strieby, August 13, 1866, AMAP, SCDAH.

39. Thomas W. Cardozo to Reverend Strieby, June 16, 1865, F. L. Cardozo to Rev. S. Hunt, October 10, 1865, AMAP, SCDAH; A.M.E. *Christian Recorder,* November 7, 1868; Willard B. Gatewood Jr., "'The Remarkable Misses Rollin': Black Women in Reconstruction South Carolina" *South Carolina Historical Magazine* 92 (July 1991): 177.

40. Thomas W. Cardozo to Reverend Strieby, June 16, 1865, F. L. Cardozo to Rev. S. Hunt, October 10, December 2, 1865, AMAP, SCDAH; C. W. Birnie, "Education of the Negro in Charleston, South Carolina, Prior to the Civil War," *Journal of Negro History* 12 (January 1927): 19; John Dennett, *The South As It Is 1865-1866* (New York: Viking Press, 1865), 217–18; *Charleston Daily News,* June 4, 1866; Drago, *Initiative, Paternalism, and Race Relations,* 61.

41. B. F. Randolph to Bvt. Maj. Genl. R. Saxton, August 3, 1865, Assistant Commissioner Letters Received, FBP, SCDAH; William Weston to Thomas Cardozo, June 24, 1865, AMAP, SCDAH.

42. E. J. Adams to *The American Missionary,* June 12, 1865, AMAP, SCDAH.

43. Tomlinson Report of Schools For Freedmen For the State of South Carolina, December 1865, AMAP, SCDAH; *Charleston Daily News,* March 4, 1868; *American Missionary Magazine* 14 (February 1870): 26.

44. *New York Times,* July 3, 1874, 2; *Charleston Yearbook,* 1880, 125.

45. *American Missionary Magazine* 14 (February 1870): 26; *American Missionary Magazine* 14 (May 1870): 98; *Charleston Daily News,* June 4, 1866; *Charleston Yearbook,* 1880, 125–26; Dennett, *The South As It Is,* 217; John P. Richardson to Mr. Cravath, January 24, 1872, M. A. Warren to Mr. Cravath, January 10, 1873, Jas. T. Ford to Rev. E. M. Cravath, June 30, 1874, Jas. T. Ford to Rev. M. E. Strieby, July 16, 1875, AMAP, SCDAH. Quoted in Richardson, *Christian Reconstruction,* 113, 194. Avery continued its importance as a major facility for the education of black teachers even into the mid-twentieth century. In 1940–41, it was one of only five South Carolina schools open to blacks that was accredited by the Southern Association of Colleges and Secondary Schools. In 1945, 60 percent of the black Charleston County teachers and 75 percent of the black teachers in the city of Charleston had been trained at Avery. E. Horace Fitchett, "The Free Negro in Charleston, South Carolina," (Ph.D. diss., University of Chicago, 1950), 265; "Avery Institute: An Accredited High School 1945" Phamphlet in possession of Mr. and Mrs. Paul Poinsette, Charleston, S.C.

46. *American Missionary Magazine* 14 (February 1870): 26; *Charleston Daily News,* June 4, 1866; Dennett, *The South As It Is,* 217–18; Jas. T. Ford to Rev. E. M. Cravath, August 5, 1874, AMAP, SCDAH; Drago, *Initiative, Paternalism, and Race Relations,* 96.

47. Examination Program for Avery Institute, March 1873, Jas. T. Ford to Rev. E. M. Cravath, August 5, 1874, AMAP, SCDAH; *Charleston*

Daily News, June 4, 1866; *Charleston News and Courier,* July 5, December 28, 1877, July 4, December 4, 1878, July 5, 1881; Fitchett, "The Free Negro," 265; Drago, *Initiative, Paternalism, and Race Relations,* 97.

48. Drago, *Initiative, Paternalism, and Race Relations,* 62, 75. Quoted in Wilbert L. Jenkins, "Chaos, Conflict and Control: The Responses of the Newly-Freed Slaves in Charleston, South Carolina, to Emancipation and Reconstruction, 1865–1877" (Ph.D. diss., Michigan State University, 1991), 182.

49. Dickson D. Bruce Jr., *Archibald Grimké: Portrait of a Black Independent* (Baton Rouge: Louisiana State University Press, 1993), 6–8, 17, 19; Charleston City Directory, 1881, 498; Williamson, *After Slavery,* 230; A.M.E. *Christian Recorder,* June 29, 1882, June 5, 1884, July 9, 1885.

50. Williamson, *After Slavery,* 230; Taylor, *The Negro in South Carolina,* 90–92, 118–19.

51. Williamson, *After Slavery,* 231–32; Tindall, *South Carolina Negroes,* 228; *Charleston Daily Courier,* January 19, 1870; Minutes of the South Carolina Annual Conference of the Methodist Episcopal Church 1879 (Charleston, SC: Marts and Holloway, 1879), 5; E. Horace Fitchett, "The Role of Claflin College in Negro Life in South Carolina," *Journal of Negro Education* 12 (Winter 1943): 46–47; Fitchett, "The Free Negro," 271; Holloway Family Papers, College of Charleston Library Special Collections (hereafter referred to as CCLSC).

52. Vaughn, *Schools For All,* 108; *New York Times,* December 25, 1867, 2.

53. Vaughn, *Schools For All,* 111, 114; *New York Times,* December 25, 1867, 2; *Charleston Daily Courier,* July 14, September 3, 1869.

54. Register of South Carolina College 1850–1877, University of South Carolina Caroliniana Library, (hereafter referred to as USCCL); A. W. Farnham to Rev. M. E. Strieby, May 2, 1876, AMAP, SCDAH; Fisk K. Brewer Scrapbook, USCCL.

55. Warren to Edward P. Smith, March 29, 1870, A. W. Farnham to Rev. M. E. Strieby, February 10, 1877, AMAP, SCDAH; Register of South Carolina College 1850–1877, USCCL; Fitchett, "The Free Negro," 273; Albert W. Pegues, *Our Baptist Ministers and Schools* (Springfield, Mass.: Willey & Co., 1892), 145–47; *Reports and Resolutions, 1874–1875* (Columbia: Republican Printing Company, 1875), 13–14.

56. A. W. Farnham to Rev. M. E. Strieby, February 10, July 21, 1877, AMAP, SCDAH; Simmons, *Men of Mark,* 757; A.M.E. *Christian Recorder,* January 6, 1876, October 13, 1881, October 19, November 9, 1882; August Meier, *Negro Thought in America 1880–1915* (Ann Arbor, Michigan: University of Michigan Press, 1963), 272.

57. Vaughn, *Schools For All,* 117.

58. *Reports and Resolutions,* 1879 (Columbia: Calvo and Patton,

1879), 362, 1879–1880, 403, 1880, 363–64; Minutes from the Commissioners of Free Schools, May 7, 1884; *Acts and Joint Resolutions,* 1882, (Columbia: Calvo and Patton, 1882) 28; *Charleston News and Courier,* September 2, 1880.

59. *Reports and Resolutions,* 1879, 362, Table 4, 1880, 363–64; *Acts and Joint Resolutions,* 1882, 28; *Charleston News and Courier,* September 2, 1880; W. H. Lawrence, *The Centenary Souvenir, Containing a History of Centenary Church, Charleston, and an Account of the Life and Labors of Rev. R. V. Lawrence, Father of the Pastor of Centenary Church* (Philadelphia: Collins Printing House, 1885), xlvi–xlvii.

CHAPTER 6

CLASS, STATUS, AND SOCIAL LIFE IN THE BLACK COMMUNITY

1. *Atlantic Monthly* (June 1877): 677.

2. Hollis R. Lynch, *The Black Urban Condition* (New York: Thomas Y. Crowell, 1973), 5; *Charleston Daily News,* February 12, 1870.

3. *Charleston News and Courier,* June 19, 1878; *Charleston Daily Republican,* October 5, 1869.

4. *Charleston News and Courier,* September 4, December 5, 1876; *Charleston Mercury,* April 24, 1867; *Charleston Daily News,* January 3, June 17, 1872.

5. Charleston Ledger of Taxpayers for 1880, Charleston County Tax Assessor's Office (hereafter referred to as CTAO); U.S. Manuscript Census of Population 1880, City of Charleston; *Charleston City Directories,* 1878, 1879–80, 1881; *Atlantic Monthly,* June 1877, 677.

6. A contemporary journalist observed: "Those who are able to work on their own account (for instance, to rent land and to farm, to keep a smithy or to be carpenters) hold themselves considerably above such as have to hire out as laborers." *Atlantic Monthly,* June 1877, 677; U.S. Manuscript Census, Industry Schedules of Manufacturers 1880, City of Charleston.

7. U.S. Manuscript Census, Industry Schedules of Manufacturers 1880, City of Charleston; Friendly Moralist Society Minutes, "Absences," March 10, 1845, College of Charleston Library Special Collections, (hereafter referred to as CCLSC).

8. U.S. Manuscript Census of Population 1870, City of Charleston; *Charleston City Directories,* 1878, 1879–80, 1881; *Charleston Daily Courier,* October 20, 1868; *Charleston Mercury,* March 26, 1867; *Northwestern Recorder,* March 1893; Jacob Schirmer Diary, July 23, 1869, South Carolina Historical Society (hereafter referred to as SCHS).

9. Oscar Lewis, *La Vida: A Puerto Rican Family in the Culture of Poverty—San Juan and New York* (New York: Random House, 1966),

xlvi; *Charleston Daily News,* December 10, 24, 1872; *Charleston News and Courier,* August 3, 1875, April 26, August 22, November 27, 1876.

10. *Charleston New Era,* September 2, 1882, November 24, December 22, 1883, February 16, 1884; *Charleston City Directory,* 1883, 58–59; *Charleston News and Courier,* May 16, September 10, 1873, August 7, 1876, August 6, 1878, June 14, 1879, May 13, August 19, 1880; *Charleston Daily News,* June 15, 1872; Caroline Gilman to Eliza, February 15, 1866, Letters of Caroline Gilman, SCHS.

11. *Charleston Daily Republican,* March 29, 1871; *Charleston Daily Courier,* August 10, 1869, May 6, 1873, August 14, October 5, 1876, April 17, July 7, August 30, October 9, 1877, June 22, 1878, July 1, 1879; *Charleston Daily News,* June 10, 1868, July 5, 1872.

12. *Charleston Daily Courier,* July 30, 1869, July 18, 1873, February 14, December 17, 1877, June 4, 1878; *Charleston Daily Republican,* September 2, 22, 1869, February 28, 1871.

13. *Charleston New Era,* March 10, 1883; *Charleston News and Courier,* January 2, May 6, 1873, July 4, 1876, July 26, 1878; *Charleston Daily Courier,* April 17, 1865; *Charleston Daily Republican,* July 5, 1870.

14. U.S. Manuscript Census of Population 1860, 1870, 1880, City of Charleston; *Charleston City Directories,* 1878, 1879–80, 1881. A similar method for analyzing the upper class is employed by Peter Kolchin. See his *First Freedom: The Responses of Alabama's Blacks to Emancipation and Reconstruction* (Westport, Conn.: Greenwood Press, 1972), chap. 6.

15. *Charleston City Directories* 1881, 1885–86; Charleston Ledger of Taxpayers for 1880, CTAO; Register of Mesne Conveyance (hereafter referred to as RMC) Book D-15, Conveyances, Mortgages, and Miscellaneous Records, 1719–1960, RMC; E. Horace Fitchett, "The Free Negro in Charleston, South Carolina" (Ph.D. diss., University of Chicago, 1950), 105; *Charleston Daily News,* December 24, 1868, June 10, 1872; *Charleston New Era,* November 3, 1883; *Charleston News and Courier,* October 18, 1877; U.S. Manuscript Census of Population 1870, 1880, City of Charleston.

16. Holloway Family Papers, CCLSC; A. T. Porter, *Led On Step By Step: Scenes From Clerical, Military, Educational, And Plantation Life In The South 1828–1898 An Autobiography* (New York: Arno Press, 1967), 285; Jacob Schirmer Diary, May 25, 1869, SCHS; A. Toomer Porter, *The History of a Work of Faith and Love In Charleston, South Carolina* (New York: D. Appleton & Co., 1882), 60.

17. See description of George Shrewsbury's activities in chap. 4; *Charleston Daily Courier,* September 13, 1869; *Charleston Daily Republican,* August 25, 1869.

18. *Charleston Daily News,* December 24, 1868; *Charleston Daily Courier,* December 17, 1866.

19. Charleston Ledger of Taxpayers for 1880, CTAO; List of the Taxpayers of the City of Charleston for 1860, SCHS; George P. Rawick, ed., *The American Slave: A Composite Autobiography,* 19 vols. (Westport, Conn.: Greenwood Press, 1972), 3: 155–56; *Charleston Daily News,* November 12, 14, 22, 1868. According to Loren Schweninger, only about 20 percent of antebellum free black property owners in the lower South owned any real estate in 1870; even the most prosperous property holders in 1860 experienced both absolute and relative declines in real holdings following the Civil War. In 1860, 121 blacks in the city of Charleston or adjacent to it owned property worth at least $2,000. By 1870 only 81 black property owners were as wealthy, and two-thirds of such persons had acquired their real estate since the war. Some former free blacks experienced property damage and loss during the war and others suffered because of the city's depressed economy. Such adversities, coupled with the freedmen's new opportunities, began to erode the position of formerly free property holders. Loren Schweninger, *Black Property Owners in the South 1790–1915* (Urbana: University of Illinois Press, 1990), 150, 193.

20. Charleston Ledger of Taxpayers for 1880, CTAO; RMC Book D-15, Conveyances Mortgages and Miscellaneous Records, 1719–1960, 3–4, Q-15, 45, RMC Book P-15, Titles to Real Estate, 1870–71, 81, RMC; Will of Richard E. Dereef, January 11, 1877, Box 243, No. 5, Charleston County Wills and Inventories (hereafter referred to as CCWI), Charleston County Courthouse (hereafter referred to as CCC); *Charleston News and Courier,* December 28, 1876, February 16, 1877.

21. Charleston Ledger of Taxpayers for 1880, CTAO; Will of William J. McKinlay, June 1873, Box 220, No. 6, Will of George Shrewsbury, February 1871, Box 230, No. 25, CCWI, CCC; *Charleston News and Courier,* June 14, 1873, March 9, 1875.

22. *Acts and Joint Resolutions,* 1874-75 (Columbia, S.C.: Republican Printing Co., 1875), 893, 1882, 54; *Charleston Daily News,* February 29, 1872; *Charleston News and Courier,* July 17, 20, 1878.

23. *Charleston Daily Republican,* February 21, March 1, 24, 1870, April 27, July 1, 1871; *South Carolina State Gazetteer and Business Directory,* 1880–81 (Charleston: R. A. Smith, 1880), 179; *Charleston News and Courier,* April 20, 1877.

24. U.S. Manuscript Census of Population 1870, City of Charleston; Thomas Holt, *Black Over White: Negro Political Leadership in South Carolina During Reconstruction* (Urbana, Ill.: University of Illinois Press, 1977), 81–83, 85–86; *Charleston Daily Republican,* June 15, August 8, 1871; *Charleston Daily News,* June 14, 1871.

25. List of the Taxpayers of the City of Charleston for 1859, 1860, SCHS; *Charleston News and Courier,* February 24, 1881; *Charleston Mercury,* February 24, 1868.

26. *Charleston Daily News,* April 9, 1872; *Charleston News and Courier,* August 29, 1873, April 20, 1877; Will of William J. McKinlay, June 1873, Box 220, No. 6, CCWI, CCC; *South Carolina State Gazetteer and Business Directory,* 1880–81, 179; Holt, *Black Over White,* 46; *Charleston City Directory,* 1881.

27. U.S. Manuscript Census of Population 1860, City of Charleston; William O. Weston to Thomas Cardozo, June 24, 1865, American Missionary Association Papers (hereafter referred to as AMAP), South Carolina Department of Archives and History (hereafter referred to as SCDAH).

28. Benj. F. Jackson to Rev. Geo. Whipple, February 18, 1868, AMAP, SCDAH; *Charleston News and Courier,* October 24, 1879, June 21, 1881.

29. U.S. Manuscript Census of Population 1860, 1870, 1880, City of Charleston; Victor Ullman, *Martin R. Delany: The Beginnings of Black Nationalism* (Boston: Beacon Press, 1971), 115–21, 297, 326.

30. *Charleston Daily News,* March 19, 1873; Holt, *Black Over White,* Table 5; *Charleston Advocate,* May 11, 1867; *Charleston Daily News,* October 8, 1872; Willard B. Gatewood, "William D. Crum, A Negro in Politics," *Journal of Negro History* 53 (October 1968): 302–03; Register of the South Carolina College, 1850-1877, University of South Carolina Caroliniana Library (hereafter referred to as USCCL); *Charleston News and Courier,* March 16, 1880.

31. *Charleston News and Courier,* July 12, 19, September 6, 1877; *Charleston New Era,* April 21, 1883; Peggy Lamson, *The Glorious Failure: Black Congressman Robert Brown Elliott and the Reconstruction in South Carolina* (New York: W. W. Norton, 1973), 75–76; Carter G. Woodson, *The Mind of the Negro as Reflected in Letters Written During the Crisis 1800–1860* (Washington: Association for the Study of Negro Life and History, 1926; reprint ed., New York: Negro Universities Press, 1969), 280–81; *Charleston Daily Republican,* August 20, 1869; *Charleston News and Courier,* December 17, 1875; Robert H. Woody, "Jonathan Jasper Wright Associate Justice of the Supreme Court of South Carolina 1870–1877," *Journal of Negro History* 18 (April 1933): 131–32.

32. *Charleston News and Courier,* December 10, 1878; O. S. B. Wall to Gen. Howard, January 23, 1866, Assistant Commissioner Letters Received, Freedmen's Bureau Papers (hereafter referred to as FBP), SCDAH; *Charleston New Era,* April 28, 1883.

33. Holloway Family Papers, CCLSC; Porter, *Led On,* 196–98; Porter, *The History of a Work of Faith and Love,* 60, 139.

34. Porter, *Led On,* 196–98; Porter, *The History of a Work of Faith and Love,* 60, 139.

35. *Charleston Daily Courier,* November 23, 1868; *Charleston News and Courier,* September 21, October 4, 6, 13, 14, 1876.

36. *Charleston News and Courier,* November 13, 30, 1868.

37. *Charleston Daily Republican,* October 3, 1870; *Charleston News and Courier,* October 13, 1876; *Charleston Daily News,* May 27, 1868.

38. Rawick, *The American Slave,* 3: 155–56; W. H. Lawrence, *The Centenary Souvenir, Containing a History of Centenary Church, Charleston, And an Account of the Life and Labors of Rev. R. V. Lawrence, Father of the Pastor of Centenary Church* (Philadelphia: Collins Printing House, 1885), xxx; *Charleston Daily News,* November 12, 14, 22, 1868.

39. *Charleston News and Courier,* June 14, 1873; Edmund L. Drago, *Initiative, Paternalism, and Race Relations: Charleston's Avery Normal Institute* (Athens, Ga.: University of Georgia Press, 1990), 32–33, 67.

40. List of the Taxpayers of the City of Charleston, for 1860 SCHS; Larry Koger, *Black Slaveowners: Free Black Slave Masters in South Carolina 1790–1860* (Jefferson, N.C.: McFarland, 1985), 198; Brown Fellowship Society Minute Book, July 1, November 4, 1869, CCLSC; State Free Negro Capitation Tax Book, Charleston, 1855, Charleston Library Society; *Charleston Daily News,* January 5, June 1, 15, 1870; Frank [Frances] A. Rollin, *Life and Public Services of Martin R. Delany* (Boston: Lee and Shepard, 1883), 191–92, 198. One of the other models of elite behavior is William Ellison, who seems never to have had an interest in identifying with his race or in promoting race goals. See Michael P. Johnson and James L. Roark, *Black Masters: A Free Family of Color in the Old South* (New York: W. W. Norton, 1986).

41. *Charleston New Era,* February 17, 1883.

42. Ibid., February 17, September 22, 1883.

43. Ibid., April 7, September 22, 1883; Lawrence, *Centenary Souvenir,* xliii.

44. *Charleston New Era,* March 3, April 14, December 15, 1883; Lawrence, *Centenary Souvenir,* xlvi, xlvii.

45. *Charleston Daily News,* June 4, 1866, July 22, 23, 1872; *Charleston News and Courier,* September 24, October 20, 1875.

46. In 1870, of 1,287 black households sampled, 51 percent (649) of the wives were employed. U.S. Manuscript Census of Population 1870, 1880, City of Charleston; *Charleston City Directory,* 1878, 243; F. L. Cardozo to Rev. E. P. Smith, July 30, 1868, A. W. Farnham to Rev. M. E. Strieby, December 7, 1877, AMAP, SCDAH; *New York Times,* July 4, 1874, 5; *Charleston New Era,* March 20, 1880; *Atlantic Monthly,* June 1877, 677; *Charleston News and Courier,* July 3, 1884; Will of George Shrewsbury, February 1871, Box 230, No. 25, CCWI, CCC.

47. Fitchett, "The Free Negro," 111, 113, 155; Woodson, *The Mind of the Negro,* 528; *Charleston Daily Republican,* October 15, 1869; *Charleston New Era,* August 25, 1883, February 16, 1884.

48. *Charleston New Era,* May 5, September 22, December 1, 1883.

49. Ibid., May 5, September 22, 1883; *Charleston News and Courier,* January 15, June 10, 1874, April 13, 1877, July 24, 1878; Brown Fellowship Society Minute Book, July 3, 1873, June 4, 1874, May 6, 1875, CCLSC; Fitchett, "The Free Negro," 153, 162–63; Holloway Family Papers, CCLSC; *Charleston City Directory, 1881,* 54–55.

50. Ibid.

51. Ibid.; *Charleston News and Courier,* November 21, 1877; Fitchett, "The Free Negro," 152–53; Holloway Family Papers, CCLSC. For more on the role played by subjective factors in the determination of status in the black community, see Willard B. Gatewood, *Aristocrats of Color: The Black Elite, 1880–1920* (Bloomington, Ind.: Indiana University Press, 1990), 9; Schweninger, *Black Property Owners,* 185.

52. Brown Fellowship Society Minute Books, 1869–1911, CCLSC; "Frances A. Rollin Whipper," Daniel Murray Papers (microfilm reel 8), 3–4, State Historical Society of Wisconsin (hereafter referred as SHSW); Koger, *Black Slaveowners,* 229; Tax List of the City of Charleston for 1860, SCHS.

53. Charleston Ledger of Taxpayers 1880, CTAO; Quoted in Willard B. Gatewood Jr., "'The Remarkable Misses Rollin': Black Women in Reconstruction South Carolina," *South Carolina Historical Magazine* 92 (July 1991): 177–79.

54. U.S. Manuscript Census of Population, City of Charleston 1860; Charleston Ledger of Taxpayers 1880, CTAO; Marina Wikramanayake, *A World in Shadow: The Free Black in Antebellum South Carolina* (Columbia, S.C.: University of South Carolina Press, 1973), 15. For more on the Noisettes, see chap. 2.

55. Will of Plowden Weston, vol. 37, Book A 1826–34, 184, Charleston County Record of Wills (hereafter referred to as CCRW), Charleston County Library (hereafter referred to as CCL); Rollin, *Life and Public Service of Martin R. Delany,* 191–92; Brown Fellowship Society Minute Book, April 6, 1871, August 7, 1873, CCLSC.

56. *Charleston New Era,* April 28, 1883, February 16, April 26, May 3, 10, 17, 1884; *Charleston News and Courier,* July 4, 1877, March 6, September 3, 1879.

57. Alfred B. Williams, *The Liberian Exodus: An Account of the Voyage of the First Emigrants in the Bark 'Azor,' and Their Reception at Monrovia With a Description of Liberia—Its Customs and Civilization, Romances and Prospects* (Charleston: News and Courier, 1878); *Charleston Daily News,* January 18, 1869, April 25, May 2, 1870, November 13, 1871; *Charleston News and Courier,* July 14, August 1, 18, 1873.

58. *Charleston New Era,* February 17, September 1, 1883, February 16, 1884; *Constitution, By-Laws and Rules of the Amateur Literary and Fraternal Association* (Charleston, SC: Edward Perry, 1873), "Preamble," Membership Roster, 12.

59. *Charleston New Era,* November 17, 1883.

60. Ullman, *Martin R. Delany,* 40; A.M.E. *Christian Recorder,* February 9, 1882.

61. Frances A. Rollin, "Diary," in *We Are Your Sisters: Black Women in the Nineteenth Century,* Dorothy Sterling, ed. (New York: W. W. Norton, 1984), 454–56, 461; A.M.E *Christian Recorder,* November 7, 1868. Beginning December 21, 1872, and continuing until perhaps March 1874, Frances A. Whipper was "editress" of the *Beaufort County Times,* a Republican weekly owned by her husband, W. H. Whipper. John Hammond Moore, *South Carolina Newspapers* (Columbia, S.C.: University of South Carolina Press, 1988), 25.

62. *Charleston News and Courier,* March 7, 1874, October 28, 1875; *Charleston City Directory,* 1883, 42, 58–59; Luis F. Emilio, *A Brave Black Regiment: History of the Fifty-Fourth Regiment of Massachusetts Volunteer Infantry 1863–1865* (Boston: Boston Book Company, 1894), 313; *Charleston Daily News,* December 25, 1866, October 5, 1871; *Acts and Joint Resolutions,* 1872 (Columbia: Republican Printing Co., 1872), 144; *Charleston Daily Republican,* August 21, 1869.

63. *Charleston City Directory,* 1883, 58–59; *Charleston News and Courier,* October 28, 1875, December 16, 22, 1876, August 21, 1883; *Charleston Daily News,* June 19, 1872; *South Carolina Leader,* October 7, 1865.

64. *Nation,* September 14, 1865, 332; Berlin, *Slaves Without Masters,* 393.

65. U.S. Manuscript Census of Population 1880, City of Charleston; Charleston Ledger of Taxpayers for 1880, CTAO; Daniel E. Huger Smith, *A Charlestonian's Recollections 1846–1913* (Charleston: Walker, Evans, Cogswell, 1950), 10; *Nation,* September 14, 1865, 332; J. V. Allen to Mr. Smith, February 16, 1867, AMAP, SCDAH; Asa H. Gordon, *Sketches of Negro Life and History in South Carolina* (Columbia, S.C.: University of South Carolina Press, 1971), 69; Septima Poinsette Clark, *Ready From Within: Septima Clark and the Civil Rights Movement* (Trenton, N.J.: Africa World Press Inc., 1991), 99.

66. *New York Times,* July 4, 1874, 5; *Charleston News and Courier,* September 29, November 30, 1885; *Charleston Mercury,* May 16, 1867; *Nation,* August 15, 1872, 105.

67. *Charleston Daily News,* June 22, 1872; *Charleston Daily Courier,* June 15, 1871; interview with Mr. and Mrs. Paul Poinsett, September 28, 1976, Charleston; Jas. T. Ford to Rev. E. M. Cravath, April 17, 1875, AMAP, SCDAH.

68. Rawick, *The American Slave,* 3: 41; *Charleston News and Courier,* September 29, 1885; *New York Times,* July 4, 1874, 5; Edward

King, *The Great South: A Record of Journeys* (Hartford, Conn.: American Publishing, 1875), 785.

69. *Charleston Daily Courier,* May 13, 1865; *Charleston Daily Republican,* August 16, 1871.

70. Smith, *A Charlestonian's Recollections,* 10; *Nation,* September 14, 1865, 332; *Charleston New Era,* December 15, 1883; interview with Mr. and Mrs. Peter Poinsette, September 28, 1976, Charleston.

CHAPTER 7

"BEHOLD A NEW ZION":
The Black Church

1. Katharine L. Dvorak, "After Apocalypse, Moses," in *Masters & Slaves in the House Of The Lord: Race and Religion in the American South, 1740–1870,* John B. Boles, ed. (Lexington, Ky: University Press of Kentucky, 1988), 175–76; Albert Raboteau, *Slave Religion: The "Invisible Institution" in the Antebellum South* (New York: Oxford University Press, 1978), 311–12; Documents Relative to the Denmark Vesey Insurrection, Document B, South Carolina Department of Archives and History (hereafter referred to as SCDAH).

2. J. K. Robinson to Mrs. Smythe, June 28, 1865, Augustine Smythe Letters, South Carolina Historical Society (hereafter referred to as SCHS); Minutes of the Charleston Baptist Association, November 1866 (n.p.:n.d.), 7; Minutes of the South Carolina Annual Conference of the Methodist Episcopal Church South, 1859 (Charleston: Advocate Office, 1860), 8; Minutes of the South Carolina Annual Conference of the Methodist Episcopal Church South, 1866 (Charleston: Weekly Record Printing, 1867), 22; *Charleston Daily News,* February 26, 1866.

3. *South Carolina Leader,* December 16, 1865; *Charleston Daily Courier,* May 30, 31, 1865; Margaret J. Sasportas Letter of Application, June 22, 1865, American Missionary Association Papers (hereafter referred to as AMAP), SCDAH.

4. *Charleston Daily News,* May 14, 1868; Minutes and Register of the First Baptist Church, Charleston County, July 1, 1866, University of South Carolina Caroliniana Library (hereafter referred to as USCCL); Minutes of the Charleston Baptist Association, 1867 (n.p.:n.d.), 32; *Charleston Daily Courier,* August 7, 1866.

5. Minutes of the Charleston Baptist Association, 1867, 32; *Charleston Daily Courier,* August 7, 1866.

6. Joel Williamson, *After Slavery: The Negro in South Carolina During Reconstruction, 1861–1877* (Chapel Hill: University of North

Carolina Press, 1965), 194; Morris Street Baptist Church Minute Book, May 9, 16, 1865, College of Charleston Avery Research Center (hereafter referred to as CCARC); Charles B. Fox, *Record of the Service of the Fifty-Fifth Regiment of Massachusetts Volunteer Infantry* (Cambridge, Mass: John Wilson & Son, 1868), 101.

7. Morris Street Baptist Church Minute Book, May 9, 16, June 10, 1865, August 3, 1868, July 15, 1886, CCARC; Ninety-Sixth Session of The Baptist Educational and Missionary Convention of South Carolina, May 8–13, 1973, in author's possession; Lawrence Faulkner to Officers and Members of First Baptist Church of This City, Minutes and Register of The First Baptist Church, Charleston County, 147–48, USCCL; *Charleston News and Courier,* January 8, 1882; Albert W. Pegues, *Our Baptist Ministers and Schools* (Springfield, Mass.: Willey & Co., 1892), 147; Edward G. Lilly, ed., *Historic Churches of Charleston* (Columbia, S.C.: R. L. Bryan Co., 1966), 7, 127.

8. *Charleston Advocate,* May 11, 1867; Morris Street Baptist Church Minute Book, December 2, 1867, CCARC; George B. Tindall, *South Carolina Negroes 1877–1900* (Baton Rouge: Louisiana State University Press, 1966), 188–89; William J. Simmons, *Men of Mark: Eminent Progressive and Rising* (Cleveland: George M. Rewell and Co., 1887; reprint ed., New York: Arno Press, 1968), 645–46.

9. Tindall, *South Carolina Negroes,* 188–189; Simmons, *Men of Mark,* 645–46; Minutes of The Second Anniversary of The Baptist Educational Missionary and Sunday School Convention of South Carolina Held With The Mount Pisgah Baptist Church Orangeburg, S.C. May 1–5, 1878, v; *Charleston News and Courier,* October 13, 1877, August 5, 1887.

10. W. H. Lawrence, *The Centenary Souvenir, Containing a History of Centenary Church, Charleston, And an Account of the Life and Labors of Rev. R. V. Lawrence, Father of the Pastor of Centenary Church* (Philadelphia: Collins Printing House, 1885), vii–viii, x, xi; *Charleston Daily News,* June 26, 1869.

11. Lilly, *Historic Churches,* 47; *Charleston Daily News,* June 15, 1866.

12. *Charleston Daily News,* June 26, 1869; F. A. Mood and H. M. Mood to the Rev. Bishop and Members of the South Carolina Conference of the Methodist Episcopal Church, March 3, 1867, Assistant Commissioner Letters Received, FBP, SCDAH; Lilly, *Historic Churches,* 146.

13. *Charleston Daily News,* October 18, 1865, June 16, 1866; "Brief Sketch," Comprehensive Record of Centenary Methodist Episcopal Church, CCARC; Lawrence, *Centenary Souvenir,* viii, ix; *Charleston Daily Courier,* September 22, 1866; Minutes of The South Carolina Annual Conference of the Methodist Episcopal Church 1881 (Charleston: Edward Perry, 1881), 38.

14. Williamson, *After Slavery,* 187–88; quoted in Francis B. Simkins and Robert H. Woody, *South Carolina During Reconstruction* (Chapel Hill: University of North Carolina Press, 1932; reprint ed., Gloucester, Mass.: Peter Smith, 1966), 374–75.

15. Simkins and Woody, *South Carolina During Reconstruction,* 375; Minutes of the South Carolina Annual Conference of the Methodist Episcopal Church 1870 (Orangeburg, SC: South Carolina Conference of the M. E. Church, 1870), 11.

16. *Charleston Daily News,* June 12, 23, July 4, 1866; June 21, 1868.

17. *Charleston Daily News,* June 12, 23, July 4, 1866, June 21, 1868; "Brief Sketch," Comprehensive Record of Centenary Methodist Episcopal Church, CCARC. When Northern and Southern Methodists held a joint meeting in 1876, an inquiry resulted in the McKee property being returned to the southern church. Its value had diminished with the general reduction of all real estate values and the Methodist Church South agreed to give Old Bethel to the black Methodists then occupying it. The precise disposition of the other property is less clear but must have been either given or sold to Northern Methodist Congregations in the city. *Charleston News and Courier,* September 6, 1876.

18. Ira Berlin stresses the elite's conservatism and adherence to antebellum values. The case of George Shrewsbury is also striking because he never joined an elite Methodist church. At his death he remained superintendent of the Sunday School at Old Bethel M.E. Church, a position he had held for years. This church would have been overwhelmingly comprised of freedmen. "Tribute of Respect," "George Shrewsbury," undated newspaper articles in Shrewsbury Papers, CCARC.

19. Williamson, *After Slavery,* 183–84; Fifteenth Session of the South Carolina Annual Conference of the Methodist Episcopal Church Held At Centenary Church Charleston, South Carolina, January 21–26, 1880 (Charleston: Edward Perry, 1880), 13.

20. Williamson, *After Slavery,* 182–83, 185; James H. Holloway, *Why I Am A Methodist: A Historical Sketch Of What The Church Has Done For the Colored Children Educationally As Early As 1790 At Charleston, S.C.* (n.p.: R. Wainwright, 1909), 5; *Charleston Daily News,* January 15, 1868; Minutes of the South Carolina Annual Conference of the Methodist Episcopal Church, 1869 (n.p.:n.d.), 6.

21. Dvorak, "After Apocalypse, Moses," 177–78; Williamson, *After Slavery,* 185–86; Lawrence, *Centenary Souvenir,* xiv–xv.

22. Williamson, *After Slavery,* 185–86; Lawrence, *Centenary Souvenir,* xiv–xvi; "Brief Sketch," Comprehensive Church Record of the Centenary Church, vol. 1, CCARC; Abraham Middleton Record Book, February 17, 1882, Papers of Abraham Middleton, USCCL.

23. Williamson, *After Slavery,* 185–86; Lawrence, *Centenary*

Souvenir, xv–xvi; "Brief Sketch," Comprehensive Church Record of the Centenary Church, vol. 1, CCARC; Thomas Holt, *Black Over White: Negro Political Leadership in South Carolina During Reconstruction* (Urbana, Ill.: University of Illinois Press, 1977), 46.

24. Holloway Family Papers, College of Charleston Library Special Collections (hereafter referred to as CCLSC); Comprehensive Record of the Centenary Methodist Episcopal Church, "Class Lists," vols. 2–3, CCARC; Holloway, *Why I Am a Methodist,* 20; Fifteenth Session of the South Carolina Annual Conference of the Methodist Episcopal Church Held At Centenary Church Charleston, South Carolina, January 21–26, 1880, 5; Minutes of the South Carolina Conference of the Methodist Episcopal Church, 1881, 38.

25. Edmund L. Drago, *Initiative, Paternalism, and Race Relations: Charleston's Avery Normal Institute* (Athens, Ga.: University of Georgia Press, 1990), 14–16; Williamson, *After Slavery,* 186; Lawrence, *Centenary Souvenir,* xiv.

26. A.M.E. *Christian Recorder,* May 6, 1865; *Charleston Daily Courier,* May 30, 1865; Daniel Payne, *History of the A.M.E. Church* (Nashville: A.M.E. Sunday School Union, 1891; reprint ed., New York: Johnston Reprint Co., 1968), 467–69; Charles S. Smith, *A History of the African Methodist Episcopal Church* (Philadelphia: Book Concern of the A. M.E. Church, 1922; reprint ed., New York: Johnson Reprint Co., 1968), 59. The sermon "I Seek My Brethren" was first preached by Reverend Wayman to freedmen in Norfolk, Virginia, and was so successful in winning adherents to the church that it became famous and was used extensively along the eastern seaboard, including the Sea Islands. Clarence E. Walker, *A Rock in a Weary Land: The African Methodist Episcopal Church During the Civil War and Reconstruction* (Baton Rouge: Louisiana State University Press, 1982), 67; William E. Montgomery, *Under Their Own Vine and Fig Tree: The African-American Church in the South 1865–1900* (Baton Rouge: Louisiana State University Press, 1993), 68.

27. A.M.E. *Christian Recorder,* May 19, 1866; Minutes of the South Carolina Annual Conference of the Methodist Episcopal Church South 1867 (Charleston: McMillan & Jowitt, 1868), 44–45.

28. Dvorak, "After Apocalypse, Moses," 187.

29. A.M.E. *Christian Recorder,* May 19, September 8, 1866; Minutes of the South Carolina Annual Conference of the Methodist Episcopal Church South 1867, 44–45; *Charleston Daily News,* October 18, 1865; Minutes of the Twelfth Session of the South Carolina Annual Conference of the African Methodist Episcopal Church 1876 (n.p.:n.d.), 12.

30. *Charleston Daily Courier,* October 21, 1865, June 2, 1866; A.M.E *Christian Recorder,* June 3, 1865, July 13, 1867.

31. A.M.E. *Christian Recorder,* April 29, 1865; *Charleston Daily Courier,* May 19, 1865.

32. A.M.E. *Christian Recorder,* March 5, 1870.

33. Ibid., May 19, 1866; *Charleston Daily Courier,* October 21, 1865.

34. Ibid.

35. A.M.E. *Christian Recorder,* June 3, 1865, February 6, 1866.

36. Ibid., June 3, 1865, February 6, May 19, 1866.

37. Simmons, *Men of Mark,* 866–68; Daniel Payne, *History of the A.M.E. Church,* 467–70; Minutes of the Seventh South Carolina Annual Conference of the African Methodist Episcopal Church Held in Bethel A.M.E. Church Columbia, S.C., January 28–February 6, 1871 (n.p.:n.d.), 22; Smith, *A History,* 504.

38. Smith, *A History,* 504; A.M.E. *Christian Recorder,* June 3, 1865, September 29, 1866; June 12, 1869; January 1, 1880, August 10, 17, 24, September 28, 1882; Daniel A. Payne, *Recollections of Seventy Years* (Nashville: African Methodist Episcopal Sunday School Union, 1888; reprint ed., New York: Arno Press, 1968), 332; *Charleston Daily News,* July 19, 1872.

39. A.M.E. *Christian Recorder,* January 11, 1880; *Charleston Daily News,* July 19, 1872.

40. Minutes of the Twelfth Session of the South Carolina Annual Conference of the African Methodist Episcopal Church 1876, 9.

41. A.M.E. *Christian Recorder,* June 3, October 14, 1865, April 8, 1875; Minutes of the Twelfth Session of the South Carolina Annual Conference of the African Methodist Episcopal Church 1876, 9.

42. "The Colored Churches," E. Willis Pamphlets 1878–1884, Charleston Library Society (hereafter referred to as CLS); A.M.E. *Christian Recorder,* September 8, 1866, November 9, 1882; *Charleston Daily News,* May 28, 1866; Lilly, *Historic Churches,* 53, 55; *Northwestern Recorder,* March 1893.

43. A.M.E. *Christian Recorder,* September 8, 1866, April 15, 1875, April 20, November 9, 1882; C. P. Gadsden to Reverend Smythe, October 27, 1867, Augustine Smythe Letters, SCHS; "The Colored Churches," E. Willis Pamphlets, CLS; *Northwestern Recorder,* March 1893; Lilly, *Historic Churches,* 55; Minutes of the Twelfth Session of the South Carolina Annual Conference of the African Methodist Church 1876, 26; Williamson, *After Slavery,* 191.

44. A.M.E. *Christian Recorder,* July 30, 1885.

45. Minutes of the Tenth Session of the South Carolina Annual Conference of the African Methodist Episcopal Church 1874 (n.p.:n.d.), 48; *Charleston News and Courier,* May 7–8, 1884.

46. *Charleston News and Courier,* May 6–8, 1884.

47. Ibid., May 6, 1884.

48. Ibid.

49. Ibid., May 6, July 1, 6, 1884; A.M.E. *Christian Recorder*, May 22, 1884.

50. *Charleston News and Courier,* May 11, July 1, 1884, January 23, 1885; Tindall, *South Carolina Negroes,* 194.

51. Thomas D. Smyth, *Autobiographical Notes, Letters and Reflections* (Charleston: Walker, Evans and Cogswell, 1914), 694–96; George A. Blackburn, ed., *The Life Work of John L. Girardeau* (Columbia, S.C.: State Co., 1916), 80–81, 136–37; *Charleston Daily Courier,* January 29, 1867, May 31,1869; Williamson, *After Slavery,* 198–99.

52. Smythe, *Autobiographical Notes,* 694–96; *Charleston Daily Courier,* January 29, 1867, May 31, 1869; Blackburn, *Life Work,* 80–81, 105, 142–43; Williamson, *After Slavery,* 198; F. D. Jones and W. H. Mills, *History of the Presbyterian Church in South Carolina Since 1850* (Columbia, S.C.: R. L. Bryan Co., 1926), 119, 146; John B. Adger, *My Life and Times 1810–1899* (Richmond: Presbyterian Committee of Publications, 1899), 176–77.

53. A.M.E. *Christian Recorder,* August 5, 1865; Andrew Murray, *Presbyterians and The Negro: A History* (Philadelphia: Presbyterian Historical Society, 1966), 142; *Charleston Daily Courier,* June 2, 1866; *Charleston Mercury,* December 24, 1866; Blackburn, *Life Work,* 142–43; Lilly, *Historic Churches,* 65.

54. A. W. Adams to Rev. Geo. Whipple, June 1, 1864, Rev. E. J. Adams to Rev. Geo. Whipple, July 27, 1865, Report of E. J. Adams, December 1865, AMAP, SCDAH; Murray, *Presbyterians and the Negro,* 142; A.M.E. *Christian Recorder,* August 5, 1865, April 28, 1866.

55. Rev. E. J. Adams to Rev. Geo. Whipple, July 27, 1865, Report of E. J. Adams, December 1865, F. L. Cardozo to Rev. E. P. Smith, January 15, 1868, AMAP, SCDAH; *Charleston Daily News,* October 5, 1872; A.M.E. *Christian Recorder,* April 28, 1866; Smyth, *Autobiographical Notes,* 694–96; *Charleston Mercury,* March 26, 1867.

56. *Charleston Daily News,* February 19, 1866; Rev. J. Stuart Hanckel, *Report on the Colored People and Freedmen of South Carolina* (Charleston: n.p., 1866), 4.

57. *Journal of the Eighty-Ninth Annual Convention of the Protestant Episcopal Church in the Diocese of South Carolina 1879* (Charleston: Walker Evans Cogswell, 1879), 26–27; *Charleston Daily Courier,* November 17, 1865, May 17, 1876.

58. *Charleston Daily Courier,* November 21, 1865, January 8, May 17–18, 1876; Tindall, *South Carolina Negroes,* 195.

59. *Charleston News and Courier,* October 26, 1875, May 17, 1876; *Journal of the Eighty-Fifth Annual Convention of the Protestant Episcopal Church,* 1875, 21.

60. *Journal of the Eighty-Fifth Annual Convention of the Protestant Episcopal Church,* 1875, 21; *Journal of the Eighty-Sixth Annual Convention of the Protestant Episcopal Church,* 1876, 35, 54, 59, 60–61.

61. *Journal of the Eighty-Fifth Annual Convention of the Protestant Episcopal Church,* 1875, 21; *Journal of the Eighty-Sixth Annual Convention of the Protestant Episcopal Church,* 1876, 25, 40, 46, 59, 63; *Journal of the Ninety-Fourth Annual Convention of the Protestant Episcopal Church,* 1884, 20–21, 26; *Charleston News and Courier,* May 13, 1876.

62. *Charleston News and Courier,* February 4, 1881, March 26, 1883; *Journal of the Ninety-First Annual Convention of the Protestant Episcopal Church,* 1881, 61.

63. *Journal of the Ninety-First Annual Convention of the Protestant Episcopal Church,* 1881, 61, 65–66, *Journal of the Ninety-Second Annual Convention of the Protestant Episcopal Church,* 1882, 12, *Journal of the Ninety-Third Annual Convention of the Protestant Episcopal Church,* 1883, 11, 18, *Journal of the Ninety-Fifth Annual Convention of the Protestant Episcopal Church,* 1885, 29–31, 35; A.M.E. *Christian Recorder,* February 24, 1881; *Charleston News and Courier,* June 21, 1884, May 14–15, 17, 1885; Albert S. Thomas, *A Historical Account of the Protestant Episcopal Church in South Carolina, 1820–1957* (Columbia, S.C.: R. L. Bryan Co., 1957), 92. The controversy over the place of black clergymen in the Diocesan convention continued until their complete exclusion was made certain by amending the Diocesan constitution. For more on the role played by Charleston aristocrats in achieving this result, see Lyon G. Tyler, "Drawing the Color Line in the Episcopal Diocese of South Carolina, 1876 to 1890: The Role of Edward McCrady, Father and Son," *South Carolina Historical Magazine* 91 (April 1990): 120–21.

64. *Charleston Daily News,* March 11, 1872; F. L. Cardozo to M. E. Strieby, March 17, 1866, F. L. Cardozo to Wm. E. Whiting, April 29, 1867, Mortimer A. Warren to Rev. E. P. Smith, May 16, 1869, James T. Ford to Rev. E. P. Smith, December 21, 1869, Jas. T. Ford to Rev. E. M. Cravath, April 17, 1871, S. C. Coles to Rev. E. M. Strieby, May 26, 1876, AMAP, SCDAH; George N. Edwards, *A History of the Independent or Congregational Church of Charleston, South Carolina Commonly Known as Circular Church* (Boston: Pilgrim Press, 1947), 86; For an extended examination of why congregationalism failed to win much support among southern blacks, see Joe M. Richardson, *Christian Reconstruction: The American Missionary Association and Southern Blacks, 1861–1890* (Athens, Ga.: University of Georgia Press, 1986), chap. 9.

65. Morris Street Baptist Church Minute Book, August 7, 1865, July 15, 1886, CCARC; A.M.E. *Christian Recorder,* April 28, 1866; "The Colored Churches," E. Willis Pamphlets, CLS; *Charleston News and Courier,* March 11, 1878; Charleston Ledger of Taxpayers for 1880,

Charleston County Tax Assessor's Office, (hereafter referred to as CTAO); U.S. Manuscript Census of Population 1880, City of Charleston; *Charleston City Directories*, 1878, 1879–80, 1881. Sometimes migrants to the city felt uncomfortable in the established churches and for this reason created new ones. In the late 1870s, one group of migrants from nearby islands began a weekly prayer meeting in their various homes and eventually organized into Greater St. Luke A.M.E. Church under Rev. W. W. Beckett in 1878. It was known as a city church with country immigrants. Bishop F. C. James, *African Methodism in South Carolina: A Bicentennial Focus* (Tappan: N.Y. Custom Book Inc., n.d.), 154.

66. W. J. Brodie, et al., to Reverend, May 23, 1867, Richard Gregorie to Rev. E. P. Smith, May 25, 1867, F. L. Cardozo to Rev. E. P. Smith, January 15, 1868, AMAP, SCDAH; Charleston Ledger of Taxpayers for 1880, CTAO; U.S. Manuscript Census of Population 1880, City of Charleston; *Charleston City Directories*, 1878, 1879–80, 1881.

67. Willard B. Gatewood, *Aristocrats of Color: The Black Elite, 1880–1920* (Bloomington, Ind.: Indiana University Press, 1990), 273, 275, 277; Comprehensive Record of Centenary Methodist Episcopal Church, "Marriage Record," Vol. 2, CCARC. The conclusion that Centenary's congregation was overwhelmingly drawn from the city was determined by an analysis of the church marriage record. During the period January 17, 1872, through 1885, out of 153 marriages where the places of residence were listed, there were only 16, or 10.5 percent of the cases, where one partner resided outside Charleston. A.M.E. *Christian Recorder,* September 8, 1866; Holloway Family Papers, CCLSC; *Charleston Daily Republican,* September 18, 1869; Lilly, *Historic Churches,* 45; Fitchett, "The Free Negro," 262; Charleston Ledger of Taxpayers for 1880, CTAO; U.S. Manuscript Census of Population 1880, City of Charleston; *Charleston City Directories*, 1878, 1879–80, 1881.

68. *Charleston Daily Courier,* November 21, 1865, March 30, 1870, April 19, 1870, January 8, 1876; *Charleston New Era,* April 3, 1880; George P. Rawick, ed., *The American Slave: A Composite Autobiography,* 19 vols. (Westport, Conn.: Greenwood Press, 1972), 2: 34–36; "St. Mark's Echo", April 1890, in author's possession.

69. E. Franklin Frazier, *The Negro Church in America* (New York: Schocken Books, 1964), 30; Vattel E. Daniel, "Ritual and Stratification in Chicago Negro Churches," *American Sociological Review* 7 (June 1942): 359; Gatewood, *Aristocrats of Color,* 274; Drago, *Initiative, Paternalism, and Race Relations,* 38; T. W. Cardozo to Rev. S. Hunt, June 23, 1865, Benj. Jackson to Dr. Brother Smith, January 13, 1868, AMAP, SCDAH.

70. Frazier, *The Negro Church,* 30; Rawick, *The American Slave,* 2: 34–36; Daniel, "Ritual and Stratification," 357; *Charleston News and Courier,* August 7, 1877.

71. *Charleston Mercury,* March 11, 1867; *Charleston News and Courier,* September 8, 1877; Benj. F. Jackson to Rev. Geo. Whipple, February 18, 1868, AMAP, SCDAH; *New York Times,* December 31, 1866, 1. Another reason for the black Charlestonians' affinity for the Baptist church may have been that certain aspects of that denomination's theology were especially consonant with traditional African religious practices. For example, the Baptists' practice of baptism by immersion was similar to river ceremonies from West and Central Africa. Sterling Stuckey, *Slave Culture: Nationalist Theory and the Foundations of Black America* (New York: Oxford University Press, 1987), 33–35; Montgomery, *Under Their Own Vine,* 107–08.

72. Frazier, *The Negro Church,* chap. 3; C. Eric Lincoln and Lawrence H. Mamiya, *The Black Church in the African American Experience* (Durham, N.C.: Duke University Press, 1990), 243–45.

73. Frazier, *The Negro Church,* chap. 3.

74. Ibid., 83; Geo. A. William to Major E. L. Deane, July 16, 1867; Assistant Commissioner Letters Received, FBP, SCDAH; *Charleston News and Courier,* April 29, September 6, 11, 1878; Carl R. Osthaus, *Freedmen, Philanthropy, and Fraud: A History of the Freedmen's Savings Bank* (Urbana: University of Illinois Press, 1976), 117–19; Montgomery, *Under Their Own Vine,* 53; *Charleston Daily Republican,* December 20, 1869.

75. Montgomery, *Under Their Own Vine,* 94–95, 114–15, 139; *Charleston News and Courier,* July 7, 1882.

76. A.M.E. *Christian Recorder,* March 5, 1870; *Charleston Daily Courier,* August 5, 1865; Leon Litwack, *Been in the Storm So Long: The Aftermath of Slavery* (New York: Alfred A. Knopf, 1979), 493.

77. Walker, *A Rock in a Weary Land,* 16, 26, 52; *South Carolina Leader,* March 31, 1866, *Charleston Daily Courier,* October 14, 1865; A.M.E. *Christian Recorder,* September 29, 1866, June 29, 1867.

78. A.M.E. *Christian Recorder,* September 29, 1866, June 29, 1867.

79. Morris Street Baptist Church Minute Book, May 16, 1865, CCARC; Pegues, *Our Baptist Ministers,* 81.

80. A.M.E. *Christian Recorder,* February 5, 1874; Minutes of The Second Anniversary of the Baptist Educational Missionary and Sunday School Convention of South Carolina Held with the Mount Pisgah Baptist Church Orangeburg, S.C., May 1–5, 1878, iii, iv, USCCL.

81. Minutes of the Baptist Educational Missionary and Sunday School Convention of South Carolina 1878, 4, 29; Minutes of The Second Anniversary of the Baptist Educational Missionary and Sunday School Convention of South Carolina Held with the Mount Pisgah Baptist Church Orangeburg, S.C., May 1–5, 1878, vii, xiv, USCCL; *Charleston News and Courier,* May 15, 1884.

82. Williamson, *After Slavery,* 187, 190–91; Minutes of the South Carolina Annual Conference of the Methodist Episcopal Church 1869, 11; *Charleston Advocate,* May 11, 1867; A.M.E. *Christian Recorder,* April 11, 1868; February 12, 1870; Minutes of the Twelfth Session of the South Carolina Annual Conference of the African Methodist Episcopal Church 1876, 15.

83. Susan M. Fickling, "The Christianization of the Negro in South Carolina 1830–1860" (M.A. thesis, University of South Carolina, 1923), 10.

84. Ibid., 10; *Journal of the Eighty-Fourth Annual Convention of the Protestant Episcopal Church, 1874,* 46; Jas. T. Ford to Rev. E. M. Cravath, February 14, 1872, Jas. T. Ford to Rev. L. Bacon D. D., June 6, 1872, AMAP, SCDAH.

85. Fickling, "Christianization of the Negro," 10.

86. Howard Brotz, ed., *Negro Social and Political Thought 1850–1920* (New York: Basic Books, 1966), 194–96; "Proceedings of the 1855 Philadelphia Colored National Convention," in *Minutes of the Proceedings of the National Negro Conventions 1830–1864,* Howard Bell, ed., (Salem, N.J: National Standard, 1856; reprint ed.; New York: Arno Press, 1969), 7; *Charleston Daily News,* March 9, 1870, Holt, *Black Over White,* 49, 81. Holt's study revealed that during Reconstruction, 22 percent of black legislators were ministers. Of the twenty-one black ministers for whom information was available in the census of 1870 for Charleston, only one could neither read nor write, while two could not write. Eighteen ministers, or 86 percent, were capable of doing both. Of these cases, all with the exception of Richard H. Cain had been born in South Carolina (Cain is listed as born in South Carolina, but this is incorrect). U.S. Manuscript Census of Population for 1870, City of Charleston. B. F. Randolph to Bvt. Maj. Gen. R. Saxton, August 31, 1865, Assistant Commissioner Letters Received, FBP; A.M.E. *Christian Recorder,* February 4, June 3, 1865. The antebellum Negro Conventions were regularly convened meetings of black leaders to discuss antislavery strategy and improvement of the quality of free black life. The Equal Rights League had similar goals, while the African Civilization Society was dedicated to promoting African emigration and evangelization.

87. Minutes of the South Carolina Annual Conference of the Methodist Episcopal Church 1869, 6; A.M.E. *Christian Recorder,* March 18, 1880; *Charleston Mercury,* February 24, 1868; Emily B. Reynolds and Joan R. Faunt, *Biographical Directory of the Senate of the State of South Carolina 1776–1964* (Columbia, S.C.: South Carolina Archives Department, 1964), 246, 248, 357; Montgomery, *Under Their Own Vine and Fig Tree,* 178–79.

88. *Charleston Daily Courier,* January 19, 1869; U.S. Manuscript Census of Population for 1860, City of Charleston; *Charleston News and*

Courier, September 25, November 12, 1873, October 8, 1875, October 9, 1877; *Charleston Daily News,* August 10, 1871, January 19, 1872; *Charleston Daily Republican,* September 27, 1869.

89. R. H. Cain to R. K. Scott, November 11, 1867, D. W. Logen to R. K. Scott, November 21, 1867, Assistant Commissioner Letters Received, FBP, SCDAH.

90. Eric Foner, *Freedom's Lawmakers: A Directory of Black Office-holders During Reconstruction* (New York: Oxford University Press, 1993), 36; Carol Bleser, *The Promised Land: The History of the South Carolina Land Commission, 1869–1890* (Columbia, S.C.: University of South Carolina Press, 1969), 28; *Charleston News and Courier,* April 28, September 25, 1885.

91. *Charleston Daily News,* February 24–25, 1870; September 27, 1869; *Charleston Daily Courier,* February 16, 1869, Walter J. Fraser Jr., *Charleston! Charleston!: The History of a Southern City* (Columbia, S.C.: University of South Carolina Press, 1989), 288.

92. *Charleston News and Courier,* October 17, 1877; Lawrence, *Centenary Souvenir,* xxx–xxxi, xxxvii–xxxviii.

CHAPTER 8

"AN EQUAL CHANCE IN THE RACE OF LIFE":
Postbellum Race Relations

1. *Charleston News and Courier,* September 16, 1885; Ellison to Janie, November 24, 1867, Adger-Smyth Flynn Family Papers, University of South Carolina Caroliniana Library (hereafter referred to as USCCL); *Charleston Mercury,* November 18, 1867; George Fredrickson, *The Black Image in the White Mind: The Debate on Afro-American Character and Destiny, 1817–1914* (New York: Harper & Row, 1971), 188.

2. *Charleston Daily News,* July 4, 1866; May 29, 1868; June 3, 1871; Sidney Andrews, *The South Since the War* (Boston: Ticknor and Fields, 1866), 22; Cousin M to Celia, June 11, 1865, Family Papers of Frederick A . Porcher, USCCL. Buckner Payne, a publisher from Nashville used the pen name "Ariel." In a pamphlet entitled "The Negro: What Is His Ethnological Status," he asserted that blacks had been created as a separate species, prior to Adam and Eve. Because some of Adam's sons intermarried with members of the allegedly inferior species, they were punished by a great flood. Fredrickson, *The Black Image in the White Mind,* 188.

3. Affy to Amie, September 5, 1865, Family Papers of Frederick A. Porcher, South Carolina Historical Society (hereafter referred to as SCHS); *Charleston Daily Courier,* July 6, 1869; Jacob Schirmer Diary, July 4, 1866, SCHS.

4. Quoted in Joel Williamson, *After Slavery: The Negro in South Carolina During Reconstruction, 1861–1877* (Chapel Hill: University of North Carolina Press, 1965), 277; James Roark, *Masters Without Slaves: Southern Planters in the Civil War and Reconstruction* (New York: W. W. Norton, 1977), 123; George P. Rawick, ed., *The American Slave: A Composite Autobiography,* 19 vols. (Westport, Conn.: Greenwood Press, 1972), 2: 119.

5. Williamson, *After Slavery,* 328–29, 334–37; Thomas Holt, *Black Over White: Negro Political Leadership in South Carolina During Reconstruction* (Urbana, Ill.: University of Illinois Press, 1977), 35, 110; *Charleston Daily News,* May 27, 1866; William C. Hine, "Frustration, Factionalism and Failure: Black Political Leadership and the Republican Party in Reconstruction Charleston, 1865–1877" (Ph.D diss., Kent State University, 1979), 460.

6. Eliza T. Holmes to ———, April 8, 1873, Williams Chestnut Manning Papers, USCCL; *Charleston Daily News,* October 9, 1869; Smythe to Janey, May 29, 1868, Augustine Smythe Letters, SCHS; Daniel E. Huger Smith, et al., eds., *Mason Smith Family Letters 1860–1868* (Columbia, S.C.: University of South Carolina Press, 1950), 277.

7. Williamson, *After Slavery,* 260–61; George W. Williams, *Sketches of Travel in the Old and New World* (Charleston: Walker Evans & Cogswell, 1871), 409–10; *Charleston Daily News,* August 12, 1868.

8. *Charleston Mercury,* October 22, 1868; *Charleston Daily Courier,* October 20, 22, 1868; R. H. Cain to R. K. Scott, October 24, 1868, Robert K. Scott Papers, South Carolina Department of Archives and History (hereafter referred to as SCDAH).

9. Arney R. Childs, ed., *The Private Journal of Henry William Ravenel* (Columbia, S.C.: University of South Carolina Press, 1947), 326; *Charleston Daily Courier,* November 2, 11, 1868.

10. *Charleston Daily Courier,* July 22, August 2, 8, 1871.

11. *Journal of the House of Representatives of the State of South Carolina,* 1869–70, (Columbia: John W. Denny, 1870), 159; *Charleston Daily Courier,* March 26, 1870.

12. Eric Foner, *Reconstruction: America's Unfinished Revolution 1863–1877* (New York: Harper and Row, 1988), 368; Holt, *Black Over White,* 143; *Charleston Daily Courier,* September 3, 4, 5, 16, 1868. A series of humiliating incidents occurring in mid- to late 1868 convinced black leaders of the importance of public accommodations legislation. On one occasion a group of black legislators had traveled to Greenville only to find that even on a stormy night there were no hotel accommodations for them. On another occasion Frances Rollin and members of her wedding party had ridden first class from Charleston to Branchville, at which point they encountered a gun-wielding train conductor at the head of a mob that

forced them into a second-class car. *Charleston Daily Courier,* August 17, 1868; "Frances Ann Rollin Whipper," Daniel Murray Papers (microfilm reel 8), 11–13, State Historical Society of Wisconsin (hereafter referred to as SHSW).

13. *Charleston Daily Courier,* April 23, 1869; *Acts and Joint Resolutions of the South Carolina Legislature,* 1869–70 (Columbia: John W. Denny, 1870), 179, 386–88; *Journal of the South Carolina House of Representatives,* 1869–70, 289.

14. *Charleston City Directory,* 1875–76, 95; *Journal of the South Carolina House of Representatives,* 1869–70, 289, 298–99; *Charleston Daily News,* February 17–18, 22, 24–25, 1870.

15. *Charleston Daily News,* February 22, March 2, 1870, *Acts and Joint Resolutions,* 1869–70, 386–88.

16. *Charleston Daily Courier,* March 31, 1870, November 3, 1883; *Charleston Daily News,* August 14, 1866, August 24, 1868, January 11, 1870.

17. Williamson, *After Slavery,* 279; *Charleston Daily Courier,* August 17, 1868; A.M.E. *Christian Recorder,* July 16, 1874; *Charleston New Era,* September 29, 1883.

18. *Charleston Mercury,* December 17, 1866, April 2, May 4, 1867; *Charleston Daily Courier,* October 15, 1866, March 27, 1867; *New York Times,* January 7, 1867, 1.

19. William C. Hine, "The 1867 Charleston Streetcar Sit-Ins: A Case of Successful Black Protest," *South Carolina Historical Magazine* 77 (April 1976): 114; Jno S. Riggs to Major Genl. R. K. Scott, May 3, 1867, Assistant Commissioner Letters Received, Freedmen's Bureau Papers (hereafter referred to as FBP), SCDAH; Williamson, *After Slavery,* 283; *New York Times,* April 5, 1867, 1, April 20, 1867, 1; *Charleston Mercury,* May 6, 1867; Jacob Schirmer Diary, May 4, 1867, South Carolina Historical Society (hereafter referred to as SCHS). For other examples of blacks freely riding street cars, see Unsigned to Lannie, October 28, 1867, Unsigned to Miss Sarah A. Smyth, October 18, 1868, Adger-Smyth Flynn Family Papers, USCCL; *Charleston Daily News,* August 20, 1872; *Charleston News and Courier,* February 6, 1877.

20. *Charleston New Era,* September 22, 1883.

21. A.M.E. *Christian Recorder,* August 26, 1865; F. L. Cardozo to William. E: Whiting, August 31, 1866, American Missionary Association Papers (hereafter referred to as AMAP), SCDAH; James B. Thomas to General, July 3, 1867, Assistant Commissioner Letters Received, FBP, SCDAH.

22. F. L. Cardozo to William. E. Whiting, July 4, 1866, AMAP, SCDAH; Willard B. Gatewood Jr., "'The Remarkable Misses Rollin': Black Women in Reconstruction South Carolina," *South Carolina Historical*

Magazine 92 (July 1991): 172, 177; Victor Ullman, *Martin R. Delany: The Beginnings of Black Nationalism* (Boston: Beacon Press, 1971), 394.

23. Capt. J. W. Clovis to R. K. Scott, July 30, 1867, Assistant Commissioner Letters Received, FBP, SCDAH; Francis B. Simkins and Robert H. Woody, *South Carolina During Reconstruction* (Chapel Hill: University of North Carolina Press, 1932; reprint ed., Gloucester, Mass.: Peter Smith, 1966), 70; Elizabeth H. Botume, *First Days Amongst the Contrabands* (Boston: Lee & Shepard, 1893; reprint ed., New York:Arno Press, 1968), 267–268; *Charleston News and Courier,* April 20, 1884.

24. *Atlantic Monthly,* June 1877, 676; *Charleston Daily Republican,* May 23, 1870. For other examples of blacks riding first class in South Carolina, see *Charleston Daily Republican,* December 12, 13, 1869; *Charleston News and Courier,* June 30, 1880.

25. *Charleston News and Courier,* October 5, November 2, 5, 1883.

26. Ibid., October 5, 16, November 5, December 4, 1883. As a means of separating the races on trains, the *News and Courier* proposed in 1883 that the railroads establish special cars that contained more expensive reserved seats only. Everyone would be allowed to purchase reserved seats, but, according to the paper, "only the better class of colored people would care to pay for reserved seats, and to such colored people little or no objection is made." This proposal is far different from the demands for strict racial separation characteristic of the turn-of-the-century South. George B. Tindall, *South Carolina Negroes 1877–1900* (Baton Rouge: Louisiana State University Press, 1966), 300.

27. *Charleston News and Courier,* August 19, 1883; *Charleston Daily Republican,* May 23, 1870, July 15, 1871; *Charleston Daily News,* August 14, 1866, April 4, 1870.

28. *Charleston Daily Republican,* August 21, 23, 1869, January 5, 1870; *Charleston Daily News,* September 29, 1869, June 1, 1870; *Charleston Daily Courier,* September 8, October 14, 1869. The case of Wilburn's Saloon was not the only one in which black aldermen used the power of the city council to punish white businessmen found guilty of racial discrimination. In 1869 Amos Brookbanks, proprietor of Brookbank's Ice Cream Garden, charged a black patron one dollar for a drink that normally cost ten cents and demurely explained, "That's the price of soda water for colored men." He was arrested for extortion but was subsequently acquitted. Brookbanks later petitioned the city council to erect a building in Meeting Street (probably for business purposes), but black and white aldermen refused to consider the matter at this time because of the petitioner's racist practices. Several weeks later the *Daily Courier* reported that the action of the city council effectively ended Brookbank's career in the ice cream business.

29. *Charleston Daily Republican,* May 23, 1870, July 15, 1871; *Charleston Daily News,* September 29, December 29, 1869, January 5,

April 4, June 1, 29, 1870; *Charleston Daily Courier,* September 8, October 14, 1869; *Charleston City Directory,* 1877–78, 256.

30. *Charleston Daily News,* March 17, 28, 29, June 23, 1870; *Charleston Daily Republican,* March 21, 1871.

31. *Charleston Daily Courier,* September 7, November 29, 1869, January 10, 1870; *Charleston Daily News,* January 10, February 16, 1870; *Charleston Daily Republican,* January 12, 1870, March 22, 1871.

32. Quoted in Williamson, *After Slavery,* 292; *Charleston News and Courier,* April 21, October 14, 1883; Tindall, *South Carolina Negroes,* 294.

33. Interview with Mr. and Mrs. Paul Poinsette, September 28, 1976, Charleston; *Charleston Daily News,* March 24, 1868, January 11, 1870.

34. U.S. Manuscript Census of Population 1880, City of Charleston; *Charleston Daily News,* October 26, 1870; *Charleston Daily Courier,* December 18, 1868, February 7, 1873, June 24, 1877, July 7, 1882; Elizabeth Boorn to Rev. E. P. Smith, February 15, 1868, AMAP, SCDAH; Tindall, *South Carolina Negroes,* 278; U. S. Bureau of the Census, *Population of the United States in 1880 Compiled from the Tenth Census: Social Statistics of Cities* (Washington: Government Printing Office, 1886), pt. 2, 18: 101.

35. *Charleston Daily Courier,* July 27–28, 1868; *Charleston Daily News,* September 11, October 2, 21, December 1, 1869.

36. *Charleston Daily News,* October 13, 1869, December 9, 1870, October 5, 1872.

37. Ibid., October 5, 1872; E. Horace Fitchett, "The Free Negro in Charleston, South Carolina" (Ph.D. diss., University of Chicago, 1950), 249; State Free Negro Capitation Book, Charleston, 1855, Charleston Library Society; Theodore D. Jervey, *The Slave Trade: Slavery and Color* (Columbia, S.C.: The State Company, 1925; reprint ed., Northbrook, Ill.: Metro Books, 1972), 227–28; *Charleston News and Courier,* November 27, December 15, 1873, January 19, 1874, January 9, February 27, 1878; Georgianna Shrewsbury Deed of Trust and Conveyance, January 15, 1885, Shrewsbury Papers, College of Charleston Avery Research Center (hereafter referred to as CCARC); Walter J. Fraser Jr., *Charleston! Charleston!: The History of a Southern City* (Columbia, S.C.: University of South Carolina Press, 1989), 306. Sometimes the question arises about the scope of the black policemen's authority during this time. They did have the power to arrest whites, an authority that they used. See *Charleston Daily News,* July 22, 1869, January 10, 1870; *Charleston News and Courier,* September 3, 1870.

38. Minutes of the Board of Firemasters, May 17, 1865, September 29, 1866, June 21, 1871, SCHS; *Charleston City Directory,* 1872–73, 302–04.

39. Minutes of the Board of Firemasters, September 27, 1865, April 15, 1868; *Charleston Daily Courier,* April 10, 1867, March 28, 1868.

40. Minutes of the Board of Firemasters, July 21, 1869, SCHS; *Charleston Daily News,* August 9, 11, 25, 1869; *Charleston Daily Courier,* July 22, 1869.

41. *Charleston Daily News,* August 9, 21, 25, 1869.

42. Ibid., August 25, September 1, 1869.

43. Ibid., August 9, 11, 1869, April 23, 26, 1870, May 21, November 21, 1872, May 2, 1874; *Charleston Daily Courier,* August 25, 1869; Jacob Schirmer Diary, April 27, 1870, SCHS.

44. Minutes of the Board of Firemasters, May 18, 1870, SCHS; *Charleston Daily News,* August 13, November 21, 1872.

45. *Charleston Daily News,* July 26, 1871, December 31, 1872; *Charleston News and Courier,* September 24, November 19, 1873, September 28, 1875. I have identified Samuel Garrett as a political independent because he ran for office in 1871 under the Democratic or Citizen's party, and in 1873 and 1875 he ran for alderman and was subsequently elected under the Republican banner.

46. *Charleston News and Courier,* April 29, 1878, January 18, 1879, January 7, 1881.

47. *Atlantic Monthly,* June 1877, 681; *New York Times,* July 4, 1874, 5; *Charleston Daily News,* June 10, 1868; *Charleston Daily Republican,* March 29, 1871; *Charleston News and Courier,* March 16, 1880.

48. *Charleston News and Courier,* May 27, 1874; U.S. Manuscript Census of Population 1880, City of Charleston.

49. U.S. Manuscript Census of Population 1880, City of Charleston; Charleston Ledger of Taxpayers for 1880, Charleston County Tax Asssessor's Office (hereafter referred to as CTAO).

50. Frederick A. Ford, *Census of the City of Charleston, South Carolina for the Year 1861* (Charleston: Evans & Cogswell, 1861). *Charleston News and Courier,* May 27, 1874.

51. *Charleston Daily News,* November 3, 14, 21, 1866; Robert Somers, *The Southern States Since the War, 1870–1871* (New York: MacMillan Company, 1871), 38–39; *Charleston Daily Courier,* May 27, 1871.

52. Manuscript Census of Population 1880, City of Charleston; Ford, *Census of the City of Charleston; Charleston Daily Courier,* September 23, 1869, February 5, August 29, 1885; *Charleston City Directories,* 1878, 1879–1880, 1881; *Charleston Daily News,* November 1, 1866; *Charleston Mercury,* July 16, 1867.

53. Communities File, Miscellaneous Article, "Charleston Street Names," SCHS; Lyman P. Powell, ed., *Historic Towns of the Southern States* (New York: Knickerbocker Press, 1900), 279; Simkins and Woody, *South Carolina During Reconstruction,* 315; Manuscript Census of Population 1880, City of Charleston. Alley dwelling grew out of the need for cheap housing and the desire of planters and other elites to have their

servants nearby. During the antebellum years, these were areas where free blacks and slaves resided, but they were not racially exclusive. Following the war, the in-migration of freedmen, coupled with Charleston's sluggish economy and the low level of construction, may have driven more people to seek residences in these locations. Many of these areas, which were mixed before the war, become heavily populated by blacks in the late nineteenth century. Horlbeck and Sires Alley are only two examples. Walter Hill, "Family, Life, and Work Culture: Black Charleston, South Carolina, 1880 to 1910" (Ph.D. dissertation, University of Maryland, 1989), 171–72.

54. *Charleston Daily Courier,* February 3, 1873; *Charleston News and Courier,* August 15, 1888.

55. John P. Radford, "Culture Economy and Urban Structure in Charleston, South Carolina, 1860–1880" (Ph.D. diss., Clark University, 1974), 206, 208; *Charleston News and Courier,* February 28, 1884; *Charleston Daily News,* January 1, 1868.

56. U.S. Manuscript Census of Population 1880, City of Charleston; *Charleston News and Courier,* July 9, 1884. Throughout the period from 1860 to 1880, there was a general shift in Charleston's population from the lower to the upper wards. In 1882 the city was redivided into twelve wards with wards nine through twelve making up the northernmost tier. Whereas, in 1860, 56 percent of the total population resided in the lower city, only 42 percent of the total resided here in 1900. For the entire period 1860–1900, the lower portion of the city lost 14 percent of its population to the upper wards. However, black and white Charlestonians experienced different degrees of population redistribution during Reconstruction and the late nineteenth century. The percentage of the white population residing in the lower wards increased from 12,948, or 55 percent, in 1860 to 13,972, or 58 percent, in 1880. But by 1900 this trend had reversed and the percentage of whites residing in the lower six wards (which correspond to the pre-1882 lower four wards) decreased to 11,997, or 49 percent. In comparison, the shift in the black population from the lower to the upper wards began earlier and was much greater. After declining from 9,728, or 58 percent, to 11,848, or 46 percent, during the period 1860–80, by 1900 only 11,215, or 36 percent, of the city's black population resided in the lower six wards. At this time, while blacks constituted 57 percent of the city's total population, in the lower city they made up this proportion of only a single ward. But in the upper six wards blacks reached and exceeded their proportion of the city's population in all but one ward. The trend toward the redistribution of the black population from the lower wards to the northern edge of the city continued throughout the twentieth century. By 1940 only 14 percent and 2 percent respectively of the population in wards one and two was black, but in wards nine through twelve, blacks made up between 51 and 71 percent of the residents. Several factors account for the continuation of

this trend. During the first half of the twentieth century, the number of domestic servants declined significantly. This must have affected housing patterns because, as a group, such persons often lived with or very near their employers. Also, the renovation of older residences in the lower historic part of the city increased property values and forced blacks out. Finally, the advent of public housing contributed to the redistribution of the black population by attracting residents away from mixed neighborhoods to new segregated public housing facilities; U.S. Bureau of the Census, *Population of the United States in 1860,* compiled from the Eighth Census (Washington: Government Printing Office, 1864), 452; *Charleston News and Courier,* July 28, 1880; U.S. Bureau of the Census, *Twelfth Census of the United States in 1900 Population* (Washington: Government Printing Office, 1901), pt. 1, 1: 642; Karl and Alma Taeuber, "Residential Segregation in the Twentieth Century South," in *The Rise of the Ghetto,* John Bracey, et al., eds. (Belmont, Calif.: Wadsworth Publishing Co., 1971), 92.

57. *Charleston Mercury,* January 26, 1865; *Journal of the Ninety-Sixth Annual Convention of the Protestant Episcopal Church in the Diocese of South Carolina 1886* (Charleston: Walker Evans Cogswell, 1886), 36; L. S. to Adele, August 22, 1865, M. W. to Ann, July 14, 1866, Vanderhorst Family Papers, SCHS; Smith, *Mason Smith Family Letters,* 188.

58. Williamson, *After Slavery,* 297; *Charleston Daily News,* September 22, 1868, March 14, 1870; see also April 16, 1868; Manuscript Census of Population 1880, City of Charleston; *Charleston Daily Courier,* August 23, 1869, August 17, 1872, September 28, 1880, May 12, 1885; *Acts and Joint Resolutions,* 1879 (Columbia, S.C.: Calvo and Patton, 1879), 3; *Charleston New Era,* December 1, 1883.

59. *Charleston News and Courier,* July 5, 1876.

60. Howard Brotz, ed., *Negro Social and Political Thought 1850–1920* (New York: Basic Books, 1966), 194–96; *Charleston News and Courier,* June 5, 8, 1877, July 20, August 29, 1878, December 27, 1881, July 22, 1885; Martin R. Delany and Robert Campbell, *Search for a Place: Black Separatism and Africa, 1860* (Ann Arbor, Mich.: University of Michigan Press, 1969), Rawick, *The American Slave,* 2: 118, 122–23, 316; A.M.E. *Christian Recorder,* December 7, 1876.

61. Alfred B. Williams, *The Liberian Exodus: An Account of the Voyage of the First Emigrants in the Bark 'Azor,' and Their Reception at Monrovia With a Description of Liberia—Its Customs and Civilization, Romances and Prospects* (Charleston: News and Courier, 1878). This was not the first time Carolinians discussed removing to Africa. Antebellum free blacks expressed an interest in immigration to Liberia, and a small number did journey there. Not all of them were the dispossessed and downtrodden of free black society, and some were quite well-to-do. Nor

did emancipation completely eliminate the desire for emigration, and the unsettled circumstances following the war spurred an interest in leaving America. In 1866 and 1867, several hundred blacks flocked to Charleston and sailed to Liberia on board the American Colonization Society ship *Golconda.* The emigrants that departed at this time were overwhelmingly from places other than the city of Charleston, most notably from Columbus and Macon, Georgia, Newbery, Columbia, and Charleston County, South Carolina. List of Emigrants for Liberia Embarked On Ship *Golconda* of Charleston, S.C., SCHS; *Charleston Daily News,* November 14, 1866. For a brief treatment of free black Carolinian immigrants to Africa, see Marina Wikramanayake, *A World in Shadow: The Free Black in Antebellum South Carolina* (Columbia, S.C.: University of South Carolina Press, 1973), 175–79; *Charleston City Directory, 1877–78,* 375.

62. *Charleston Daily Republican,* August 23, 1871; *Charleston News and Courier,* July 20, 1877; July 20, 1878, May 5, 9, 1885; Robert Starobin, ed., *Blacks In Bondage: Letters of American Slaves* (New York: New Viewpoints Press, 1974), 163.

63. Minutes of the Tenth Session of the South Carolina Annual Conference of the African Methodist Episcopal Church 1874 (n.p.:n.d.), 46; A.M.E. *Christian Recorder,* August 2, 1877.

64. *Charleston News and Courier,* July 28, 1877; Azor Clipping Collection, SCHS; A.M.E. *Christian Recorder,* March 7, 1878.

65. A.M.E. *Christian Recorder,* March 8, 1877; W. G. Marts to Rev. Dr. Strieby, July 7, 1877, AMAP, SCDAH.

66. "History of the Liberian Movement," Azor Clipping Collection, SCHS; *Charleston News and Courier,* August 15, 1877, October 14, 1879.

67. *Charleston News and Courier,* August 15, 18, 1877, March 16, 19, 22, 1878; "History of the Liberian Movement," Azor Clipping Collection, SCHS.

68. *A.M..E. Christian Recorder,* February 10, June 30, July 7, 1881; Charles S. Smith, *A History of the African Methodist Episcopal Church* (Philadelphia: Book Concern of the A.M.E. Church, 1922; reprint ed., New York: Johnson Reprint Co., 1968), 127–28, 175, 179. The Missionary activities of Reverend S. F. Flegler marked the initial entry of the A. M. E. Church into the field of African missions. Little Bethel was established by Flegler in Brewerville fifteen miles from Monrovia and was the first A. M. E. Church in Africa. He established Brown's Chapel and Mount Carmel shortly thereafter in Royseville and Arthington respectively, approximately twenty-four miles from Monrovia. In 1891 the Liberian Annual Conference was organized and incorporated into the Twelfth Episcopal District under the supervision of Bishop Henry M. Turner. *Charleston News and Courier,* March 23, April 3, 20, 22, 23 1878, May 10, 1880; Azor Clipping Collection,

SCHS; Minutes of The Second Anniversary of The Baptist Educational Missionary and Sunday School Convention of South Carolina Held with the Mount Pisgah Baptist Church, Orangeburg, S. C., May 1–5, 1878; William J. Simmons, *Men of Mark: Eminent Progressive and Rising* (Cleveland: George M. Rewell and Co., 1887; reprint ed., New York: Arno Press, 1968), 910, 952.

69. One area of research that merits more thorough investigation is how Afro-American emigrants fared once in Liberia. We know that many returned to America sadly disappointed with life in Africa, but several of the emigrants became prosperous. Jesse Sharp, a free black painter, migrated to Liberia in 1852. After obtaining land on the St. Paul's River, he began to cultivate sugar. Later, he purchased a mill for two thousand dollars to process his crop and shipped the first cargo to the United States in 1859. In the fall of 1865, Sharp produced twenty thousand pounds of sugar and nine thousand gallons of molasses, and his agents were purchasing additional equipment valued at two thousand dollars to allow more efficient production. In another case the Charlestonian Saul Hill immigrated to Liberia in 1866 under the auspices of the American Colonization Society. Although he left with few visible means of support, by 1877 he had established a coffee plantation in Bopora (about sixty-five miles northeast of Monrovia) that was planted with nine thousand trees. Hill's annual income from planting was approximately three thousand dollars at this time, and he hoped to expand the tillable land and increase the number of trees planted by six thousand in the near future. The case of Clement Irons is also revealing. Irons had been a prosperous machinist in Charleston and was the inventor of the Irons' cotton gin. After immigrating to Liberia in 1878, he made his living as a millwright and later constructed the first steam-propelled ship to operate on the St. Paul's River. Always active in the A.M.E. church, Clement Irons was elected a trustee for the first A.M.E. church in Liberia, and after the Liberian Annual Conference was organized, he became one of its itinerant deacons. *Charleston Daily Courier,* November 16, 1866, November 16, 1877, July 22, 1885; *African Repository* 54 (July 1878): 78; Tindall, *South Carolina Negroes,* 163–66; "History of The Liberian Movement," Azor Clipping Collection, SCHS; Smith, *A History,* 127–28, 175, 179.

70. In *After Slavery,* a study that draws heavily on social custom, Joel Williamson contends that "well before the end of Reconstruction, separation had crystallized into a comprehensive pattern which, in its essence, remained unaltered until the middle of the twentieth century." In another important post–Civil War study, Howard Rabinowitz argues that change in urban race relations during Reconstruction must not only be measured against the segregation-integration dichotomy. Changing black-white relations must also consider that postwar defacto segregation usually replaced

the antebellum exclusion of blacks from public facilities. See Williamson, *After Slavery,* 275, 298 and Howard Rabinowitz, *Race Relations in the Urban South 1865–1890* (New York: Oxford University Press, 1978), 331–32.

A POSTSCRIPT

THE LEGACY OF RECONSTRUCTION

1. Hampton M. Jarrell, *Wade Hampton and the Negro: The Road Not Taken* (Columbia, S.C.: University of South Carolina Press, 1949), 73; Lewis P. Jones, "Two Roads Tried—And One Detour," *South Carolina Historical Magazine* 79 (July 1978): 211.

2. Ibid.; *Charleston News and Courier,* July 10, 11, 1876.

3. J. Morgan Kousser, *The Shaping of Southern Politics: Suffrage Restriction and the Establishment of the One Party South, 1880–1910* (New Haven, Conn.: Yale University Press, 1974), 84, 91, 147; William J. Cooper Jr., *The Conservative Regime: South Carolina, 1877–1890* (Baltimore: Johns Hopkins Press, 1968), 103–05, 109; George B. Tindall, *South Carolina Negroes 1877–1900* (Baton Rouge: Louisiana State University Press, 1966), 309–10.

4. Kousser, *The Shaping of Southern Politics,* 91, 147; Cooper, *The Conservative Regime,* 105, 108–09; William Archer, *Through Afro-America: An English Reading of the Race Problem* (London: Chapman & Hall, 1910; reprint ed., Westport, Conn.: Negro Universities Press, 1970), 171–73.

5. Tindall, *South Carolina Negroes,* 300–02; I. A. Newby, *Black Carolinians: A History of Blacks in South Carolina from 1895 to 1968* (Columbia, S.C.: University of South Carolina Press, 1973), 47–48; Archer, *Through Afro-America,* 176.

6. *Charleston News and Courier,* January 10, 1881, January 1, 1882; Laylon W. Jordan, "Police and Politics: Charleston in the Gilded Age 1880–1900," *South Carolina Historical Magazine* 81 (January 1980): 46; Theodore D. Jervey, *The Slave Trade: Slavery and Color* (Columbia, S.C.: The State Company, 1925; reprint ed., Northbrook, Ill.: Metro Books, 1972), 228; Archer, *Through Afro-America,* 169–70.

7. Septima Poinsette Clark, *Ready from Within: Septima Clark and the Civil Rights Movement* (Trenton, N.J.: Africa World Press Inc., 1991), 91; Mamie G. Fields, *Lemon Swamp and Other Places: A Carolina Memoir* (New York: Free Press, 1983), 52–53, 57–58.

8. Quoted in C. Van Woodward, *The Strange Career of Jim Crow* (New York: Oxford University Press, 1974), 96, 98.

9. "Frances A. R. Whipper," Daniel Murray Papers (microfilm reel 8), 11, State Historical Society of Wisconsin.

BIBLIOGRAPHY

PRIMARY SOURCES

GOVERNMENT RECORDS AND REPORTS

FEDERAL

Report of the Joint Committee on Reconstruction. Washington: Government Printing Office, 1866.

U.S. Bureau of the Census. *Manuscript Census of Population 1850–1880, City of Charleston.*

U.S. Bureau of the Census. *Manuscript Industry Schedules of Manufactures 1880, City of Charleston.*

U.S. Bureau of the Census. *Negro Population of the United States 1790–1915.* Washington: Government Printing Office, 1918.

U.S. Bureau of the Census. *Population of the United States in 1850 Compiled from the Seventh Census Statistics of Population, Tables 1–8.* Washington: Government Printing office, 1864.

U.S. Bureau of the Census. *Population of the United States in 1860 Compiled from the Eighth Census.* Washington: Government Printing Office, 1864.

U.S. Bureau of the Census. *Population of the United States in 1870 Compiled from the Ninth Census.* Washington: Government Printing Office, 1872.

U.S. Bureau of the Census. *Population of the United States in 1880 Compiled from the Tenth Census: Social Statistics of Cities,* vol. 18. Washington: Government Printing Office, 1886.

U.S. Bureau of the Census. *Twelfth Census of the United States in 1900, Population,* vol. 1. Washington: Government Printing Office, 1901.

U.S. Bureau of the Census. *Twelfth Census of the United States in 1900, Special Reports: Occupations.* Washington: Government Printing Office 1904.

U.S. Bureau of Labor. *Cargo Handling and Longshore Labor Conditions,* by Boris Stern. Bulletin of the U. S. Bureau of Labor Statistics No. 550. Washington: Government Printing Office, 1932.

STATE

Acts and Joint Resolutions of the General Assembly of the State of South Carolina. Columbia: various. 1866–1885.

The Constitution of South Carolina, Adopted April 16, 1868, and the Acts and Joint Resolutions of the General Assembly Passed at the Special Session of 1868. Columbia, S.C.: John W. Denny, 1868.

Cooper, Thomas and McCord, David J., ed. *The Statutes at Large of South Carolina; Edited, Under Authority of the Legislature,* 10 vols. Columbia, S.C.: State Co, 1930.

Journal of the Convention of the People of South Carolina Held in Columbia, S.C. September 1865 Together with the Ordinances Reports Resolutions, etc. Columbia, S.C.: J. A. Selby, 1865.

Petitions Relating to Slavery.

Petitions To The General Assembly of the State of South Carolina. 1865–1877.

Proceedings of the Constitutional Convention of South Carolina. Charleston, S. C.: Denny & Perry, 1868. Reprint ed., New York: Arno Press, 1968.

Report of the Attorney General to the General Assembly of South Carolina Concerning the Phosphate Interest of the State. Columbia, S. C.: Calvo and Patton, 1877.

Reports and Resolutions of the General Assembly of the State of South Carolina. 1866–1885.

South Carolina *Statutes at Large.* 1865–1885.

State Free Negro Capitation Tax Books for Charleston 1811–1864.

CITY AND COUNTY

Charleston County Record of Wills and Estate Inventories.

Charleston County Register of Mesne Conveyance.

Charleston Ledgers of Taxpayers for 1869, 1871, 1880.

Charleston *Yearbooks,* 1865–1885.

Dawson, J. L., and DeSaussure, H. W. *Census of the City of Charleston, South Carolina, for the Year 1848.* Charleston: J. B. Nixon, 1849.

A Digest of the Ordinances of the City Council of Charleston from the Year 1783 to October 1844 to Which Are Annexed the Acts of the Legislature Which Relate to the City of Charleston. Charleston, S. C.: n.p., 1844.

Edwards, Alexander, ed. *Ordinances of the City Council of Charleston*

From *In the State of South Carolina Passed Since the Incorporation of the City.* Charleston, S.C.: n. p., 1802.

Ford, Frederick A. *Census of the City of Charleston, South Carolina for the Year 1861.* Charleston: Evans & Cogswell, 1861.

Hamilton, James Jr. *An Account of the Late Intended Insurrection Among a Portion of the Blacks of this City Published by the Authority of the Corporation of Charleston.* Charleston, S.C.: A. E. Miller, 1822.

Lists of the Taxpayers of the City of Charleston, 1859, 1860.

Ordinances of the City Council of Charleston From in the State of South Carolina Passed Since the Incorporation of the City. Charleston, n.p., 1802.

Ordinances of the City of Charleston from the 19th of August 1844 to the 14th of September 1854 and the Acts of the General Assembly. Charleston: A. E. Miller, 1854.

Report on the Free Colored Poor of the City of Charleston. Charleston, S.C.: Burgess & James, 1842.

PERIODICALS

A.M.E. *Christian Recorder,* 1865–85.
American Missionary Magazine, 1865–74.
Atlantic Monthly, 1865–85.
Charleston Advocate, 1867.
Charleston Daily Courier, 1859–73.
Charleston Daily News, 1865–73.
Charleston Daily Republican, 1869–72.
Charleston Mercury, 1865–68.
Charleston New Era, 1882–84.
Charleston News and Courier, 1873–85.
Nation, 1865–85.
New York Times, 1860–85.
Northwestern Recorder, 1893.
South Carolina Leader, 1865.

MANUSCRIPT COLLECTIONS

Papers of Abiel Abbott.
Abraham Middleton Papers.
Adger-Smyth Flynn Family Letters.
Allston Family Papers.
American Missionary Association Papers.
Azor Clipping Collection.
Fisk K. Brewer Scrapbook.
Brown Fellowship Society Minute Books.

Bureau of Refugees, Freedmen and Abandoned Land Records.
Charleston Scrapbook: Clippings Chiefly from Charleston Newspapers.
Comprehensive Records of Centenary Methodist Episcopal Church.
Elias Horry Deas Papers.
Papers Relating to Peter Desverneys Free Person of Color.
Friendly Moralist Society Minute Books.
William H. Gilliland Papers.
Caroline Gilman Letters.
Holloway Family Papers.
List of Emigrants for Liberia Embarked On Ship Golconda
    of Charleston, S.C.
Letters of Louisa Lord.
Williams Chestnut Manning Papers.
The Autobiography of Francis Asbury Mood (typescript).
Morris Street Baptist Church Minute Book.
Franklin J. Moses Papers.
Noisette Family Papers.
Philippe Noisette Papers.
James L. Orr Papers.
Family Papers of Frederick A. Porcher.
William Ravenel Family Papers
Henry Raymond Family Letters.
Record of Colored Members of the Methodist Episcopal Church,
    Charleston, South Carolina, 1821–1880.
Register of the South Carolina College, 1850–1877.
Letters of Rusticus.
Jacob Schirmer Diary.
Robert K. Scott Papers.
Shrewsbury Family Papers.
Slave Conspiracy in Charleston File.
Augustine Smyth Papers.
Vanderhorst Family Papers.
Documents Relative to the Demark Vesey Insurrection.
Weyman Family Papers.
W. P. A. Notes on the Brown Fellowship Society.

MINUTES, RECORDS, AND PROCEEDINGS

*Journal of the Annual Convention of the Protestant Episcopal Church in
    the Diocese of South Carolina,* 1865–1886.
Minutes and Register of The First Baptist Church, Charleston County,
    1847–1875.
Minutes from the Commissioners of Free Schools, 1865–1885.

Minutes of The Baptist Educational, Missionary and Sunday School Convention of South Carolina, 1878.

Minutes of the Board of Firemasters, 1845–1885.

Minutes of the Charleston Baptist Association, 1865–1885.

Minutes of The Second Anniversary of The Baptist Educational, Missionary and Sunday School Convention of South Carolina Held with the Mount Pisgah Baptist Church, Orangeburg, S.C., May 1–5, 1878.

Minutes of the South Carolina Annual Conference of the African Methodist Episcopal Church, 1865–1885.

Minutes of the South Carolina Annual Conference of the Methodist Episcopal Church, 1866–1885.

Minutes of the South Carolina Annual Conference of the Methodist Episcopal Church South, 1859–1885.

Ninety-Sixth Session of the Baptist Educational and Missionary Convention of South Carolina, May 8–13, 1973.

TRAVEL ACCOUNTS, REPORTS, AND MISCELLANEOUS WORKS

Achates. *Reflections Occasioned By the Late Disturbances in Charleston 1822.* Charleston, S. C.: A. E. Miller, 1822.

Adams, F. C. *Manuel Pereira, Or the Sovereign Rule of South Carolina.* Washington: Buell & Blanchard, 1853.

Adger, John B. *My Life and Times 1810–1899.* Richmond: Presbyterian Committee of Publication, 1899.

Alvord, J. W. *Letters from the South Relating to the Condition of the Freedmen Addressed to Major General O. O. Howard.* Washington: Howard University Press, 1870.

Andrews, Sidney. *The South Since the War.* Boston: Ticknor & Fields, 1866.

Archer, H. P. *Local Reminiscences: A Lecture Delivered by Mr. H. P. Archer.* Charleston: S.C.: Daggett Printing Co., 1893.

Archer, William. *Through Afro-America: An English Reading of the Race Problem.* London: Chapman & Hall, 1910. Reprint, Westport, Conn.: Negro Universities Press, 1970.

Avary, Myrta. *Dixie After the War.* New York: Doubleday, Page & Co., 1906.

Bernhard, Karl, Duke of Saxe-Weimar-Eisenach. *Travels Through North America During the Years 1825 and 1826,* 2 vols. Philadelphia: Carey, Lea & Blanchard, 1833.

Botume, Elizabeth H. *First Days Amongst the Contrabands.* Boston: Lee & Shepard, 1893. Reprint, New York: Arno Press, 1968.

Bremer, Fredrika. *The Homes of the New World: Impressions of America,* 2 vols. New York: Harper and Bros., 1853.

Clark, Septima P. *Ready from Within: Septima Clark and the Civil Rights Movement.* Trenton, N.J.: Africa World Press Inc., 1990.

Coker, Daniel. "A Dialogue Between a Virginian and an African Minister." In *Negro Protest Pamphlets: A Compendium.* Comp. Dorothy Porter. New York: Arno Press, 1969.

Constitution, By-Laws and Rules of the Amateur Literary and Fraternal Association. Charleston, S. C.: Edward Perry, 1873.

Crowe, Eyre. *With Thackeray in America.* London: Cassell and Co., 1893.

Delany, Martin R. *The Condition, Elevation, Emigration and Destiny of the Colored People of the United States.* New York: Arno Press, 1969.

Dennett, John. *The South As It Is 1865–1866.* New York: Viking Press, 1865.

Emilo, Luis F. *A Brave Black Regiment: History of the Fifty-Fourth Regiment of Massachusetts Volunteer Infantry 1863–1865.* Boston: Boston Book Company, 1894.

An Exposition of the Late Schism in the Methodist Episcopal Church in Charleston in the Year 1833 up to November 28 of that Year. Charleston: J. S. Burges, 1834 .

Fields, Mamie Garvin. *Lemon Swamp and Other Places: A Carolina Memoir.* New York: Free Press, 1983.

Fox, Charles B. *Record of the Service of the Fifty-Fifth Regiment of Massachusetts Volunteer Infantry.* Cambridge, Mass: John Wilson & Son, 1868.

Hamilton, Thomas. *Men and Manners in America.* Philadelphia: Carey, Lea and Blanchard, 1833.

Hardy, Lady Duffus. *Down South.* London: Chapman & Hall, 1883.

Hodgson, Adam. *Letters from North America,* 2 vols. London: Hurst & Robinson, 1824.

Holloway, James H. *Why I Am A Methodist: A Historical Sketch of What the Church Has Done for the Colored Children Educationally As Early As 1790 at Charleston, S.C.* N.p.: R. Wainwright, 1900.

Jervey, Theodore D. *The Slave Trade: Slavery and Color.* Columbia, S.C.: State Company, 1925. Reprint ed., North Brook, Ill.: Metro Books, 1972, 220–21.

Jervey, Susan R., and Ravenel, Charlotte St. J. *Two Diaries from Middle St. John's Berkeley South Carolina, February–May, 1865: Journals Kept by Miss Susan R. Jervey & Miss Charlotte St. J. Ravenel at Northampton and Poshee Plantation & Reminiscences of Mrs. Waring Henagan.* N.p.: St. John's Hunting Club, 1921.

Kemble, Frances A. *Journal of a Residence on a Georgia Plantation in*

1838–1839. London: Longman, Green, et al., 1863. Reprint, New York: Alfred A. Knopf, 1961.

King, Edward. *The Great South: A Record of Journeys.* Hartford, Conn.: American Publishing, 1875.

Lambert, John. *Travels Through Lower Canada and the United States of North America in the Years 1806, 1807, and 1808,* 3 vols. London: Richard Phillips, 1810.

Laurens, Edward R. An Address Delivered in Charleston, Before the Agricultural Society of South Carolina On September 18, 1832. Charleston, S.C.: A. E. Miller, 1832.

———. A Letter to the Hon. Whitemarsh B. Seabrook of St. John's Colleton; In *Explanation and Defense of an Act to Amend the Law in Relation to Slaves and Free Persons of Color.* Charleston, S.C.: Observor Press, 1835.

Lawrence, W. H. *The Centenary Souvenir, Containing a History of Centenary Church, Charleston, and an Account of the Life and Labors of Rev. R. V. Lawrence, Father of the Pastor of Centenary Church.* Philadelphia: Collins Printing House, 1885.

Lyell, Sir Charles. *A Second Visit to the United States of North America,* 2 vols. London: John Murray, 1849.

Martineau, Harriet. *Retrospect of Western Travel,* 2 vols. London: Sanders & Otley, 1838.

Mills, Robert. *Statistics of South Carolina Including A View of Its Natural Civil and Military History, General and Particular.* Charleston: Hurlbut and Lloyd, 1826.

Mood, F. A. *Methodism in Charleston.* Nashville: E. Stevenson & J. E. Evans, 1856.

Payne, Daniel. *History of the A.M.E. Church.* Nashville: A.M.E. Sunday School Union, 1891. Reprint, New York: Johnson Reprint Co., 1968.

———. *Recollections of Seventy Years.* Nashville: A. M. E. Sunday School Union, 1888. Reprint, New York: Arno Press, 1968.

Pegues, Albert W. *Our Baptist Ministers and Schools.* Springfield, Mass.: Willey & Co., 1892.

Pollard, Edward. *Black Diamonds Gathered in the Darkey Homes of the South.* New York: Pudney & Russell, 1859. Reprint ed., New York: Negro Universities Press, 1968.

Porter, A. T. Led On Step By Step: Scenes from Clerical, Military, Educational and Plantation Life in the South 1828–1898, An Autobiography. New York: Arno Press, 1967.

———. *The History of A Work of Faith and Love in Charleston, South Carolina.* New York: D. Appleton & Co., 1882.

Powell, Lyman P., ed. *Historic Towns of the Southern States.* New York: Knickerbocker Press, 1900.

Power, Tyrone. *Impressions of America During the Years 1833, 1834 and 1835*, 2 vols. London: Richard Bentley, 1836.

Proceedings of the Colored People's Convention of the State of South Carolina Held in Zion Church Charleston. Charleston: South Carolina Leader, 1865.

Public Proceedings Relating to Calvary Church and the Religious Instruction of Slaves. Charleston, S. C.: Miller and Browne, 1850.

Redpath, James. *The Roving Editor: or Talks With Slaves in the Southern States.* New York: A. B. Burdick, 1859. Reprint, New York: Negro Universities Press, 1968.

Rollin, Frank [Frances] A. *Life and Public Services of Martin R. Delany.* Boston: Lee and Shepard, 1883.

Rules and Regulations of the Brown Fellowship Society—Established at Charleston, S.C. Charleston, S.C.: J. B. Nixon, 1844.

Seventeenth Annual Report of the Executive Committee of the Christian Benevolent Society, March 1856. N.p.: n.d.

Simmons, William, J. *Men of Mark: Eminent Progressive and Rising.* Cleveland: George M. Rewell & Co., 1887. Reprint, New York: Arno Press, 1968.

Smith, Daniel E. Huger. *A Charlestonian's Recollections, 1846–1913.* Charleston: Carolina Art Association, 1950.

Smyth, Thomas D. *Autobiographical Notes, Letters and Reflections.* Charleston, S.C.: Walker, Evans and Cogswell, 1914.

Somers, Robert. *The Southern States Since the War, 1870–1871.* New York: Macmillan & Company, 1871.

Stirling, James. *Letters From the Slave States.* London: John W. Parker, 1857.

Stuart, James. *Three Years in North America,* 2 vols. New York: J. J. Harper, 1833.

Thornwell, J. H. *The Rights and Duties of Masters: A Sermon Preached at the Dedication of a Church Erected in Charleston S.C. for the Benefit and Instruction of the Colored Population.* Charleston, S. C.: Walker and James, 1850.

Thornwell, Reverend Dr. *A Review of Reverend J. B. Adger's Sermon on the Religious Instruction of the Coloured Population.* Charleston, S.C.: Burgess, James and Paxton, 1847.

Trapier, Paul. *The Religious Instruction of the Black Population: The Gospel to be Given to Our Servants.* Charleston: Miller and Brown, 1847.

Waters, Brian, ed. *Mr. Vessey of England Being the Incidents and Reminiscences of Travel in a Twelve Weeks Tour Through the United States and Canada in the Year 1859.* New York: Putnam's Sons, 1956.

Wightman, William M. *Life of William Capers D. D.* Nashville: Publishing House of the Methodist Episcopal Church South, 1896.

Williams, Alfred B. *The Liberian Exodus. An Account of the Voyage of the First Emigrants in the Bark "Azor," and Their Reception at Monrovia With a Description of Liberia—Its Customs and Civilization, Romances and Prospects.* Charleston: News and Courier, 1878.

Williams, George W. *Sketches of Travel in the Old and New World.* Charleston, S.C.: Walker, Evans & Cosgwell, 1871.

PUBLISHED PRIMARY SOURCES

Aptheker, Herbert, ed. *A Documentary History of the Negro People in the United States,* 2 vols. New York: Citadel Press, 1969.

Bell, Howard, ed. *Minutes of the Proceedings of The National Negro Conventions 1830–1864.* New York: Arno Press, 1969.

Bergh, Albert E., ed. *The Writings of Thomas Jefferson.* Washington: Thomas Jefferson Memorial Association, 1905.

Blassingame, John, ed. *Slave Testimony: Two Centuries of Letters Speeches, Interviews and Autobiographies.* Baton Rouge: Louisiana State University Press, 1977.

Brotz, Howard, ed. *Negro Social and Political Thought 1850–1920.* New York: Basic Books, 1966.

Catteral, Helen T., ed. *Judicial Cases Concerning American Slavery and the Negro,* 5 vols. Washington: Carnegie Institution, 1929.

Childs, Arney R., ed. *The Private Journal of Henry William Ravenel.* Columbia, S.C. : University of South Carolina Press, 1947.

Donnan, Elizabeth, ed. "Papers of James A. Bayard 1796–1815." *Annual Report of the American Historical Association,* 2 vols. Washington: Government Printing Office, 1913.

Johnson, Michael P., and James L. Roark, ed., *No Chariot Let Down: Charleston's Free People of Color on the Eve of the Civil War.* Chapel Hill: University of North Carolina Press, 1984.

Leland, Isabella Middleton. "Middleton Correspondence 1861–1865." *South Carolina Historical Magazine* 65 (April 1964): 98–109.

Lynch, Hollis R., ed. *The Black Urban Condition.* New York: Thomas Y. Crowell, 1973.

McPherson, Edward, ed. *The Political History of the United States of America During the Period of Reconstruction.* Washington: Solomon & Chapman, 1875. Reprint, New York: Negro University Press, 1969.

Pinckney, Elise, ed. *Register of St. Philip's Parish Church Charleston, South Carolina, 1810 Through 1822.* Charleston: National Society of the Colonial Dames of America in the State of South Carolina, 1973.

Rawick, George P., ed. *The American Slave: A Composite Autobiography,* 19 vols. Westport, Conn.: Greenwood Press, 1972.

Said, Omar ibn. "Autobiography of Omar ibn Said." *American Historical Review* 30 (July 1925): 787–95.

Smith, Daniel E. Huger, et al., ed. *Mason Smith Family Letters 1860–1868.* Columbia, S.C.: University of South Carolina Press, 1950.

Starobin, Robert, ed. *Blacks in Bondage: Letters of American Slaves.* New York: New Viewpoints Press, 1974.

———. *Denmark Vesey: The Slave Conspiracy Of 1822.* Englewood Cliffs, N.J.: Prentice Hall Inc., 1970.

Sterling, Dorothy, ed. *We Are Your Sisters: Black Women in the Nineteenth Century.* New York: W. W. Norton, 1984.

Stuckey, Sterling, ed. *The Ideological Origins of Black Nationalism.* Boston: Beacon Press, 1972.

Thornbrough, Emma Lou, ed. *Black Reconstructionists.* Englewood Cliffs, N.J.: Prentice Hall, 1972.

Woodson, Carter G. *Free Negro Heads of Families in the United States in 1830.* Washington: Association for the Study of Negro Life and History, Inc., 1925.

———. ed. *The Mind of the Negro as Reflected in Letters Written During the Crisis 1800–1860.* Washington: Association for the Study of Negro Life and History, 1926. Reprint, New York: Negro Universities Press, 1969.

SECONDARY SOURCES

ARTICLES

Abbott, Martin. "The Freedmen's Bureau and Negro Schooling in South Carolina." *South Carolina Historical Magazine* 57 (April 1956): 65–81.

Aptheker, Herbert. "South Carolina Conventions 1865." *Journal of Negro History* 31 (January 1946): 91–97.

Birnie, C. W. "Education of the Negro in Charleston, South Carolina, Prior to the Civil War." *Journal of Negro History* 12 (January 1927): 13–21.

Browning, James B. "Beginnings of Insurance Enterprise Among Negroes." *Journal of Negro History* 22 (October 1937): 417–32.

Carter, Dan T. "The Anatomy of Fear: The Christmas Day Insurrection Scare of 1865." *Journal of Southern History* 42 (August 1976): 345–64.

Daniel, Vattel E. "Ritual and Stratification in Chicago Negro Churches." *American Sociological Review* 7 (June 1942): 352–61.

Donnan, Elizabeth. "The Slave Trade into South Carolina Before the Revolution." *American Historical Review* 33 (July 1928): 804–28.

Durden, Robert F. "The Establishment of Calvary Protestant Episcopal Church for Negroes in Charleston." *South Carolina Historical Magazine* 65 (April 1964): 63–84 .

Eisterhold, John A. "Charleston: Lumber and Trade in a Declining Southern Port." *South Carolina Historical Magazine* 74 (April 1973): 61–72.

Fitchett, E. Horace. "The Role of Claflin College in Negro Life in South Carolina." *Journal of Negro Education* 12 (Winter 1943): 42–68.

Floyd, Viola C. "The Fall of Charleston." *South Carolina Historical Magazine* 66 (December 1975): 115–26.

Fordham, Monroe. "Nineteenth-Century Black Thought in the United States: Some Influences of the Santo Domingo Revolution." *Journal of Black Studies* 6 (December 1975): 115–26.

Gatewood, Willard B. "William D. Crum, A Negro in Politics." *Journal of Negro History* 53 (October 1968): 301–20.

———. "'The Remarkable Misses Rollin': Black Women in Reconstruction South Carolina." *South Carolina Historical Magazine* 92 (July 1991): 172–88.

Gutman, Herbert G. "Persistent Myths About the Afro-American Family." *Journal of Interdisciplinary History* 6 (Autumn 1975): 181–210.

———. "The World Two Cliometricians Made." *Journal of Negro History* 60 (January 1975): 53–227.

Hamer, Marguerite B. "A Century Before Manumission." *North Carolina Historical Review* 17 (July 1940): 232–36 .

Harris, Robert L. "Charleston's Free Afro-American Elite: The Brown Fellowship Society and the Humane Brotherhood." *South Carolina Historical Magazine* 82 (October 1981): 289–310.

Hindus, Michael S. "Black Justice Under White Law: Criminal Prosecutions of Blacks in Antebellum South Carolina." *Journal of American History* 63 (December 1976): 575–99.

Hine, William C. "The 1867 Charleston Streetcar Sit-Ins." *South Carolina Historical Magazine* 77 (April 1976): 110–14.

———. "Black Politicians in Reconstruction Charleston: A Collective Study." *Journal of Southern History* 49 (November 1983): 555–84.

———. "Black Organized Labor in Reconstruction Charleston." *Labor History* 25 (Fall 1984): 504–17.

January, Alan F. "The South Carolina Association: An Agency for Race Control in Antebellum Charleston." *South Carolina Historical Magazine* 78 (July 1977): 191–201.

Jones, Lewis P. "Two Roads Tried—And One Detour." *South Carolina Historical Magazine* 79 (July 1978): 206–18.

Jordan, Laylon W. "Police and Politics: Charleston in the Gilded Age 1880–1900." *South Carolina Historical Magazine* 81 (January 1980): 35–50.

———. "Education for Community: C. G. Memminger and the Origination of Common Schools in Antebellum Charleston." *South Carolina Historical Magazine* 83 (April 1982): 99–115.

Lander, Ernest. "Ante-Bellum Rice Milling in South Carolina." *South Carolina Historical Magazine* 52 (July 1951): 125–32.

Moore, Jamie W. "The Lowcountry in Economic Transition: Charleston Since 1865." *South Carolina Historical Magazine* 80 (April 1979): 156–71.

Northrup, Herbert. "The New Orleans Longshoremen." *Political Science Quarterly* 57 (December 1942): 526–44.

Schweninger, Loren. "Slave Independence and Enterprise in South Carolina, 1780–1865." *South Carolina Historical Magazine* 93 (April 1992): 101–25.

Shick, Tom W. and Doyle, Don H. "The South Carolina Phosphate Boom and the Still Birth of the New South, 1867–1920." *South Carolina Historical Magazine* 86 (January 1985): 1–31.

Simpson, George. "The Belief System of Haitian Vodun." *American Anthropologist* 47 (January 1945): 35–59.

Starobin, Robert. "Disciplining Industrial Slaves in the Old South." *Journal of Negro History* 53 (April 1968): 111–28.

Stuckey, Sterling. "Through the Prism of Folklore: The Black Ethos in Slavery." *Massachusetts Review* 9 (Summer 1968): 417–37.

Tyler, Lyon G. "Drawing the Color Line in the Episcopal Diocese of South Carolina, 1876 to 1890: The Role of Edward McCrady, Father and Son." *South Carolina Historical Magazine* 91 (April 1990): 107–24.

Wilkie, Jane R. "Urbanization and Deurbanization of the Black Population Before the Civil War." *Demography* 13 (August 1976): 311–28.

Wish, Harvey. "American Slave Insurrections Before 1861." *Journal of Negro History* 22 (July 1937): 299–320.

Woody, Robert H. "Jonathan Jasper Wright Associate Justice of the Supreme Court of South Carolina 1870–1877." *Journal of Negro History* 18 (April 1933): 114–31.

BOOKS

Abbott, Martin. *The Freedmen's Bureau in South Carolina.* Chapel Hill: University of North Carolina Press, 1967.

Alexander, Adele L. *Ambiguous Lives: Free Women of Color in Rural Georgia, 1789–1879.* Fayetteville: University of Arkansas Press, 1991.

Anderson, James D. *The Education of Blacks in the South, 1860–1935.* Chapel Hill: University of North Carolina Press, 1988.

Bellows, Barbara L. *Benevolence Among Slaveholders: Assisting the Poor in Charleston, 1670–1860.* Baton Rouge: Louisiana State University Press, 1993.

Berlin, Ira. *Slaves Without Masters: The Free Negro in the Antebellum South.* New York: Pantheon Press, 1974.

Betts, Albert D. *History of South Carolina Methodism.* Columbia, S.C.: Advocate Press, 1952.

Blackburn, George A. *The Life Work of John L. Girardeau.* Columbia, S.C.: State Co., 1916.

Blassingame, John. *Black New Orleans 1860–1880.* Chicago: University of Chicago Press, 1973.

Bleser, Carol. *The Promised Land: The History of the South Carolina Land Commission, 1869–1890.* Columbia, S.C.: University of South Carolina Press, 1969.

Borchert, James. *Alley Life in Washington: Family, Community, Religion, and Folklife in the City, 1850–1970.* Urbana: University of Illinois Press, 1980.

Bracey, John, et al. *The Rise of the Ghetto.* Belmont, Calif.: Wadsworth Publishing Co., 1971.

Bruce, Dickson D. *Archibald Grimké: Portrait of a Black Independent.* Baton Rouge: Louisiana State University Press, 1993.

Burton, E. Milby. *The Siege of Charleston 1861–1865.* Columbia, S. C.: University of South Carolina Press, 1970.

Channing, Steven A. *Crisis of Fear: Secession in South Carolina.* New York: W. W. Norton, 1974.

Cooper, William J., Jr. *The Conservative Regime: South Carolina 1877–1890.* Baltimore: Johns Hopkins Press, 1968.

Cornelius, Janet D. *When I Can Read My Title Clear: Literacy, Slavery, and Religion in the Antebellum South.* Columbia, S.C.: University of South Carolina Press, 1991.

Coulter, E. Merton. George W. Williams: *The Life of a Southern Merchant and Banker 1820–1903.* Athens, Ga.: Hibriten Press, 1976.

Creel, Margaret Washington. *A Peculiar People: Slave Religion and Community-Culture Among the Gullahs.* New York: New York University Press, 1988.

Curtin, Philip D. *The Atlantic Slave Trade: A Census.* Madison: University of Wisconsin Press, 1969.

Derrick, Samuel. *Centennial History of the South Carolina Railroad.* Columbia, S.C.: State Co., 1930.

Doyle, Don. *New Men, New Cities, New South: Atlanta, Nashville, Charleston, Mobile, 1860–1910.* Chapel Hill: University of North Carolina Press, 1990.

Drago, Edmund L. *Initiative, Paternalism, and Race Relations: Charleston's Avery Normal Institute.* Athens, GA: University of Georgia Press, 1990.

DuBois, W. E. B., ed. *The Negro Artisan.* Atlanta: Atlanta University Press, 1902. Reprint ed., New York: Arno Press, 1969.

———. *Black Reconstruction in America 1860–1880.* New York: Russell & Russell, 1935. Reprint, New York: Atheneum Press, 1971.

Dvorak, Katherine L. "After Apocalypse, Moses." In *Masters and Slaves in the House of the Lord: Race and Religion in the American South 1740–1870.* Ed. John B. Boles. Lexington, Ky.: University Press of Kentucky, 1988.

Eaton, Clement. *The Growth of Southern Civilization 1790–1860.* New York: Harper & Row, 1961.

Edwards, George N. *A History of the Independent or Congregational Church of Charleston, South Carolina Commonly Known As Circular Church.* Boston: Pilgrim Press, 1947.

Fogel, Robert, and Stanley Engerman. *Time on the Cross: The Economics of American Negro Slavery.* Boston: Little, Brown & Co., 1974.

Foner, Eric. *Reconstruction: America's Unfinished Revolution 1863–1877.* New York: Harper and Row, 1988.

———. *Freedom's Lawmakers: A Directory of Black Officeholders During Reconstruction.* New York: Oxford University Press, 1993.

Foote, Shelby. *The Civil War: A Narrative,* 3 vols. New York: Random House, 1974.

Fraser, Walter J., Jr. *Charleston! Charleston!: The History of a Southern City.* Columbia: University of South Carolina, 1989.

Frazier, E. Franklin. *Black Bourgeoisie: The Rise of a New Middle Class in the United States.* New York: Collier Press, 1962.

———. *The Negro Church in America.* New York: Schocken Books, 1964.

Fredrickson, George. *The Black Image in the White Mind: The Debate on Afro-American Character and Destiny 1817–1914.* New York: Harper & Row, 1971.

Freehling, William W. *Prelude to Civil War: The Nullification Controversy in South Carolina 1816–1836.* New York: Harper & Row, 1965.

Gatewood, Willard B. *Aristocrats of Color: The Black Elite, 1880–1920.* Bloomington: Indiana University Press, 1990.

Glatthaar, Joseph T. *Forged in Battle: The Civil War Alliance of Black Soldiers and White Officers.* New York: Free Press, 1990.

Goldin, Claudia. *Urban Slavery in the American South 1820–1860: A Quantitative History.* Chicago: University of Chicago Press, 1976.

Gordon, Asa H. *Sketches of Negro Life and History in South Carolina.* Columbia, S.C.: University of South Carolina Press, 1971.

Harding, Vincent. "Religion and Resistance Among Antebellum Negroes, 1800–1860." In *The Making of Black America: Essays in Negro Life and History,* 2 vols. Ed. August Meier and Elliott Rudwick. New York: Athenueum, 1969.

Herskovits, Melville. *The Myth of the Negro Past.* Boston: Beacon Press, 1958.

Holt, Thomas. *Black Over White: Negro Political Leadership in South Carolina During Reconstruction.* Urbana, Ill.: University of Illinois Press, 1977.

James, Bishop F. C. *African Methodism in South Carolina: A Bicentennial Focus.* Tappan, N.Y.: Custom Book Inc., N.D. 154.

James, C. L. R. *Black Jacobins.* New York: Vintage Press, 1963.

Jarrell, Hampton M. *Wade Hampton and the Negro: The Road Not Taken.* Columbia, S.C.: University of South Carolina Press, 1949.

Jenkins, Warren M. *Steps Along the Way: The Origin and Development of the South Carolina Conference of the Central Jurisdiction of the Methodist Church.* Columbia, S.C.: Socamead Press, 1967.

Jones, F. D., and W. H. Mills. *History of the Presbyterian Church in South Carolina Since 1850.* Columbia, S.C.: R. L. Bryan Co., 1926.

Jones, Jacqueline. *Labor of Love, Labor of Sorrow: Black Women, Work, and the Family From Slavery to the Present.* New York: Basic Books, 1985.

Jones, Norrece T. *Born a Child of Freedom Yet a Slave: Mechanisms of Control and Strategies of Resistance in Antebellum South Carolina.* Middletown, Conn.: Wesleyan University Press, 1990.

Joyner, Charles. *Down by the Riverside: A South Carolina Slave Community.* Urbana: University of Illinois Press, 1984.

———. "'If You Ain't Got Education': Slave Language and Slave Thought in Antebellum Charleston." In *Intellectual Life in Antebellum Charleston.* Ed. Michael O'Brien and David Moltke Hansen. Knoxville, Tenn.: University of Tennessee Press, 1986.

Knight, Edgar W. *The Influence of Reconstruction on Education in the South.* New York: Columbia University, 1913. Reprint, New York: Arno Press, 1969.

Koger, Larry. *Black Slaveowners: Free Black Slavemasters in South Carolina 1790-1860.* Jefferson, N.C.: McFarland & Co., 1985.

Kolchin, Peter. *First Freedom: The Responses of Alabama's Blacks to Emancipation and Reconstruction.* Westport, Conn.: Greenwood Press, 1972.

Kousser, J. Morgan. *The Shaping of Southern Politics: Suffrage Restriction and the Establishment of the One-Party South, 1880–1910.* New Haven, Conn.: Yale University Press, 1974.

Lamson, Peggy. *The Glorious Failure: Black Congressman Robert Brown Elliott and the Reconstruction in South Carolina.* New York: W. W. Norton, 1973.

Lewis, Oscar. *La Vida: A Puerto Rican Family in the Culture of Poverty—San Juan and New York.* New York: Random House, 1966.

Lilly, Edward G., ed. *Historic Churches of Charleston.* Columbia, S.C.: R. L. Bryan Co., 1966.

Lincoln, C. Eric and Lawrence H. Mamiya. *The Black Church in the African American Experience.* Durham, N.C.: Duke University Press, 1990.

Litwack, Leon. *Been in the Storm So Long: The Aftermath of Slavery.* New York: Alfred A. Knopf, 1979.

McLeod, Jonathan W. *Workers and Workplace Dynamics in Reconstruction-Era Atlanta: A Case Study.* Los Angeles: Center for Afro-American Studies and Institute of Industrial Relations, University of Califorinia Press, 1989.

Meier, August. *Negro Thought in America 1880–1915.* Ann Arbor, Mich.: University of Michigan Press, 1963.

Montgomery, William E. *Under Their Own Vine and Fig Tree: The African-American Church in the South, 1865-1900.* Baton Rouge: Louisiana State University Press, 1992.

Moore, James H. *South Carolina Newspapers.* Columbia: University of South Carolina Press, 1988.

Mullin, Gerald W. *Flight and Rebellion: Slave Resistance in Eighteenth Century Virginia.* New York: Oxford University Press, 1972.

Murray, Gerald W. *Presbyterians and the Negro: A History.* Philadelphia: Presbyterian Historical Society, 1966.

Newby, I. A. *Black Carolinians: A History of Blacks in South Carolina from 1895 to 1968.* Columbia, S.C.: University of South Carolina Press, 1973.

Osthaus, Carl R. *Freedmen, Philanthropy, and Fraud: A History of the Freedmen's Savings Bank.* Urbana: University of Illinois Press, 1976.

Phillips, U. B. *American Negro Slavery.* Baton Rouge: Louisiana State University, 1969.

Quarles, Benjamin. *The Negro in the Civil War.* Boston: Little, Brown & Co., 1969.

Rabinowitz, Howard. *Race Relations in the Urban South 1865–1890.* New York: Oxford University Press, 1978.

Raboteau, Albert J. *Slave Religion: The "Invisible Institution" in the Antebellum South.* New York: Oxford University Press, 1978.

Ransom, Roger, and Richard Sutch. *One Kind of Freedom: The Economic Consequences of Emancipation.* London: Cambridge University Press, 1977.

Ravenel, Mrs. St. Julien. *Charleston: The Place and the People.* New York: Macmillan Co., 1927.

Reynolds, Emily B., and Joan R. Faunt. *Biographical Directory of the Senate of the State of South Carolina 1776–1964.* Columbia, S.C.: South Carolina Archives Department, 1964.

Rhett, Robert G. *Charleston: An Epic of Carolina.* Richmond: Garrett & Massie, 1940.

Richardson, Joe. *Christian Reconstruction: The American Missionary Association and Southern Blacks, 1861–1890.* Athens, Ga.: University of Georgia Press, 1986.

Roark, James. *Masters Without Slaves: Southern Planters in the Civil War and Reconstruction.* New York: W. W. Norton, 1977.

Rosengarten, Dale, et al. "Between the Tracks: Charleston's East Side During the Nineteenth Century." *Archaelogical Contributions No. 17.* Charleston: Charleston Museum, 1987.

Schweninger, Loren. *Black Property Owners in the South, 1790–1915.* Urbana: University of Illinois Press, 1990.

Seabrook, Isaac Dubose. *Before and After Or: The Relations of the Races at the South.* Baton Rouge: Louisiana State University Press, 1967.

Simkins, Francis, and Robert Woody. *South Carolina During Reconstruction.* Chapel Hill: University of North Carolina Press, 1952.

Smith, Charles S. *A History of The African Methodist Episcopal Church.* Philadelphia: Book Concern of The A. M. E. Church, 1922. Reprint, New York: Johnson Reprint Co., 1968.

Smith, Samuel D. *The Negro in Congress 1870–1901.* Chapel Hill: University of North Carolina, 1940.

Spero, Sterling, and Abram Harris. *The Black Worker.* New York: Columbia University Press, 1931. Reprint, New York: Atheneum Press, 1974.

Starobin, Robert. *Industrial Slavery in the Old South.* New York: Oxford University Press, 1970.

Stuckey, Sterling. *Slave Culture: Nationalist Theory and the Foundations of Black Nationalism.* New York: Oxford University Press, 1987.

Swint, Henry L. *The Northern Teacher in the South 1862–1870.* New York: Octagon Books, 1967.

Taylor, Alrutheus A. *The Negro in South Carolina During Reconstruction.* Washington: Association for the Study of Negro Life and History, 1924.

Taylor, Rosser H. *Antebellum South Carolina: A Social and Cultural History.* New York: Da Capo Press, 1970.

Thernstrom, Stephan. *Poverty and Progress: Social Mobility in a Nineteenth-Century City.* New York: Atheneum Press, 1971.

Thomas, Albert S. *A Historical Account of the Protestant Episcopal Church in South Carolina 1820–1957.* Columbia, S.C.: R. L. Bryan, 1957.

Tindall, George B. *South Carolina Negroes 1877–1900.* Baton Rouge: Louisiana State University Press, 1966.

Turner, Lorenzo D. *Africanisms in the Gullah Dialect.* Ann Arbor, Mich.: University of Michigan Press, 1974.

Ullman, Victor. *Martin R. Delany: The Beginnings of Black Nationalism.* Boston: Beacon Press, 1971.

Uya, Okon Edet. *From Slavery to Public Service: Robert Smalls 1839–1915.* New York: Oxford University Press, 1971.

Vaughn, William P. *Schools For All: The Blacks and Public Education in the South 1865–1877.* Lexington, Ky.: University Press of Kentucky, 1974.

Vlach, John. *Charleston Blacksmith: The Work of Philip Simmons.* 2d ed. Columbia, S.C.: University of South Carolina Press, 1992.

Wade, Richard C. *Slavery in the Cities: The South 1820–1860.* London: Oxford University Press, 1964.

Walker, Clarence E. *A Rock in a Weary Land: The African Methodist Episcopal Church During the Civil War and Reconstruction.* Baton Rouge: Louisiana State University Press, 1982.

Wikramanayake, Marina. *A World in Shadow: The Free Black in Antebellum South Carolina.* Columbia, S.C.: University of South Carolina Press, 1973.

Williamson, Joel. *After Slavery: The Negro In South Carolina During Reconstruction 1865–1877.* Chapel Hill: University of North Carolina Press, 1965.

———. *New People: Miscegenation and Mulattoes in the United States.* New York: New York University Press, 1984.

———. *The Crucible of Race: Black-White Relations in the American South Since Emancipation.* New York: Oxford University Press, 1984.

Woodson, Carter G. *The Education of the Negro Prior to 1861: A History of the Education of the Colored People of the United States from the Beginning of Slavery to the Civil War.* New York: Arno Press, 1968.

———. and Charles H. Wesley. *The Negro in Our History.* Washington: Associated Publishers, 1962.

Woodward, C. Van. *The Origins of the New South 1877–1913.* Baton Rouge: Louisiana State University Press, 1971.

———. *The Strange Career of Jim Crow.* New York: Oxford University Press, 1974.

DISSERTATIONS AND THESES

Fickling, Susan M. "The Christianization of the Negro in South Carolina 1830–1860." M.A. thesis, University of South Carolina, 1923.

Fitchett, Horace E. "The Free Negro in Charleston, South Carolina." Ph.D. diss., University of Chicago, 1950.

Henry, Howell M. "Police Control of the Slave in South Carolina." Ph.D. diss., Vanderbilt University, 1914.

Hill, Walter. "Family, Life, and Work Culture: Black Charleston, South Carolina, 1880 to 1910." Ph.D. diss., University of Maryland, 1989.

Jenkins, Wilbert L. "Chaos, Conflict, and Control: The Responses of the Newly-Freed Slaves in Charleston, South Carolina, to Emancipation and Reconstruction, 1865–1877." Ph.D. diss., Michigan State University, 1991.

Martin, Josephine Walker. "The Educational Efforts of the Major Freedmen's Aid Societies and the Freedmen's Bureau in South Carolina 1862–1870." Ph.D. diss., University of South Carolina, 1972.

Moore, Burchill R. "A History of the Negro Public Schools of Charleston, South Carolina 1867–1942." M.A. thesis, University of South Carolina, 1942.

Radford, John P. "Culture, Economy and Urban Structure in Charleston, South Carolina 1860–1880." Ph.D. diss., Clark University, 1974.

OTHER MISCELLANEOUS SOURCES

Charleston City Directories 1872–1873, 1878, 1879–80, 1881, 1885–86.

E. Willis Pamphlets, 1878–1884.

South Carolina State Gazeteer and Business Directory 1880–81. Charleston: R. A. Smith, 1880.

INDEX

Pillsbury, Gilbert, 88–90, 97, 141, 154, 167, 241–44
Plymouth Congregational Church, 214, 216, 222. *See also* American Missionary Association
Porter, A. Toomer, 140, 146, 167, 173–74
Porter, Benjamin F., 154, 224, 255, 257–58
Protestant Episcopal Church: antebellum origins of black membership, 211; discourages black defections, 211; postwar growth, 211; controversy over black clergy, 213–14

race relations: 7, 75–76, 79–80, 94–95; three tier model, 58–60, 73, 291n; Constitution of 1868 Bill of Rights, 94–95, 231; and education, 94, 137, 140–43, 155–56; integration, 156–57, 235–37, 240–46, 338n; church related matters, 197, 212–14, 224; racist perceptions, 227; and politics, 228–33; segregation practiced, 234–36, 238–39, 240–41, 264–65; residential patterns, 246–47. *See also* racial segregation
racial segregation: legal opposition, 231–33, 235–36, 239–40; opposed by civil disobedience, 233–35; residential patterns, 246–53
Randolph, Benjamin F.: 151; and politics. 87, 94–95, 142–43; biography, 89, 149, 230; and Northern Methodists, 198
Ransier, Alonzo, 43, 84–85, 90–91, 93, 95–96, 116, 143, 153, 182, 215
Reconstruction Acts, 86, 89
Redpath, James, 137–38, 142
Republicans: Committee of Thirteen, 86–87; party establishment, 86–89; election of 1868, 95–97, 230; aldermanic appointees (1868), 96; ratify the Constitution of 1868, 96; blacks as Charleston aldermen, 228; black state legislators, 228; political assassinations, 230; racial rift over civil rights, 231–33
Riley, Stepney B., 168, 175, 224
Rollin, Charlotte, 150
Rollin, Frances: 60; as an educator, 150; biography, 180–81; marriage to William Whipper, 181; biographer of Martin R.

Delany, 183; challenges racial segregation, 236
Rollin, William, 59–60, 181
Roper Hospital, 241

Salem Baptist Church, 192
Saltus, Thaddeus, 156, 213–14
Santo Domingo, 22, 180. *See also* Denmark Vesey conspiracy; Haitian Revolution;
Sasportas, Frederick, 53, 169–70
Sasportas, Joseph, 53, 155, 198
Sasportas family, 66, 149, 169–70, 191, 215
Saxton, Rufus, 69, 101, 145
Saxton School, 138–40, 146–48, 150, 152
Scot's Presbyterian Church, 211
Scott, Cornelius C., 156
Scott, Robert, 89, 91, 96, 223, 235
Seabrook, Joseph, 211
Second Presbyterian Church, 210
Shaw, Robert G., 139, 312n
Shaw Memorial School, 139, 151, 154, 163
Shaw Orphan Asylum, 241
Shrewsbury, George, Jr.: Lieutenant on city detective force, 242
Shrewsbury, George, Sr.: successful businessman and Democrat, 123; employs blacks, 163–64; relationship with A. Toomer Porter, 167, 173–74; financial investments, 168; property dispute with Methodist Episcopal South Church, 196–97
Sickles, Daniel, 76, 85, 89, 109, 235–36
Sierra Leone, 210, 255
slave: slave trade, 2–3, 283n; urban slavery, 9–10, 14, 25–26, 34, 117, 122; occupations, 10–11, 14–15, 116–17, 122–23; hiring practices 12–13, 37, 117, 127–28; literacy, 15–16, 136; religious life, 15, 17–21, 189–90; behavior, 22–24, 33–34; housing, 24–25; family, 25–26; sex ratio, 26; resistance, 27–32; selective manumission, 37, 41, 71; emancipation restrictions, 38–40; nominal enslavement, 39–40; Civil War service, 66
Smalls, Charles, 192–93
Smalls, Robert, 11, 19, 67, 70, 165, 169–70, 232

Smyth, Thomas D., 209–10
Society of Free Dark Men, 52
South Carolina Agricultural College and
    Mechanical Institute, 155
South Carolina Association, 32, 56
South Carolina Bureau of Emigration, 111
South Carolina Land Commission, 92, 223
Spencer, Nathaniel T., 126
St. Domingue, 28–30. *See also* Denmark
    Vesey conspiracy; Haitian Revolution;
    L'Ouverture, Toussaint
Sterrett, Norman Bascom, 154, 206
Steward, Theophilis G., 200, 204
St. Mark's Protestant Episcopal Church:
    146; founding and early growth, 211–12;
    controversy over admission to South
    Carolina Diocese, 212–13; elite status,
    212, 215–16. *See also* Protestant
    Episcopal Church
Stoddard, George B., 130

task system, 126
Thirty-third Regiment of the U.S.C.T., 67
Thornwell, James H., 18
Tillman, Benjamin, 264
Tomlinson, Reuben, 138, 141, 147
Trapier, Paul, 18, 20
Trinity Methodist Episcopal Church, 20, 54,
    190, 195, 198–201
Tully, Thomas, 166–67, 174
Turner, Henry M., 208
Twenty-first Regiment of the U.S.C.T.,
    68–69, 78
Twenty-sixth Regiment of the U.S.C.T., 89,
    149

U.S. Civil Rights Act of 1866, 232. *See also*
    civil rights
Union League, 89–90, 128, 165
Unity and Friendship Society, 52, 179

Vanderhorst, Richard, 204–5
Vesey, Robert, 70, 205

violence: fear of freedmen, 74–75; due to
    the presence of black troops, 75–77;
    freedmen versus policemen, 76–77; and
    labor conflict, 129–33; politically
    inspired, 228–31, 263. *See also* race rela-
    tions

Wagener, John, 111, 123, 132, 230–31, 244
Wall, Edward P., 58, 88, 96–98, 113, 119,
    175, 215, 239
Wall, Orindatus S. B., 70, 83
Wallingford Academy, 139, 148, 152
Wallingford United Presbyterian Church,
    210
Warren, Mortimer A., 148
Washington, Samuel, 154
Washington Race Course, 25, 164
Webster, Alonzo, 194, 198
Wesley Methodist Episcopal Church,
    194–95, 198
Weston, Anthony, 42, 50, 65, 168, 176, 181
Weston, Jacob, 40, 54
Weston, Maria, 50
Weston, Mary, 150
Weston, Nancy, 154
Weston, Plowden, 181
Weston, Samuel, 16, 39, 53–54, 155, 171,
    179, 195, 198, 221
Weston, William, 53, 96, 151
Weston family, 149, 179, 181–82, 215,
    256–57
West Point Rice Mills, 10, 113
Whipper, Williams J., 169, 172, 181, 233
white labor: hostility to slave and free black
    workers, 14, 44–45, 62–64, 109; occupa-
    tional distribution, 42, 108, 115
Williams, Bruce, 154–55
Williams, George W., 102
Wilson, Joshua L, 123
Wright, Jonathan J., 93, 95, 155, 172–73, 257

Zion Presbyterian Church, 17–18, 33, 69, 82,
    102, 139, 178, 190, 206, 209–10